RESEARCH IN ORGANIZATIONAL BEHAVIOR

Volume 18 • 1996

RESEARCH IN ORGANIZATIONAL BEHAVIOR

An Annual Series of Analytical Essays and Critical Reviews

Editors: **BARRY M. STAW**
Haas School of Business
University of California, Berkeley

L.L. CUMMINGS
Carlson School of Management
University of Minnesota

VOLUME 18 • 1996

JAI PRESS INC.

Greenwich, Connecticut   *London, England*

Copyright © 1996 JAI Press Inc.
55 Old Post Road No. 2
Greenwich, Connecticut 06830

JAI PRESS LTD.
The Courtyard
28 High Street
Hampton Hill
Middlesed TW12 1PD
England

All rights reserved. No part of this publication may be reproduced, stored on a retrieval system, or transmitted in any form or by any means, electronic, mechanical, photocopying, recording, filming or otherwise without prior permission in writing from the publisher.

ISBN: 1-55938-938-9

Manufactured in the United States of America

CONTENTS

LIST OF CONTRIBUTORS   vii

PREFACE
    Barry M. Staw and L.L Cummings   ix

AFFECTIVE EVENTS THEORY: A THEORETICAL
DISCUSSION OF THE STRUCTURE, CAUSES
AND CONSEQUENCES OF AFFECTIVE
EXPERIENCES AT WORK
    Howard M. Weiss and Russell Cropanzano   1

MOTIVATIONAL AGENDAS IN THE WORKPLACE:
THE EFFECTS OF FEELINGS ON FOCUS OF
ATTENTION AND WORK MOTIVATION
    Jennifer M. George and Arthur P. Brief   75

WHY DO WORKERS BITE THE HANDS THAT
FEED THEM? EMPLOYEE THEFT AS A
SOCIAL EXCHANGE PROCESS
    Jerald Greenberg and Kimberly S. Scott   111

CULTURE AS SOCIAL CONTROL:
CORPORATIONS, CULTS, AND COMMITMENT
    Charles A. O'Reilly and Jennifer A. Chatman   157

CONSEQUENCES OF PUBLIC SCRUTINY FOR
LEADERS AND THEIR ORGANIZATIONS
    Robert I. Sutton and D. Charles Galunic   201

ENTRAINMENT: PACE, CYCLE, AND RHYTHM IN
ORGANIZATIONAL BEHAVIOR
    Deborah Ancona and Chee-Leong Chong   251

CUSTOMER-SUPPLIER TIES IN
INTERORGANIZATIONAL RELATIONS
  Mark Fichman and Paul Goodman   285

INTERFIRM RELATIONSHIPS:
A GRAMMAR OF PAIRS
  Blair H. Sheppard and Marla Tuchinsky   331

LIST OF CONTRIBUTORS

Deborah Ancona	Sloan School of Management MIT
Arthur P. Brief	Freeman School of Business Tulane University
Jennifer A. Chatman	Haas School of Business University of California, Berkeley
Chee-Leong Chong	Sloan School of Management MIT
Russell Cropanzano	Department of Management Colorado State University
Mark Fichman	Graduate School of Industrial Administration Carnegie Mellon University
D. Charles Galunic	Department of Organizational Behavior INSEAD
Jennifer M. George	Department of Management Texas A&M University
Paul Goodman	Graduate School of Industrial Administration Carnegie Mellon University
Jerald Greenberg	Department of Management and Human Resources The Ohio State University

Charles A. O'Reilly	Graduate School of Business Stanford University
Kimberly S. Scott	Department of Management and Human Resources The Ohio State University
Blair H. Sheppard	Fuqua School of Business Duke University
Robert I. Sutton	Department of Industrial Engineering and Engineering Management Stanford University
Marla Tuchinsky	Fuqua School of Business Duke University
Howard M. Weiss	Department of Psychological Science Purdue University

PREFACE

Like most academic fields, research in organizational behavior has gone through an ebb and flow, through various periods of theoretical bloom and empirical consolidation. Yet, regardless of the particular cycle in which our field has been, *Research in Organizational Behavior* has always attempted to be a safe haven for new ideas. We have tried to make *Research in Organizational Behavior* a place where scholars can look for new theoretical approaches as well as the reformulation of existing concepts in organizational behavior.

Volume 18 continues this tradition of breaking new theoretical ground. The volume begins with two reformulations of the field's most central research topics. First, in an effort to replace the vast but rather stagnant literature on job satisfaction, Howard Weiss and Russell Cropanzano present an affective events theory. They draw on recent psychological research on mood and emotion to show how dispositional and situational factors shape our affective experiences at work. Then, Jennifer George and Arthur Brief revise our theories of motivation. They outline how emotions can alter a person's motivational attention, changing the individual's focus from work to family concerns, as well as influencing the dynamics underlying his or her work motivation.

Next, the volume moves to the social fabric of organizational life. Jerald Greenberg and Kimberly Scott explain the nature of employee theft using norms and social exchange as their organizing concepts. They show how a cycle of acceptance can occur when people are willing to victimize organizations, when theft is infrequently prosecuted, and when guilt over theft is minimal. In the following chapter, Charles O'Reilly and Jennifer Chatman explore the notion of organizational culture as a social control system based on shared norms and values. They show how social control works in a variety of strong culture organizations, drawing explicit parallels from business organizations to religious sects and cults. Robert Sutton and Charles Galunic then move the discussion from social control *inside* organizations to the scrutiny of leaders from *outside* the organization. They gather a wide range of examples and literature to form new propositions about the consequences of public scrutiny for organizations and the people who lead them.

The last group of chapters in this volume concern the behavior of organizations as entities devoted to the production of goods and services. Deborah Ancona and Chee-Leong Chong first introduce the concept of entertainment to show how temporal cycles and rhythms govern organizational activities. Instead of the usual focus on what organizations do, entrainment suggests that *when* activities take place may be critical to their success. From the notion of entrainment this volume then moves to an analysis of customer-supplier relations. Mark Fichman and Paul Goodman go beyond the usual individual perspective on customer interactions, stressing the dyadic and network view of relationships between firms in industrial markets. This emphasis on business relationships is pushed even further by the final chapter in this volume. Here Blair Sheppard and Marla Tuchinsky develop a grammar for theorizing about organizational pairs. They go past the argument that interfirm relationships are as important as markets and hierarchies. Drawing upon concepts from social anthropology and psychology, they embark on the necessary but more difficult task of specifying the nature of interfirm relationships over time.

As a collection, we believe these essays are provocative and risky endeavors. They do not challenge the way we currently view organizational behavior, but also provide the kind of diversity needed to keep organizational behavior a vibrant and productive field. They are, in short, the kind of chapters this Series strives to bring to its readers on a regular basis.

Barry M. Staw
L.L. Cummings
Series Editors

AFFECTIVE EVENTS THEORY:
A THEORETICAL DISCUSSION OF THE STRUCTURE, CAUSES AND CONSEQUENCES OF AFFECTIVE EXPERIENCES AT WORK

Howard M. Weiss and Russell Cropanzano

ABSTRACT

In spite of accepted definitions of job satisfaction as "affect" very little is known about the causes and consequences of true affective experiences in work settings. Working from the basic literature on moods and emotions, we introduce a theory of affective experience at work which emphasizes the role of work events as proximal causes of affective reactions. We discuss the structure of affective experiences, their situational and dispositional causes and their effects on performance and job satisfaction.

Cranny, Smith, and Stone (1992) define job satisfaction as "an affective (that is, emotional) reaction to a job that results from the incumbent's comparison of actual outcomes with those that are desired (expected, deserved, and so on)" (p. 1). This is a rather curious definition of a construct, including as it does both the essential variable (affective reaction) *and* its presumed causes (outcome-standard comparisons). The fact that there is general agreement with this definition (their conclusion) makes the inclusion of a theory of the construct's causes in the definition of the construct no less troublesome.

However, confusion of construct and causes is not the most troublesome aspect of this definition. More difficult is the fact that job satisfaction *is not* an affective or emotional reaction to a job, or at least it is not as it typically has been studied and operationalized. Judging from the nature of most job satisfaction questionnaires it would be more accurate to argue that *job satisfaction is a positive or negative evaluative judgment of one's job or job situation*. This is decidedly not the same thing as an affective or emotional reaction.

What then is the connection between affect and satisfaction? The answer to this question is found by clearly distinguishing cause and effect. Satisfaction is an evaluative judgment about one's job that partly, but not entirely, results from emotional experiences at work. It also partly results from more abstract beliefs about one's job. Together, affective experiences and belief structures result in the evaluation we call job satisfaction.

Treating job satisfaction as a summary evaluation with both affective and belief antecedents is quite consistent with current positions on attitude formation. While it has long been recognized that attitudes have affective and cognitive correlates, the real meaning of this point, as well as research on the interplay of the two components, is only now taking shape. Breckler and Wiggens (1989) provide a very cogent discussion of this issue. They argue that attitudes are general evaluations encompassing both affect and cognition. The affective component refers to feelings that are "engendered" by the attitude object and "represents emotional experience associated with the attitudinal object." The cognitive component refers to beliefs about the object, the location of the object on dimensions of judgment. Overall evaluations are influenced by both of these components to greater or lesser degrees.

Making this distinction between satisfaction as judgment and the affective experiences which influence this judgment leads quickly to the conclusion that satisfaction and affective experience should be treated as separate phenomena with distinct but overlapping causes and consequences. This, in turn, suggests the importance of studying affective reactions at work independent of job satisfaction.

Paradoxically, in spite of the "accepted" definition of satisfaction as affect or emotion, we know precious little about emotional reactions at work. In this paper we intend to describe a theoretical position on affective reactions which we hope will serve as a guide to research on the topic. We will suggest a structure for emotional reactions as well as ideas about their causes and consequences. One of the consequences is job satisfaction or dissatisfaction and thus one could argue that a piece of the total position constitutes a piece of a theory of job satisfaction. Theory is perhaps too pretentious. The term is meant only to suggest that there will be conceptual variables integrated into a general framework. In any case, this paper is offered in the spirit of William James (1890) who said "At a certain stage in the development of any science a degree of vagueness is what exists with profit."

THREE THEORETICAL APPROACHES TO JOB SATISFACTION

While the position we will outline focuses on the structure, causes, and consequences of affective experiences, it rests squarely in the overall tradition of research on job satisfaction. Therefore, we begin with a general overview of the previous positions on job satisfaction, and then contrast these positions with one that focuses on affective experiences.

Most specific theoretical positions on job satisfaction can be taken as variants of three general approaches, which we refer to as the "Cognitive Judgment Approach," the "Social Influence Approach," and the "Dispositional Approach." In discussing elements of these positions we will avoid any evaluation of the research literature as good reviews exist elsewhere (Arvey, Carter, & Buerkley, 1991; Locke, 1976).

Cognitive Judgment Approach

By far, the cognitive judgment approach has dominated the theoretical landscape. It is represented most generally by what Lawler (1973) referred to as Discrepancy Theory, and in specific forms, for example, by Katzell's (1964) and Locke's (1976) outcome-value discrepancies, by Ilgen's (1971) discussion of outcome-expectancy discrepancies and by Porter's (1962) position on outcome-need discrepancies. It is also represented by Lofquist and Dawes' (1969) Theory of Work Adjustment, by theories of job satisfaction within the expectancy-value-instrumentality tradition (Mitchell, 1974) and by equity/justice theories of satisfaction (Greenberg, 1982). Lest anyone believe that the advanced age of these seminal references suggests that the position is no longer considered useful, recent papers from these positions continue to appear (Dawes, 1992; Konovsky, Folger, & Cropanzano, 1987; Rice, McFarlin, & Bennett, 1989; Stone, 1992).

While each of the theories has its particular constructs, a general structure exists for all theories in this tradition (see Figure 1). In this general structure the work environment is represented as a set of concrete or abstract features (job characteristics, pay levels, promotion opportunities, etc.). These features are perceived, not always accurately, by job incumbents who compare their perceptions to some set of standards (values, needs, etc.). In some versions the features have meaning only in a work context (e.g., pay levels, career opportunities) while in other versions more abstract psychological properties are used (e.g., autonomy). In any case, some sort of arithmetic function (differences, weighted differences, ratios, etc.) is used to assess the match between perceptions and standards and this match is the proximal cause of job satisfaction. Over the years the nature of the standards has been a major point of disagreement (see Locke, 1976, for the classic discussion) but the fundamental and underlying structure of the cognitive judgment approach is consistent across different theories in this tradition.

The overarching domination of this approach suggests that it might be useful to examine some of its assumptions. For the most part, these assumptions turn out not to be logical necessities. Rather, they are simply characteristic of research and writing from this tradition.

To begin with, implicit in the cognitive judgment approach is the relative stability of job satisfaction and, consequently, the general unimportance of time as a factor in the study of work attitudes. Certainly environmental features can change and so too can standards, but by and large these constructs are treated as being relatively stable on a day-to-day basis. As such, it makes little difference whether we measure satisfaction on Monday or Wednesday, July or September. Clearly, the cognitive judgment approach would not suggest the usefulness of measuring affective reactions on a daily basis or treating fluctuations as anything but error.

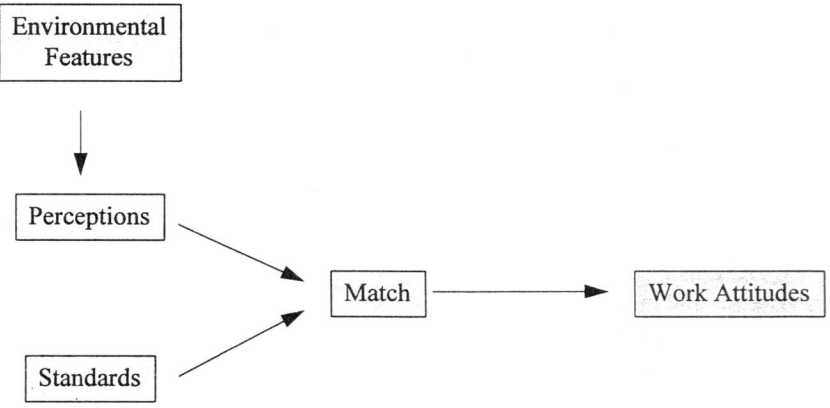

Figure 1. Cognitive Judgment Approach

This point is ironic because much has been made recently of the stability of work attitudes and the implication of that stability for dispositional versus environmental explanations (Gerhart, 1987; Staw & Ross, 1985). The basic conclusion that any demonstrated stability is compatible with both positions (Davis-Blake & Pfeffer, 1989; Gerhart, 1987) is exactly what one would expect because in the cognitive judgment approach both the person and the environment are described in "dispositional" terms. Characteristics of people interact with characteristics of the environment.

Within the cognitive judgment approach a dimensional structure for satisfaction has evolved which focuses on the attributes or features of the environment. This is the distinction generally made between overall and facet satisfaction and it is a natural result of a feature evaluation model of work attitudes. On the other hand, with one very notable exception (see Herzberg, Mausner, & Snyderman, 1959), satisfaction itself is treated as a unitary concept. We may ask, "How satisfied are you with" this or that but the experience of satisfaction is not broken down any further.

This is reasonable for studying satisfaction, the overall evaluative judgment about one's job. However, if it is affect we are after then we must recognize that affective reactions have their own phenomenal structure. For example, a person may be angry, frustrated, sad, or ashamed. All are negative affective reactions yet they may result in quite different behavioral consequences. The possibility of meaningfully distinct affective experiences at work has been ignored by researchers accepting job satisfaction as a measure of affect.

In addition, the focus on feature evaluation has led to a simultaneous neglect of the study of what actually happens at work. A pat on the back, receiving a bonus, an award at a dinner are the real experiences that somehow influence responses to the item "my job provides recognition." Yet, we know very little about these experiences, how people react to them, and how they affect overall evaluations.

Finally, and in spite of the definition of satisfaction as emotion, one could honestly ask "where is the emotion in the study of job satisfaction?" How do we account for the reservationist in Studs Terkel's (1974) *Working* who says about her job "I hated it with a passion. Getting up in the morning, going to work feeling, Oh my God, I've got to go to work." Certainly not by asking her to tell us how much of some feature she wants and how much of some feature she thinks she gets.

Social Influences Approach

In the late 1970s the Social Influences approach, most notably in the form of Social Information Processing Theory (SIP) (Salancik & Pfeffer, 1977, 1978), was presented to the field. An excellent review of this position is provided by Zalesny and Ford (1990).

The basic idea of SIP is that the social environment has both direct and indirect influences on judgments about work. It has direct influences on overall attitudes (Adler, Skov, & Salvemeni, 1985) as well as indirect influences on the perceptions (Weiss & Shaw, 1979) and standards (Weiss, 1977) which feed into attitude judgments.

Over the years, many authors have taken great pains to generate a controversy over whether Social Information Processing is a valid alternative to the traditional cognitive judgment approach (see, most recently, Stone, 1992). At its core, with regard to most of SIP's elements, there is nothing inherently contradictory about the SIP and traditional Cognitive Judgment approaches (see Figure 2). Social Information Processing is more a complement than an alternative to Cognitive Judgment in that it fills in some loose ends about factors which influence the basic variables in the judgment process. That is, the Cognitive Judgment approach argues that we make evaluative job satisfaction judgments based on our perceptions of whether or not some desired standards are being met. The Social Influences approach maintains this cognitive process. It simply adds the caveat that social information is a major input into our perceptions and standards.

What then is the source of the idea that SIP and Cognitive Judgment are antagonistic positions? In our opinion, part of the problem is the loose language of the original Salancik and Pfeffer articles which introduced new and unnecessary constructs that were difficult to understand and operationalize. In addition, part of the problem is their presenting "need fulfillment" as representative of all discrepancy positions (thus criticizing all by criticizing the concept of needs).

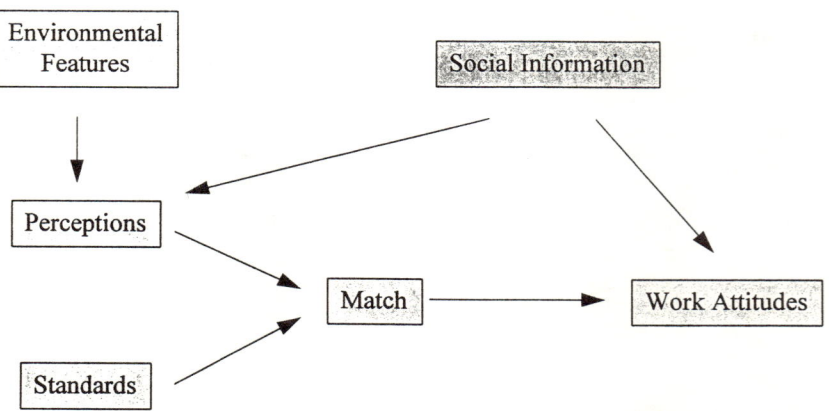

Figure 2. Cognitive Judgment and Social Influences Approaches

However, we also believe that there is a genuine source of conflict between the positions and it centers on one "controversial" aspect of Salancik and Pfeffer's (1977) initial position. That aspect is the frequent reference to the "Social Construction of Reality," as if attitudes were continuously being constructed and reconstructed in a social context. This, we would argue, suggested to some readers that job attitudes have an ephemeral, artificial quality, independent of the reality of an external world of job and work characteristics. The importance of this point is illustrated by this question: "With regard to the construction of job attitudes, is this construction/judgment made and stored and then recalled when attitudes are requested, or is the construction/judgment made and remade each time the attitude is requested, with potentially different information used on each occasion?" Traditional Cognitive Judgment theorists would take the former position, as indicated earlier, although they would not suggest that these attitudes could not be revised in the face of new information. Social Information Processing, some might argue (Zalesney & Ford, 1990), suggests the later position. To a great extent this element of Salancik and Pfeffer's position, an element frankly not well articulated in the initial papers nor ever empirically explored in the literature, does not sit well with those advocating the traditional approach. It has led to a broad brush painting of the whole SIP position as somehow antagonistic to the Cognitive Judgment approach.

We will not try to resolve this controversy. We will only say that current thinking on attitude expression is giving more and more weight to the idea that attitudes generally are not stored and recalled but are "constructed" on demand (Wilson & Hodges, 1992). Further, each construction involves the integration of both stored information relevant to the attitude object and contextual information unrelated to the attitude object. Social information can easily be understood as important contextual information.

Dispositional Approach

The basic idea of the Dispositional approach is this: to some degree, a person's job satisfaction reflects his or her general tendency to feel good or bad about all aspects of life and this general tendency is independent of the specific nature of the job, its positive or negative features. Recently, Judge (1992) has provided an excellent review of the Dispositional position and so we will only touch on the highlights, again focusing more on the nature of the approach than on any evaluation of the research results.

Joseph Weitz first discussed a dispositional approach to job satisfaction and developed what he called the gripe scale to measure it (Weitz, 1952), but current interest on the topic has been stimulated by the work of Staw and Ross (1985). Staw and Ross argued that previous theories of job satisfaction had overemphasized situational causes at the expense of dispositional ones. To find support for their position they examined the stability of job attitudes over a five-year period for a national sample of men. Their sample did in fact show attitudinal stability, as judged by the correlations of attitudes measured in different years. In spite of the fact that these correlations were smaller among those men who had changed jobs or careers than among those who did not, their data can be taken as providing support for some stability in job attitudes.

As has been noted by a number of people (Davis-Blake & Pfeffer, 1989; Gerhart, 1987), stability by itself does not provide particularly strong evidence for dispositional factors, as the stability could just as easily be a function of stable job features as dispositions. More compelling would be the identification of the relevant individual differences variables underlying the dispositional component. In fact, Staw and Ross (1985) speculated on the nature of the underlying personality variables suggesting that individual differences in affective tendencies, perhaps biologically based, might be responsible.

Since Staw and Ross (1985), research on the dispositional component of job satisfaction has followed two paths. One path has tried to explicate the particular personality traits responsible for the dispositional nature of satisfaction. The other path is embodied in the work of Arvey, Bouchard, Segal, and Abraham (1989) who have attempted to demonstrate an inherited tendency to report satisfaction/dissatisfaction.

Personality Determinants of Dispositional Satisfaction

Almost all of the recent research on personality and job satisfaction has looked at the two personality traits of Positive Affectivity and Negative Affectivity. These are personality traits which predict general emotional tendencies in people. People who are high on Positive Affectivity (PA) tend to be lively, sociable, and often in a positive mood. People who are high on Negative Affectivity (NA) tend to be more distressed and unhappy, focusing on the negative side of things.

Because job satisfaction, like all attitudes, has affective as well as belief components, it is not surprising that differences in affective tendencies have been shown to be associated with differences in job satisfaction. For example, Levin and Stokes (1989) conducted a laboratory study in which they asked people who were either high or low on NA to work on interesting or boring tasks. They found that quite independent of the type of task, their satisfaction with the task was influenced by their degree of Negative Affectivity. Similarly, in two field studies Cropanzano, James, and Konovsky (1993) showed that both NA and PA correlated with global satisfaction. Recently, Watson and Slack (1993) found that PA predicted job satisfaction as long as two years later.

Clearly, general affective tendencies are partly responsible for dispositional aspects of job satisfaction, but what is the significance of this finding? In our opinion, simply knowing that some personality variables account for more variance in satisfaction is not by itself very interesting. Accounting for more variance is much less important than building a theoretical framework with both dispositions and situations existing harmoniously in the service of explanation. Ultimately, the disposition has to enlighten underlying process.

Do these findings on affective dispositional correlates of job satisfaction help to expand our conceptual understanding of this construct? We think they do in an important but limited way. An underlying theme in this research is the significance of affect. Unlike early correlational approaches to satisfaction, current dispositional studies have been focused on affective tendencies. It appears that these dispositions are capturing the affective, as opposed to the belief, component of job attitudes (Brief & Roberson, 1989). This in turn suggests that the effect of these dispositions is mediated by affective processes. For example, George (1989) and Weiss, Nicholas, and Daus (1993) suggest that emotional dispositions like Negative and Positive Affectivity influence mood states at work and these mood states can influence satisfaction as well as other important work behaviors. The findings on affective dispositions remind us that there are affective influences on satisfaction judgments. It remains to more fully explicate those affective based processes.

Genetic Influences on Job Satisfaction

Staw and Ross (1985) suggested that there may be biologically based explanations for their dispositional findings. Arvey, Bouchard, Segal, Abraham (1989) took this suggestion a step further and examined the possibility of a genetic component to satisfaction by way of estimating its hereditability, hereditability being the proportion of phenotypic variance accounted for by genetic factors (Willerman, 1979).

In the Arvey, Bouchard, Segal, and Abraham (1989) study, 34 pairs of monozygotic twins reared apart (MZA) were administered the Minnesota Satisfaction Questionnaire and the intraclass correlation for the twins' satisfaction levels was taken as an estimate of hereditability. Using this method, Arvey et al. (1989) estimated an hereditability level of .31 for overall satisfaction. They also concluded that the hereditability of intrinsic facets is stronger (.32) than is the hereditability of extrinsic factors (.11). Furthermore, partialling out the effects of similarity in job types had minimal effects on these hereditability estimates, leading Arvey et al. to conclude that self-selection into similar jobs could not account for the satisfaction results.

Arvey, McCall, Bouchard, and Taubman (1994) reported a replication of the earlier results, this time using both monozygotic and dizygotic twins, not necessarily reared apart. In this type of study, hereditability is estimated by comparing the correlations for the MZ twins, who share all genetic components, with the correlations for DZ twins, who on average share only 50% of genetic components. Here Arvey et al. (1994) found results consistent with the earlier findings but with generally smaller hereditablity estimates (less than 20%).

In spite of methodological criticisms raised by one of us (Cropanzano & James, 1990) our belief is that Arvey's results suggest that there is some genetic influence on satisfaction (see also Bouchard, Arvey, Keller, & Segal, 1992). However, that effect is apparently small. Even using Arvey's initial estimate, the hereditability is not higher than .30 and, given some of the methodological issues raised by Cropanzano and James and also the results from Arvey's own replication, an herititability somewhat lower than .30 is probable.

As it is with personality correlates, simply knowing that there is a genetic component to satisfaction is not the same thing as understanding it. For us, the key question with regard to hereditability, as with dispositions generally, is "does this finding enlighten us about the processes involved in job satisfaction?" By themselves, these hereditability findings do not offer much in the way of psychological explanation. However, they can point in productive directions, if carefully examined.

One direction, naive in our opinion, would be to search for physiological process explanations to substitute for psychological ones. This would be naive given the small hereditability coefficients and the fact that even strong genetic effects typically define a "range of reaction" further influenced by environmental factors. Besides, as Plomin (1990) suggests, it seems likely that genetic effects on behavior are the results of the interactions of many genes making small interactive contributions. Physiological and psychological explanations can certainly complement and enrich each other. However, the history of attempts to baldly substitute physiology for psychology is simply not impressive.

A more useful direction is to search for psychological processes that can incorporate these genetic findings and their likely physiological consequences. What we mean is that future theories can ill afford to ignore these hereditability findings. They have to be incorporated into general theories of job satisfaction, but not as boxes labeled "heredity" with arrows pointing to job satisfaction but as signposts pointing the way to appropriate proximal, psychological causes.

AFFECTIVE EVENTS THEORY: AN OVERVIEW

Our own reading of the "signposts" directs us toward affective reactions and we will now present an overview of our position, a position we call Affective Events Theory or AET. Our overview will highlight some of the more important elements of AET, contrasting our position with more traditional positions on job satisfaction along the way. More detailed discussions of the components will constitute the remainder of the paper.

In contrasting Affective Events Theory with traditional theories the first point of departure is that Affective Events Theory focuses on the *structure, causes and consequences of affective experiences at work*. As described earlier, satisfaction is an evaluative judgment made about one's job. While affective experiences may influence that judgment, satisfaction and affect are not equivalent constructs. In its delineation of the factors which influence job satisfaction, Affective Events Theory focuses on affective experiences as a counterbalance to theories which exclusively focus on judgment processes. However, here affective experiences are the more central phenomena of interest with job satisfaction being one consequence.

As a second point of departure, Affective Events Theory directs attention away from features of the environment and towards *events as proximal causes of affective reactions*. Things happen to people in work settings and people often react emotionally to these events. These affective experiences have a direct influence on behaviors and attitudes and the nature of these effects has not been explored. We are not dismissing the relevance of features but we are tentatively suggesting that environmental features influence affect primarily by making affective events (or the recall or imagination of affective events) more or less likely.

Affective Events Theory also adds *time* as an important parameter when examining affect and satisfaction. Research on mood and emotion clearly indicates that affect levels fluctuate over time and that the patterns of these fluctuations are predictable to a great extent. We are proposing that these patterns of affective reactions influence both overall feelings about one's job and discrete behaviors at work.

Paying attention to patterns of affective experience over time is in direct contrast to traditional approaches to job satisfaction in which the time of measurement is given no theoretical importance. In such approaches, satisfaction, as well as indices of predictors and consequences (performance, for example) are assessed at some arbitrary point in time. Ignoring time is consistent with a theoretical position which focuses on the effects of environmental features because such features are considered relatively stable. Unfortunately, this approach ignores the importance of affective variation, a mistake which may contribute to the failure to find affect-performance relationships of any substance.

Finally, Affective Events Theory considers the *structure of affective reactions* as important as the structure of environments. Dimensional structures of job satisfaction focus on dimensions of the attitude object. That is, the job is the object and its dimensions are features like pay or supervision. AET recognizes that affect itself is multidimensional and emphasizes the importance of the structure of the psychological experience. People can feel angry, frustrated, proud or joyful and these different reactions have different behavioral implications.

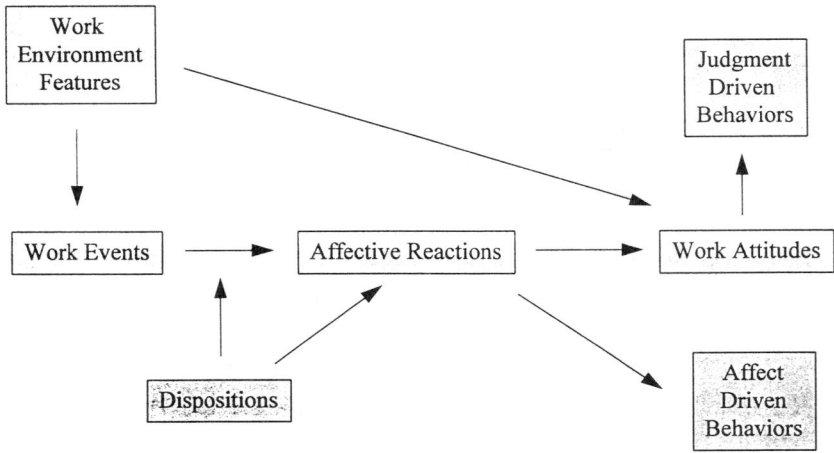

Figure 3. Affective Events Theory: Macro Structure

In Figure 3 we have presented a tentative macro structure to the affective events position. While we will use the remainder of the paper to describe its components in more detail, it seemed useful to begin by walking through the basic elements.

At the core of the position are affective experiences. A key question involves how these experiences are to be described. Moods are different from emotions and emotions, at least, can be described at different levels of differentiation. We will address this question later and will suggest that the appropriate structure depends on the problem being addressed.

Fundamental to the theory is the idea that affect levels fluctuate over time and that the causes of these patterns of affect can be examined in terms of endogenous components, such as known cycles in mood or affective dispositions, and exogenous components, such as affectively relevant events which constitute shocks to existing patterns. Dispositions can also influence the way events produce affective reactions. Work environments are seen as having an indirect influence on affective experience by making certain events, real or imagined, more or less likely.

The consequences of affective experience are both attitudinal and behavioral. Affective experiences have a direct influence on job satisfaction. This influence corresponds to the affective aspect of attitudes. Features have both direct and indirect influences: directly by evaluation in the "cognitive" judgment part of satisfaction and indirectly through their influence on the likelihood of various events. Note, however, that this reference is made to features generally. We are not suggesting that each feature of the work environment has both direct and indirect effects.

Finally, behaviors are grouped into two categories: affect driven behaviors and judgment driven behaviors. Affect driven behaviors follow directly from affective experiences and are not mediated by overall attitudes. They are influenced by processes like coping or mood management or by direct effects of affect on cognitive processing or judgment biases. Judgment driven behaviors are mediated by satisfaction. They are the consequences of decision processes where one's evaluation of one's job is part of the decision matrix.

PREVIOUS RESEARCH CONSISTENT WITH AET

While it is obviously tempting to argue that no important research has focused on the role that affective events play in job satisfaction or that affect has been ignored entirely, this would be far from the truth. As we indicated earlier, affective dispositions are currently enjoying some popularity (see Judge, 1992) and the effects of mood on various aspects of work behavior has received some attention (see, for example, George, 1989, 1992). These efforts, however, do not represent attempts to provide coherent theoretical perspectives on the topic. Historically, we believe, two such endeavors are close to what we offer and therefore should be discussed in this paper. Both, by and large, have been forgotten in today's discourse on the topic.

Hersey (1932)

In 1932 Rexford Hersey published his research on *Workers' Emotions in Shop and Home*. Hersey's research is now mostly forgotten yet it still stands as the seminal piece on emotional reactions at work. For one year Hersey intensively studied the emotions and behaviors of 17 skilled workers in two departments of a railroad car and locomotive repair facility of a large public utility. Each man was interviewed four times a day, first for 13 weeks and then for periods of 10 weeks and 13 weeks after periods of eight and four weeks, respectively, during which no measurements took place. The interview was composed of a number of questions including what would today be called a mood checklist (22 items such as happy, hopeful, tense, angry, etc.). Hersey was also able to assess daily productivity as well as individual differences in physical and psychological attributes.

Hersey's general "theoretical" position focused on the concept of life crises. He argued that life, including work life, is filled with a variety of major and minor crises which demand adjustment. The effects of these crises could be seen by examining daily patterns of emotional reactions. While Hersey did not empirically examine this proposition he did obtain some interesting findings with regard to mood and behavior. For our purposes, three findings are of particular interest. First, Hersey was able to chart daily mood levels, scored

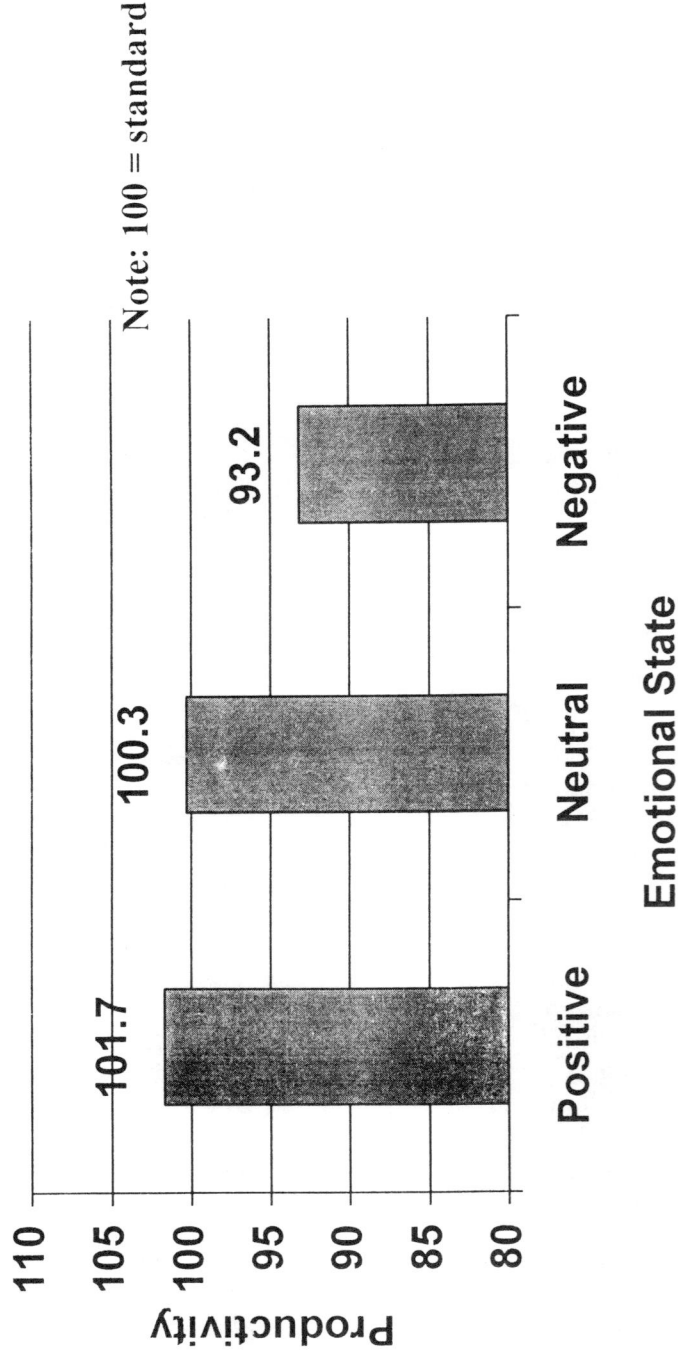

Figure 4. Relationship Between Productivity and Emotional State

Source: Adapted from Hersey (1932).

as positive and negative, and document daily fluctuations in affect. Second, by assessing both daily mood levels and daily performance levels he was able to demonstrate a definite relationship between emotional state at work and productivity. Interestingly, this relationship was not symmetrical in that the negative effects of a negative emotional state were much more pronounced than were the positive effects of a positive state (see Figure 4).

Third, without benefit of modern statistical techniques Hersey was able to discern definite mood cycles over the course of the year. These cycles varied across individuals. Different workers had longer or shorter periods to their cycles.

Hersey's research approximately coincided with the Hawthorne studies and with Hoppock's research on job satisfaction. For whatever reasons, it is certainly true that both the Hawthorne and Hoppock studies are mentioned in almost all current Industrial and Organizational Psychology textbooks while Hersey is virtually unknown to today's researchers. Yet it is probably true that Hersey's work could be published intact today (albeit with a little analytical updating) while neither Hawthorne nor Hoppock would withstand current review processes.

Herzberg, Mausner, and Snyderman (1959)

Herzberg maintained that satisfaction and dissatisfaction were not poles of a single continuous dimension but separate and distinct dimensions. The field responded with cries of "methodological artifact," "confusion of agents and events," and "attributional processes." It seems clear that if a modern day Herzberg were to arrive on today's scene with the Two Factor Theory in hand the reactions would be substantially muted. After all, today we have Positive and Negative Affect (Watson & Tellegen, 1985, as discussed later) and Herzberg's dimensions of satisfaction would be perfectly consistent with that particular dimensional organization of mood self-reports.

For our purposes it is useful to note a few relatively unique aspects of Herzberg's work, apart from his Two Factor conceptualization. To begin with, Herzberg understood and emphasized the variability of work attitudes. Using his critical incidents method he asked respondents to "think of a time when you felt especially good or bad about your job." Nothing in this question suggested that people respond in terms of different jobs or that they had to separate these incidents by any particular length of time. In fact, he said that implicit in his new approach is "the notion that job attitudes varied for each individual from one period to another" (p. 13) and that these variations could be linked to variations in diverse criteria.

For Herzberg, the primary causes of these periods of satisfaction or dissatisfaction were specific work events. "I felt terrible when I was passed over for the promotion" (p. 42), "When I finally knew I had the problem licked,

I felt higher than a kite" (p. 42), "A warehouse checker is ordered by his supervisor to go out in the rain and check a group of freight cars" (p. 21). Careful review of these incidents indicate that some of the responses described specific events and others described longer term "situations." Herzberg referred to them all as events but clearly some respondents answered in terms of shorter time frames and described specific occurrences on the job and others answered in terms of longer time frames and described general features of the work situation. However, even these "long range sequences" as Herzberg referred to them, had implicit shorter term events at their core. For example, a salesman describes a long-term situation of frustration but includes in his description that "the boss was too busy to train him and seemed annoyed whenever (he) asked questions" (p. 22); or, as another example, an engineer expresses career frustrations but says that he felt bad because there was a strike going on and management refused to let him participate in the negotiations (p. 22).

Interestingly, while Herzberg described the proximal causes of satisfaction as work events, he did not stay at this level of analysis for long. Instead, he used his events to develop descriptions of environments which facilitated the events (interesting work, possibility for advancement, possibility for growth, etc.) and then kept his focus on these environmental features as he developed his concepts of "motivators" and "hygienes." This focus on features made it easier to incorporate his findings with a need satisfaction approach to satisfaction, specifically Maslow's Hierarchy of Needs (Maslow, 1954). However, a careful reading of Herzberg clearly indicates that in his theory *features operate by making certain events more or less likely.*

If we keep the distinctions between events and features and the distinctions between affective reactions and overall evaluations in mind, the great controversy between one factor and two factor theories of job satisfaction seems rather inconsequential. Our overall evaluation of our job is unidimensional, consistent with a one factor approach. Further, at any given time our current affective state is either positive or negative (Diener & Emmons, 1984) and the affective consequences of work events can be either positive or negative. However, certain kinds of features can be conducive to the occurrence of positive but not negative events and other kinds of features can be conducive to negative events but have little influence on the frequency of positive events. But, again, the construct we refer to as job satisfaction is still a unidimensional evaluation of one's job.

THE NATURE OF EMOTIONS AND MOODS

At this point we will start to examine the elements of AET in more detail. We will begin at the core of the theory, with a discussion of the nature of affective reactions, their definitions and structural representations. This will be followed, in turn, by discussions of the way events come to elicit affective reactions, what is known about other antecedents of mood and emotion, affective cycles, the influence of affective reactions on job satisfaction and, finally, our ideas about the performance implications of affective reactions.

We should say immediately that the study of emotion has a long history and the literature is enormous and fragmented (see Plutchik, 1994, for an up-to-date summary.) In fact, the scientific study of emotion predates the formal birth of psychology with the writings of Charles Darwin (1872[1965]). Emotion was there, too, at the birth of psychology, as two of psychology's "fathers," William James and Wilhelm Wundt, wrote extensively on the topic.

Our objective cannot be to review all that is known about affect, moods, and emotions. Rather, we hope to summarize those facts and theories which have relevance to work experience. We are intentionally selective without trying to imply that the theories we have chosen to present are the accepted positions in the field. No theory currently meets this criterion.

The objective we do acknowledge is to convince the reader of the validity of the basic structure of our theory, the importance of events, the difference between affect driven and judgment driven behaviors, and so forth and then selectively use the current literature on moods and emotions to fill in the details of the structure while suggesting certain avenues of research. In doing this we recognize that other organizational researchers might accept the overall framework but be guided by different positions in filling in the details.

Defining Emotions

Emotions and moods are both affective states yet rarely have psychologists made explicit attempts to differentiate them. This curious situation is mostly due to the fact that these two types of affective experiences have two different research traditions. The research tradition involving emotions is long and varied. The tradition focusing on moods is shorter and more focused.

Emotions are intuitively well understood yet a definitive definition of emotion has been difficult to come by. The difficulty in developing a definition seems to arise from the observation that an emotional reaction is not one reaction, but a constellation of related reactions. Nonetheless, most definitions seem to settle on a few essential components. We will use Frijda's (1993) summary to introduce these components. According to Frijda, every emotional experience has four main components. To begin with there is the experiential component of affect, "the irreducible aspect that gives feelings their emotional, noncognitive character" (p. 383). Next, Frijda argues, a person is generally not aware of feeling good or bad but rather one is aware of the pleasantness or unpleasantness of the eliciting event and therefore the experience of affect is intricately tied to the appraisal of that event. Most definitions of emotions include the idea that there is an overall affective experience and a consequent cognitive appraisal process (Plutchik, 1994). Third, for Frijda and for most theorists, emotions are also characterized by a wide variety of physiological bodily changes. Finally, Frijda suggests that the experience of an emotion includes an action readiness, a general readiness to deal with the environment through increased arousal and vigilance.

Implicit in all definitions is that an emotion is a reaction to an event. It is not a trait, although there can be trait differences in chronic affect levels or in reactivity to specific events. Also implicit in all definitions is that emotions have event or object specificity. As Frijda (1993) says "Emotions have an object, they are about something... One is happy about something, angry at someone, afraid of something" (p. 381). Finally, even when one acknowledges the multiple components of the emotional experience (affect, physiology, etc.) it is the *experience* that remains fundamental.

Defining Moods

Frijda (1993) and Morris (1989) both tell us that moods are most frequently distinguished from emotions by three features: intensity, duration, and diffuseness. More specifically, moods, as compared to emotions, are thought to be less intense, of longer duration and lack specificity with regard to a particular object or behavioral response.

Frijda (1993) and Morris (1989) also tell us that the first two criteria are not very useful. To begin with, moods can vary greatly in their duration. One often thinks of moods lasting for hours or even days, yet mood manipulations in the laboratory can last less than a few minutes and still have the effects attributed to real mood experiences. Emotions, on the other hand, can last for long periods of time. In addition, diffuse affective states like anxiety or depression can be of very high intensity while specific emotional reactions can be rather mild.

Frijda (1993) and Morris (1989) conclude that the real distinguishing feature between moods and emotions is diffuseness in terms of both object and response. Emotions are affective states directed at someone or something (Frijda, 1993). Moods, on the other hand, lack an object to which the affect is directed. Lazarus (1991a) makes a similar point when he says that moods are vague and "lack a contextual provocation."

None of these authors are suggesting that moods do not have specific causal antecedents, only that the phenomenal experience of the mood does not include the causal factor. The importance of the experiential disconnection between the affect state and its cause is further emphasized in Frijda's (1993) suggestion that an emotion turns into a mood when one loses the focus on the precipitating event or object. Similarly, making the cause of the mood salient may transform a mood into a weak emotion. This latter position is consistent with research which demonstrates that when people are made aware of the cause of their mood state many of the global effects of mood are eliminated (Clore, 1992).

Mood researchers also argue that moods, more than emotions, are diffuse in terms of elicited responses in that they influence a wide variety of cognitive and behavioral responses which are not connected to the original source of the mood (Isen, 1984; Morris, 1989). Obviously, we agree with the argument that moods have diverse effects but we would caution that this distinction between mood and emotion can be taken too far. While it is true that the effects of emotions tend to be more targeted toward dealing with either the source of the emotion or the emotional state, they too can have generalized behavioral effects mediated by activation or arousal levels. In addition, many of the global effects of moods may result from rather specific attempts to manage one's subjective state. This being said, it still remains that the effects of mood tend to be less dependent on the nature of the cause of the mood. This is consistent with the idea that the cause is not part of the phenomenal experience.

The Stucture of Emotions

Researchers on moods and emotions have spent a good amount of time and energy trying to dimensionalize, classify and categorize these two types of affective responses. In this section and the next we will present a summary of these efforts. It is our observation that the dimensionalization or categorization objectives of emotion researchers appears to be quite different from the objectives of psychologists who study mood. From the beginning, emotion researchers have been interested in categorization, developing lists of primary emotions. Even those researchers who criticize the idea that there are so called "basic" emotions provide lists of emotions or emotion families (e.g., anger, love, frustration, joy, etc.). Mood researchers, on the other hand, seem to be less interested in the phenomenal experience of discrete moods and more interested in reducing the mood experience to its underlying dimensions (e.g., pleasantness, intensity, etc.). While this difference may be the result of historical accident, it certainly is consistent with the differences between the affective experiences of moods and emotions. Mood is affect disconnected from its causal object. As such, the specificity of a mood may have fewer behavioral implications than its position on some underlying dimensions. Emotions, on the other hand, are object oriented and the object, causal circumstances and specific emotional reaction are therefore important for understanding and predicting responses.

Intuition tells us that there are many different kinds of emotions, each of which involves a unique phenomenological experience, with different consequences for individuals and their employing organizations. As a result of this diversity, researchers have found a need for some structure to act as a guide for future research. The problem with emotions, however, is not a lack of structure but, instead, a surfeit of perspectives, points-of-view, and theoretical models. We have more structures than we could possibly use. There are many different frameworks each based on the needs of particular researchers (Lazarus, 1991a). Consequently, there is no one structure on which everyone agrees (Ortony & Turner, 1990).

Plutchik (1994) has recently reviewed attempts to develop lists of "basic" emotions. He points out that this is not a new endeavor. Descartes and Spinoza both proposed emotional classification schemes as philopsophers attempted to wrestle with the "passions" of humankind. All emotional positions, whether they arise from an evolutionary perspective, a cognitive perspective, or a psychoanalytic perspective have attempted to summarize the multitude of ways we refer to emotions. Inherent in all of these attempts is a distinction between primary and secondary emotions. Primary emotions refer to fundamental or basic emotions and secondary emotions are emotional states derived from a combination these primary emotions. This distinction is designed to summarize the variety of emotional reactions and still retain the nuances among the many different emotions we experience and can recognize in others.

Emotional researchers from an evolutionary perspective tend to look for evidence of primary emotions in displays of common emotions across cultures and also in similar displays of emotions among different species, particularly humans and primates. This last approach is traceable to Darwin's work in *The Expression of Emotions in Man and Animals* (1872[1965]).

Ekman (1992) recently applied these biological criteria to various emotion lists and concluded that there are at least six basic emotions: anger, fear, sadness, enjoyment disgust and surprise. Plutchik (1994) also working from the evolutionary perspective, offers the following eight basic emotions: joy, sadness, acceptance, disgust, fear, anger, expectation and surprise. Izard (1977), following a more physiological approach, offers fear, anger, enjoyment, interest, disgust, surprise, shame, contempt, distress, guilt.

Research by Shaver, Schwartz, Kirson, and O'Connor (1987) represents a semantic classification to reduce the wide variety of experienced emotions to a few categories (see Figure 5). This approach uses the semantic similarity of emotion words to develop categories of emotions. Shaver and his colleagues had a group of subjects rate 213 words with respect to their "emotionness." These ratings were then subjected to cluster analysis. Subjects identified six categories of emotions: love, joy, surprise, anger, sadness, and fear. These six primary categories were then meaningfully subdivided into 24 subcategories. Eventually, all 213 words could be classified using either the 24 subcategories or the 6 primary categories.

The Shaver et al. structure is intuitively meaningful but it is unclear what the semantic analysis has to say about the structure of actual emotions. It may be true that the cognitions pertaining to emotion words can be hierarchically organized but even Shaver et al. are cautious in their willingness to extrapolate

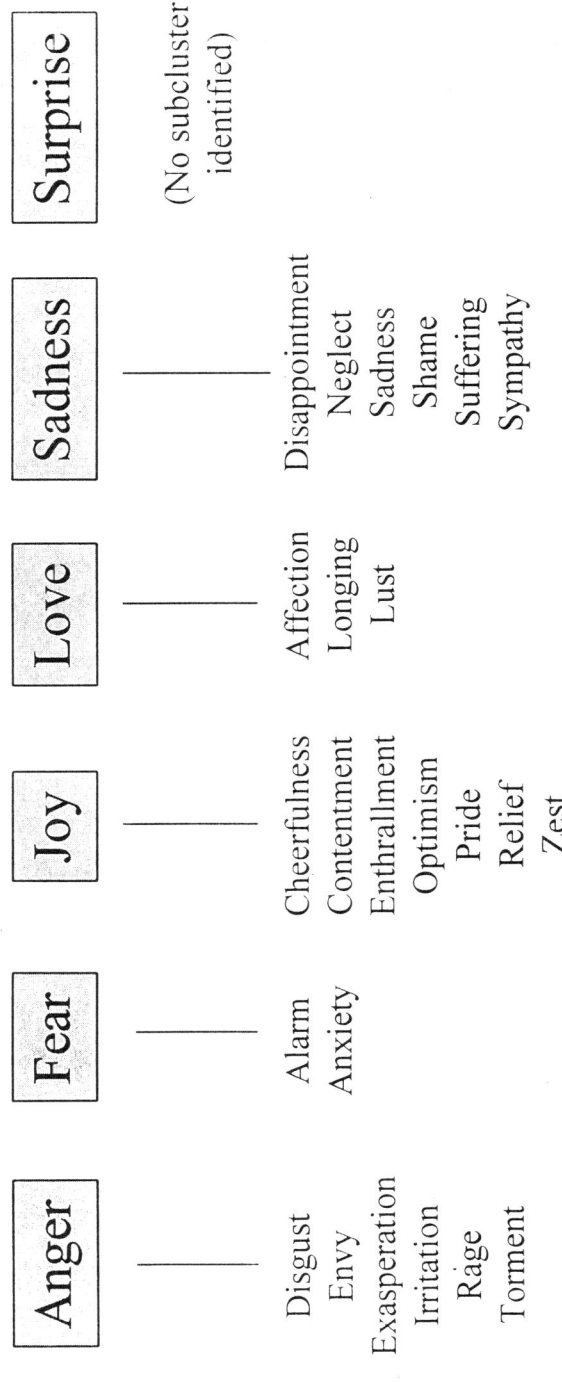

Figure 5. Semantic Organization of Emotion Words

Source: Adapted from Shaver, Schwartz, Kirson, and O'Conner (1987).

to actual emotion categories. However, one cannot help notice the degree of overlap between the Ekman, Izard, Plutchik, and Shaver lists.

Finally, we should point out that for many researchers in the cognitive appraisal tradition, the search for "basic" emotions is of little value. Ortony, Clore, and Collins (1988) regard such a search as unprofitable because, in their opinion, there is no way to choose among lists. Their approach, like other cognitive appraisal theorists, argues for sets of relatively independent emotion categories or families based on common appraisal processes. We will have more to say about this appraisal process later. Here we will only point out that these appraisal theorists still present various lists of emotions (Clore et al. talk about such things as joy, pride, shame, distress, love, hate, etc.) as the end product of the appraisal process.

Implications for Affective Events Theory

Applied psychologists are going have to await more research before the issue of basic emotions is completely resolved. However, work to date has already given us sufficient grounding to proceed.

First, all researchers agree that emotions can be plausibly organized into families. These categories can provide a guiding foundation for future research. A short list of these families would at least include anger, disgust, joy, fear, and sadness. It might also include surprise. It should be noted that this list is based on convergence between evolutionary and cognitive appraisal research. These particular emotional states seem to show up time and time again—regardless of the empirical paradigm. Consequently, at least these six emotional families, and possibly some others, should receive future research attention.

Second, everyone concurs that specific emotional states do exist. In fact, these states include some of our most memorable experiences, including jubilation, loathing, grief, and terror. In every major theory, these specific emotions are brought about by the action of cognitive appraisals. Interestingly, appraisals are even central to theories of basic emotion. However, basic emotion theorists generally see the appraisals as automatic, rapid, and hardwired (Ekman, 1992). Regardless, for a person to experience an emotion some event in the individual's environment has to be appraised. Ultimately, appraisals involve events—in the broad sense of the word—including people and things. Consequently, it follows that any theory of emotion must also be a theory of how people adapt to events in their environment.

Third, some emotion terms seem to be more specific, whereas others are more general. It is not clear whether or not the general emotions are shaped into the specific ones. However, it is clear that some words refer to broader states than do others. For example, we usually regret some loss that happened in the past. However, we can be sad about some loss that did happen or that will happen. Sadness is more general with respect to time. Likewise, fear can refer to either a very intense or a mild emotional state, whereas the term horror is generally reserved for something very intense. Fear is more general with respect to intensity.

This has implications for the prediction of behavior. It seems likely that specific emotions will prove especially useful for the prediction of specific behaviors. Consider, for example, the emotion of sadness. How would a sad person behave at work? That might depend on the specific variant of sadness being experienced. A person who was disappointed over something might behave one way. A person who felt guilty might behave another. Pity would likely lead to the prediction of a third set of responses. According to Shaver and his colleagues, disappointment, guilt, and pity are all part of the sadness family. People experiencing any of these three specific emotions might all describe themselves as sad. However, in each instance very different behaviors are apt to result.

In spite of the difficulty of the task, organizational researchers cannot be deterred from borrowing or developing classification schemes for describing emotional reactions at work. If one assumes that discrete emotions have limited and specific action tendencies, an assumption held by most emotion researchers (see, e.g., Lazarus, 1991a), then a full understanding of the behavioral implications of emotional reactions at work requires the use of some classification scheme. We believe that ultimately the environment-emotion-behavior chain will include a situation-emotion matrix that presents the key situational features which are conducive to specific emotional reactions. It seems to us that at the very least the analysis of the structure of work emotions is as important as the analysis of the dimensions of job satisfaction.

The Structure of Mood

So far we have been discussing mood as if it were a single thing. However, experience tells us otherwise. Intuitively, when we describe our mood we tend to do so in terms of two words: "good" and "bad." In psychological jargon, we might say that people articulate their feelings with reference to hedonic tone, "positive" for "good" and "negative" for "bad." We also categorize our moods in terms of their intensity. We can say, for example, that we feel "okay" or "very good." Both are generally positive, but the latter is more so.

Researchers, of course, attempt to describe mood more systematically and, as we have said, mood researchers have been particularly concerned with reducing the mood experience to underlying dimensions. The most common paradigm for doing this task has been to administer a large number of mood items to a group of respondents. These responses are then subjected to a dimensional analysis (cluster analysis, factor analysis, etc.) (Mayer & Gaschke, 1988; Watson & Tellegen, 1985). The obtained factors/clusters are taken to indicate the underlying dimensional structure of mood. Although this and similar paradigms are widely used, the dimensions obtained vary somewhat among researchers. In general, two different two-dimensional structures have received wide currency. One structure, frequently adopted in the organizational sciences, conceptualizes mood in terms of Positive Affectivity (PA) and Negative Affectivity (NA). Another widely discussed structure, less frequently used in organizational research, dimensionalizes mood states in terms of Hedonic Tone (with positive and negative affect as anchors on a single continuum) and Intensity. The evidence for each of these models is reviewed below.

Positive and Negative Affectivity

The empirical literature on state and trait mood has been extensively reviewed by Watson and Clark (1984) and Watson and Tellegen (1985). According to these authors, both state and trait mood can be best represented in terms of two distinct dimensions: Positive Affectivity (basically good feelings) and Negative Affectivity (basically bad feelings). At the high pole, PA is characterized by such adjectives as "energetic," "exhilaration," and "joy." People who report high positive affectivity exhibit a zest for living. At the low end, however, low PA is not the presence of negative affect. Rather, the low pole is characterized by the absence of positive affect. Individuals scoring low on PA are best seen as apathetic and listless. NA manifests itself in a different complex of feeling states. People score high on NA when they report anger, nervousness, anxiety, guilt, sorrow, and so on. At the low pole, NA does not involve the presence of positive affect. Rather, it involves the absence of negative affect. In this sense, it functions in a manner analogous to PA. Individuals scoring low on NA often report being placid and content.

Seminal work on this NA/PA model of mood was conducted by Zevon and Tellegen (1982). These researchers had 23 subjects fill out the same mood adjective checklist for 60 consecutive days. Afterwards, they conducted 23 within subjects factor analyses. For 21 of the 23 individuals, two strong and independent factors emerged, one characterized by positive affect and the other by negative affect. These data provided clear support for the PA/NA model.

Since the initial work of Zevon and Tellegen (1982), several others studies have uncovered the two basic PA and NA dimensions (e.g., Gotlib & Meyer, 1986; Watson & Clark, 1991; Watson, Clark, & Carey, 1988; Watson, Clark, & Tellegen, 1988; Watson & Tellegen, 1985). For example, one representative study was reported by Watson (1988). In this study 80 undergraduate students were administered a daily mood checklist for 6-8 weeks. These mood reports were than factor analyzed and the PA and NA dimensions were again recovered. Watson (1988) also reported that social activity and exercise were most strongly related to PA, while perceived stress was strongly related to NA. Physical symptom reports were related to both NA and PA.

Although still limited, cross-cultural investigations have also produced consistent findings. For example, using a method similar to the one reported above, Watson, Clark, and Tellegen (1984) uncovered the same two factor structures in a sample of Japanese citizens. Similar results were also obtained in another cross-cultural study by Almagor and Ben-Porath (1989).

The NA/PA model of mood structure has been extremely influential within the organizational sciences (see George, 1992, for a review). Nevertheless, it is not the only useful way for dimensionalizing mood states. A second model has also obtained a great deal of empirical support. It is to this alternative approach that we now turn.

Hedonic Tone and Intensity

As with NA/PA model, various researchers have argued that mood can be thought of as involving two dimensions but have proposed a different set of dimensions (for reviews see Larsen & Diener, 1992; Russell, 1979). The first dimension of this alternative structure is sometimes referred to as Hedonic Tone and other times as Pleasantness. The Hedonic Tone or Pleasantness dimension describes mood states as falling on a scale from very positive to very negative with many points in between. The positive pole of this Hedonic Tone dimension would include such things as "happy" and "carefree," while the low pole would be characterized by such markers as "sober" and "distressed." Note that this is a single bi-polar continuum.

The second dimension in this alternative structure is the level of intensity. That is, feelings can range from very intense to very mild. So, for example, we can see the high end as including such adjectives as "restless" and "changeable," while the low end is characterized by such adjectives as "controlled" and "peaceful."

As with NA and PA, the Hedonic Tone and Intensity structure has received empirical support. Much of this support comes from the work of Russell and his colleagues who have found evidence for two broad dimensions that he calls "Degree of Arousal" and "Pleasantness-Unpleasantness" (e.g., Russell, 1978, 1979; Russell & Mehrabian, 1977; Russell & Ridgeway, 1983).

Why the Confusion Over Factor Structures?

At first glance the two previous sections appear to completely contradict one another but, in fact, it is possible that both models can provide a good mathematical fit to the data. To understand why this is so one needs to consider that the NA/PA and Hedonic Tone/Intensity solutions have in common the fact that each describes mood in terms of two orthogonal factors. Both models provide a simplified representation of a more complex reality. Let us look at this in more detail.

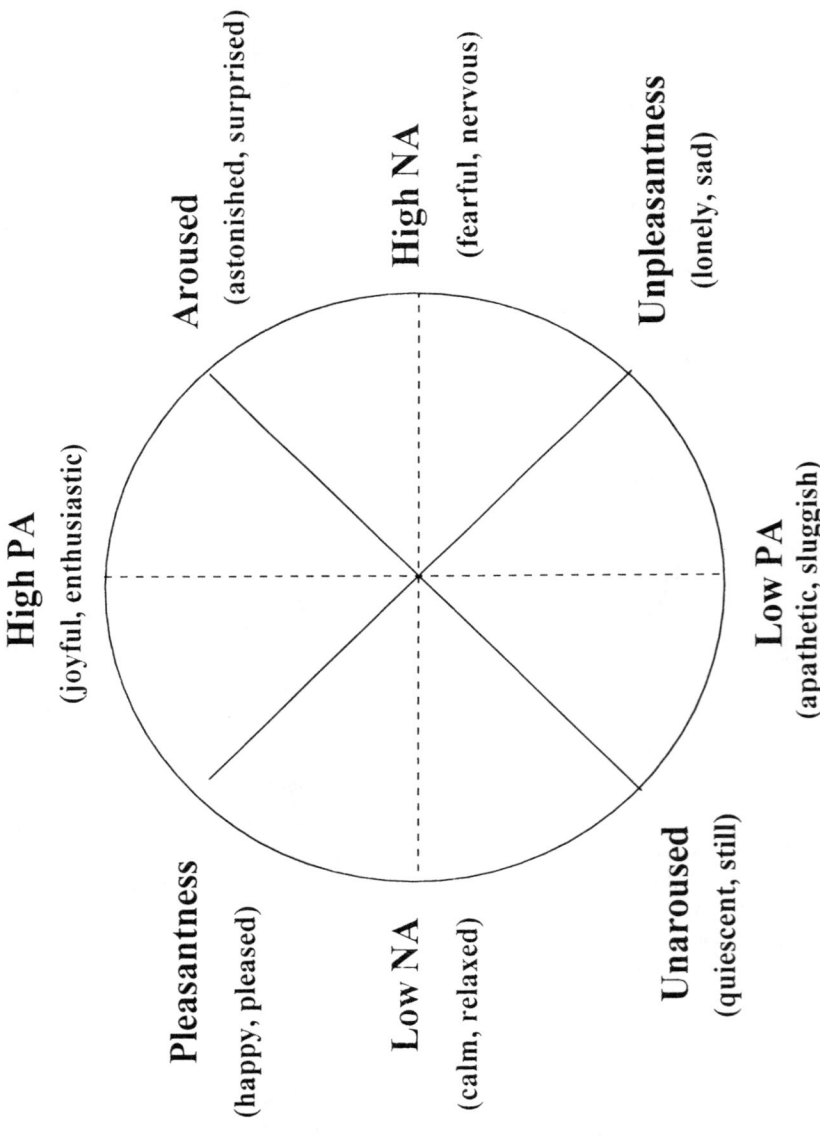

Figure 6. Circumplex Model of Mood

Several authors have noted that when words referring to mood are judged in terms of similarity, the relationships among the words can be visually depicted in terms of a circular or "circumplex" model (see Figure 6) (Larsen & Diener, 1992; Mayer & Gaschke, 1988; Meyer & Shack, 1989; Russell, 1980; Watson & Tellegen, 1985).

What is especially important for our purposes is how one might represent this circumplex in two-dimensional space. Given the circular relationship among the words, multiple two-dimensional structures are possible. As shown in Figure 6, the two structures we have been discussing are simply different axis rotations of the same data. Both summarize the relationships equally well in that both structures can be used to precisely locate a given mood in the dimensional space.

Because, mathematically speaking, both models generally fit the observed data the value of either approach cannot be decided on mathematical grounds alone. Rather, the worth of either solution becomes, not so much a matter of truth, as a matter of methodological and theoretical clarity. Consequently, both "camps" have looked to other evidence to make the case for their preferred structures. We will review some of these arguments.

Robustness Across Multiple Operations

As we have seen, both the NA/PA and the Hedonic Tone/Intensity dimensions have been recovered from factor analytic studies of survey responses. However, the Hedonic Tone/Intensity model has been demonstrated with other paradigms as well. For example, much of the work of Russell and his colleagues has used multi-dimensional scaling techniques (e.g., Russell, 1979; Russell & Ridgeway, 1983). Similarly, the Hedonic Tone/Intensity solution also shows up when pictures and not words are used as stimulus materials (Russell, Lewicka, & Niit, 1989). Conversely, evidence for the NA/PA model has been limited to factor analytic research on verbal scales.

Conceptual Descriptions

There has been some conceptual ambiguity regarding the two dimensions of NA and PA that is relevant to choosing an appropriate dimensional structure. Essentially, most adjectives that load on either NA or PA describe only the high pole for each adjective. Take, for example, the case of the Positive and Negative Affectivity Schedule (or PANAS, see Watson, Clark, & Tellegen, 1988). The PANAS is probably the most widely used measure of PA and NA. The schedule was constructed by using exploratory factor analysis to identify items with high loadings on one dimension (either NA or PA) and low loadings on the other. Interestingly, this procedure left the scale's authors with only items indicative of high positive affect (such as "energetic") or high negative affect (such as "anxious").

Other factor analytic research has also produced mixed results. On the supportive side, Mayer and Gaschke (1988) report that "drowsy" and "tired" had a highly negative (−.39 and −.36, respectively) loading on PA and very low loadings on NA (−.04 and −.09, respectively). Similarly, "calm" was adequately loading on NA (−.59) and had a low loading on PA (.06). The results for "content" were less definitive but still supportive. "Content" had a lower loading on PA (.39) than NA (−.43). In the Mayer and Gaschke (1988) study, therefore, there were at least a few clean markers of low PA and low NA.

However, not all of the research has been this supportive. In one study, Meyer and Shack (1989) collected self-ratings on a variety of different mood adjectives. These data were then factor analyzed and subjected to a varimax rotation. Theoretically speaking, several adjectives would seem to have been good markers for low NA, including such things as "relaxed," "calm," "pleased," "content," "satisfied," "quiet," and "still." However, none of these items produced clear results. Most contained similar loadings on both NA and PA. In fact, "pleased," "content," "satisfied," "quiet" all had higher absolute loadings on PA than they did on NA. Of the remaining three that had higher loadings on NA, the clearest solution was for "calm," which loaded −.27 on NA and .19 on PA. Thus, "calm" was the only reasonable marker of low NA while it was also more or less independent of PA. Of course, −.27 is not a decisive loading.

Similar results were obtained for Meyer and Shack's low PA adjectives. Four items seemed to be good candidates for low PA: "sluggish," "drowsy," "sleepy," and "quiet." However, the first three of these adjectives all had higher (positive) absolute loadings on NA. That is to say, they were better markers of high negative affect than they were of low positive affect. In fact, the item that came closest to being a clean marker of low PA was "quiet." It had a −.31 loading on PA and a .26 loading on NA. Every other item with a negative loading on PA had a higher (and positive) loading on the NA dimension. Put differently, there were no clear indices of low PA.

NA and PA may be more independent at the high pole than at the low pole. This phenomenon has long been known. For example, Zevon and Tellegen (1982, p. 112) maintained that NA and PA were "descriptively bipolar but affectively unipolar dimensions." To state the matter differently, NA and PA seem only to be independent constructs at the high end of their poles.

What this means theoretically has yet be fully articulated. It is difficult to understand a dimension that is one thing on the low end and two things on the high. Certainly, this makes the NA/PA model more difficult to interpret, as most constructs have two poles, not one. The Hedonic Tone/Intensity model avoids these concerns. Hedonic Tone and Affect Intensity are (at least in

The Issue of Error Variance

A series of studies by Green, Goldman, and Salovey (1993) is also problematic for the NA/PA model of mood. These authors conducted confirmatory factor analyses of various mood adjectives. They found that when measurement error was taken into account, the two factor NA/PA model provided a poor fit to the data. A better fitting model involved a single bi-polar dimension of mood, with PA and NA fitting as opposite ends of this continuum. This bi-polar dimension, of course, is similar to the factor of Hedonic Tone. Similar arguments have been made by Russell (1979).

The Issue of Time Frame

As noted above, it has been argued that NA and PA are basic dimensions of both state and trait mood (Watson, 1988). However, some research suggests that the structure of mood may vary based upon the time perspective taken by the respondent. For example, studies by Diener and Emmons (1984) and Diener and Iran-Nejad (1986) were able to replicate the independent NA and PA dimensions only when individuals were asked to describe their mood in general. When subjects were asked to describe their current mood state (as opposed to their general predispositions), negative and positive affect exhibited a significant, negative correlation. Diener and his colleagues argued that it is difficult to feel both good and bad *at the exact same time*. If this is so, then NA and PA might be useful personality dimensions, but less useful as dimensions of state mood.

It should be emphasized that not all of the data are consistent. For example, Watson (1988) and Mayer and Gaschke (1988) were able to recover the NA/PA factor structure with judgments of one's present mood. The point here is that the NA/PA structure is only inconsistently obtained with ratings of current mood, while the Hedonic Tone/Intensity structure seems to be more stable. It would seem that the more stable factor structure is likely to be the more useful one.

Other evidence seems to suggest that people tend not to experience both types of affect simultaneously. Experimental and field evidence presented by Baron (1976, 1984) suggests that when incompatible mood states exist the stronger one tends to cancel the weaker. Baron (1976, 1984), in fact, has found that these incompatible responses are a useful tool for conflict management.

Once again, we should emphasize that independent mood states do not necessarily imply independent mood traits. Personality dispositions to experience moods may well be interdependent. This is a separate empirical question. Our concern here is with mood states. Both experimental (Baron, 1984) and correlational (Baron, 1976; Diener & Emmons, 1984; Diener & Iran-Nejad, 1986) evidence suggests that individuals experiencing a positive mood state will not be experiencing a negative one. Thus, when mood is assessed as a state, there is at least some evidence that NA and PA are (negatively) correlated. This would suggest the greater usefulness of an Hedonic Tone/Intensity Structure over the NA/PA structure.

Integration With Other Research

Watson and Clark (1984), recognizing the inability to choose between the two structures on mathematical grounds, argued that a more informed choice could be made by looking at the way in which the two structures fit with other relevant literature. The NA/PA model clearly has some strengths in this regard. As noted by Watson and Clark (1984), Watson (1988) and Watson, Clark, and Tellegen (1988), the same NA/PA factor structure can be used to describe both state and trait mood. NA corresponds to the personality dimension of Neuroticism and PA to the dimension of Extraversion. Thus, the use of the NA/PA solution allows for a clear connection between states and traits. On the other hand, as Larsen and Diener (1987) have shown, very similar links can also be established between Hedonic Tone/Intensity and other personality dimensions such as Affect Intensity. Similarly, the Hedonic Tone/Intensity model is also consistent with much research on attitudes (Osgood, Suci, & Tannenbaum, 1957). Consequently, the advantages of either structure using this criterion are unclear.

For purposes of Affective Events Theory, there is at least one respect in which the Hedonic Tone/Intensity model might be more useful. It is our belief that a common structure for moods and emotions would be advantageous and that the Hedonic Tone/Intensity structure better fits that bill. As we will describe in the next section, emotional states result from a two stage appraisal process (Frijda, 1986; Lazarus, 1991a, 1991b). The first part of the appraisal involves an assessment of the "goodness" or "badness" of the event, as well as an assessment of the event's importance. Appraisals of "goodness" lead to positive affective states, the intensity of which is relatively high for important events and relatively low for unimportant events. Similarly, appraisals of "badness" lead to negative affective states, whose intensity is likewise modulated by importance. We shall have more to say about emotion formation later. For now it should suffice to indicate how closely the appraisal of "good-bad" corresponds to Hedonic Tone, while the appraisal of "important-unimportant" impacts intensity. The observations suggest that the Hedonic Tone/Intensity model might be more parsimonious and more easily integrated with various theories of emotion.

THE EFFECTS OF EVENTS ON EMOTION AND MOOD

Emotion Generating Events

Our theory gives primary emphasis to the role of events as proximal causes of affective reactions and then as more distal causes of behaviors and attitudes through affective mediation. Consequently, at this point we feel obligated to discuss what we mean by event. This obligation is easily met because we mean nothing more than what the word event means in ordinary language. The World Book Dictionary gives the primary definition of event as "a happening, especially an important happening." The Random House Dictionary goes on to add "something that occurs in a certain place during a particular period of time." Implied in both of these definitions is the idea of change, a change in circumstances, a change in what one is currently experiencing.

Some, but by no means all, events have affective significance in that they generate an emotional reaction or mood change in people. It is these changes that we need to focus on. To do so requires that we try to answer at least two questions. First, what kinds of changes have affective significance? Second, how do specific representations of events eventuate in the experience of specific emotions?

It turns out that these two questions correspond nicely to a two stage appraisal process advocated by most cognitively oriented emotion researchers (Lazarus, 1991a, 1991b; Ortony, Clore, & Collins, 1988; Roseman, 1984; Smith & Ellsworth, 1987; Stein, Tribasso, & Liwag, 1993). We present an overview of the common elements of their theories to describe the processes involved when events elicit emotional reactions. We should say from the outset that emotion theories come in many different forms. Plutchik (1994) has described four different categories: motivational theories, psychoanalytic theories, evolutionary theories, and the cognitive theories which we focus on. All theories assume that emotional reactions generally begin with an appraisal of an event (Plutchik, 1994); however, cognitive theories focus their attention on just this point. Because this is the issue we need to focus upon, we feel that the cognitive theories have more to say to us. However, we invite our readers to examine other mediators of event-emotion relationships.

There appears to be a common emotion elicitation process at the core of all cognitive appraisal theories. This process begins with an event which is initially evaluated for relevance to well being in simple positive or negative terms. This initial evaluation also contains an importance evaluation which influences the intensity of the emotional reaction. Initial appraisal leads to further, more specific, appraisal of context focusing on consequences, attributions, coping potential, and so forth. While different theorists offer different appraisal dimensions, all suggest that it is this secondary level of appraisal which results in the experience of discrete emotions like anger, sadness, or joy.

Primary Appraisal

Initial or primary appraisal appears based on "concern relevance" (Frijda, 1993), relevance to well being. Just what does this mean? Most theorists suggest that concern relevance is intricately tied to one's personal set of goals and values. Lazarus (1991a) is very specific when he says that "harms or benefits depend on goal commitments which reside in the person and are either thwarted or facilitated by the behavior of the environment" (p. 92). He concludes that initial appraisal involves an assessment of "goal relevance," does the event touch on some issue of personal desire or concern, and "goal congruence," is the event consistent (beneficial) or inconsistent (harmful) with those desires or concerns. Similar positions are offered by Ortony, Clore, and Collins (1988), Frijda (1993), Stein, Tribasso, and Liwag (1993), among others. Recently, Berkowitz (1989) has reformulated the classic frustration-aggression theory of Dollard, Doob, Miller, Mowrer, and Sears (1939) in these terms, concluding that frustration is a blockage of goal gratification and the aggression effect is mediated by negative affective responses.

In addition, theorists who argue that goal relevance is essential to the emotional reactions to events generally add that the intensity of the emotion is directly correlated with the importance or desirability of the goal. Ortony, Clore, and Collins (1988) add other variables which influence the intensity of the emotional reaction to an event, including unexpectedness and existing arousal levels.

Although both positive and negative goal relevant events can occur, producing positive and negative emotional reactions, respectively, Taylor (1991) reviews evidence which suggests that the effects of positive and negative events are not symmetrical. More specifically, she concludes that negative events produce stronger reactions than do positive events. Although the research which examines this issue suffers from the difficulty of equating event strength, the body of the work suggests that negative events produce stronger physiological responses and stronger subjective feelings of affect.

The connection between the goal relevance involved in general emotional appraisals and the motivational and affective consequences of work goals is obvious. Locke and Latham (1990) have provided a useful discussion of the relationship between work goals and affective reactions and we will add only a few points relevant to emotional appraisal. First, the type of goals relevant to emotional appraisal go well beyond the performance goals which form the core of organizational study in this area. People have a wide variety of goals and objectives. These preferred states can be what people strive for, what they seek to avoid, what they hope to maintain, what they want to see occur, and so forth (Cropanzano, James, & Konovsky, 1993). All are relevant to emotional appraisal.

Second, in agreement with most cognitive appraisal theorists (Lazarus, 1991a; Ortony, Clore, & Collins, 1988; Stein, Trabasso, & Liwag, 1993) we assume that goals are hierarchically organized (cf. Cropanzano et al., 1993). People have broad, distal goals as well as proximal subgoals which are instrumental to the attainment of these higher level objectives. In addition, the goal-subgoal connections within hierarchy structures can be described with different types of instrumentality. Some subgoals are necessary but not sufficient for the attainment of broader objectives, as, for example, the instrumentality of a college degree for professional success. Some subgoals are sufficient but not necessary for the attainment of broader objectives, as, for example, winning the lottery as a way of achieving wealth. We expect that the importance of any particular goal, and therefore the intensity of emotional arousal, is influenced by the position of the event implicated goal in the hierarchy and well as the nature of the instrumental relationship with other goals. For example, it might be that the failure to obtain a necessary but not sufficient goal may have greater negative implications than the actual achievement of that goal has positive emotional implications. Similarly, meeting a sufficient but necessary goal may have greater positive emotional significance than the failure to meet that goal would have negative significance.

Third, people can and do focus on different elements of their goal structures at any particular time. It is logical to assume, therefore, that goal attention influences the reaction to specific events.

We wish to make one last point on this issue of goals and emotional appraisal. After reading what we have written about the nature of emotional appraisal, one might argue that the appraisal of the goal significance of events greatly resembles the process of standard comparison which we ascribed to the Cognitive Judgment approach. The similarity is not lost on us, but we must point to some important differences. To begin with, our focus here is on the formation of discrete emotional reactions not general evaluations. Second, our focus is on the appraisal of the emotional significance of an event, not the goal significance of a feature of the environment. Third, with regard to emotional experiences, goal significance is just the beginning of the full appraisal process. This all being said, one fundamental point of similarity remains and that is the ubiquity of goals as frame of reference for evaluating one's personal state of affairs.

Secondary Appraisal

All cognitive appraisal theorists argue that primary appraisal is followed by a secondary appraisal, an interpretive "meaning analysis" (Smith & Pope, 1992) in which specific cues from the environment and the person are evaluated and discrete emotional responses elicited. Where the theories differ is in the specific dimensions they propose as relevant to the appraisal process. So, for example,

Smith and Ellsworth (1985) proposed that emotional events are appraised in terms of five dimensions: pleasantness, certainty, self vs. other agency, attentional direction (toward or away from), and effort needed to deal with the event. Roseman (1984) proposed that events are appraised in terms of whether the situational state is consistent or inconsistent with motives, certainty of outcome, agency, motivational state (consistent with a positive or negative motive), and coping potential. Lazarus (1991a) offered blame or credit (who is responsible), coping potential and future expectancy of the situation improving or getting worse as the key appraisal dimensions. Other dimensional structures have been offered by Frijda (1987), Ortony, Clore, and Collins (1988), and Scherer (1984) among others.

Although most appraisal theories do not specify any particular sequence to secondary appraisal, essential elements of the process can be captured by using a decision tree as a model. Figure 7 illustrates this using the configuration set forth by Stein, Trabasso, and Liwag (1993). We use this configuration as an example, without endorsing this dimensional structure over any other.

Research on the validity of this appraisal process can be illustrated by a recent study by Roseman, Spindel, and Jose (1990). They asked subjects to recall events for 16 specific emotions and then to respond to a set of appraisal questions for each. They showed that the responses to the appraisal questions were able to differentiate among the specific emotions. Other studies done by Weiner (1985), Smith and Ellsworth (1985), and Frijda (1989), among others, have generally supported each researcher's conception of appraisal dimensions, although no definitive conclusion about the usefulness of one configuration over another can yet be made.

Mood Generating Events

There exists quite a substantial empirical literature which speaks to the antecedents of moods. Interestingly, this literature exists primarily as a catalogue of mood manipulations in studies conducted to examine some hypothesis about mood effects. Most of these manipulations seem rather intuitive and ad hoc, allowing for little to be gleaned about their underlying conceptual similarities. Theoretical discussions of the antecedents of mood have been far less frequent than have similar discussions about the antecedents of emotions. All this is meant to indicate that there is much less to say about the antecedents of mood then there was to say about the antecedents of emotion.

Nonetheless, Morris (1989) has contributed a useful discussion of this topic which we will summarize. He suggests that there are four positions on the sources of experienced moods. Position 1 states that moods are the result of mildly positive or mildly negative events. This is the position which guides most of the laboratory research on the effects of moods. Indeed, experimental studies

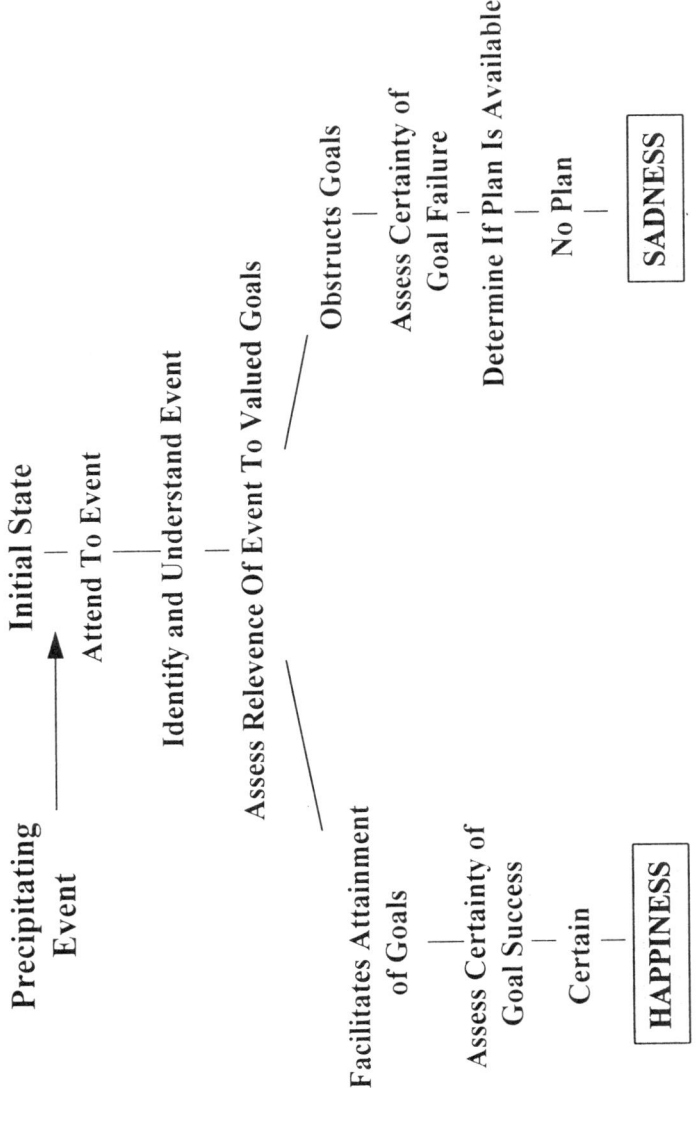

Figure 7. Appraisal Flow for Happiness and Sadness

Source: Adapted from Stein, Trabasso, and Liwag (1993).

have demonstrated the efficacy of manipulating mood by showing brief videos, providing subjects with cookies, playing pleasant or unpleasant music, helping subjects "find" a small amount of money, inducing success on experimental tasks, and so forth. While these studies show that mild events of "hedonic relevance" induce a mild affective state more consistent with moods than emotions they do little to tell us what it is about these events that produce the state. Morris says they are events of hedonic relevance, but this says nothing more than they induce affect. We acknowledge their effectiveness but also suggest that however intuitive they may seem a fuller statement of what kinds of events are of mild hedonic relevance is absent.

The second position noted by Morris is that moods result from the offset of emotional reactions. Whether they are believed to be residues of the emotions, simultaneous affective experiences initially overwhelmed by the emotion or opponent process reactions to the end of the emotion varies. In each case, the mood follows the emotion. Morris (1989) says that it is difficult to comment on the validity of this position because there are too few relevant empirical studies.

Position 3 states that moods can result from the recollection of emotional events. It seems clear that mood states can be directly affected by cognitive processes of recall and imagination in the absence of actual, current affective events. Many popular mood manipulations count on it. So too do authors and screenwriters. Morris (1989) argues that the affective response is likely to be "mood like" in that it will be of low intensity with no specific response tendencies. While we do not argue that moods can result from recall or imagination we would add that so too can full blown emotional responses. Many people know all too well that thinking about a deceased loved one can generate real sadness, not undifferentiated background affect.

Finally, Position 4 states that inhibition of a full blown emotional response can result in a residual mood. Wharton and Erickson (1993) argue that "emotional display rules" exist in organizations and that there are increasing expectations to control emotional displays at work. To the extent that Position 4 is valid, these expectations of emotional suppression may increase the prevalence of negative moods, with accompanying consequences.

OTHER CAUSES OF AFFECT LEVELS AT WORK

Dispositional Influences on Affect

Thus far we have presented evidence that affective traits are one cause of job satisfaction. We have further maintained that these traits are partially rooted in the individual's biology, and may have some genetic basis as well.

Despite this, we were careful to note that these observations do nothing to rule out the important role played by situational determinants.

Main Effects of Affective Dispositions

Research suggests that affective dispositions exert main effects on job satisfaction. One of the best illustrations of this is a large survey of 1,816 drivers conducted by Czajka (1990). Czajka (1990) reports that job satisfaction was predicted by both positive affectivity ($r = 0.43$) and negative affectivity ($r = -0.46$). Additionally, after controlling for salary and tenure, NA and PA together account for 29% of the variance in job satisfaction. Czajka's (1990) findings are important for our present purposes, as he reports no evidence of a disposition by situation interaction. Instead, situational variables (i.e., pay and tenure) and person variable (i.e., NA and PA) each contributed additive main effects. Similar results were obtained in two studies by Cropanzano, James, and Konovsky (1993). Findings of this type would suggest that both affective traits and situational attributes impact job satisfaction. However, a closer look suggests that reality might be a little more complicated than this.

Affective traits appear to act as latent predispositions that help set the stage for individuals to have more or less intense bouts of emotion. These traits are affective predispositions and not the experience of affect, per se. Thus, we can further see that a given affective trait manifests itself only under particular environmental conditions. This is to say, for example, that an individual high in trait Negative Affectivity or neuroticism, need not go through life with a chronic sense of discontentment. Rather, such an individual is predisposed to react more strongly to negative events when they happen to occur. When no negative event takes place, individuals high and low in trait NA should have similar levels of mood and job satisfaction.

This observation has some interesting conceptual implications. If affective dispositions are defined as manifestations of repeated bouts with negative and positive emotion, and if such bouts of emotion are partially dependent upon the situation, then affective traits are (partially) defined in reference to the environmental context. Concrete evidence for this can be gleaned from a study by Werner and Pervin (1986). Werner and Pervin content analyzed the items from six widely used personality inventories. This included, but was not limited to, scales that measured dispositional affectivity. Across the six inventories, 55.7% of the items made specific reference to situations. Thus the personality traits were being measured, and to some extent defined, as to how they were manifested in particular settings.

This does not mean that researchers can or should not study traits and environments separately. In fact, the very complexity of the problem demands that we do so. Nevertheless, a full understanding of the way in which affective dispositions manifest themselves demands that we simultaneously consider both the trait and the eliciting situation. Below, we consider this issue from two perspectives. First, we consider statistical interactions between affective dispositional and situational stimuli. Second, we explore the reciprocal transactions between the person and the environment.

Statistical Interactions

Bolger (1990) surveyed pre-medical students in the period leading up to and shortly after taking the MCAT exam. Bolger also assessed each individual's level of neuroticism. Neuroticism is closely related to trait NA (Meyer & Shack, 1989; Watson & Clark, 1984). Bolger (1990) found that individuals high in neuroticism were more reactive to the stress of the exam. In particular, the high neuroticism individuals reported more anxiety in the week preceding the MCAT, but were not more anxiety ridden in other weeks. Negative emotion was only manifested as the stressor approached. When the stressor was further away in time, all individuals were about equally low in mood negativity.

Similar findings were also obtained in another longitudinal study by Bolger and Schilling (1991). Within a community sample of adults, Bolger and Schilling (1991) found that participants high in neuroticism had much more negative responses to various daily hassles, such as interpersonal conflict.

In a field study of working individuals, Parkes (1990) drew similar conclusions. When placed in a stressful environment, teachers who were high in NA reported more symptoms of distress than did teachers low in NA. Conversely when the environment was less stressful, teachers reported similar levels of distress, regardless of their level of negative affectivity.

All of these findings were replicated and extended by Marco and Suls (1993). These later researchers also discovered that individuals high in trait NA were more reactive to negative events. Moreover, Marco and Suls (1993) also found that high NAs take longer to recover from a stressor. Once again, the emotional outcomes associated with NA were only present when a negative event occurred. At other times, individuals high in trait NA demonstrated levels of emotion that were comparable to their low NA counterparts.

These ideas were experimentally tested by Larsen and Ketelaar (1991). Larsen and Ketelaar (1991) first assessed undergraduate students on their levels of neuroticism and extroversion. (PA is highly correlated with extroversion, but extroversion includes other things as well. For a discussion, see Meyer and Shack [1989] and Johnson and Ostendorf [1993]). Larsen and Ketelaar (1991) then exposed subjects to three kinds of stimuli: positive affect provoking, negative affect provoking, and nonaffect provoking (neutral). As one might expect, individuals high in neuroticism reacted primarily to the negative events. They were relatively nonreactive to the neutral and positive stimuli. Conversely, individuals high in extroversion reacted mainly to the positive events. They, in turn, were relatively nonreactive to the negative and neutral stimuli. Again, we see evidence that affective traits serve as predispositions to respond within a particular environmental context.

It is noteworthy that this reasoning has been directly applied to job satisfaction. In an experimental study Bittle and Hausenstein (1990) found that dispositional affectivity was only related to job satisfaction when the work environment was generally unenriched and negative. However, while in a relatively enriched environment individuals were generally satisfied with their work, regardless of whether or not they were predisposed to negative affectivity.

Trait affectivity does seem to be related to both one's mood and also one's level of job satisfaction. However, in both cases, the personality trait acts as an affective predisposition. That is, it predisposes people to respond with greater or lesser intensity to either a positive or a negative event.

The Dynamic Transaction Between the Person and the Environment

It is important to note that individuals are not passive recipients of environmental pressure. Instead, individuals move through their lives both influencing and being influenced by their environments. This is true for all personality traits, but we are here concerned with the evidence pertaining to affective predispositions. Unfortunately, virtually all of the research has been conducted with only predispositions for negative emotion. It is likely (albeit still unclear) that trait PA behaves in a similar fashion. In any case, these limitations in the literature have caused us to limit our discussion to trait NA and related dispositions.

Individuals high in trait negative affectivity behave differently than their counterparts who are low on this trait. In particular, they are more likely to engage in contentious interpersonal tactics by being obstinate or argumentative. For example, Buss, Gomes, Higgins, and Lauterbach (1987) found that individuals predisposed to negative emotion were more likely to quarrel with their spouses.

These findings were extended in a longitudinal field study by Bolger and Schilling (1991). In various settings, including the workplace, individuals high in neuroticism were more likely to argue and quarrel with others. Bolger and Schilling (1991) also found that this tendency to fight was actually one cause of the experienced negative mood. That is, by their contentiousness, individuals high in neuroticism elicited hostility from others. This hostility, in turn, caused them to experience negative emotion.

Although little direct evidence exists, it also seems possible that the work environment can affect individual levels of trait NA. In one longitudinal study, Kohn and Schooler (1982) found that trait levels of personal distress were accentuated by oppressive working conditions. For example, workers forced to labor under heavy work loads with tight deadlines were likely to show higher levels of trait-based distress. Kohn and Schooler's (1982) study is highly suggestive. However, more research is needed to replicate and extend these findings.

Environmental Causes

Environmental psychologists have uncovered a variety of factors which can change the level of reported affect (see Bell, Fisher, & Loomis, 1978, for a good review). Such environmental conditions as weather, air pollution, noise, and negative ion level appear to influence affect and related behaviors. Generally these factors operate in the background, influencing mood states rather than specific emotions.

In general, several aspects of weather are related to self-reported mood. Laboratory studies have shown that exposing subjects to uncomfortable levels of heat produces negative mood states (Bell, Garnand, & Heath, 1984; Griffitt & Veitch, 1971). Similarly, Cunningham (1979) found that a hot temperature during the summer reduced mood levels while in the winter, a warmer temperature was associated with a better mood. It has been shown that sunshine has a positive effect on mood states (Persinger, 1975) and high humidity is associated with negative affect (Cunningham, 1979; Persinger, 1975).

Laboratory research has shown that exposing people to noxious pollutants can worsen their moods (Rotton, 1983) but the picture is complicated by research indicating that different pollutants have different effects during different seasons. For example, Cunningham (1979) found that higher levels of carbon monoxide were associated with better moods during the summer and worse moods in the winter. Obviously, these results and other results like them must be interpreted in the context of severe potential for spurious effects of other variables. Baron, Russell and Arms (1985) have shown that negative ions in the environment affect mood levels. However, in their research the direction of the effect depended upon other environmental stimuli.

Crowding is another environmental variable that can have negative consequences for mood levels (Freedman, 1975). Oldham and Fried (1987) found that perceptions of crowding were associated with lower levels of job satisfaction. However, the negative mood effects of crowding can be reduced when people believe they have personal control (Fleming, Baum, & Weiss, 1987).

Overall, the evidence suggests that a wide variety of environmental factors influence individual affect levels. By and large, these operate in the background to influence mood levels but it seems clear that their consequences on organizational behaviors, as mediated by mood states, are likely to be important.

EMOTION EPISODES: THE EBB AND FLOW OF EMOTIONAL EXPERIENCE

Our own discussion of emotions, guided as it is by theories and research on the topic, has so far characterized emotions as discrete reactions precipitated by specific events. Although we believe this to be a useful characterization of any specific emotional reaction, in a very important sense it misses a fundamental aspect of emotional experience. Frijda (1993) notes that when people are asked to describe an emotional experience, often they do not simply report a single emotion precipitated by a single event. Instead they report a series of emotional transactions with the environment, all coherently organized around a single underlying theme. Frijda refers to this coherent and dynamic series of emotional experiences as an emotion episode, a situation in which a single event of affective significance leads to the unfolding of a series of subevents, also with affective significance. Each of the subevents can produce a distinct, even opposite, emotional response but the full episode is driven by what Lazarus (1991a) would call a core relational theme.

Frijda (1993) goes on to say that during this episode the person remains in a state of "continuous emotional engagement" (p. 387). Emotional engagement refers to a heightened level of arousal and attention. To us, this suggests that during the emotion episode, the person's attention is focused on issues related to the underlying theme, possibly leaving fewer resources to commit to job performance. It also suggests that small events, coworker comments, organizational memos, and so forth take on increased, and perhaps unwarranted, emotional significance. Finally, it suggests that people may overreact to emotional events unrelated to the underlying core theme as their heightened level of arousal produces a misrepresentation of the event's emotional import. A likely consequence of emotional engagement is that people will experience more intense and diverse affective reactions then they would otherwise.

The effects of emotional engagement on affect levels during emotion episodes can be seen in research examining Zillman's Excitation Transfer Theory (Zillman, 1979). Excitation Transfer Theory proposes that individuals' emotional experiences are enhanced when people are already in aroused states, regardless of the source of the original arousal or of its initial hedonic direction. However, this excitation transfer should only occur when the arousal experience has become "disconnected" from its original cognitive label. Supporting data is found in a number of studies by Zillman and his associates (e.g., Cantor, Zillman, & Bryant, 1975; Zillman & Bryant, 1974; but also see, Branscombe, 1985). Of course, the persistent effects of mood on how we interpret the world (Morris, 1989), which we will discuss later, also illustrates the affective consequences of continuous emotional engagement.

Imagine a worker who hears about the possibility of a large scale layoff in his organization. This event, being of relevance to his well being, is likely to elicit an emotional reaction. Because it has negative implications it will elicit a negative reaction and because it involves the anticipation of future harm that negative reaction is likely to be fear or anxiety. This layoff possibility, in turn, instigates a series of subevents, many caused by the coping mechanisms of the worker himself, each of which can have some emotional significance. For example, the worker may talk to his supervisor who tries to reassure him of his worth to the company and these reassurances produce a positive affective state. The worker may talk to other workers who relate tales of downsizing or outplacement, each with emotional implications. During the "episode" the worker will experience wide swings of affect in both positive and negative directions. He will also engage in coping processes which can divert resources away from job activities and consequently reduce job performance.

The key element of the concept of emotion episodes is that these episodes represent the ebb and flow of emotional experience over time. While each of the events during the episode can be described in discrete terms, the episode itself has a coherence and a set of features that suggest it should be treated as a unit of analysis.

AFFECTIVE CYCLES: EXOGENOUS AND ENDOGENOUS CAUSES

Earlier, we stated than any analysis of affect as either a dependent or independent variable would require a full consideration of the fluctuation of affect levels over time. We are now prepared to offer a more detailed, albeit speculative, statement of our position.

We begin by suggesting that affect states can be described at two levels. First, one can describe an immediate affective state at a general or "primary" level. This description would refer to the state as being either positive or negative and of being at a certain level of intensity. In some cases, affective states can only be described at this primary level. A person's current mood, divorced as it is from specific references, is the notable example. In other cases, when specific emotions are involved, the affective state can be described at two levels, a general description involving valence and intensity (corresponding to the primary appraisal of emotion generation) and a secondary level which references the specific emotion(s) involved. Even where specific emotions are experienced, description and analysis at the primary level can still be useful.

Primary affective states can and do fluctuate over time. Particular trends in affect levels are the result of both endogenous and exogenous factors. Endogenous factors which influence affect trends include affective dispositions, established cycles of mood levels and chronic, situational circumstances of affective significance. Exogenous factors are affective events which serve as "shocks" that disrupt the regularity of underlying affect patterns. They can be either work related or nonwork related.

In most cases, these shocks will constitute events which generate an emotional reaction consisting of both primary and secondary appraisal. Consequently, the affective state can be described both in terms of the general evaluative dimension and in terms of the specific emotion experienced. However, in some cases events of "mild hedonic relevance" may elicit a change in mood state without accompanying secondary appraisal and therefore without the experience of a specific emotion.

Finally, affective "shocks" produce "after shocks." Here we are referring to the emotion episodes we described earlier. To remind the reader, an emotion episode refers to a series of emotional experiences precipitated by a single emotional event. During the emotion episode the person is in a state of continuous affective or emotional engagement and the series of after shocks should continue to alter the normal affective pattern.

In Figures 8 and 9 we have tried to visually depict what we have been suggesting. Figure 8 shows a hypothetical picture of a pattern of affect for a single individual. Figure 9 shows ones subject's data from a study by Weiss, Nicholas, and Daus (1993). Weiss et al. asked managers to provide self-reports of affect levels 4 times a day over a 3-week period. Figure 9 shows the results for one manager over 4 days, 16 total observations, presenting only the results for self-reports of being in a pleasant or unpleasant mood state.

It can readily be seen that the collection of affect data over any period of time allows for analysis of a number of parameters in affect trends, including means and variances of the aggregate set as well as the frequency and severity of "affect spikes." These parameters can serve as both dependent and independent variables in organizational analysis. For example, one might examine the relationship between dispositional variables and the mean or variance in affect states. Spikes serve as evidence for the occurrence of affective events which disrupt more typical affect trends and, therefore, can be examined in relation to these events. All of these parameters can be examined with regard to their association with traditional organizational criteria.

However, focusing on parameters which summarize these data hides the richness of the information inherent in data examined over time, its rhythm and its deviations from an underlying rhythm. Oscillating patterns or cycles of mood have been examined in nonwork settings by Larsen and Kasimatis (1990) and McFarlane, Martin, and Williams (1988) among others. Such cycles can be examined in terms of the amplitude of response as well as the frequency or period of the cycle. Larsen and Kasimatis (1990), reminiscent of Hersey (1932), showed that the extent to which a 7-day cycle described mood fluctuations was predicted by individual personality factors, with introverts showing a more cyclical pattern than extroverts. Studies of mood cycles within

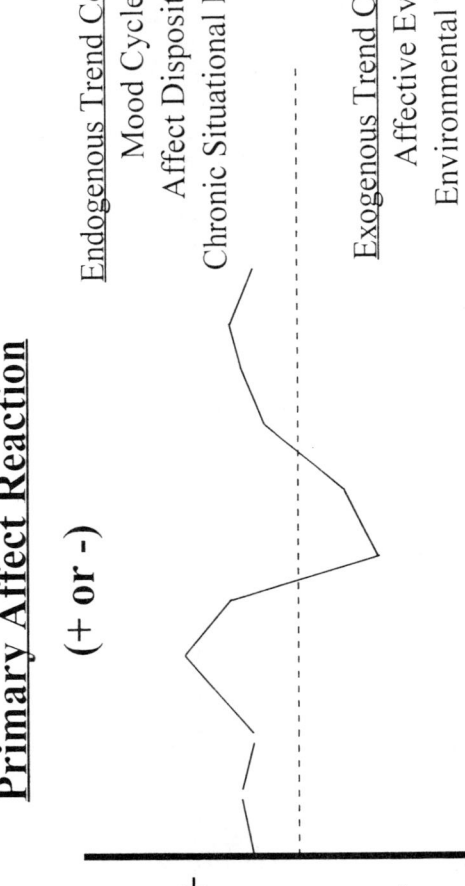

Figure 8. Affect Cycles

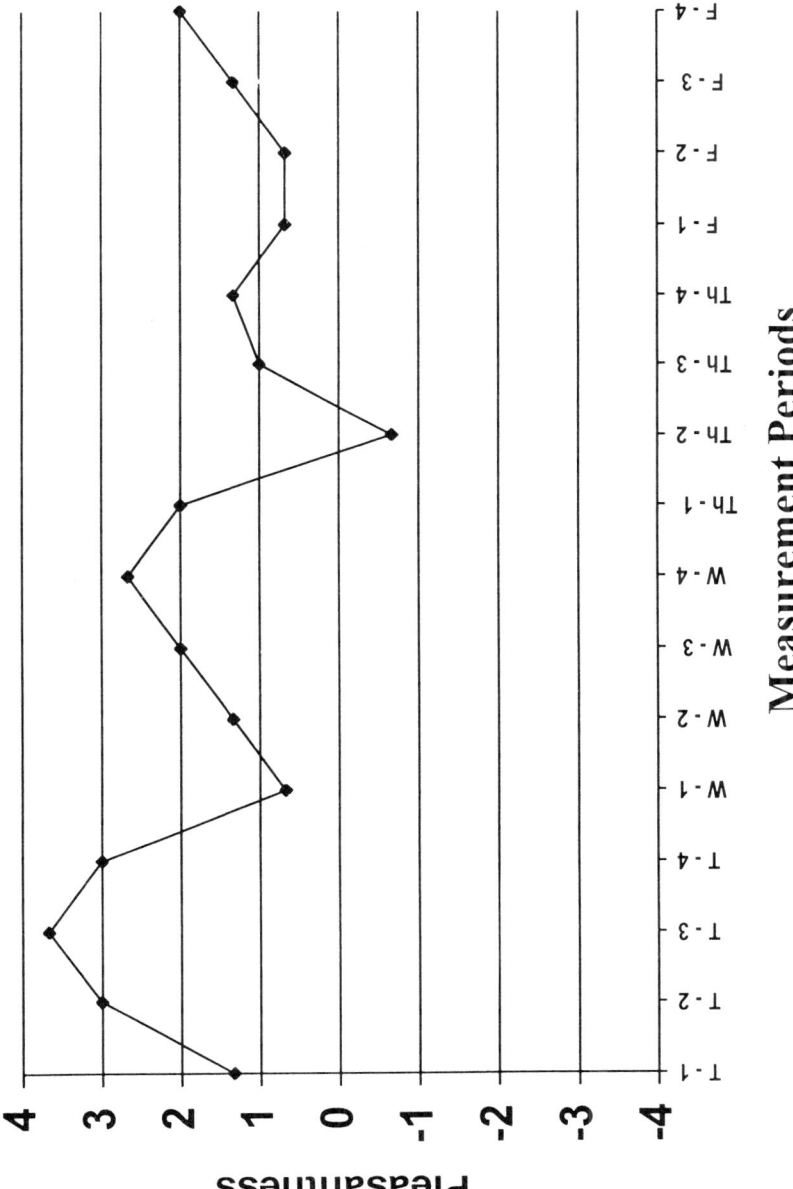

Figure 9. Affect (Pleasantness) Trends for a Single Manager (Sixteen Recordings Over Four Days)

days, requiring multiple measurements throughout the day, are less frequent and apart from Hersey's speculations, formal analyses of mood cycles with data collected in work settings do not exist.

As an example of the possible advantage of looking at patterns of affect, we offer the study of the relationship between affect and performance. While reported associations of job satisfaction with performance are basically negligible, such analyses involve correlating aggregrate performance with "aggregate" satisfaction. In our opinion, examining the correspondence of affect patterns over time and performance patterns over time would be a more productive approach.

Cycles represent the endogenous components of the mood trends while exogenous components are represented by deviations from the cycles. One can focus on the stable patterns and treat the exogenous events as error, as do researchers searching for mood cycles, or one can detrend the data to examine effects of exogneous shocks. Each approach has a role to play in organizational analyses of affect.

While we think that the examination of the trends in affect is of real significance we do not want to misrepresent our position. To us, the affect trends are simply the history of affective experience over a period of time. As a documentation of that history, it may have predictive significance. However, the real action lies with the affective state at any particular time.

AFFECT AND SATISFACTION JUDGMENTS

A basic premise of this paper is that affective experiences at work influence overall judgments about satisfaction with one's job and do so independent of the influences of feature assessments. This position is consistent with more basic research on the affective and "cognitive" influences on general attitudes. In two separate studies, Abelson, Kinder, Peters, and Fiske (1982) asked survey participants to describe Presidential candidates in affective and trait terms. More specifically, participants were asked whether a candidate "has ever made you feel (angry, hopeful, etc.)" and also to evaluate that candidate in terms of specific traits (honest, smart, etc.). Regression analyses were conducted to examine the independent influence of both affective and trait ratings on overall evaluations of the candidates. In both studies the affect ratings consistently predicted the overall evaluations independent of the trait ratings. The trait ratings in fact were less useful.

More recently, Breckler and Wiggens (1989) reported two studies attempting to validate the distinction between affective and what they referred to as "evaluative" or belief influences on overall attitudes. In the first study students were given a list of objects or activities (e.g., computers, blood donations). Using scales developed for the study they were asked to indicate their beliefs about the objects/activities and how each makes them feel. These were then correlated with global ratings of each object/activity. Partial correlational analyses indicated that the affective and belief components had independent influences on the overall attitudes. The second study replicated the first and also showed that the affective component better predicted behavior then did the belief component.

Taking the distinction between affective and belief components a step farther, Edwards (1990) showed that attitudes can develop out of both affective experiences and information about the attitudinal object. Moreover, the effectiveness of persuasion attempts depends on whether the nature of the attempt is consistent with the original mode of attitude formation. In addition, Miller and Tesser (1986) argued that instrumental behaviors are driven by the belief component and consummatory behaviors by the affective component. They demonstrated that by getting people to focus on one of the components they could influence subsequent behaviors involving the attitudinal object.

All four papers proceeded from the basic premise that attitudes are general evaluations which are influenced by both affective experiences with the object and sets of more abstract beliefs about the object. While these are often referred to as the affective and cognitive components of attitudes, Breckler and Wiggins (1989) correctly point out that because cognitive processes are an important part of affective reactions it is better to make a distinction between those influences which represent emotional experiences with the object and those influences which relate to sets of beliefs about characteristics of the object. Taken together, these studies demonstrate the usefulness of making that distinction.

The relevance of this work to the nature of job satisfaction is easy to see. The affective component of job satisfaction reflects the recall of affective episodes on the job and the belief component represents evaluations of the job in terms of its features, as operationalized in the various versions of cognitive/judgment theories.

With regard to job satisfaction, the importance of the belief component has been frequently demonstrated. The contribution of the affective component has been less well established. To help rectify this situation, Weiss, Nicholas, and Daus (1993) had a sample of managerial/professional employees complete diaries in which they reported their mood levels four times daily over a 3-week period. At the end of the three weeks and independent of the diary procedure, participants completed a questionnaire which included a 5-item overall job satisfaction scale as well as a VIE based belief assessment containing questions about the instrumentality of the job for receiving each of 10 outcomes and the valence of those outcomes.

While the intrusiveness of the data collection procedure limited participation to only 24 subjects, the results clearly support the relevance of affect as a predictor of satisfaction and the relative independence of affective and belief based influences. Based on considerations described earlier, four different operationalizations of the mood self-reports were used: pleasantness, activation, positive affect, and negative affect. Average mood levels were computed (4 times daily over 16 days) and correlated with overall satisfaction. Three of the four correlations were statistically significant ($r = .66$ for pleasantness, $r = .47$ for positive affect, $r = -.41$ for negative affect) while the fourth ($r = .36$ for activation) approached significance.

Perhaps more importantly, regression analyses in which overall satisfaction was regressed on mood and VIE beliefs together demonstrated that both components had significant, independent influences on job satisfaction. Without getting into the question of which component is more important, the answer to which is probably "it depends," it is clear that with regard to judgments of job satisfaction both affective experiences and more abstract belief systems play a role.

The distinction between mood and emotion further complicates the analysis of affective influences on job satisfaction. We have argued, based upon Morris (1989), that moods are general affective states disassociated from particular events. They can arise as residual states after events or in response to the recall of previous emotional events. They can also arise from factors like the weather, having nothing to do with particular events. While, as in Weiss, Nicholas, and Daus (1993), one can chart the mood levels of individuals over the course of a day, it is more likely that specific events and not general mood levels are stored and recalled. Consequently, it may be that average mood level over a period of time predicts satisfaction (as in Weiss et al., 1993) because it is an indicant, however imprecise, of the frequency and/or intensity of affective events. It may also be the case that the average mood level predicts satisfaction because both share affective dispositional variance.

These positions are not incompatible and both suggest that part of a relationship between average mood level and satisfaction is spurious. If so, a better analysis of affective events and subsequent job satisfaction would focus on the occurrence of the events themselves and the affective reactions they generate or, at the very least, focus on significant changes in affect levels as indicants of affective events.

Not all of the relationship is likely to be spurious. To begin with, mood may color the interpretation of events. As such, being in a negative mood may result in a neutral event being interpreted as negative. More directly, a person's mood may trigger an actual event of affective relevance (e.g., an argument, a reprimand).

As certain as the dual influences of affect and belief on attitudes appear to be, the evidence for these influences does not speak to the basic question of whether attitudes are formed stored, revised, and recalled or whether they are constructed on demand. With regard to job satisfaction, is the evaluative judgment continuously revised by experience and therefore in place when required by the satisfaction questionnaire or does the questionnaire instigate an attitude construction process and a new judgment?

Hastie and Parke (1986) have made the distinction between "on-line" and memory based judgments in person perception and this distinction has relevance here. With "on-line" judgments, evaluations are made at the time of exposure to the events or information relevant to the judgment. Later, a stored judgment is retrieved. With memory based judgments, the judgment is made later and based upon retrieval of representations of the initial events or information.

Wilson and Hodges (1992) have provided an important discussion of this topic with regard to attitudes. They begin their discussion with what they refer to as the traditional viewpoint, a viewpoint which states that attitudes are stable and persistent evaluations. According to the traditional view, when people are asked to report their attitudes toward some object, their job, their supervisor, and so forth, they open a "mental file containing their evaluation" and report it. Presumably, this evaluation is the result of on-line judgment processes.

The alternative position, which they advocate, states that people often construct their attitudes at the time the attitude is called for. In constructing these attitudes they consult a large "database" of relevant information including, presumably, affective experiences with the attitudinal object and belief based information. When constructing these attitudes the full database is never tapped. Rather, at any given time, people generate their attitudes from a subset of the "database" and the subset they use can itself be influenced by current contextual factors. Consequently, attitudes can be quite unstable because they are influenced by situational factors which determine which information is utilized.

Wilson and Hodges (1992) offer a good amount of evidence to support their alternative position, focusing on the extensive evidence on contextual effects on attitudes. Of particular importance is research showing that current mood state can influence attitudinal reports. From this literature it seems quite clear that the mood of a person at the time satisfaction is being assessed can also influence responses to satisfaction scales, independent of the history of affect or the nature of belief systems. Recently, Brief, Butcher, and Roberson (1995) rather dramatically demonstrated this phenomenon. Employees filled out an attitude survey in small groups. In some groups, prior to completing the survey, employees were given cookies, soft drinks and an inexpensive gift, a manipulation designed to enhance positive mood. Employees in other groups were simply asked to complete the survey. Reported job satisfaction was higher in the positive mood groups than in control groups.

Wilson and Hodges (1992) go on to say that not all attitudes are constructed at the time of attitude evaluation. Some are, in fact, stored and recalled. Wilson and Hodges offer a number of suggestions about which attitudes are likely to be constructed and which are likely to be stored but perhaps the most well worked explanation is offered by Fazio (1986). Fazio describes attitudes as differing in "accessibility" which is simply the strength of the association between an object and an evaluative response. Attitudes gain in accessibility when then the association is strengthened by repeated calls for the evaluation or when the attitude has been formed by direct experience with the object.

Given the validity of Fazio's position, one could argue that attitudes formed on the basis of personal experience would be less influenced by contextual factors such as current mood. One could further argue that attitudes toward certain job facets, facets that have to do with "concrete" or tangible aspects of one's job, like coworkers or supervisors, are more likely to be formed by personal experience and are therefore less likely to be affected by context. More abstract features, security, trust, career development, as examples, are more likely to result from indirect informational influences and would be more affected by context. The study by Brief, Butcher, and Roberson (1995) examined only overall satisfaction and therefore does not allow for a test of this proposition.

Finally, if job satisfaction is at least partially constructed on demand one could reasonably ask about the way affective experiences are used in the judgment process. The nature of the storage and recall process is unclear. When attitude judgments are made, are affectively meaningful events somehow counted? Are they averaged over events with different intensities? If averaged, are they weighted by recency?

Very little research has been done on these questions. Diener and his colleagues (Diener, Colvin, Pavot, & Allman, 1991; Diener, Sandvick, & Pavot, 1990) have shown that the Subjective Well Being, a general judgment about satisfaction with one's life, depends more on the frequency of positive events than on their intensity. Diener speculates about a number of processes which lead to "psychic costs" following the experience of intense positive affect, thereby dampening their influence as well as the influence of subsequent positive experiences. Regardless of the processes involved, the suggestion that the frequency rather than the intensity of positive experiences has a more pronounced influence on satisfaction has implications for organizational practice. It suggests that major but infrequent affectively meaningful events such as recognition ceremonies or bonuses will be less important determinants of overall satisfaction than will working in an environment which provides daily, if only minor, positive experiences.

Affective experiences and object relevant beliefs together influence evaluative judgments. This much we know. Basic information about the cognitive processes involved remains speculative.

AFFECT AND PERFORMANCE

Perhaps the most disappointing aspect of decades of study on work attitudes is the failure to locate the holy grail of satisfaction research, an effect of satisfaction on performance. The typical study examining satisfaction-performance relationships has taken the following form: satisfaction, assessed as a bipolar construct with positive (satisfaction) and negative (dissatisfaction) poles is measured at some arbitrary point in time and correlated with some aggregate measure of performance. It is generally known that such studies have produced basically nothing. Satisfaction shows negligible correlations with performance (Iaffaldano & Muchinsky, 1985; Podsakoff & Williams, 1986) and when correlations are found causal direction is ambiguous. Correlations with indices of withdrawal (turnover, absenteeism, lateness) are perhaps more consistent but still quite small (Hulin, 1991).

Over the years numerous attempts have been made to explain the discrepancy between the intuitive appeal of the proposition and the absence of supportive results. So, for example, Fisher (1980) and Fisher and Locke (1992) have suggested that the lack of a relationship between satisfaction and performance was due to the discrepancy between the "generality" of attitudes and the "specificity" of most criterion indices. Solutions to this problem of inconsistent generality involve either making the attitude more specific, assessing "attitudes toward the act," or making the behavior more general, assessing aggregated patterns of multiple behaviors.

Neither solution is particularly satisfying. The former solution essentially changes the concept of job satisfaction in the service of theoretically uninteresting predictability. The second is perhaps more interesting but runs the risk of creating aggregations that have little practical meaning to organizations, also in the service of predictability.

Interestingly, rather than trying to explain the absence of findings one might ask why any relationship would be expected. What is not often said is that in the form in which the key constructs are conceptualized and measured there is very little reason to expect any relationship to begin with. With regard to productivity, one is hard pressed to develop a rationale for why a worker's overall evaluation of his or her job should in any way influence how hard he or she works on the job, what strategies he or she employs when doing the job or any of the other factors which affect task performance. With regard to withdrawal, the behavioral processes are perhaps easier to accept, generally involving decisions in which job satisfaction is one factor entering into a withdrawal decision. Even here, however, the decision process seems better suited to turnover than absenteeism or lateness which appear to be more spontaneous and less "thoughtful."

Our interest is, of course, affect and our objective in this last section is to examine the conceptual relationships between affective states and job performance, broadly defined. Generally, we will keep our reviews of the literature brief, as good reviews exist elsewhere (see Morris, 1989, for the basic literature on the effects of moods and Isen & Baron, 1991, for a more organizationally focused review of the effects of positive affect). Our focus will

Affect versus Attitude Driven Behaviors

To begin with, any understanding of the relationship between affect levels and work behaviors must begin by drawing the distinction between affect driven behaviors and attitudinally driven behaviors. Certain work behaviors are direct responses to affective experiences. So, for example, mood influences helping behaviors, information processing strategies and probability judgments (Morris, 1989). Similarly, more overt negative emotional experiences are likely to lead to specific coping responses (Lazarus, 1991a, 1991b). The particular pattern of responses can have important effects on work performance and these effects are not mediated by any relationship between affective experiences and satisfaction judgments. Thus, for affect driven behaviors, direct affect-performance relationships without nonspurious satisfaction-performance relationships would be expected. Further, because affect levels can fluctuate we would expect these affect driven behaviors to be of a relatively short duration and be high variability. This would suggest that any relationship would be best captured by analyses which assess to congruence of patterns of affect and performance.

Other work relevant behaviors are attitudinally driven. Attitude driven behaviors are directly influenced by overall evaluations of one's job and consequently any relationship between affect levels and these behaviors will be mediated by job satisfaction. These are likely to be behaviors which result from well considered decisions and specifically, those behaviors where the overall evaluation of the job enters into that decision.

Hulin (1991) has suggested that discrete withdrawal behaviors like lateness, absenteeism, turnover, and retirement are in fact all manifestations of an underlying latent withdrawal propensity. In his view, the common finding of low correlations among these behaviors is primarily due to attenuation resulting from their low base rates. Working from this position, Hanisch and Hulin (1990) attempted to show that retirement is one manifestation of this underlying withdrawal construct. In fact, what they showed was that the four withdrawal behaviors sorted into two factors, "work withdrawal" which included indices of unfavorable work behaviors, lateness and absenteeism, and "job withdrawal" which included turnover intentions and desire to retire. In addition, regression analyses suggested that JDI factors like pay satisfaction or work satisfaction were better predictors of job withdrawal then work withdrawal. This last finding is consistent with a generally better association between satisfaction and turnover than satisfaction and absenteeism (Hackett & Guion, 1985). (Lateness has been too infrequently studied to draw any conclusions.)

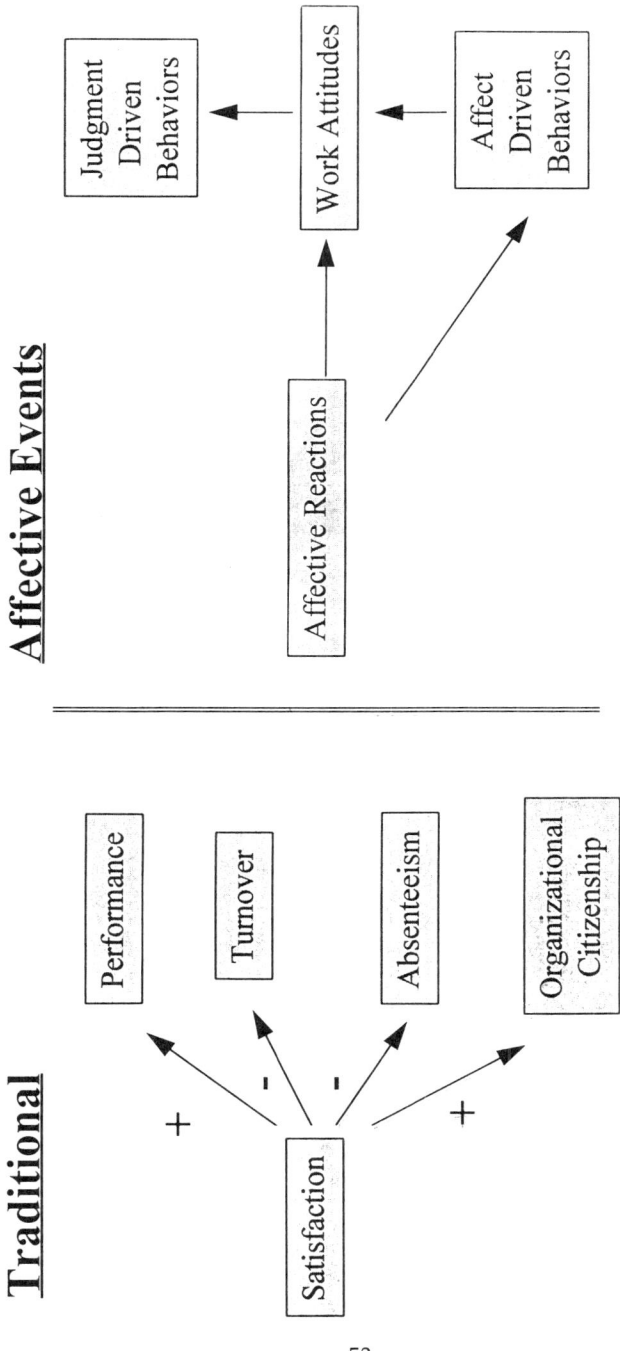

Figure 10. Affect and Performance: Two Models

While this two factor solution and the JDI correlations require replication, the findings are clearly consistent with our distinction between affect driven and attitude driven behaviors. Turnover and retirement are behaviors that require a thoughtful decision and satisfaction, the overall evaluation of one's current job situation, is likely to be one factor entering into that decision. Lateness and turnover are less "considered," tend to be more spontaneous, and are likely to be more a function of immediate affect levels.

The distinction between affect driven and attitude driven behaviors rests on the assumption that affect levels have direct behavioral consequences. In the next sections we point to the evidence with regard to the effects of emotions and moods.

Affect Driven Behaviors: Emotions

Throughout this paper we have distinguished between affective states which are unfocused, relatively mild and exist as background to our daily experiences (mood) and more overt emotional reactions of greater intensity of which people are aware (emotions). Discussion of the nature of affect driven behaviors will be facilitated by maintaining this distinction. Partly this is due to the fact that the emotion and mood literatures tend to be distinct and partly this is due to the fact that the effects of affective states, particularly negative ones, may depend on the degree of awareness of the state. Nevertheless, it is important to note that this distinction can be pushed too far. Certainly, most researchers from both traditions rarely worry about a difference between mood and emotion and therefore manipulations can overlap. Further, as mentioned earlier, overt emotional events may be one cause of longer lasting mood states.

Emotional reactions are often characterized as dysfunctional, disorganizing states. We believe, following Lazarus (1991a), that this is a misconception. Emotional responses are generally quite functional, but they are functional qua the emotion. They do not disorganize behavior as much as they reorganize or redirect it. Emotions do interupt ongoing behavior (Lazarus, 1991a; Mandler, 1984). They have what Frijda (1993) refers to as "control precedence." People in an emotional state tend to be controlled by that state, they tend to be preoccuppied by the emotion and there is a persistance to behaviors designed to deal with the emotion. This control precedence is particulary dramatic in the case of the emotion episodes which we described earlier. From the perspective of the previous behavior, this may seem disorganized and disruptive. However, from the point of view of the emotional problem it seems less so. Emotions "organize" behavior around the demands of the preciptiating situation and "disorganize" the activities that were disrupted.

For our purposes, we need to examine the effects of this "reorganization" response on job performance. In our opinion, the analysis of the performance implications of emotional states reduces to a distinction between two domains of behavior. Behaviors in the job domain are those behaviors required to do one's job. Behaviors in the emotion domain are those behaviors driven by the emotional state. The only question of relevance to job performance is this: "How are the behaviors in the emotion domain related to the behaviors in the job domain?"

Three answers are apparent. First, behaviors in the emotion domain can interfere with behaviors in the job domain. Emotional reactions can produce responses incompatable with job demands or can use up cognitive resources needed for job performance. Second, behaviors in the emotion domain can facilitate job performance, perhaps by increasing arousal levels or by instigating performance compatable behaviors (e.g., increased social behavior for a salesperson). Third, the behaviors in the emotion domain may be unrelated to those in the job domain. The key point, of course, is that behavior is not performance. The performance implications of emotions will depend on the match or mismatch between behaviors generated by the emotion or the resources used by the emotion response process and the behaviors and resources required by the task.

This being said, it is our contention that in most cases the emotion responses will tend to be incompatable with behavior in the job domain, producing performance decrements. Interestingly, these decrements are likely to occur as a consequence of both positive and negative emotions, because the management of both types of emotions will require resources which could be used for task performance and both types of emotions are more likely to produce job incompatable rather than job compatable behaviors. This prediction is in direct contradiction to the inuitive prediction of a positive performance effect for positive emotions and a negative effect for negative emotions.

In addition, we suggest that the performance implications of negative emotions will be more pronounced than those of positive emotions. Negative emotions serve as signals that some state of affairs is problematical. The sequence of activity involves primary appraisal, secondary appraisal and the development of a coping strategy designed to correct the situation. These activities are likely to be more extensively and continuously disruptive than are the activities resulting from the appraisal of a positive state.

We would therefore predict greater decrements in performance for negative emotional states than for positive states and certainly would be hard pressed to predict increments in performance for either state except under those rare circumstances where the behaviors in the emotion domain and job domain are compatable. Certainly, predicting simple linear associations between affective states (positive to negative) and performance (positive to negative) seems overly simple. The asymmetry for the performance implications of positive and negative emotional states is consistent with the research by Hersey (1932) which we cited earlier.

The behavioral implications of negative emotional states are generally discussed under the topic heading of coping strategies. It is not our desire to review this extensive literature. We do, however, want to comment on the important position offered by Lazarus and Folkman (Folkman & Lazarus, 1990; Lazarus, 1991a). Their theory identifies eight different coping strategies in response to a negative emotional event. These eight can be further reduced to two categories: problem focused coping and emotion focused coping. Problem focused coping deals directly with the emotion eliciting situation, through problem solving or confrontation. Emotion focused coping tries to deal with the affective state rather than its cause by denial, personal control of affect, social support, and so forth.

The choice of strategy has obvious performance implications but one should not be misled into thinking that problem focused coping is more performance efficient than is affect focused coping. Problem focused coping involves planning to deal with the emotional situation. This can be consuming of time and resources and can have negative effects on performance. On the other hand, affect strategies which involve denial might be more efficient in the short run because they allow the person to focus on the job.

However, we also need to make the distinction between short-term and long-term solutions. If we assume that elimination of the problem is the most performance effective strategy in the long run then strategies which avoid problem solving are not long-term efficient. In any case, research on the relationships between typical coping strategies and performance on jobs with different behavioral demands would be a useful activity.

Affect Driven Behaviors: Moods

The effects of mood on memory, judgments and behaviors have been studied quite extensively in the last decade. Research by Alice Isen has stimulated much of this work and extensive reviews of the literature can be found in Isen and Baron (1991) and Morris (1989). While Morris' book primarily reviews the basic research on the topic, Isen and Baron present reviews of both the basic and organizational literatures.

Before proceeding, it will be useful to again remember the distinction between behavior and performance. Mood has well documented effects on such things as memory, judgment, and social behaviors but the performance implications of these effects depend upon task demands. So, for example, mood appears to influence the depth of processing on cognitive tasks (Sinclair & Mark, 1992). The effect on performance will depend on the processing requirements of the job.

Three additional factors complicate efforts to draws definitive implications for organizational behavior from the basic literature on moods. First, mood effects themselves are complex. Effects are often inconsistent and researchers have most recently reduced efforts to document main effects and instead have searched for moderators and theoretical explanations that provide coherent organization to apparent inconsistences. Consequently, we will provide an overview of both basic findings and theoretical perspectives.

Second, the effects of mood are not always symmetric (Morris, 1989; Taylor, 1991). In the basic literature, much of the research has independently manipulated positive mood or negative mood and then compared the mood induced group to a control group not experiencing the mood manipulation. Even where both positive and negative moods are manipulated in the same study, results have been generally interpreted independently for the effects of positive mood, compared to a neutral mood, or negative mood, compared to a neutral mood. These paradigms can hide the fact that when being in a positive mood has effect A, being in a negative mood does not necessarily have an effect opposite to A. For example, being in a positive mood often (but not always) increases helping behavior when compared to a control condition of a neutral mood (Isen & Baron, 1991). However, being in a negative mood can also increase helping behavior, again when compared to a neutral condition (Morris, 1989).

Third, positive mood effects are almost entirely demonstrated by way of experimental studies where mood is manipulated with events of minor positive hedonic relevance. Isen's work (Isen, 1984; Isen & Baron, 1991) best illustrates this approach. People find money in telephone booths, they are given small prizes, they are shown funny movies or listen to pleasant music. Negative mood effects, on the other hand, are demonstrated in two distinct ways. First, events of minor negative hedonic relevance are manipulated. People are told they have failed some task or see a depressing movie or are asked to read sad stories. These kinds of studies parallel the positive affect studies and their results can be more or less compared to examine the differential effects of positive and negative moods. Negative mood effects are also demonstrated by comparing chronically, clinically depressed people with normals or sometimes by comparing less severe but still chronically dysphoric people with normals (Conway & Giannopoulos, 1993). These studies raise all of the traditional concerns of causal direction and spuriousness as well as new issues of the effects of mood intensity. We believe that the results of studies where negative mood is manipulated are of greater relevance to work issues than are results drawn from research with the chronically depressed.

The effects of mood have generally been organized into four categories: mood effects on memory, mood effects on evaluative judgements, mood effects on processing strategies, and mood effects on social behaviors. All have relevance to job performance and we will discuss each in turn.

Mood and Memory

One of the most extensively researched topics is the effect of mood on memory. Most of the research has been stimulated by Bower's (1981) integration of mood and emotion with an associative network model of memory. In this model emotions, like ideas and events, are represented as nodes in a network of associations or linkages. Whenever a node is stimulated, for whatever reason, activation spreads to connected nodes. If the activation level crosses some threshold the idea represented by the connected node is brought into consciousness (remembered). A number of predictions for the effects of mood on memory can be generated by this model but the two that have received the most attention have been the predictions of "state dependent memory" and "mood congruent memory."

State dependent memory refers to a facilitation of memory when the psychological or physiological state at the time of learning matches the state at the time of recall. So, for example, if you are in a negative mood when you learned some material your later recall of that material should be facilitated when you are again in a negative mood. This prediction derives from the idea that the material and the mood are associated at the time of learning. Activation of the mood at time of recall spreads to the learned material increasing the likelihood of the material reaching the activation threshold and thereby being brought into awareness. The hedonic tone of the learned material (positive, neutral, or negative) is of no relevance to the facilitation of recall.

Initial research by Bower and his associates seemed to support this position (Bower, 1981). Subsequent research has been neither strong nor consistent (Clore, Schwarz, & Conway, 1994; Morris, 1989) leading even Bower (Bower & Mayer, 1985) to question its robustness. (But, see Eich, 1995, for a discussion of some conditions which may facilitate the state dependent memory effect.)

Mood congruence effects are demonstrated when memory is facilitated by a match between the hedonic tone of the material being recalled and the mood at the time of recall. So, for example, one might ask whether being in a good mood facilitates the recall of positive as opposed to negative material. This issue of recall congruence has been considered important to mood researchers because the phenomenon has implications for the effects of mood on judgments and behaviors that rely on the recall of information. Consequently, a good amount of research has accumulated on the topic.

Overall, mood congruence finds more support than does state dependent memory, but the results are still not entirely straightforward. Clore, Schwarz, and Conway (1994) have most recently reviewed the literature on mood congruent recall and conclude that results support a congruence position, but not as would be predicted from an associative network model. More specifically, they argue that while positive moods facilitate the recall of positive materials and inhibit the recall of negative materials negative moods inhibit the recall of positive material but do not facilitate the recall of negative material. Clore et al. suggest that this asymmetry may be due to a mood management or mood repair process, whereby people in a negative mood deliberately avoid the recall of negative material in order to reduce their negative mood. However, as Clore et al. (1994), Blaney (1986), and Morris (1989) all point out, this mood repair process also suggests that people in a negative mood will deliberately recall positive material as well as repress negative material and this is not generally found. In any case, this issue of incongruence in the way positive and negative moods affect the recall of positive and negative material does not invalidate the basic finding; people in a positive mood recall more positive items from memory than negative items (recall of positive items is facilitated and negative items inhibited) and people in a negative mood recall more negative items than positive items (recall of positive items is inhibited).

Mood and Evaluative Judgments

Given the effects of mood on memory, one would naturally expect to find a biasing effect of mood on memory based judgments. In fact, this bias has been repeatedly demonstrated. So, for example, mood influences the evaluation of the positiveness or negativeness of events, the evaluation of neutral objects, the evaluation of other people and the perceived likelihood of positive or negative events occurring (Morris, 1989). All of these influences are in a mood congruent direction.

A good organizational example of this biasing effect is provided by the Brief, Butcher, and Roberson (1995) paper which we discussed earlier. They had two groups of employees complete a traditional job satisfaction questionnaire. Recall that prior to filling out the survey, some employees were placed in a positive mood while the remainder of the employees were not given a positive mood induction and served as the control group. As expected, employees in the positive mood reported higher job satisfaction than did employees in the control group.

The biasing effect of mood on evaluative judgments would appear to be a direct outcome of mood congruent memory effects. That is, when people are called upon to make judgments of evaluation, event probabilities, and so forth, they search their memories for information relevant to the judgment. If the mood they are in influences what they recall, as it does, then it should also influence the judgments that are based on these recollections.

As compelling as the memory based explanation is for these effects of mood on judgment, it does not appear to account for the phenomenon. Two findings, in particular, cast doubt on the memory based explanation. Johnson and Tversky (1983) had subjects read newspaper stories about deaths from different causes (illness, murder, fire) and then complete a questionnaire asking about the risks of dying by various causes. As intended, the newspaper articles produced a negative affective state in the subjects and subjects in these negative states reported greater concerns about dying from various causes than did controls. Of particular interest is the finding that the concerns were unrelated to the type of death that produced the original negative mood state. That is, people whose negative mood was caused by reading about someone dying from leukemia showed no greater concern about dying from illness than about dying from an accident. This finding, as Johnson and Tversky pointed out, is inconsistent with a memory based process because such a process would predict that the mood induction information would be most likely to cue memories related to that event.

Schwarz and Clore (1983) asked people in positive and negative mood conditions to respond to a life satisfaction questionnaire. Ordinarily, as predicted from any memory based explanation, one would expect that current mood would influence reports of life satisfaction. However, Schwarz and Clore also provided some subjects with an explanation for why they were in the mood they were in. Their findings clearly showed that current mood only influenced life satisfaction evaluations when subjects *were not* given a reason for their mood state. This finding, replicated on numerous occasions (Clore, Schwarz, & Conway, 1994), is difficult for any memory based explanation since these explanations posit mood as a memory cue regardless of any attributional information which might be available.

How is the mood effect on evaluative judgments to be explained if not by biased recall from memory? An alternative position, gaining popularity, is the "mood as information" position advocated by Schwarz and Clore (1988; Clore, 1992). The basic idea of this position is that the mood you are in is a piece of information you use to tell you how you feel about the object being judged. Essentially, you misattribute your affective state to the object or issue being evaluated and your judgment is biased accordingly. Let us illustrate this position by referring back to the paper by Brief, Butcher, and Roberson (1995). The reader will recall that employees placed in a positive mood at the time of completing a job satisfaction questionnaire reported higher job satisfaction than did control subjects. A memory based explanation for these results would suggest that the positive affect facilitated the recall of positive information used in making the satisfaction judgment. The mood as information position would suggest that the employees misattributed their current mood to the topic of the questionnaire, thereby assuming they felt better about their jobs than they would have in a neutral mood state. The mood as information position would also predict that the mood biasing effects on satisfaction can be eliminated by providing attributional information when the survey is administered.

The mood as information position suggests conditions when the biasing of effects of mood should be reduced. The existence of these moderating conditions does not, however, reduce the importance of mood on organizationally relevant evaluative judgments. We have previously defined mood as affect disconnected from its causes. In the Schwarz and Clore paradigm subjects are provided with clear, but false, explanations for their moods. This does not imply that in natural contexts such clear attributional factors will be readily available or that people in particular moods will be actively searching for these attributions. Consequently, it seems likely that the moderating condition of clear mood explanations is a low probability event in work contexts and therefore main effects of moods on evaluative judgments are more likely than not. Because so many organizational behaviors involve judgments and decisions based on evaluations of the likelihood of positive and negative outcomes the impact of mood states seems clear.

Mood and Processing Strategy

Sinclair and Mark (1992) have recently organized the diverse effects of mood on judgment in terms of the effect of mood on processing strategy. They argue that the findings consistently point to the conclusion that people in a positive mood are more likely to engage in simplified, heuristic processing strategies when making judgments and decisions while people in a negative mood are more likely to engage in systematic processing. The evidence they marshall for this general phenomenon is quite convincing . For example, in persuasion studies people in a positive mood are more influenced by peripheral cues such as source attractiveness while people in a negative mood are more influenced by central cues like message quality (Worth & Mackie, 1987). Such a difference in cue use is generally attributed to differences in depth of processing (Eagly & Chaiken, 1993). In addition, when making judgments about others, people in positive moods tend to rely more on stereotyping information while people in negative moods rely more on individuating information (Bodenhausen, 1993). Positive mood appears to increase halo among judgments on different dimensions when compared to neutral and negative moods (Sinclair, 1988). Finally, when compared to controls, people in a positive mood use fewer categories to group objects (Isen & Daubman, 1984).

In aggregate, these findings seem to converge on a general processing difference between people in positive and negative moods. People in a positive mood are less likely to engage in effortful, systematic processing than are people in negative moods. This consistent use of heuristic processing can, of course, be dysfunctional when tasks demand more effortful processing. For example, Sinclair and Mark (1992) found that statistics students placed in a positive mood were less accurate in their estimation of correlation coefficients from scatterplots than were students placed in a negative mood.

Sinclair and Mark (1992) examine the potential explanations for this general finding of processing differences and conclude that a combination of two seem reasonable. The first explanation involves mood maintenance or mood repair processes. People in a positive mood may avoid systematic processing because engaging in effortful cognitive processing may eliminate the positive mood. People in a negative mood, on the other hand, may be more inclined to engage in systematic processing as a distraction to help eliminate the negative mood.

The second and possibly coexisting explanation involves the mood as information explanation described earlier. This explanation assumes that current mood states are used as cues for judgments about the satisfactoriness of situations. People in negative moods judge the situation as somehow unsatisfactory, are motivated to rectify the situation and engage in the cognitive activity necessary to accomplish that goal. People in positive moods judge the situation as more satisfactory, less problematic, and therefore feel that systematic processing is unnecessary.

We would be remiss if we did not comment on a line of research which appears, on the surface, to be inconsistent with the conclusions of Sinclair and Mark (1992). Ellis and Ashbrook (1988) have suggested that chronically depressed individuals engage in more self-focused attention and negative thinking than do normals. This, in turn, reduces the cognitive processes available for problem solving producing a performance decrement on tasks that require extensive cognitive processing.

Recently, Conway and Giannopoulos (1993) provided evidence to support the Ellis and Ashbrook position. They provided depressed and non depressed subjects with information about 70 different jobs along five dimensions and asked the subjects to provide overall evaluations of the jobs. Using a regression based policy capturing procedure they found that the depressed subjects used fewer dimensions in generating their evaluations than did the controls.

Clearly, this data and the Ellis and Ashbrook position generally need to be reconciled with the evidence provided by Sinclair and Mark. One obvious difference is that Ellis and Ashbrook focus on the effects of chronic depression, a negative affective state of longer duration and greater severity than the mood manipulations used in studies cited by Sinclair and Mark. Whether this accounts for differences in results remains to be determined. However, if the effects of negative mood on processing strategy are curvilinear then questions of appropriate levels for generalization to organizational contexts become significant.

Recently, Staw and Barsade (1993) examined the effects of affective traits on managerial processing strategies. First year MBA students participated in an assessment center which included an in basket exercise measuring decision-making strategies (use of information, accuracy of judgments, etc.). Individuals assessed as having either high, medium, or low trait positive affect were compared. Results indicated that compared to subjects with medium or high trait positive affect, subjects with low trait positive affect used less data, requested less information and were less accurate in their judgments. Staw and Barsade's results are more consistent with the Ellis and Ashbrook position than they are with the Sinclair and Mark position. However, it must be noted that

Affective Events Theory 63

Staw and Barsade focused on trait affect levels rather than state affect levels. It is worth investigating whether trait based affect differences evoke different cognitive processes than state changes in normals. In any case, the Staw and Barsade findings in addition to the apparent conflict between the Ellis and Ashbrook and Sinclair and Mark positions provides further evidence of the complexity of mood predictions.

Mood and Behavior

Helping behavior is the most frequently studied behavioral consequence of mood, stemming directly from the work by Isen and her colleagues (Isen, 1984; Isen & Baron, 1991). Given the potential relevance of helping to such important organizational relevant variables as citizenship behavior and customer service, it is not surprising that Isen's work has received a good amount of attention in the organizational literature (see, for example, George, 1991; George & Brief, 1994). The very general finding of Isen's work on this topic is that positive mood enhances helping behavior and cooperation while reducing aggressiveness. Both Isen (1984) and Isen and Baron (1991) review considerable laboratory evidence indicating that being in a positive mood makes people more generous, helpful, and cooperative, when compared to neutral mood controls. While in a good mood people report greater liking for others and evaluate people more favorably.

Moreover, it appears that it is easier to resolve conflicts among people in a positive mood. For example, in the context of organizational negotiations, people in a good mood are more likely to reach "win-win" integrative bargaining solutions (Carnevale & Isen, 1986) and are more likely to make cooperative concessions during negotiations (Baron, 1990).

The one caveat to the general finding of increased helping and cooperation is that the effect is lost if people believe that helping may interfere with the mood (Isen & Baron, 1991). Isen explains this exception to the general finding by invoking two explanations. First, there is a basic tendency for positive moods to increase helping. Second, there is a coexisting desire to maintain a positive mood. When the helping interferes with the second desire it is avoided.

As often turns out to be the case, the effects of negative mood are more complicated. Because Isen's work compares positive mood subjects to controls, the findings do not enlighten us as to the effects of negative mood. However, one might expect that if being in a positive mood increased helping and cooperation being in a negative mood would decrease it. This turns out not to be the case. In fact there is extensive evidence to indicate that being in a negative mood also can serve to increase helping behavior (Carlson & Miller, 1987). The most likely explanation for this effect involves self-regulatory processes wherein people in negative moods engage in helping behavior to eliminate the negative mood (Morris, 1989). When people are led to believe that their helping will not reduce their moods they do not help (Manucia, Baumann, & Cialdini, 1984).

Although both Isen and Baron (1991) and George and Brief (1994) provide thoughtful discussions of the relevance of the mood and helping literature to organizational behavior not much empirical research has been conducted. George (1991) found that a state measure of Positive Affect did correlate with a measure of helping and also with a measure of customer service behavior. No other quality empirical studies exist. However, given the complexity of the basic findings, the moderators of the effect of positive mood on helping, and the possibility that negative mood can also increase helping behaviors under certain circumstances, predictions in organizational settings will not be straightforward.

Given that being in a positive mood increases the estimated probabilities of the occurrence of positive events and being in a negative mood increases the estimated probabilities of the occurrence of negative events (Wright & Bower, 1992) an effect of mood on behaviors based on probability estimation would be expected. In fact, the relationship between mood and risk taking has been well researched and consistent effects are found, but, as before, these effects are not what one might initially expect. In fact, it is with risk taking that the push and pull of cognitive processing and mood maintenance seem to show up most clearly. In the classic study on the topic, Isen and Patrick (1983) showed that subjects given a hypothetical risk situation were willing to risk more than controls, but when they were placed in a real situation where their own resources were put at real risk they engaged is less risky behavior. Later Isen, Nygren, and Ashby (1988) showed that people in a positive mood expressed higher negative utilities for loss than did controls, apparently overcoming any event probability differences when making decisions about risky outcomes.

Throughout this section, we have emphasized the complex nature of mood effects on judgments, processing strategies, and behaviors. Nothing in this area appears to be straightforward. However, the complexity of findings should not be confused with an absence of findings. Mood effects, while complex and interactive, are also consistent and pronounced.

Overall, it seems that mood effects are a complex interplay of both cognitive and motivational factors. On the cognitive side, mood effects on memory, attributions and processing strategies play a role. On the motivational side, mood repair (for negative mood states) and mood maintenance (for positive mood states) also influence responses. A particular prediction in any situation depends on the mood state, the task, and the aforementioned cognitive and motivational processes.

FINAL COMMENTS

What we have attempted to do in this paper is to flesh out a structure for an event based approach to affective experiences at work and to fill in some of the details by referring to the basic literature on emotions and moods. Along the way, we have contrasted our position with some more traditional positions on similar topics. In some cases we offer our position as a complement to those traditional positions, in other cases as an alternative. In all cases we hope to encourage readers to rethink some issues they may have taken for granted.

Because we summarized our position early in the paper, we think it unnecessary to do so again. Nevertheless, there are some key points and implications which need to be reiterated.

To begin with, job satisfaction is not affect and it is time we stopped saying it is. Over the years we have developed a construct called job satisfaction. This construct, as defined by its most popular operations, is the overall evaluation one has towards one's job. There may be differences of opinion about the usefulness of the construct but the construct exists as what it is and it is not affect.

Second, affective experiences in their traditional forms as emotions and moods are potentially important aspects of work experience. These affective states influence performance and job satisfaction but their performance implications are, by and large, independent of their relationships with satisfaction. It is the failure to realize this point, in conjunction with the aforementioned confusion of affect and satisfaction, that has led to the dismal record of satisfaction-performance research.

Third, affective states can and do fluctuate over time and the performance implications of affect depend on affect states at particular times. Satisfaction is also influenced by current affect levels, along with affect histories. Consequently, time of assessment cannot be arbitrary and patterns of change over time become primary dependent variables. When change becomes our focus of attention, we have to modify the structure of our causal explanations as a consequence. Explanations for change cannot be found in stable, steady characteristics of people or situations. Instead they are found in discrete events.

Take the orbits of the planets as an example. The continued stable pattern of planetary movement is "explained" in terms of the functional relationships of the stable characteristics of the system (e.g., the mass of the planets and the sun, etc.). How would we explain a planet pulling out of its orbit? Any explanation would require the addition of a discrete event, like a meteor.

So too with our organizational variables. We must understand when we are interested in stable patterns and search for functional relationships among state variables, and when we are looking at changes and search for precipitating events. In this paper, our focus has been on changes in affect levels, their causes in events and their consequences in changes in performance. However, we have also recognized that there are endogenous elements to the levels and patterns of affective states which are most efficiently explained in terms of stable attributes.

Finally, it is perhaps somewhat injudicious for us to admit that as we developed our position our thoughts kept returning to the work of Frederick Herzberg. We say injudicious because we are well aware of the way Herzberg's theory is treated in current I/O Psychology. About the only thing positive anyone has to say about his work is that it focused attention on intrinsic task characteristics as influences on motivation and satisfaction. Beyond this, the ideas remain only of "historical interest" (see, for example, Dipboye, Smith, & Howell, 1994).

Certainly, we did not write this paper to defend Herzberg. We are well aware of the methodological flaws in the research and conceptual problems with the theory as a whole. Yet, in our opinion, Herzberg began with some fundamental assumptions, the validity of which can be evaluated independent of the theory in its entirety. People react to the events of their work lives. These events drive their immediate affective states and these states can vary over time. Some events are positive, some events are negative, some features are more likely to generate positive events some features are more likely to generate negative events. These were Herzberg's basic assumptions and these ideas inform our own position.

ACKNOWLEDGMENT

We wish to thank Seymour Adler, Arthur Brief, Rebecca Henry, and Carolyn Jagacinski for their helpful comments on earlier versions of this manuscript.

REFERENCES

Abelson, R.P., Kinder, D.R., Peters, M.D., & Fiske, S.T. (1982). Affective and semantic components in political person perception. *Journal of Personality and Social Psychology, 42*, 619-630.

Adler, S., Skov, R.B., & Salvemini, N.J. (1985). Job characteristics and job satisfaction: When cause becomes consequence. *Organizational Behavior and Human Decision Processes, 35*, 266-278.

Almagor, M., & Ben-Porath, Y.S. (1989). The two-factor model of self-reported mood: A cross-cultural replication. *Journal of Personality Assessment, 53*, 10-21.

Arvey, R.D., Bouchard, T.J., Segal, N.L., & Abraham, L.M. (1989). Job satisfaction: Environmental and genetic components. *Journal of Applied Psychology, 74*, 187-192.

Arvey, R.D., Carter, G.W., & Buerkley, D.K. (1991). Job satisfaction: Dispositional and situational influences. In G.L. Cooper & I.T. Robertson (Eds.), *International review of industrial and organizational psychology* (Vol. 6, pp. 359-383). Chichester, England: John Wiley & Sons.

Arvey, R.D., McCall, B.P., Bouchard, T.J., & Taubman, P. (1994). Genetic influences on job satisfaction and work values. *Personality and Individual Differences, 17*, 21-33.

Baron, R.A. (1976). The reduction of human aggression: A field study of the influence of incompatible responses. *Journal of Applied Social Psychology, 6,* 260-274.

Baron, R.A. (1984). Reducing organizational conflict: An incompatible response approach. *Journal of Applied Psychology, 69,* 272-279.

Baron, R.A. (1990). Environmentally-induced positive affect: It's impact on self-efficacy, task performance, negotiation, and conflict. *Journal of Applied Social Psychology, 20,* 368-384.

Bell, P.A., Fisher, J.D., & Loomis, R.J. (1978). *Environmental psychology.* Philadelphia, PA: Saunders.

Bell, P.A, Garnand, D.B., & Heath, D. (1984). Effects of ambient temperature and seating arrangement of personal and environmental evaluations. *Journal of General Psychology, 110,* 197-200.

Berkowitz, L. (1989). Frustration-aggression hypothesis: Examination and reformulation. *Psychological Bulletin, 106,* 59-73.

Bittle, M.L., & Hausenstein, N.M.A. (1990, August). *Determinants of job satisfaction: Social cues, task structure, and predisposition.* Paper presented at the annual meeting of the American Psychological Association, New Orleans, LA.

Blaney, P.H. (1986). Affect and memory: A review. *Psychological Bulletin, 99,* 229-246.

Bodenhausen, G.V. (1993). Emotions, arousal, and stereotypic judgments: A heuristic model of affect and stereotyping. In D.M. Mackie & D.L. Hamilton (Eds.), *Affect, cognition, and stereotyping: Interactive processes in group perception* (pp. 13-37). San Diego: Academic Press.

Bolger, N. (1990). Coping as a personality process. *The Journal of Personality and Social Psychology, 59,* 525-537.

Bolger, N., & Schilling, E.A. (1991). Personality and the problems of everyday life: The role of neuroticism in exposure and reactivity to daily stressors. *Journal of Personality, 59,* 355-386.

Bouchard, T.J., Jr., Arvey, R.D., Keller, L.M., & Segal, N.L. (1992). Genetic influences on job satisfaction: A reply to Cropanzano and James. *Journal of Applied Psychology, 77,* 89-93.

Bower, G.H. (1981). Mood and memory. *American Psychologist, 36,* 129-148.

Bower, G.H., & Mayer, J.D. (1985). Failure to replicate mood congruent retrieval. *Bulletin of the Psychonomic Society, 23,* 39-42.

Branscombe, N.R. (1985). Effects of hedonic valence and physiological arousal in emotion: A comparison of two theoretical perspectives. *Motivation and Emotion, 9,* 153-169.

Breckler, S.J., & Wiggins, E.C. (1989). Affect versus evaluation in the structure of attitudes. *Journal of Experimental Social Psychology, 25,* 253-271.

Brief, A.P., Butcher, A.B., & Roberson, L. (1995). Cookies, disposition, and job attitudes: The effects of positive mood inducing events and negative affectivity on job satisfaction in a field experiment. *Organizational Behavior and Human Decision Processes, 62,* 55-62.

Brief, A.P., & Roberson, L. (1989). Job attitude organization: An exploratory study. *Journal of Applied Social Psychology, 19,* 717-727.

Buss, D.M., Gomes, M., Higgins, D.S., & Lauterbach, K. (1987). Tactics of manipulation. *Journal of Personality and Social Psychology, 52,* 1219-1229.

Cantor, J.R., Zillman, D., & Bryant, J. (1975). Enhancement of experienced sexual arousal in response to erotic stimuli through misattribution of unrelated residual excitation. *Journal of Personality and Social Psychology, 32,* 69-75.

Carlson, M., & Miller, N. (1987). Explanation of the relation between negative mood and helping. *Psychological Bulletin, 102,* 91-108.

Carnevale, P.J.D., & Isen, A.M. (1986). The influence of positive affect and visual access on the discovery of integrative solutions in bilateral negotiation. *Organizational Behavior and Human Decision Process, 37,* 1-13.

Clore, G.L. (1992). Cognitive phenomenology: Feelings and the construction of judgment. In L.L. Martin & A. Tesser (Eds.), *The Construction of social judgments* (Vol. 10, pp. 133-163). Hillsdale, NJ: Lawrence Erlbaum Associates.

Clore, G.L., Schwarz, N., & Conway, M. (1994). Affective causes and consequences of Social Information Processing. In P.S. Wyer Jr. & T.K. Srull (Eds.), *Handbook of social cognition* (Vol. 1, pp. 323-417). Hillsdale, NJ: Lawrence Erlbaum Associates.

Conway, M., & Giannopoulos, C. (1993). Dysphoria and decision making: Limited information use in the evaluation of multiattribute targets. *Journal of Personality and Social Psychology, 64*, 613-623.

Cranny, C.J., Smith, P.C., & Stone, E.F. (1992). *Job satisfaction: How people feel about their jobs and how it affects their performance.* New York: Lexington Press.

Cropanzano, R., & James, K. (1990). Some methodological considerations for the behavioral genetic analysis of work attitudes. *Journal of Applied Psychology, 75*, 433-439.

Cropanzano, R., James, K., & Konovsky, M.A. (1993). Dispositional affectivity as a predictor of work attitudes and job performance. *Journal of Organizational Behavior, 14*, 595-606.

Cunningham, M.R. (1979). Weather, mood, and helping behavior: Quasi-experiments with the sunshine samaritan. *Journal of Personality and Social Psychology, 37*, 1947-1956.

Czajka, J. (1990). The relation of positive and negative affectivity to workplace attitudes. In L.R. Jauch & J.L. Wall (Eds.), *Academy of management bestpapers proceedings, 1990.* Ada, OH: Academy of Management.

Darwin, C. (1872[1965]). *The Expression of emotions in man and animals.* Chicago, IL: University of Chicago Press.

Davis-Blake, A., & Pfeffer, J. (1989). Just a mirage: The search for dispositional effects in organizational research. *Academy of Management Review, 14*, 385-400.

Dawes, R.V. (1992). The structure of occupations: Beyond RIASEC. *Journal of Vocational Behavior, 40*, 171-178.

Diener, E., Colvin, C.R., Pavot, W.G., & Allman, A. (1991). The psychic costs of intense positive affect. *Journal of Personality and Social Psychology, 61*, 492-503.

Diener, E., & Emmons, R.A. (1984). The independence of positive and negative affect. *Journal of Personality and Social Psychology, 47*, 1105-1117.

Diener, E., & Iran-Nejad, A. (1986). The relationship in experience between different types of affect. *Journal of Personality and Social Psychology, 50*, 1131-1138.

Diener, E., Sandvick, E., & Pavot, W. (1990). Happiness is the frequency, not the intensity of positive versus negative affect. In F. Strack, M. Argyle, & N. Schwarz (Eds.), *Subjective well-being: An interdisciplinary approach* (Vol. 8, pp. 119-139). Oxford, England: Pergamon Press.

Dipboye, R.L., Smith, C.S., & Howell, W.C. (1994). *Understanding industrial and organizational psychology: An integrated approach.* Ft. Worth, TX: Harcourt Brace College Publishers.

Dollard, J., Doob, L.W., Miller, N.E., Mowrer, O.H., & Sears, R.R. (1939). *Frustration and aggression.* New Haven, CT: Yale University Press.

Eagly, A.H., & Chaiken, S. (1993). *The Psychology of attitudes.* Ft. Worth, TX: Harcourt Brace Jovanovich College Publishers.

Edwards, K. (1990). The interplay of affect and cognition in attitude formation and change. *Journal of Personality and Social Psychology, 59*, 202-216.

Eich, E. (1995). Searching for mood dependent memory. *Psychological Science, 6*, 67-75.

Ekman, P. (1992). An argument for basic emotions. *Cognition and Emotion, 6*, 169-200.

Ellis, H.C., & Ashbrook, P.W. (1988). Resource allocation model of the effects of depressed mood states on memory. In K. Fiedler & J. Forgas (Eds.), *Affect, cognition, and social behavior* (pp. 25-43). Toronto: C.J. Hogrefe.

Fazio, R.H. (1986). How do attitudes guide behavior? In R.M. Sorrentino & E. T. Higgens (Eds.), *Handbook of motivation and cognition* (pp. 204-243). New York: Guilford Press.

Finn, S.E. (1986). Stability of personality self-ratings over 30 years: Evidence for an age/cohort interaction. *Journal of Personality and Social Psychology, 50,* 813-818.
Fisher, C. (1980). On the dubious wisdom of expecting job satisfaction to correlate with performance. *Academy of Management Review, 5,* 607-612.
Fisher, C.D., & Locke, E.A. (1992). The new look in job satisfaction research and theory. In C.J. Cranny, P.C. Smith, & E.F. Stone (Eds.), *Job satisfaction: How people feel about their jobs and how it affects their performance* (Vol. 1, pp. 165-194). New York: Lexington Press.
Fleming, I., Baum, A., & Weiss, L. (1987). Social density and perceived control as mediators of crowding stress in high-density residential neighborhoods. *Journal of Personality and Social Psychology, 52,* 899-906.
Folkman, S., & Lazarus, R.S. (1990). Coping and emotion. In N.L. Stein, B. Leventhal & T. Trabasso (Eds.), *Psychological and biological approaches to emotion* (pp. 313-322). Hillsdale, NJ: Erlbaum.
Freedman, J.L. (1975). *Crowding and behavior.* San Francisco, CA: Freeman.
Frijda, N.H. (1986). *The emotions.* Cambridge: Cambridge University Press.
Frijda, N.H. (1987). Emotion, cognitive structure, and action tendency. *Cognition and Emotion, 1,* 115-143.
Frijda, N.H. (1989). Aesthetic emotions and reality. *American Psychologist, 44,* 1546-1547.
Frijda, N.H. (1993). Moods, emotion episodes and emotions. In M. Lewis & J.M. Haviland (Eds.), *Handbook of emotions* (pp. 381-403). New York: Guildford Press.
George, J.M. (1989). Mood and absence. *Journal of Applied Psychology, 74,* 317-324.
George, J.M. (1991). State or trait: Effects of positive mood on prosocial behaviors at work. *Journal of Applied Psychology, 76,* 299-307.
George, J.M. (1992). The role of personality in organizational life: Issues and evidence. *Journal of Management, 18,* 185-210.
George, J.M. & Brief, A.P. (1992). Feelingn good—doing good: A conceptual analysis of the mood at work-organizational spontaneity relationship. *Psychological Bulletin, 112,* 310-329.
Gerhart, B. (1987). How important are dispositional factors as determinants of job satisfaction? Implications for job design and other personnel programs. *Journal of Applied Psychology, 72,* 366-373.
Gotlib, I.H., & Meyer, J.P. (1986). Factor analysis of the multiple affect adjective check list: A separation of positive and negative affect. *Journal of Personality and Social Psychology, 50,* 1161-1165.
Green, D.P., Goldman, S.L., & Salovey, P. (1993). Measurement error masks bipolarity in affect ratings. *The Journal of Personality and Social Psychology, 64,* 1029-1041.
Greenberg, J. (1982). Approaching equity and avoiding inequity in groups and organizations. In J. Greenberg & R.L. Cohen (Eds.), *Equity and justice in social behavior* (pp. 389-435). New York: Academic Press.
Griffitt, W., and Veitch, R. (1971). Hot and crowded: Influence of population density and temperature on interpersonal affective behavior. *Journal of Personality and Social Psychology, 17,* 92-98.
Hackett, R.D., & Guion, R.M. (1985). A reevaluation of the absenteeism-job satisfaction relationship. *Organizational Behavior and Human Decision Processes, 35,* 340-381.
Hanisch, K.A., & Hulin, C.L. (1990). Job attitudes and organizational withdrawal: An examination of retirement and other voluntary withdrawal behaviors. *Journal of Vocational Behavior, 37,* 60-78.
Hastie, R., & Parke, B. (1986). The relation between memory and judgment depends on whether the judgment task is memory-based or on-line. *Psychological Review, 93,* 258-268.
Hersey, R.B. (1932). *Worker's emotions in shop and home: A study of individual workers from the psychological and physiological standpoint.* Philadelphia: University of Pennsylvania Press.

Herzberg, F., Mausner, B., & Snyderman, B.B. (1959). *The motivation to work*. New York: John Wiley & Sons.

Hulin, C. (1991). Adaptation, persistence and commitment in organizations. In M.D. Dunnette & L.M. Hough (Eds.), *Handbook of industrial and organizational psychology* (Vol. 25, pp. 445-505). Palo Alto, CA: Consulting Psychologists Press.

Iaffaldano, M.T., & Muchinsky, P.M. (1985). Job satisfaction and job performance: A meta-analysis. *Psychological Bulletin, 97*, 251-273.

Ilgen, D.R. (1971). Satisfaction with performance as a function of the initial level of expected performance and the deviation from expectations. *Organizational Behavior and Human Performance, 6*, 345-361.

Isen, A.M. (1984). Toward understanding the role of affect in cognition. In R.S. Wyer, Jr. & T.K. Srull (Eds.), *Handbook of social cognition* (Vol. 3, pp. 179-236). Hillsdale, NJ.: Erlbaum.

Isen, A.M., & Baron, R.A. (1991). Positive affect as a factor in organizational behavior. In L.L. Cummings & B.M. Staw (Eds.), *Research in organizational behavior* (Vol. 13, pp. 1-53). Greenwich, CT: JAI Press.

Isen, A.M., & Daubman, K.A. (1984). The influence of affect on categorization. *Journal of Personality and Social Psychology, 47*, 1206-1217.

Isen, A.M., Nygren, T.E., & Ashby, F.G. (1988). Influence of positive affect on the subjective utility of gains and losses: It is just not worth the risk. *Journal of Personality and Social Psychology, 55*, 710-717.

Isen, A.M., & Patrick, R. (1983). The effect of positive feeling on risk-taking: When the chips are down. *Organizational Behasior and Human Peformance, 31*, 194-202.

Izard, C.E. (1977). *Human emotions*. New York: Plenum.

Izard, C.E. (1992). Basic emotions, relations among emotions, and emotion-cognition relations. *Psychological Bulletin, 99*, 561-565.

James, K., Clark, K., & Cropanzano, R. (1994). *Positive and negative creativity in groups, institutions, and organizations: A review and theoretical extension*. Manuscript under review.

James, W. (1884). What is an emotion? *Mind, 9*, 188-205.

James, W. (1890). *Principles of psychology*. New York: Holt.

Johnson, E., & Tversky, A. (1983). Affect, generalization, and the perception of risk. *Journal of Personality and Social Psychology, 45*, 20-31.

Johnson, J.A., & Ostendorf, F. (1993). Clarification of the five-factor model with the abridged Big Five Dimensional Circumplex. *Journal of Personality and Social Psychology, 65*, 563-576.

Judge, T.A. (1992). Dispositional perspective in human resources research. In G.R. Ferris & K.M. Rowland (Eds.), *Research in personality and human resources management* (Vol. 10, pp. 31-72). Greenwich, CT: JAI Press.

Katzell, R.A. (1964). Personal values, job satisfaction, and job behavior. In H. Borow (Ed.), *Man in a world of work*. Boston: Houghton Mifflin.

Kohn, M.L., & Schooler, C. (1982). Job conditions and personality: A longitudinal assessment of their reciprocal effects. *American Journal of Sociology, 87*, 1257-1286.

Konovsky, M.A., Folger, R., & Cropanzano, R. (1987). Relative effects of procedural and distributive justice on employee attitudes. *Representative Research in Social Psychology, 17*, 15-24.

Larsen, R.J., & Diener, E. (1987). Affect intensity as an individual difference characteristic: A review. *Journal of Research in Personality, 21*, 1-31.

Larsen, R.J., & Diener, E. (1992). Promises and problems with the circumplex model of emotions. *Review of Personality and Social Psychology, 13*, 25-29.

Larsen, R.J., & Kasimatis, M. (1990). Individual differences in entrainment of mood to the weekly calendar. *Journal of Personality and Social Psychology, 58*, 164-171.
Larsen, R.J., & Ketelaar, T. (1989). Extraversion, neuroticism, and susceptibility to positive and negative mood induction procedures. *Personality and Individual Differences, 10*, 1221-1228.
Larsen, R.J., & Ketelaar, T. (1991). Personality and susceptibility to positive and negative emotional states. *The Journal of Personality and Social Psychology, 61*, 132-140.
Lawler, E.E. (1973). *Motivation in work organizations.* Monterey, CA: Brooks/Cole Publishing.
Lazarus, R.S. (1991a). *Emotion and adaptation.* New York: Oxford University Press.
Lazarus, R.S. (1991b). Progress on a cognitive-motivational-relational theory of emotion. *American Psychologist, 46*, 819-834.
Lazarus, R.S. (1991c). Cognition and motivation in emotion. *American Psychologist, 46*, 352-367.
Levin, I., & Stokes, J.P. (1989). Dispositional approach to job satisfaction: Role of negative affectivity. *Journal of Applied Psychology, 74*, 752-758.
Locke, E.A. (1976). The nature and causes of job satisfaction. In M.D. Dunnette (Ed.), *Handbook of industrial and organizational psychology.* Chicago: Rand McNally.
Locke, E.A., & Latham, G.P. (1990). *A theory of goal setting and task performance.* Englewood Cliffs, NJ: Prentice-Hall.
Lofquist, L.H., & Dawes, R.V. (1969). *Adjustment to work: A psychological view of man's problems in a work-oriented society.* New York: Appleton-Century-Crofts, Educational Division.
MacFarlane, J., Martin, C.L., & Williams, T.M. (1988). Mood fluctuations: Women versus men and menstrual versus other cycles. *Psychology of Women Quarterly, 12*, 201-223.
Manucia, G.K., Baumann, D.J., & Cialdini, R.B. (1984). Mood influences in helping: Direct effects or side effects? *Journal of Personality and Social Psychology, 46*, 357-364.
Marco, C.A., & Suls, J. (1993). Daily stress and the trajectory of mood: Spillover, response assimilation, contrast, and chronic negative affectivity. *The Journal of Personality and Social Psychology, 64*, 1053-1063.
Maslow, A.H. (1954). *Motivation and personality.* New York: Harper.
Mayer, J.D., & Gaschke, Y.N. (1988). The experience and meta-experience of mood. *Journal of Personality and Social Psychology, 55*, 102-111.
Meyer, G.J., & Shack, J.R. (1989). Structural convergence of mood and personality: Evidence for old and new directions. *The Journal of Personality and Social Psychology, 57*, 691-706.
Miller, M.G., & Tesser, A. (1986). Effects of affective and cognitive focus on the attitude behavior relation. *Journal of Personality and Social Psychology, 51*, 270-276.
Mitchell, T.R. (1974). Expectancy models of job satisfaction, occupational preferences and effort: A theoretical, methodological, and empirical appraisal. *Psychological Bulletin, 81*, 1053-1077.
Morris, W.N. (1989). *Mood: The frame of mind.* New York: Springer-Verlag.
Oldham, G.R., & Fried, Y. (1987). Employee reactions to workspace characteristics. *Journal of Applied Psychology, 72*, 75-80.
Ortony, A., Clore, G.L., & Collins, A. (1988). *The cognitive structure of emotions.* Cambridge: Cambridge University Press.
Ortony, A., & Turner, T.J. (1990). What's basic about basic emotions? *Psychological Bulletin, 97*, 315-331.
Osgood, C.E., Suci, G.J., & Tannenbaum, P.H. (1957). *The measurement of meaning.* Urbana: University of Illinois Press.
Parkes, K.R. (1990). Coping, negative affectivity, and the work environment: Additive and interactive predictors of mental health. *Journal of Applied Psychology, 75*, 399-408.

Persinger, M.A. (1975). Geophysical models for parapsychological experiences. *Psychoenergetic Systems, 1*, 63-74.

Plomin, R. (1990). The role of inheritance in behavior. *Science, 248*, 183-188.

Plutchik, R. (1994). *The psychology and biology of emotion.* New York: Harper Collins College Publishers.

Podsakoff, P.M., & Williams, L.J. (1986). The relationship between job performance and job satisfaction. In E.A. Locke (Ed.), *Generalizing from laboratory to field settings* (pp. 207-253). Lexington, MA: Lexington Press.

Porter, L.W. (1962). Job attitudes in management: I. Perceived deficiencies in need fulfillment as a function of job level. *Journal of Applied Psychology, 46*, 375-384.

Rice, R.W., McFarlin, D.B., & Bennett, D.E. (1989). Standards of comparison and job satisfaction. *Journal of Applied Psychology, 74*, 591-598.

Roseman, I.J. (1984). Cognitive determinants of emotions: A structural theory. In P. Shaver (Ed.), *Review of personality and social psychology* (Vol. 5, pp. 11-36). Beverly Hills, CA: Sage.

Roseman, I.J., Spindel, M.S., & Jose, P.E. (1990). Appraisal of emotion eliciting events: Testing a theory of discrete emotions. *Journal of Personality and Social Psychology, 59*, 99-915.

Rotton, J. (1983). Affective and cognitive consequences of malodorous pollution. *Basic and Applied Social Psychology, 4*, 171-191.

Russell, J.A. (1978). Evidence of convergent validity on the dimensions of affect. *Journal of Personality and Social Psychology, 36*, 1152-1168.

Russell, J.A. (1979). Affective space is bipolar. *Journal of Personality and Social Psychology, 37*, 345-356.

Russell, J.A. (1980). A circumplex model of affect. *Journal of Personality and Social Psychology, 39*, 1161-1178.

Russell, J.A., Lewicka, M., & Niit, T. (1989). A cross-cultural study of a circumplex model of affect. *The Journal of Personality and Social Psychology, 57*, 848-856.

Russell, J.A., & Mehrabian, A. (1977). Evidence for a three-factor theory of emotion. *Journal of Research in Personality, 11*, 273-294.

Russell, J.A., & Ridgeway, D. (1983). Dimensions underlying children's emotion concepts. *Developmental Psychology, 19*, 795-804.

Salancik, G.R., & Pfeffer, J.R. (1977). An examination of need-satisfaction models of job attitudes. *Administrative Science Quarterly, 22*, 427-456.

Salancik, G.R., & Pfeffer, J.R. (1978). A social information processing approach to job attitudes. *Administrative Science Quarterly, 23*, 224-252.

Scherer, K.R. (1984). On the nature and function of emotion: A component process approach. In K.R. Scherer & P. Ekman (Eds.), *Approaches to emotion* (pp. 293-318). Hillsdale, NJ: Lawrence Erlbaum Associates.

Schwarz, N., & Clore, G.L. (1983). Mood, misattribution, and judgments of well-being: Informative and directive functions of affective states. *Journal of Personality and Social Psychology, 45*, 513-523.

Schwarz, N., & Clore, G.L. (1988). How do I feel about it? Informative functions of affective states. In K. Fiedler & J. Forgas (Eds.), *Affect, cognition, and social behavior* (pp. 44-62). Toronto: Hogrefe International.

Shaver, P., Schwartz, J., Kirson, D., & O'Connor, C. (1987). Emotion knowledge: Further exploration of a prototype approach. *Journal of Personality and Social Psychology, 52*, 1061-1086.

Sinclair, R.C. (1988). Mood, categorization breadth, and performance appraisal: The effects of order of information acquisition and affective state on halo, accuracy, information retrieval, and evaluations. *Organizational Behavior and Human Decision Processes, 42*, 22-46.

Sinclair, R.C., & Mark, M.M. (1992). The influence of mood state on judgment and action: Effects on persuasion, categorization, social justice, person perception and judgmental accuracy. In L.L. Martin & A. Tesser (Eds.), *The construction of social judgments* (pp. 165-193). Hillsdale, NJ: Lawrence Erlbaum.

Smith, C.A., & Ellsworth, P.C. (1985). Patterns of cognitive appraisal in emotion. *Journal of Personality and Social Psychology, 48*, 813-838.

Smith, C.A., & Ellsworth, P.C. (1987). Patterns of appraisal and emotion related to taking an exam. *Journal of Personality and Social Psychology, 52*, 475-488.

Smith, C.A., and Pope, L.K. (1992). Appraisal and Emotion: The interactional contributions of dispositional and situational factors. In M.S. Clark (Ed.), *Review of personality and social psychology*, Vol. 14: *Emotion and social behavior* (pp. 32-62). Newbury Park, CA: Sage.

Staw, B.M., & Barsade, S.G. (1993). Affect and managerial performance: A test of the sadder-but-wiser vs. happier-and-smarter hypotheses. *Administrative Science Quarterly, 38*, 304-331.

Staw, B.M., & Ross, J. (1985). Stability in the midst of change: A dispositional approach to job attitudes. *Journal of Applied Psychology, 70*, 469-480.

Stein, N.L., Trabasso, T., & Liwag, M. (1993). The representation and organization of emotional experience: Unfolding the emotion episode. In M. Lewis and J.M. Haviland (Eds.), *Handbook of emotions* (Vol. 13, pp. 279-300). New York: Guilford Press.

Stone, E.F. (1992). A critical analysis of Social Information Processing models of job perceptions and job attitudes. In C.J. Cranny, P.C. Smith, & E.F. Stone (Eds.), *Job satisfaction: How people feel about their jobs and how it affects their performance* (Vol. 1, pp. 21-44). New York: Lexington Press.

Taylor, S.E. (1991). The asymmetrical impact of positive and negative events: The mobilization-minimization hypothesis. *Psychological Bulletin, 110*, 67-85.

Terkel, S. (1974). *Working: People talk about what they do all day and how they feel about what they do.* New York: Pantheon Books.

Watson, D. (1988). Intraindividual and interindividual analyses of positive and negative affect: Their relation to health complaints, perceived stress, and daily activities. *Journal of Personality and Social Psychology, 54*, 1020-1030.

Watson, D., & Clark, L.A. (1984). Negative affectivity: This disposition to experience negative emotional states. *Psychological Bulletin, 96*, 465-490.

Watson, D., & Clark, L.A. (1991). Self-versus-peer ratings of specific emotional traits: Evidence of convergent and discriminant validity. *The Journal of Personality and Social Psychology, 60*, 927-940.

Watson, D., Clark, L.A., & Carey, G. (1988). Positive and negative affectivity and their relation to anxiety and depressive disorders. *Journal of Abnormal Psychology, 97*, 346-353.

Watson, D., Clark, L.A., & Tellegen, A. (1984). Cross-cultural convergence in the structure of mood: A Japanese replication and a comparison with U.S. findings. *Journal of Personality and Social Psychology, 47*, 127-144.

Watson, D., Clark, L.A, & Tellegen, A. (1988). Development and validation of brief measures of positive and negative affect: The PANAS scales. *Journal of Personality and Social Psychology, 54*, 1063-1070.

Watson, D., & Slack, A.K. (1993). General factors of affective temperament and their relation to job satisfaction over time. *Organizational Behavior and Human Decision Processes, 54*, 181-202.

Watson, D., & Tellegen, A. (1985). Toward a consensual structure of mood. *Psychological Bulletin, 98*, 219-235.

Weiner, B. (1985). An attributional theory of achievement motivation and emotion. *Psychological Review, 92*, 548-573.

Weiss, H.M. (1977). Subordinate imitation of supervisor behavior: The role of modeling in organizational socialization. *Organizational Behavior and Human Performance, 19*, 89-105.

Weiss, H.M., Nicholas, J.P., & Daus, C. (1993). *Affective and cognitive influences on job satisfaction.* San Francisco, CA: Society of Industrial/Organizational Psychology.

Weiss, H.M., & Shaw, J.B. (1979). Social influences on judgments about tasks. *Organizational Behavior and Human Performance, 24*, 126-140.

Weitz, J. (1952). A neglected concept in the study of job satisfaction. *Personnel Psychology, 5*, 201-205.

Werner, P.D., & Pervin, L.A. (1986). The content of personality items. *The Journal of Personality and Social Psychology, 51*, 622-628.

Wharton, A.S., & Erickson, R.J. (1993). Managing emotions on the job and at home: Understanding the consequences of multiple emotional roles. *Academy of Management Review, 18*, 457-486.

Willerman, L. (1979). *The psychology of individual and group differences.* San Francisco: W.H. Freeman.

Wilson, T.D., & Hodges, S.D. (1992). Attitudes as temporary constructions. In L. Martin & A. Tesser (Eds.), *The construction of social judgments* (Vol. 10, pp. 37-65). Hillsdale, NJ: Lawrence Erlbaum Associates.

Worth, L.T., & Mackie, D.M. (1987). Cognitive mediation of positive mood in persuasion. *Social Cognition, 5*, 76-94.

Wright, W.F., & Bower, G.H. (1992). Mood effects on subjective probability assessment. *Organizational Behavior and Human Decision Processes, 52*, 276-291.

Zalesny, M.D., & Ford, J.K. (1990). Extending the social information processing perspective: New links to attitudes, behaviors, and perceptions. *Organizational Behavior and Human Decision Processes, 47*, 205-246.

Zevon, M.A., & Tellegen, A. (1982). The structure of mood change: An idiographic/nomothetic analysis. *The Journal of Personality and Social Psychology, 43*, 111-122.

Zillman, D. (1979). *Hostility and aggression.* Hillsdale, NJ: Lawrence Erlbaum Associates.

Zillman, D., & Bryant, J. (1974). The effect of residual excitation on the emotional response to provocation and delayed aggressive behavior. *Journal of Personality and Social Psychology, 30*, 782-791.

MOTIVATIONAL AGENDAS IN THE WORKPLACE:
THE EFFECTS OF FEELINGS ON FOCUS OF ATTENTION AND WORK MOTIVATION

Jennifer M. George and Arthur P. Brief

ABSTRACT

We propose that feelings, an integral aspect of the human experience, are central to obtaining a richer understanding of work motivation. Contrary to an implicit assumption in much of the work motivation literature, we suggest that workers strive to become many things, with the self as an accomplished worker being just one of many possible selves potentially in need of motivational attention. Feelings, in the form of emotions, help to determine which possible self is focused on motivationally at any point in time and when shifts in this attention take place (e.g., from the self as accomplished worker to the self as caring parent). Because the self as an accomplished worker is of prime concern for understanding work motivation, we address how feelings, in the form of moods, impact motivation within this possible self. Moods, with their origins in person-context interactions, are posited to impact both distal and proximal work motivation. Given the complexity of the issues involved, we explore the potential effects of positive mood on some of the constructs and processes underlying distal and proximal work motivation in an exemplary fashion. The paper concludes with a discussion of the types of questions a theory of work motivation *with feelings* should address and the tentative answers to those questions we have provided.

- A caring parent, a loving spouse, a devoted child, a good friend, an involved citizen, an accomplished professional, and a happy person all represent some of the "possible selves" (Markus & Nurius, 1986) an individual may be motivated to become.
- While a person may strive to be many things, he or she does not have the "capacity" (e.g., Kahneman, 1973; Kanfer & Ackerman, 1989) to focus motivationally on all of them simultaneously.
- Feelings—excitement, fear, enthusiasm, distress, elation, and so forth—can "signal" (Frijda, 1988) which possible selves require motivational attention.
- Once a possible self has come into focus, feelings additionally serve to "guide" (Weiner, 1985) strivings towards realizing that self.

In this paper, we will argue that each of the above assertions is plausible and serves to enrich our understanding of human motivation. Moreover, we will contend that even though these assertions are potentially enlightening, they largely have been ignored by students of work motivation. While some of these assertions have been considered in the organizational behavior literature (for example, in regards to the relationship between work and nonwork—see Brett, 1980; Dubin, Hedley, & Taveggia, 1976; Gardner, Dunham, Cummings, & Pierce, 1987, 1989; Rice, Near, & Hunt, 1980), they have not been considered as a set. Additionally, the assertions have not been integratively linked in an explicit way to work motivation. That is, based on our reading of the literature, we believe extant theories of work motivation do not adequately capture the notions that (a) people have motivational agendas comprised of something in addition to being a high performer at work; and (b) feelings influence the ways people proceed through their motivational agendas. The following cases begin to exemplify the bases for these beliefs. This is so because we know of no theory of work motivation that provides an adequate explanation for any of the cases, even though they seem to depict rather commonplace incidents.

- Jane was so distressed with her lack of progress, she just could not force herself to stare at the damn manuscript any longer. For weeks on end, she had been trying to revise the manuscript to resubmit to a journal. After hours of sitting at her desk struggling with the reviewer's comments, Jane said "To hell with it" and left the office to go for a run. "Come hell or high water," she was convinced she would at least break a five-minute mile today.
- Roger had never been this far along on his delivery route by noon. He was bursting with energy. Melissa said "yes" last night; they were to be married next June. Now he knew what it felt like to be on top of the world.

- Bob was gripped with fear as he sped away from the garage. Moments earlier, he was engrossed in re-building a carburetor when his boss gave him the message: Sarah, Bob's six year old, had been hit in the head with a swing during recess and was on the way to Mercy Hospital. When he heard, Bob dropped his tools and ran to his car without saying a word.
- "God, what a beautiful day" Lisa thought to herself on the way to work. After several cold, rainy days, the clear sky and warmth of the sun just made her feel great. Then an idea popped into her mind: "When I get to the office, I'll see if that new claims adjuster, Doug, wants to join the diversity task force I'm chairing. He might have some insights from the last company he worked for and he does seem like a nice guy."

The remainder of our paper unfolds as follows. First, we explain how theories of work motivation largely fail to portray workers as people with strivings to become many things and with feelings to signal which of these strivings demand attention. Next, we show how feelings, even when they do not produce a shift in attention, have motivational consequences by guiding actions towards realizing any particular possible self that may be the focus of attention. For example, we specify how feelings might stimulate a change in the standards a person uses to judge his/her progress toward becoming a particular possible self. Finally, we conclude the paper by considering the sorts of questions a more complete theory of work motivation should be able to answer.

CURRENT APPROACHES TO WORK MOTIVATION

Mowday and Sutton (1993) recently echoed O'Reilly's (1991) conclusion that organizational behavior was in a fallow period. O'Reilly's judgment was based on his review of work published between 1987 and 1990 in five specific areas, including motivation. Focusing on work published since 1990 in the same five areas, Mowday and Sutton went so far as to observe that papers in these areas, for the most part, "continued to offer incremental conceptual advance or focused on methodological rather than conceptual issues"; and, therefore, that "novelty and intellectual excitement were largely absent" (p. 196). While we generally concur with the observation that progress in understanding motivation in the workplace has been incremental, we do not believe that the last few years have been fallow. Incrementalism is a normal route to the accumulation of scientific knowledge, allowing for the production of such insightful works as Kanfer and Ackerman's (1989) integrative resource model of ability—motivation interactions for attentional effort and Locke and Latham's (1990) theory of goal setting and task performance. In addition, a more catholic view of the social science enterprise would recognize that intellectual excitement, in part, is in the eye of the beholder. We agree, however, with Mowday and Sutton's assertion that organizational behavior is preoccupied with cognitive processes which at its worst "can lead to theory and research that portrays organization members as cognitive stick figures whose behavior is unaffected by emotions" (p. 197). Following the leads of Cummings (1982), Cappelli and Sherer (1991), and O'Reilly (1991), Mowday and Sutton suggest that a remedy to this preoccupation with cognitive processes is an increased emphasis on the context of organizational behavior. Also, and as we have suggested, this emphasis on context should incorporate the role of feelings.

Here, we take Mowday and Sutton's (1993) advocacy for contextualism in organizational behavior a step farther in terms of understanding work motivation. That is, while we recognize that work motivation is influenced by the organizational context in which workers are embedded, we also emphasize that workers are people too, with lives beyond the workplace. This idea is neither new nor completely neglected by students of work motivation. Rexford B. Hersey (1932), in his study *Workers' Emotions in Shop and Home,* concluded "The fact that our emotions, and with them our interests, are thus so deeply tied up with our situations outside the plant may cause the influence and problems of the worker's home life to be a more important factor in even his plant behavior than his purely plant problems" (p. 399). Like Hersey, our focus is on how feelings (moods as well as emotions) affect work behaviors; and, also like him, we recognize that such influential feelings need not arise out of the workplace.

The fact that current approaches to motivation neglect the role of feelings is illustrated by the following observations. About ten years ago, Craig C. Pinder's (1984) *Work Motivation* was published. In the book, Pinder reviewed the then well known theoretic approaches to work motivation, for example, Maslow's (1943) hierarchical theory of needs, Deci's (1975) cognitive evaluation theory, Adam's (1963) equity theory, Vroom's (1964) valence-instrumentality-expectancy theory, Locke's (1975) goal setting theory, and Hackman and Oldham's (1980) job characteristics theory. The book, as a reflection of these approaches, supplies an interesting database. Terms indicative of strong feelings (i.e., emotions) or more low-level feeling states (i.e., moods) appear nowhere in the book's table of contents or subject index. The closest construct we could find in the book was "job satisfaction"; and, it was dismissed as irrelevant to the motivation to perform assigned job tasks (i.e., work motivation) in less than two pages.

Jumping ahead to the 1990s and Ruth Kanfer's chapter in the *Handbook of Industrial and Organizational Psychology* (Dunnette & Hough, 1990) titled "Motivation Theory and Industrial and Organizational Psychology," we found the motivational functions of feeling to fare somewhat better, but only marginally so. Kanfer, for instance, does review Weiner's (1985) attributional theory of motivation and emotion; however, she cites no organizational studies employing the approach.

Pinder's (1984) and Kanfer's (1990) reviews were used to make a point we believe is readily apparent. Feelings, be they emotions or moods, do not occupy a central role in current theoretic approaches to work motivation (Ashforth & Humphrey, 1995). Glimmers of change, however, are evident. Pekrun and Frese (1992) for example, opened a recent "review" on work and emotions by noting "we are convinced that industrial and organizational psychologists *ought* to take the issue of emotions at work more seriously"; but, they also observed "there is little research that speaks directly to the issue of work and emotion" (p. 153). Additionally, research by Staw and colleagues has focused on affect as it relates to actual performance (e.g., Staw & Barsade, 1993; Staw, Sutton, & Pelled, 1994). To help guide the additional research we believe is required, an alternative approach to understanding work motivation is presented in this paper.

According to Frijda (1988) "emotions exist for the sake of signaling states of the world that have to be responded to, or that no longer need response and action" (p. 354). That is, one way to view feelings is as information (Schwarz, 1990) people can use to direct motivational attention.[1] "Motivational attention" refers to the allocation of cognitive resources to a possible self, to the pathways leading to that end, and to the consequences of arriving there. Such a view "personalizes motivation" (Nuttin, 1984) in that "possible selves" can be thought of as individualized representations of goals that, when cognitively attended to, incite and direct self-relevant actions (Markus & Ruvolo, 1989). The role that emotions are likely to play in focusing attention on one or more possible selves is described by Klinger (1982) as follows:

> The flow of attention and thought content seems to be steered from moment to moment by the mental and environmental flow of concern-related cues. Thus, as each cue is sensed, it appears nonconsciously to be accorded a kind of priority that determines the likelihood of its being processed further.... It seems very likely that what determines the priority accorded a concern-related cue is its capacity to elicit an affective response.... Thus, it appears that attentional mechanisms are themselves steered in part by emotional response, which is in turn anchored in goal striving. (pp. 139-140)

Before continuing to explore the effects of feelings on motivational attention, it is important to elaborate on the focus of that attention, possible selves. This is so, in part, because the mere recognition of "possible selves" as a construct causes one to re-frame the study of work motivation.

WORKERS ARE PEOPLE TOO

"Possible selves" are what people want to become or avoid becoming; they function as incentives for future behaviors and as a means for evaluating and interpreting current views of the self (Markus & Nurrius, 1986). Thus, it is clear that possible selves entail and are intimately connected to feelings. While possible selves is a distinct concept, a number of ideas in psychology are related to it: for example, "current concerns" (Klinger, 1975), "life themes" (Schank & Abelson, 1977), "personal goals" (Staub, 1980), "personal projects" (Cropanzano, James, & Citera, 1993; Little, 1983), "self-definitions" (Gollwitzer & Wicklund, 1985), "desired selves" (Schlenker, 1985), "psychological careers" (Raynor & McFarlin, 1986), and "life tasks" (Cantor & Kihlstorm, 1987). These ideas are all alike in that they explicitly link knowledge about the self (e.g., enduring goals, aspirations, feelings, hopes, fears, and fantasies) to the regulation of behavior (Markus & Ruvolo, 1989). For our purposes, however, what is most salient about their similarity is that each idea, in its own way, emphasizes that people's lives are not singularly directed; rather, we strive to be many things. This simple notion that individuals are not always occupied just with realizing *a* possible self or completing *a* personal project or performing *a* life task largely has been unrecognized by work motivation theorists. These theorists seem to implicitly assume that workers always are motivationally attending to their possible self as a job performer when they are in the workplace. More generously and, perhaps, more realistically stated, theories of work motivation, in large part, do not address the question of when the possible self as job performer comes into focus. Vroom's theory, for instance, is concerned with the level of task-related effort a worker chooses to expend on his or her job. The theory is not concerned with when such choices are made.

If, as was noted in the introduction of our paper, individuals may strive to be a caring parent, a loving spouse, a devoted child, a good friend, an involved citizen, a happy person as well as an accomplished job performer, then our understanding of work motivation would be enriched to the degree that theory can explain when any given possible self captures motivational attention. Of course, such a conclusion assumes that people do not have the capacity to focus motivationally on all of their possible selves simultaneously. Various views of human cognitive capacity (or attentional resources) (e.g., Kahneman, 1973; Kanfer & Ackerman, 1989; Norman & Bobrow, 1975) support this assumption. Also supportive of the idea that one's attentional resources are limited is how the working, on-line, or accessible self-concept has been conceived (e.g., Cantor & Kihlstrom, 1987; Rhodewalt, 1986; Schlenker, 1985). That conception implies "not all self-representations or identities that are part of the complete self-concept will be accessible at any one time. The working self-concept of the moment, is best viewed as a continually active, shifting array of accessible self knowledge" (Markus & Wurf, 1986, p. 306); and thus, "At any one time a subset of these various representations is accessed and invoked to regulate or accompany the individual's behavior" (Markus & Wurf, 1986, p. 307). A worker, therefore, can be thought of as having a motivational agenda, a set of possible selves, with his or her attention likely focused, at any one point in time, on only a subset of agenda items.

One could argue that context per se drives motivational attention; that while in the workplace, the agenda item focused on is the self as a job performer. But, data are available that suggests this is not so. Roberson (1989) assessed the personal work goals of a group of 172 employees. The mean number of work goals subjects reported was 32, with only 15% pertaining to the completion of actual job tasks (i.e., to job performance). Other work goals concerned such content areas as interpersonal relationships with coworkers and supervisors [e.g., "continue to nurture my relationships with the store manager" (p. 357)], working conditions, training, and future job situation. Thus, Roberson's findings clearly show that people's motivational agendas, even when limited to those items directly applicable to the workplace, contain many possible selves (e.g., a high job performer and a good coworker). The problem of interest here is identifying what may cause a worker to shift her motivational focus, for example, from being a high job performer to being a friendly coworker or from being a high job performer to a caring parent, a loving spouse, or some other non-workplace possible self. As we have suggested earlier in the paper and will demonstrate further below, we believe a plausible solution to this problem lies in considering the worker's feelings.

A question that the previous paragraph may raise is "If workers, while in the workplace, are not motivationally focused on their job performance, what then explains their on-going task behaviors?" An answer to this question is provided by the research of Langer and her associates (e.g., Langer, Blank, & Chanowitz, 1978). She argues people do not always derive behavioral strategies based on current incoming information; rather, a situation, because of the regularity of the information it contains, can elicit stereotypically re-enacted behaviors. Stated somewhat differently, Langer (e.g., Chanowitz & Langer, 1981; Langer, 1975) asserts that when one has overlearned a task and knows it very well, the task often is performed without thinking about it, in an automatic way. Thus, workers can be motivationally focused on a possible self completely detached from their on-going, job-related behaviors yet may perform their jobs in a routine fashion.

Given our concern is with currently motivated behaviors and, not, stereotypically enacted ones, we return below to the topic of feelings. Again, we believe a worker's feeling can cause him or her to shift attention from one motivational agenda item or possible self to another.

Workers' Feelings

Hersey's (1932) intensive study of a relatively small number of workmen employed at a railroad repair shop supplies ample evidence consistent with the belief that feelings affect motivational attention. For example, take the case of worker "M" whose productivity, according to Hersey's observations, dropped on average by more than 5% when he was in a negative emotional state (e.g., angry, disgusted, sad, apprehensive, or worried). Hersey further observed that "M's" negative emotional states were attributable to "worry over wife's failure to menstruate," "interruption of sex relations with his wife on account of childbirth" (p. 360), and other concerns centering on his home life. These observations could be explained in terms of "M's" feelings leading him to shift his focus of motivational attention away from being a high job performer to a possible self tied to his home life.

Our explanation of "M's" changes in job performance also can be applied to the case of "A.B.," a driver employed by the Yellow Cab Company of Philadelphia. According to Viteles' (1932) description of "A.B.," the driver was reported by the garage superintendent to a "Weak-Sister Committee," in part, because of "a slump in earnings" and "a low state of mind" (p. 599). The committee's purpose was to outline programs for the "rehabilitation" (p. 599) of poor earning drivers. "A.B.'s" problems, as diagnosed by a psychologist working for the committee, were tied to his wife's recent suicide. According to the psychologist, "A.B." had become occupied with blaming himself for his wife's death and, even more so, with concern for his two children who had been placed in an orphan asylum. Again, we would attribute "A.B.'s" slump in job performance to his understandably negative emotional state inducing him to shift the focus of motivational attention away from himself as a job performer to himself as father and spouse.

Consistent with our explanations of "M" and "A.B.'s" behavior is considerable theorizing. Simon (1967), for instance, argues emotions can interrupt ongoing behavior; and, Carver and Scheier (1990) suggest a potential consequence of this interruption is a reconsideration and reprioritization of one's goals.

Our interest here is not with the micro-cognitive processes described by Simon (1967), Carver and Scheier (1990), Klinger (1982), and others; rather, it is with the more general idea that feelings can "signal" (Frijda, 1988), likely in conjunction with the situational cues that triggered them, which possible selves require motivational attention. The importance of this idea to understanding work motivation is obvious. If one accepts, for instance, Vroom's (1964) description of the thought processes workers engage in when choosing a level of effort to expend on performing their jobs, it would be hard to conceive of such a decision making process always taking place. That is, people's thoughts are not always focused on the performance of their jobs even when they are on the job. Something must cause workers to focus on themselves as job performers; and, we posit one such possible "something" are worker's feelings. Imagine organizational behavior in context and the stream of thoughts presumably standing behind that behavior. Are we to presume in that context, a worker's mind is occupied exclusively, for example, by thoughts of the valence, expectancy, and instrumentality of his or her job performance? Or, is the data suggesting such a focus merely a product of researchers directing the attention of their respondents by the questions they ask. By now, it should be clear that we believe the possible self as a job performer shifts into and out of focus. Moreover, we believe changes in job performance could be understood better if one could explain when a worker's construal of him or herself as a job performer enters into the working self-concept (i.e., becomes a focused-upon motivational agenda item.)

Summary

Thus far, we have asserted that workers have many possible selves they motivationally can attend to, and their feelings signal which of these possible selves require motivational attention. In making the case for these assertions, we turned to data from the 1930s. We did so merely because we were unaware of any later treatments of feelings and motivational agendas in the workplace. Such lack of awareness further supports our claim that current understandings of work motivation do not capture adequately the array of possible selves workers can choose to focus on or the effects of worker's feelings on those choices. While shifts in focus of attention might also be explained by cognitive mechanisms, we believe that emotion does play a significant and prominent role and has been under-attended to in the literature.

Everyday, casual observations are consistent with our reasoning. Colleagues, for instance, having troubles at home often seem preoccupied at work with those concerns rather than focusing on improving their teaching effectiveness or the quality of their scholarship; rather, in regards to these job tasks, they seem to go through the motions. In addition, the popular culture we are surrounded by tells us that the emotional lives of workers are motivationally important and that they do make choices about which components of their self-concepts are in need of attention, even when they are on the job. The lead character in the television show "Murphy Brown," for example, is depicted as the epitome of a stereotypic career-oriented woman; yet, much of the show's air-time focuses on Murphy's feelings and how she deals with them as a lover, mother, and friend. At this point we would like to note that while our current focus on emotion is in terms of its influence on the focus of attention, it is likely that emotion also has other effects (both indirect and direct) on motivation.

Assuming we adequately have defended the position that our theoretical concerns are not detached from the lives of thinking *and* feeling men and women who engage in paid work and who have conceptions of themselves beyond the workplace, we will proceed with our story. For what we have told so far is incomplete. This is the case, in part, because we have tried to keep our story-line simple, presenting only an idea or two and, thereby, avoiding, at this stage of development, getting caught up in the cognitive mechanics of a remarkably complex phenomenon, human motivation.

FEELINGS AND MOTIVATION WITHIN A POSSIBLE SELF

Up until this point, we have discussed how feelings cause workers to shift among their many possible selves. Just as a worker who has learned that his child has had an accident immediately disengages from his possible self as job performer and engages his possible self as caring parent, so too can a worker who was daydreaming about a romantic weekend out of town with his fiance shift attention back to his possible self as job performer when he learns that he has just landed a major account. As we have demonstrated in the previous section, feelings generated by these negative and positive events are responsible for causing shifts in motivational focus or attention (Frijda, 1988). These feelings are relatively intense and are commonly referred to as emotions. Due to their intensity, emotions interrupt cognitive thought processes and behaviors (Simon, 1982). Moreover, emotions are normally associated with specific events or occurrences and, thus, are tied to particular possible selves. People normally do not feel a constant state of euphoria that is not tied to a particular event or happening within a possible self, for example. But people do feel euphoria when exceptionally good things happen to them which are linked to possible selves such as being offered a much sought after new job or deciding to get married.

Feelings also play another important, albeit more subtle, role in workers' motivational agendas. In this case, the feelings do not so much cause a shift from one possible self to another but rather impact the nature of motivation within a possible self. The feelings we are concerned with here are less intense than emotions and commonly are referred to as moods. Moods are generalized feeling states that are not necessarily focused on any particular target (Brady, 1970; Nowlis, 1970; Ryle, 1950) nor necessarily linked to any given possible self. Moods are distinguished from intense emotional experiences in that they usually do not interrupt ongoing thought processes and behaviors and are not typically identified with a particular stimulus (Clark & Isen, 1982; Thayer, 1989). Moods refer to typical feelings experienced on a day-to-day basis which provide the affective context for thought processes and behaviors (George, 1989). While moods do not usually interrupt thought processes, they can profoundly influence them (Clark & Isen, 1982). As Clark (1982, p. 264) suggests "there is now little doubt that subtle feeling states, or ... moods, are capable of influencing a wide variety of judgments and behaviors." The fact that moods do appear to have such widespread effects on cognitions and behavior is consistent with their nonspecific, pervasive character (Morris & Reilly, 1987).

In everyday language, mood is typically viewed as a unidimensional concept ranging from good to bad or positive to negative. While this is an intuitively appealing conceptualization, a substantial and growing body of literature, however, suggests that mood is most appropriately characterized by at least two dominant and independent dimensions, positive mood and negative mood, rather than a single dimension (e.g., Burke, Brief, George, Roberson, & Webster, 1989; Costa & McCrae, 1980; Meyer & Shack, 1989; Watson & Pennebaker, 1989; Watson & Tellegen, 1985).[2] As Meyer and Shack (1989, p. 691) have stated "in recent years a consensus has formed that a two-dimensional structure adequately describes self-rated affect at its broadest level" (Diener, Larsen, Levine, & Emmons, 1985; Larsen & Diener, 1985; Russell, 1978; Watson, Clark, & Tellegen, 1984; Watson & Tellegen, 1985; Zevon & Tellegen, 1982). Positive moods are characterized by feeling, for example, attentive, interested, alert, excited, enthusiastic, inspired, proud, determined, strong, and active while negative moods often entail feeling distressed, upset, hostile, irritable, scared, afraid, ashamed, guilty, nervous, and jittery (Watson & Tellegen, 1985).

While these adjectives are descriptive of positive and negative mood states, respectively, they also are descriptive of positive and negative emotions. It is the intensity of the feeling which distinguishes moods from emotions. The boundary between emotions and moods thus is fuzzy. Again, a useful heuristic is that experiencing an emotion can interrupt cognitive processes and behaviors and demand attention whereas moods provide the context for cognitive processes and behaviors without necessarily interrupting them and do not demand attention.

Emotions can also feed into moods. A significant event within a possible self may invoke an emotional response which interrupts ongoing activities. Once the individual has gotten used to the idea of the event or habituated to the emotion experienced (Frijda, 1988), the event can still have lingering effects on feelings in the form of moods. For example, learning that you have just been promoted is likely to demand attention and produce a positive emotional state. As you get used to the idea and your level of elation subsides somewhat, the recent promotion may still impact feelings in the form of moods. The rest of the day at work you may be feeling "on top of the world" and may be especially nice to those around you.[3] When you go home, you may have an overall sense of well-being and be especially likely to notice how attractive your spouse looks and how clever your children are. While your positive feelings were generated by a particular event (i.e., the promotion), their "afterglow" in the form of a positive mood has effects which go beyond the event or possible self in question.

More generally, while moods, unlike emotions, are not necessarily tied to a particular event or occurrence in a possible self, like emotions, moods are subject to a multitude of influences. Many of these influences or determinants of moods stem from the contexts within which behaviors occur while other influences derive from internal factors (i.e., personality) and their interaction with the context or situation. In fact, we propose that some of the effects that context has on motivation operate through the mediating mechanism of mood. Before getting back to the more central concern of our paper, namely the effects of feelings on motivation, it probably is useful for us to take a brief detour and discuss the etiology of mood states.

DETERMINANTS OF MOODS

As mentioned above, moods are determined by the interaction[4] of personality and contextual factors. In terms of personality, positive affectivity or extraversion is an important dispositional antecedent of positive mood while negative affectivity or neuroticism is a dispositional determinant of negative mood (Tellegen, 1982, 1985; Watson & Clark, 1984; Watson & Pennebaker, 1989). Hence, simply by virtue of their personality traits, some workers will be more likely to experience positive or negative moods than others. [For applications of positive and negative affectivity constructs in the organizational literature see, for example, Brief, Burke, George, Robinson, and Webster (1988), Burke, Brief, and George (1993), and George (1992).]

However, personality is not the whole story. Contextual factors have powerful effects on moods. True to our conception of workers as whole people who cannot check the rest of their lives at the workplace door, we take a broad view of the contextual determinants of moods experienced at work. Moreover, these contextual determinants are found at several levels of analysis, the individual level, the group level, and higher levels. These contextual determinants, some of which have been recently described by George and Brief (1992), are as follows.

Individual-level Determinants of Moods

The individual-level contextual determinants of moods refer to life events occurring across possible selves which impact general mood levels. These events can pertain to work (e.g., good performer) and nonwork (e.g., loving spouse) possible selves. These events can be major such as death of a loved one or minor such as getting new office furniture; both kinds of events can influence moods across possible selves. For example, an argument with your spouse may put a damper on your feelings the next day across possible selves even though you are not currently thinking or attending to the fact that you recently had an argument.

Group-level Determinants of Moods

George (1990) proposed that work groups may vary in terms of their affective tone, or the characteristic feelings experienced by group members. Some work groups tend to be very upbeat, energetic, and enthusiastic while other groups tend to be much more low key, disinterested, and apathetic. A variety of factors have the potential to impact group affective tone such as the composition of the group (in terms of personality characteristics, demographics, size, etc.), characteristics of the group's leader, and the level of interaction within the group (George, 1996). Being a member of an upbeat, enthusiastic work group is likely to promote positive moods in group members just as being a member of a distressed and angry group is likely to foster negative moods. Indeed, contagion models of feelings specify how people are affected by the moods and emotions of those around them (Hatfield, Cacioppo, & Rapson, 1994; Sullins, 1991). While we have relied on work group examples to make our point, there is no reason to believe that other groups (e.g., family and friends) do not serve that same mood-inducing functions. Being part of a family characterized by feelings of hostility, shame, and guilt is likely to have an effect on one's mood outside of the home.

Organizational and Environmental Determinants of Moods

Factors emanating from the wider organizational context in which one works also have the potential to affect moods. Similar to the case of life events, these factors can be either major or minor. Examples of major organizational determinants of moods include the organization's rewards systems and organizational culture, goals, and performance levels. For instance, Ben and Jerry's Ice Cream Company's culture and goals emphasize the importance of social responsibility and of employees having fun at work. To the extent that Ben and Jerry's is successful on these counts, positive feelings may be generated. As another example, negative moods are likely to be prevalent in organizations facing decline or imminent demise (Sutton & Callahan, 1987). Relatively minor, but not necessarily less influential, organizational determinants of moods include the physical surroundings in an organization, the layout of the work area and office density, and environmental conditions (e.g., Baron, Russell, & Arms, 1985; Brebner, 1982; Eden & Leviaton, 1974; Oldham & Rotchford, 1983; Pfeffer, 1982).

Mood also is influenced by the larger context in which individuals and their groups and organizations are embedded. The economic conditions of one's community, for example, have been shown to have rather profound effects on mood states (e.g., Catalano & Dooley, 1977). Also, at the nation-state level, one readily can image conditions of economic growth or decline as well as war or peace and social upheaval or tranquility influencing how people generally feel on a day-to-day basis. The moods of people currently living in those eastern European countries experiencing economic turmoil, ethnic violence, or sharp increases in crime must be adversely affected. Based upon a review of the research examining differences in happiness across countries, Headey and

Wearing (1992) assert that citizens of some countries (e.g., Denmark, Sweden, and Switzerland) are happier than citizens of other countries (e.g., Hungary, France, and Italy) because the former countries tend to be more democratic, wealthy, egalitarian (in terms of income distributions), and sexually equitable as well as have citizens that are relatively high on extraversion and low on neuroticism.

The notion of a personality by context interaction helps explain why individuals exposed to the same life events or belonging to the same work group and organization can experience different moods. Recognizing the potential for such variance in responses to life events and settings in no way should be taken to downplay the importance of context as a determinant of mood. Rather, our position is that person and contextual factors combine, in perhaps complex ways, to produce mood and to ignore either set of factors as determinants of mood represents a failure to appreciate the richness of the human experience.

Summary

The interaction of personality and contextual factors result in the moods people experience. Contextual factors are found at several levels of analysis, individual, group, and higher levels. While we have provided examples of contextual features within each of these levels, our discussion of these influences only was meant to be suggestive of the wide range of factors which have the potential to impact mood and, obviously, was not intended to be exhaustive. Now that we have some idea of where moods come from, we return to our prime concern with the effects of moods on motivation within a particular possible self. Given what we have said about the origins of moods, these effects of mood could be construed as a mechanism linking context and personality to work motivation.

MOOD AND WORK MOTIVATION

In trying to untangle the effects of mood on motivation within a particular possible self, we were confronted with a seemingly endless array of theoretical propositions and empirical results pertaining to the complex interplay between moods, cognitions, and motivation. A comprehensive treatment of these interrelationships and their net effect on work motivation would be virtually impossible in the confines of any one paper. An alternative path to take and the one we have chosen here is to explore the implications of mood for motivation within a particular possible self in a more exemplary fashion. This has forced us to make some choices regarding the focus of our efforts. First, because our prime concern is with work motivation, we will focus on the possible self as a job performer.[5] Second, given the existence of several currently popular theories of work motivation, we will use these theories as a backdrop for exploring the effects of feelings on motivation within this possible self. Finally, given the substantial evidence which suggests that positive and negative mood states do not have symmetrical effects on cognitive processes and motivation (Isen & Baron, 1991), we have decided to focus on the effects of positive mood. We based this decision, in part, on pragmatic concerns. That is, the mood effects that are relevant here are much more clear-cut in the case of positive mood and more ambiguous and difficult to interpret in the case of negative mood. Given the complexities of the issues involved and the fact that currently popular approaches to work motivation in large part have neglected to consider the effects of positive or negative moods, we have chosen to focus on the former. However, in no way is this meant to imply that negative mood is not important for understanding work motivation or that positive mood is more important than negative mood.

In thinking about motivation within the possible self as job performer, a useful distinction can be made between distal and proximal motivation. As described by Kanfer (1990), distal motivation refers to how workers make choices about what specific job behaviors to engage in and how much initial effort to exert while proximal motivation is concerned with how workers regulate their behaviors once they are engaged in the chosen task. Distal theories of motivation focus on constructs and processes which influence the choice of tasks or goals and intended effort levels. Proximal theories, on the other hand, focus on constructs and processes that guide actions during engagement with the task. As their descriptions imply, distal and proximal theories are complementary rather than competing perspectives on motivation. As largely ignored by others but recognized by Kanfer, currently popular theories of work motivation differ in terms of how richly they can explain distal and proximal phenomenon.

After reviewing and reflecting on the literatures pertaining to moods, cognitions, and motivation, we propose that positive mood enhances distal motivation by facilitating initial involvement, interest, and enthusiasm for work tasks. Moreover, once a worker is in the process of performing a task, positive mood also enhances proximal motivation in that it results in a worker, for example, persisting. Take the earlier mentioned case of Jane, the aspiring journal author. Being in a positive mood might lead her to tackle once again her revision and to become completely engrossed in fashioning the manuscript's arguments. Once into the task, that same positive mood may lead her to estimate that she is rapidly progressing towards her goal of completing a successful revision, thereby, causing her to persist at the task. Below we discuss how an analysis of the effects of positive mood on cognitions underlying work motivation has directed us to these overall conclusions.

Positive Mood and Distal Motivation

How might positive mood impact the choices workers make concerning tasks and effort levels (i.e., their distal motivation)? One way to trace these potential effects is to explore the implications of positive mood for the constructs and processes which have been shown to influence distal motivation. For example, constructs and processes from expectancy theory have been used to explain distal motivation. Moreover, while certainly in need of further development, this theoretical perspective receives support in the literature. Essentially, expectancy theory offers an explanation of how a worker chooses among tasks and among levels of initial effort expenditure and is supported by considerable empirical evidence (e.g., Matsui, Kagawa, Nagamatsu, & Ohtsuka, 1977; Matsui & Ohtsuka, 1978). Thus, once a person's motivational attention becomes focused on the self as a job performer, expectancy theory offers a plausible, albeit incomplete, heuristic for thinking about the choices (i.e., what job task to tackle and, initially, how much effort to expend on that task) a person might make.

The basic expectancy theory model proposes that workers choose among alternative courses of action based upon their assessments of valence, instrumentality, and expectancy. Valence refers to the strength of a person's preference for an outcome or his or her anticipated satisfaction from receiving the outcome. Vroom (1964) points out that for many outcomes, valence is not based on anticipated satisfaction or dissatisfaction upon receipt of the outcome itself. Rather, some outcomes (i.e., first level outcomes) are valent because they are perceived to be instrumental for attaining other valent outcomes (i.e., second level outcomes). Instrumentality is the perceived link between these two types of outcomes. Expectancy is the perceived probability that an act will result in a particular first level outcome such as a worker's belief that a high level of effort will result in a high level of performance. Expectancy, instrumentality, and valence are posited to combine in a multiplicative fashion to yield distal motivation or choice of activities and effort levels.

Expectancy theory and the research it has spawned has focused exclusively on the cognitive processes presumed to underlie distal motivation irrespective of the effects of workers' feelings (Ashforth & Humphrey, 1995). However, an extensive and growing body of literature highlights the high degree of interdependence between thoughts and feelings; particularly relevant here is theorizing and research pertaining to the effects of positive mood on cognitions. This work suggests that positive mood will affect valence, instrumentality, and expectancy judgments in a positive manner and hence, distal motivation within the possible self as job performer.

There are at least three mechanisms through which we expect positive mood to influence distal motivation analyzed through an expectancy theory lens, these being mood-congruent judgment, mood-congruent recall, and mood effects on attributions. With regard to the first mechanism, considerable evidence suggests that positive mood influences judgments of a wide variety of stimuli (Clark & Isen, 1982). That is, people in positive moods tend to see things in a positive light and be optimistic about the future. For example, people in a positive mood have been shown to evaluate consumer products more favorably (Isen, Shalker, Clark, & Karp, 1978), to rate ambiguous scenes as more pleasant (Forest, Clark, Mills, & Isen, 1979; Isen & Shalker, 1982), to rate ambiguous facial expressions more positively (Schiffenbauer, 1974), and to have more positive conceptions of people and report more liking for others (Forgas & Bower, 1987; Griffitt, 1970; Veitch & Griffitt, 1976), than people who are not in a positive mood. Likewise, being in a positive mood has been shown to influence task perceptions and satisfaction (Brief, Butcher, & Roberson, 1995; Kraiger, Billings, & Isen, 1989). Being in a positive mood also influences judgments of the future. For instance, people in positive moods tend to have elevated probability estimates of positive future events and reduced estimates of negative future events compared to those in neutral and more negative moods (Bower & Cohen, 1982; Masters & Furman, 1975) and to have higher expectations of future success (Feather, 1966). Hence, when people are in a good mood they tend to judge a diverse range of stimuli more positively than when they are in a neutral or negative mood.

Particularly relevant to the concept of motivation is the fact that positive mood also appears to influence judgments such as expectations about future performance (Kavanagh & Bower, 1985). For example, Forgas, Bower, and Moylan (1990) found that people in positive moods made higher self-efficacy judgments. Likewise, Baron (1990) found that positive mood induced by pleasant scents resulted in higher reported self-efficacy on a clerical task among men.

The basic tendency to form mood-congruent judgments suggests that positive mood will enhance work motivation viewed in expectancy theory terms. Workers in positive moods are likely to have expectancies which are biased in a positive direction. Thus, when a worker is focused on him/herself as a job performer and is in a positive mood, he or she is likely to have higher expectancies for difficult tasks than if he or she was not in a positive mood. Assuming Jane is in a particularly positive mood, for example, she is more likely to tackle her manuscript revision than when she is not feeling so good. In terms of valence, it is likely that workers generally will judge outcomes to be more positively valent when they are in positive moods than when they are not. Because people in positive moods tend to be more optimistic, instrumentality judgments also are expected to be influenced by mood such that workers in positive moods will perceive stronger linkages between positively valent first and second level outcomes. These positive mood effects on valences and instrumentalities likely would lead to workers choosing to expend relatively higher levels of initial effort on the tasks they chose to perform. This is so because they see a greater pay-off attached to their performance.

Thus, Jane, in approaching the revision, not only would envision producing a manuscript that would be accepted but also would see her article in a journal leading to highly attractive rewards (e.g., fame and tenure); therefore, she, at least initially, commits her full mental and physical resources to working on the revision. Hence, distal motivation is likely to be higher when workers are in positive moods, with one caveat. That is, we know that people seek to maintain positive moods (Carlson, Charlin, & Miller, 1988; Clark & Isen, 1982; Mischel, Ebbesen, & Zeiss, 1973; Morris & Reilly, 1987). If a worker is in a positive mood and thinks that a given action or effort level will dampen his or her positive feelings, then positive mood may not result in enhanced distal motivation because of the desire to maintain the positive mood. But, in the case we have made for Jane's engagement in revising her manuscript, she does so with the belief that her efforts will be efficacious and rewarding, thereby, sustaining her positive feelings. Of course, her actual experiences in dealing with the revision could lead to a different outcome.

The remaining two mechanisms through which positive mood is likely to impact distal motivation from an expectancy theory perspective are mood-congruent recall and mood effects on attributions. Mood-congruent recall refers to the tendency to recall material from memory which is consistent with current mood state at the time of recall (Bower, 1981; Ehrlichman & Halpern, 1988; Schwarz & Clore, 1988). Thus, when people are in a positive mood they are more likely to recall positive material from memory than when they are not in a positive mood. While mood-congruent recall has received impressive support in the literature, it is a complex phenomenon with some remaining unanswered questions (Blaney, 1986; Parrott & Sabini, 1990). Here, we attempt to provide a simplified account of the operation of mood-congruent recall based upon the overall thrust of the existing literature.

When people recall material from memory regarding themselves or some other target (e.g., a person, situation, or event), they usually do not recall all potentially relevant information but rather cut short the search process as soon as enough information has come to mind to form the judgment at hand (Bodenhausen & Wyer, 1987; Schwarz & Clore, 1988; Wyer, 1980). As already noted, material which is congruent with one's current mood state is more accessible from memory and hence is recalled more easily (Bower, 1981; Isen et al., 1978). Thus, for positive moods, material of a similar affective tone to current mood state will be overrepresented in the selective database which is relied upon to form evaluations and judgments from memory (Schwarz & Clore, 1988).

While expectancy theory deals with contemporaneous events, expectancy, valence, and instrumentality judgments also have a basis in the past. In making these types of judgments, workers rely on their past experiences recalled from memory. As we have argued, these memories will be biased positively for workers in a positive mood. So, for example, suppose you are trying to decide whether you should deliver a paper at an academic conference or ask your co-author to do it. Assuming you are in a positive mood when you make the choice, here is what could happen. You recall the times you did a good job presenting, not the case when you felt you looked foolish. These memories contribute to your conclusion that you are probably going to deliver another good performance at the upcoming conference (i.e., your expectancy is high). You also remember that, when you performed well at other conferences, people came up to you afterwards to offer flattering words; and, once a researcher you respected a lot but had not met previously even ask you to join her for a drink. You recall the attention felt good; you did not remember how, when you failed, it was a real embarrassment. These memories lead you to believe that performing well at the upcoming conference will result in additional, pleasurable interactions with your peers (i.e., your instrumentalities for positively valent outcomes are high). In sum, you are motivated to present the paper, in part, because you made the choice while in a positive mood.

Research on depression suggests a potential link between mood and attributions, particularly regarding the self. That is, people who are clinically depressed are more likely to attribute personal failures to stable, internal causes (Anderson, Horowitz, & French, 1983; Garber & Holdon, 1980). The results for depression are germane to our focus on positive mood. This is so because depression entails not only high negative affect or mood but also low levels of positive mood (Clark & Watson, 1988; Tellegen, 1985). In a series of experiments, Forgas et al. (1990) demonstrated that mood influences attributions of "normal" people as well. More specifically, they found that people in a negative mood made more internal and stable attributions for failures than for successes with the reverse pattern occurring for people in positive moods. Interestingly enough, people in positive moods made more internal attributions for success than failure both for themselves and others whereas people in negative moods made more internal attributions for their own failures but not for the failures of others. As Forgas et al. (1990, p. 817) indicate "mild affective states not unlike those commonly experienced in daily mood fluctuations have surprisingly powerful and nonobvious consequences for achievement attributions."

The obvious way mood effects on attributions could influence distal motivation is through a worker's belief about effort-performance relationships (i.e., expectancy). A worker in a positive mood likely would attribute successes to such an internal, stable factor as high ability and failure to such an external, unstable factor as bad luck. Thus, returning to your decision about whether or not to deliver a conference paper, you would see your previous successes as a presenter as a result of your talent for succinctly yet provocatively conveying to an audience of your peers the theses of your papers; and, see your prior embarrassing delivery as a product of the misfortune to have had in your audience a particularly nasty and vocal critic. These sorts of favorable attributions contribute to your belief that, if you adequately prepare, you would do just fine delivering the paper; and, therefore, because of this expectancy belief, you are more motivated to take on presenting the paper. For more about the interrelations between feelings, attributions, and motivation, see, for example, Weiner (1985).

In sum, our aim was to demonstrate how being in a positive mood can enhance distal work motivation construed from an expectancy theory frame-of-reference. We showed how enhanced distal motivation could result in the choice of difficult work tasks and the initial expenditure of relatively high levels of effort on whatever task was chosen. To explain how these effects of positive mood can come about, three alternative but compatible cognitive mechanisms were described. Our descriptions of these mechanism should not be taken as proof of viewing workers as "cognitive stick figures" (Mowday & Sutton, 1993, p. 197). Our view of workers fully recognizes their feelings as well as their thoughts. Not only have we attended to the effects of mood on distal work motivation; we also have argued that the focus of attention on such motivational concerns (i.e., on the self as a job performer) can be driven by emotions. Moreover, we have reasoned that these feelings (moods and emotions) are a product of person-context interactions. Thus, the current treatment of cognitive mechanisms largely was used to demonstrate how feeling can affect motivation; but, it also served another purpose. By treating the thoughts *and* feelings of workers as well as their personalities and the contexts in which they are embedded, we have moved toward a more complete recognition of the sources of work motivation. In keeping with our goal to help formulate a richer understanding of work motivation, we now turn to a consideration of the effects of mood on proximal motivation.

Positive Mood and Proximal Motivation

While distal motivation is what drives workers' choices of tasks and initial effort levels, proximal motivation guides behavior while workers are actually performing the tasks they have chosen. We propose that positive mood influences not only the choice of tasks and effort levels (i.e., distal motivation), but also ongoing motivation during task engagement (proximal motivation). One of the principal approaches to proximal motivation is control theory. Motivational control theory is a metatheoretical perspective which has been viewed as an integrative framework in which elements of other theories of motivation can be incorporated (e.g., goal setting theory; Locke, Shaw, Saari, & Latham, 1981) (Hyland, 1988; Klein, 1989). Rather than getting into the finer details of control theory and its variants, we will try to explain the key elements of control theory and explore their relationship to positive mood at work. The core element in control theory is the negative feedback loop; essentially, a perceptual input is compared to a reference criterion and the difference between the two results in a signal called detected error. Detected error motivates behavior to lessen the discrepancy between the perceptual input and the reference criterion.

Hyland (1988) suggests that there are four types of reference criterion. First, the criterion could refer to some end state such as a completed piece of work. Second, the criterion could reflect a rate of progress towards a particular end state such as making a certain amount of progress on a research project. Third, the criterion could reference a mode of being or doing such as achieving or affiliating. The final type of reference criterion concerns some internal state or mental content such as thinking positively about one's supervisor.

The perceptual input refers to an individual's perception of how they stand with regards to the reference criterion; the nature of this input depends, therefore, on the nature of the reference criterion. For example, if the reference criterion is a particular end state (e.g., finishing a project), then the perceptual input is one's perceptions regarding whether or not the project is completed. If an error is detected (i.e., there is a difference between the reference criterion and perceptual input), then behavior may be initiated to reduce the discrepancy. Hence, the negative feedback loop. Error sensitivity refers to the salience of this discrepancy to the individual and is reflected in the intensity of the behavior initiated to reduce it (Carver & Scheier, 1981).

Control theory contains both cognitive and affective components (Klein, 1989). The cognitive component is comprised of all the information processing activities that take place with respect to the reference criterion, perceptual input, and their comparison. Affect is involved in two ways. First, as mentioned above, the reference criterion could involve, for example, maintenance of a particular affective state. For instance, an individual's reference criterion may be to avoid feeling nervous. Second, perceived discrepancies may give rise to affective reactions (Carver & Scheier, 1990) such as an individual experiencing negative emotions upon failing to attain some goal.

As was the case with distal motivation, we focus here on the effects of positive mood in an exemplary fashion. In regards to positive moods, we posit that they influence the perceptual input, detection of a discrepancy, and choice of a reference criterion level. By doing so, we intend to demonstrate how feelings affect proximal motivation and, thereby, guide ongoing task behaviors.

As a worker performs a task, he or she periodically acquires information related to his/her progress on the task. Because people in positive moods tend to perceive stimuli more positively, this information (referred to as the perceptual input in control theory) can be influenced by feelings, particularly for inputs which are somewhat ambiguous.[6] Thus, workers in positive moods may judge themselves as making more progress towards a goal than those not in a positive mood. Obviously, when the perceptual input is very clear-cut (e.g., you are trying to write an abstract with a 250-word limitation and you count you have written 312 words), positive mood will have little or no effect on the perceptual input because it is not amenable to alternative interpretations. Frequently, however, perceptual inputs are ambiguous, and, in these circumstances, positive mood is likely to play a role. For example, if, in the process of revising a paper, you reread a section you have just finished working on, you will be more likely to be satisfied with the changes you have made if you are in a positive mood when you reread the section than if you are not in a positive mood.

Additionally, Schwarz and Clore (1988) and others (e.g., Forgas & Moylan, 1987) argue that mood can serve an informational function. That is, current mood states may be used as information in forming judgments. For example, if a worker is in a positive mood while performing a task, he or she may use this piece of information as positively reflecting on task progress. Schwarz and Clore report the results of a number of experiments which provide evidence for this effect. Moreover, they posit that mood is most likely to be used as an input on complex judgmental tasks when competing information is less accessible and salient (Schwarz, Strack, Kommer, & Wagner, 1987; Strack, Schwarz, & Gschneidinger, 1985), or, in a sense, more ambiguous. Let us return to the case of Jane, who is into her revision, to show the effects of positive moods on perceptual inputs. Jane stops writing a moment to sense where she is in revising her arguments in ways that will satisfy the journal's reviewers. It is safe to assume the information Jane gets from reading what she has written is not clear-cut. Given she is in a positive mood, Jane is more likely to perceive this information positively and use her good feelings as additional favorable input. By comparing these positively biased data to her goal, Jane also is more likely to judge her progress on the revision to be satisfactory.

There are at least two additional ways in which positive mood is likely to result in favorable comparisons of perceptual inputs and reference criteria; again, such comparisons being at the heart of proximal motivation, from a control theory perspective. More specifically, (a) the effects of positive mood on categorization flexibility and (b) the motivation to maintain positive mood states, are each likely to cause workers to favorably evaluate their ongoing task activities and progress towards goals (or reference criteria). In regards to categorization flexibility, Isen and her colleagues, for instance, have shown that people in positive mood states tend to make more connections and integrations of divergent stimulus materials (Isen & Daubman, 1984; Isen, Daubman, & Nowicki, 1987; Isen, Johnson, Mertz, & Robinson, 1985). In other words, positive moods promote people to see more interrelatedness among stimuli and to use broader, more inclusive categories.

Consistent with these findings, Sinclair (1988) found, in a performance appraisal context, that people in positive moods used broader categories or exhibited more halo error than people in negative moods. More recently,

Murray, Sujan, Hirt, and Sujan (1990) demonstrated that people in positive moods created and used more inclusive categories (i.e., they were more flexible in approaching categorization tasks). As Isen and Baron (1991, p. 21) assert "persons who are feeling happy are more cognitively *flexible*—more able to make associations, to see dimensions, and to see relations among stimuli— than are persons in a neutral state." Thus, workers in positive moods may perceive a wider range of perceptual inputs as equalling the reference criterion. This conclusion, coupled with the previously discussed idea that people are motivated to maintain their positive moods, suggests happy workers are less likely to judge that they have failed to make adequate progress towards their task goals. Again, of course, if perceptual inputs and reference criteria are very clear-cut and objective, this result would not hold. But, Jane, at work on her revision with the goal in mind of writing to satisfy a set of journal reviewers, would be more likely to judge the information she has collected regarding her progress to fall into the acceptable range. To repeat, this likelihood is a function of her good mood leading to an increase in the breadth of this acceptable range and of her motivation to stay happy.

Finally, we address choice of a reference criterion level or, more broadly, responses to the above sort of comparisons. A number of possibilities can result from comparing perceptual inputs to the reference criterion. When Jane, for example, decides to work on her journal revision she might set, as her reference criterion level for the day, completing the revisions on the first section of the paper. Around lunch time, she reads the changes she has made to this section and as a partial result of her good mood, is truly pleased with her progress and decides that she will strive not only to finish revising this section but also the next section as well. This increase in her reference criterion level causes her to become even more immersed in the manuscript. Thus, perceiving her current performance to compare favorably with her goal causes her to raise her goal and persist at revising the paper to achieve this now, more difficult, goal. Evidence in support of such a scenario is available. Carver (1979) suggests that a person's response to the comparison of a perceptual input to a reference criterion is influenced by the person's expectations about future actions leading to goal accomplishments. As we already have argued, people in a positive mood see themselves as more self-efficacious and, therefore, believe they are capable of accomplishing more. In this case, the consequence of such expectations may be the setting of a higher reference criterion level. Moreover, what we have said about mood-congruent recall and mood's effects on attributions are supportive of the idea of a positive mood-higher reference criterion level relationship. Given that past accomplishments are a basis for choosing a reference criterion level and that people in positive moods recall more positive experiences from memory, it is plausible the choice of a reference criterion level likely would be biased upward by being in a positive mood. Likewise, the tendency for people in positive moods to make more internal attributions for success should contribute to them setting higher reference criterion levels than workers who are not in positive moods.

The essence of our analyses so far suggests that workers in a positive mood may be more likely to judge progress towards their task goals positively and, following these judgments, set higher goal levels for themselves. If this were so, then workers in positive moods would be expected to exhibit higher levels of proximal motivation by persisting longer and exerting more effort on the tasks they are engaged in performing.[7] But, this conclusion is too limited. For example, in the process of performing a task, workers, independent of their moods, may be confronted with information indicating progress towards their goals is not satisfactory; and, such information may lead them to lower their goal levels, shift work tasks, or even shift their motivational attention to another possible self. For example, upon reading the section she is working on and despite her positive mood, Jane may detect a major logical contradiction which not only causes her to conclude that she will not be able to finish revising the section that day but also makes her very depressed. This might cause her to shift to her possible self as a teacher and grade student papers the rest of the day. Control theory recognizes such possibilities and, more generally, the fact that the world is not static. While it is possible to explore the potential effects of positive mood at a point in time, the dynamic nature of performing a task, of experiencing feelings, and of workers' task and nontask related selves, make the construction of generalizable predictions remarkably complex. At this point, this complexity precludes us from making exact predictions concerning precisely when positive mood will and will not result in enhanced proximal motivation, a shift in focus of attention, a lowering of goals, or a raising of goals. Nevertheless, we can better understand the proximal motivation of workers by explicitly recognizing that their feelings do play a role; and, here, we have demonstrated what that role might be. More generally, we recognize that feelings may directly and indirectly influence both proximal and distal motivation in multiple ways, in addition to those considered here.

WHAT MIGHT A THEORY OF WORK MOTIVATION WITH FEELINGS LOOK LIKE?

The various subjects we have covered so far may be construed as some of the elements in the outline of a new theory of work motivation, one that takes into account the effects of emotions and moods. We do not claim that all of the elements have been articulated or that an outline constitutes a set of interrelated propositions. But, the ideas we have presented do provide starting points for constructing explanations of worker motivation potentially richer than those provided by theories currently in use. Here, by summarizing and integrating these ideas, we intend to show what such a richer theory might look like.

Our approach to suggesting what an alternative theory might look like is to present and respond to a small set of questions we believe a theory of work motivation ought to address:

1. Given workers can think about many things, what causes them to focus their motivational attention on performing their jobs?

A theory of work motivation should provide some clues as to when workers are likely to make choices about expending their efforts at work and not assume, even implicitly, that workers' thoughts always are occupied with such concerns. The clue that we provided as to when motivational attention shifts to a focus on job performance was emotions. More precisely, we posited, as depicted in Figure 1, person-context interactions are capable of producing intense feelings that drive individuals to become concerned with realizing such possible selves as an accomplished worker. While we did not attempt to detail the nature of these interactions, we do suggest interested readers examine the reasoning behind Lazarus' (1991) assertion that to understand any given emotion requires one to spell out the *particular* person-environment relationships underlying it. They will find that Lazarus (as we do) rejects the idea that emotions are exclusively a product of either contexts or traits; rather, both, in a relational sense, are important to understanding how specific emotions are generated.

Not only is our story about emotions that produce shifts in motivational attention incomplete. Obviously, we also have ignored many other factors that may cause workers to focus on themselves as job performers. We *intentionally* did so to emphasize workers are people with feelings, not, "cognitive stick figures." By solely attending to emotions, we in a sense challenge other work motivation theorists to articulate additional clues as to when workers are likely to think about themselves as job performers.

2. Given workers are focusing on themselves as job performers, how is the choice of particular tasks and effort levels on those tasks affected by feelings?

Workers can be thought of as occupying jobs that require them to choose where to direct their effort and how much of it to expend in the direction chosen. Without the conceptualization of such choices, distal work motivation theorists would have a limited subject matter to pursue. Not surprisingly, therefore, some current theories (e.g., expectancy theory) do attend to these sorts of choices. Somewhat understandably, they do so in rather mechanistic ways, suggesting workers, in essence, make effort direction and level choices based upon the subjective expected utilities of the options faced. Such a mechanical view of distal work motivation processes is not very troublesome to us. What is a concern is that, in the apparent press to rationalize understandings of work motivation, feelings have been left aside.

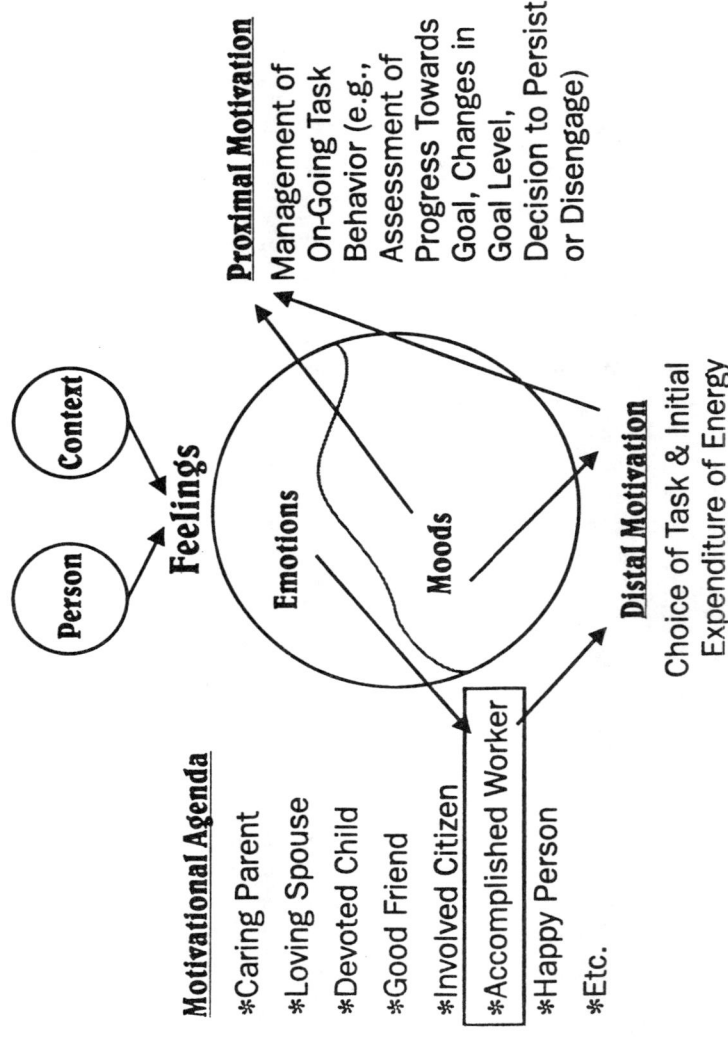

Figure 1. Some Effects of Feelings on Work Motivation

To remedy the view of workers as unfeeling decision makers, we brought mood into the distal work motivation process. We posited that being in a positive mood favorably affects work motivation by contributing to workers choosing to tackle more difficult tasks and to exert more effort on those tasks. Three cognitive explanations (mood-congruent judgment, mood-congruent recall, and mood effects on attributions) were provided in support of these propositions. Beyond describing how mood affects distal motivation, we specified certain person and context factors that interact to produce typically unfocused, generalized feeling states (i.e., moods). The person or personality factors discussed were positive and negative affectivity. Examples of the context factors included life events, work group affective tone, organizational culture, and nation-state factors.

The posited effects of positive mood on distal motivation, the explanations provided for these effects, and the specified determinants of mood all represent new considerations for students of work motivation. These considerations likely raise numerous issues not previously dealt with by those students. From a methodological perspective, for example, work motivation researchers may not be familiar with either measuring or manipulating mood, assessing mood effects on recall from memory, gauging dispositional traits, or tracing the effects of mood at some higher level of analysis to the moods of individual workers. Simply, bringing feelings into distal work motivation research probably requires more than accepting a foreign set of ideas; it also likely will entail adopting research techniques from other areas of inquiry and developing new ones, including those more phenomenological in nature.

3. Given workers are engaged in performing a task, how is the process of managing ongoing task behaviors affected by feelings?

While proximal theories of motivation have been evoked in the area of work with increasing frequency, they, with few exceptions (e.g., Kanfer & Ackerman, 1989), have been used in a snapshot fashion. That is, control theory, as we have employed it, is a way of viewing how individuals manage their *ongoing* task behaviors; but, most work motivation researchers seemed to have measured control variables at one point in time to predict performance at some second point in time. Alternatively, our predictions regarding the effects of feelings on proximal motivation appear to us to cry out for repeated measures of mood, the control theory constructs (e.g., perceptual inputs, detected discrepancies, and reference criterion levels), as well as behaviors in order to tease out the dynamic relationships among these variables. Performing a task is not necessarily a simple, linear process and to capture how workers manage its discontinuities requires intermittent measurement.

Regarding our predictions, we posited positive mood states favorably affect (a) judged progress towards a task goal, particularly when perceptual inputs are ambiguous; and (b) the setting of reference criterion levels. These predictions imply workers in positive moods may exhibit high levels of proximal motivation by persistently exerting effort to reach relatively ambitious goals. This implication, however, must be viewed as temporally bound, for as task behaviors unfold, workers may be confronted with information that only could be interpreted as negative in terms of progress towards their goals. Such information may, for example, lead to lowered goal levels or to a change in or from work tasks. Moreover, events not related to task performance might produce emotions that induce a shift in motivational attention to another possible self. But, this, of course is where we began our story.

Finally, the methodological implications of our theorizing have only very briefly been addressed above. Researchers in this area face several methodological challenges that, we believe, our worth striving to meet. First, it is likely that empirical exploration of many of the ideas presented in this paper would necessitate the use of within-person designs which explore how feelings impact focus of attention, distal motivation, and proximal motivation over time. The pragmatic difficulties of conducting such studies in field settings are obvious. Second, the appropriate time periods for sampling and the appropriate data collection techniques to use are open to question. For instance, is asking people to self-report their feelings at different points in time and using a protocol analysis paradigm to help uncover key relationships too obtrusive a methodology that may bias any results obtained? Third, the inherent difficulty of assessing motivation, per se, and not actual performance or time on task is well known to researchers in the area. These are just a few examples of the methodological challenges researchers in this area face. They are not insurmountable, however, and to the extent that they are satisfactorily met, our understanding of work motivation may be considerably enhanced.

CONCLUSIONS

By emphasizing workers are whole people with aspirations in addition to becoming high job performers and feelings that affect their thoughts, we generated new ways to think about work motivation. These new ways portray moods and emotions as central to understanding where workers apply their efforts, the magnitudes of those efforts, and how long they persist. And, these feeling states were recognized as products of person-context interactions. Thus, our ideas should be useful for helping to explain the effects, for example, of mood dispositional traits *and* organizational context on work motivation. Put simply, we propose that a rich understanding of work motivation necessitates the consideration of feelings, their origins in person-context interactions, and how feelings combine with thoughts to determine the direction and level of motivation. The importance of this proposal is supported by Herbert Simon's

(1995, p. 508) observation, "we need to reconnect cognition with affect and motivation, probably via the mechanisms that determine the focus of attention."

NOTES

1. Alternatively, feelings may sometimes signal the need for additional information.
2. There are what can be considered to be alternatives to this view, however. See, for example, Russell's (1980) circumplex model. Additionally, some researchers have attended to the two dimensions of pleasantness/unpleasantness and extent of arousal or activation (Purcell, 1982; Watson & Tellegen, 1985).
3. Potentially to clarify matters, it should be noted that we are concerned with the experience of emotions and moods and not the display of feelings that are incongruent with one's internal states. On the later point, see, for example, Hochschild (1979, 1983) and Rafaeli and Sutton (1989).
4. We use the term interaction here in a broad sense to include the five forms of person-situation interactions in interactional psychology (e.g., Pervin & Lewis, 1978). Hence, interaction can refer to a situation wherein personality and context have additive or main effects on moods or to a situation wherein there is a statistical interaction between personality and context in determining moods. Our concern here is not so much with the specific forms that are more or less likely but rather with interactions as the basic determinants of moods.
5. An alternative approach to the one we propose here entails considering motivation within the possible self as job performer in terms of the extent to which people are engaged in or disengaged from work roles (Kahn, 1990). However, this alternative approach does not recognize explicitly the variety of work- and nonwork-related roles that could affect motivation in the workplace.
6. Since people in positive moods tend to perceive stimuli more positively, there is the potential that their perceptions may be somewhat inaccurate or biased in a positive direction. Additionally, some research suggests that people in negative affective states may be especially accurate in their perceptions (e.g., Sinclair, 1988).
7. We have not considered the possibility that, because people in a positive mood are less likely to detect a negative discrepancy between ongoing performance and the reference criterion, they might be less motivated. This alternative assumes people would have been motivated to eliminate the undetected negative discrepancy by trying harder to obtain the reference criterion. We choose not to attend to this plausible case simply to keep our exposition as straight-forward as possible.

REFERENCES

Adams, J.S. (1963). Toward an understanding of inequity. *Journal of Abnormal and Social Psychology, 67,* 422-436.

Anderson, C.A., Horowitz, L.M., & French, R.D. (1983). Attributional style of lonely and depressed people. *Journal of Personality and Social Psychology, 45,* 127-136.

Ashforth, B.E., & Humphrey, R.H. (1995). Emotion in the workplace: A reappraisal. *Human Relations, 48,* 97-125.

Baron, R.A. (1990). Environmentally-induced positive affect: Its impact on self-efficacy, task performance, negotiation, and conflict. *Journal of Applied Social Psychology, 20,* 368-384.

Baron, R.A., Russell, G.W., & Arms, R.L. (1985). Negative ions and behavior: Impact on mood, memory, and aggression among Type A and Type B persons. *Journal of Personality and Social Psychology, 48,* 746-754.

Blaney, P.H. (1986). Affect and memory: A review. *Psychological Bulletin, 99,* 229-246.
Bodenhausen, G.V., & Wyer, R.S. (1987). Social cognition and social reality: Information acquisition and use in the laboratory and the real world. In H.J. Hippler, N. Schwarz, & S. Sudman (Eds.), *Social information processing and survey methodology* (pp. 6-41). New York: Springer-Verlag.
Bower, G.H. (1981). Mood and memory. *American Psychologist, 36,* 129-148.
Bower, G.H., & Cohen, P.R. (1982). Emotional influences in memory and thinking: Data and theory. In M.S. Clark & S.T. Fiske (Eds.), *Affect and cognition* (pp. 291-331). Hillsdale, NJ: Erlbaum.
Brady, J.V. (1970). Emotion: Some conceptual problems and psychophysiological experiments. In M.B. Arnold (Ed.), *Feelings and emotions: The Loyola Symposium* (pp. 69-100). New York: Academic Press.
Brebner, J. (1982). *Environmental psychology in building design.* London: Applied Science.
Brett, J.M. (1980). The effect of job transfer on employees and their families. In C.L. Cooper & R. Payne, *Current concerns in occupational stress* (pp. 99-136). New York: John Wiley & Sons.
Brief, A.P., Burke, M.J., George, J.M., Robinson, B.S., & Webster, J. (1988). Should negative affectivity remain an unmeasured variable in the study of job stress? *Journal of Applied Psychology, 73,* 199-207.
Brief, A.P., Butcher, A.H., & Roberson, L. (1995). Cookies, disposition, and job attitudes: The effects of positive mood-inducing events on job satisfaction in a field experiment. *Organizational Behavior and Human Decision Processes, 62,* 55-62.
Burke, M.J., Brief, A.P., & George, J.M. (1993). The role of negative affectivity in understanding relationships between self-reports of stressors and strains: A comment on the applied psychology literature. *Journal of Applied Psychology, 78,* 402-412.
Burke, M.J., Brief, A.P., George, J.M., Roberson, L., & Webster, J. (1989). Measuring affect at work: Confirmatory analyses of competing mood structure with conceptual linkage to cortical regulatory systems. *Journal of Personality and Social Psychology, 57,* 1091-1102.
Cantor, N., & Kihlstrom, J.F. (1987). *Personality and social intelligence.* Englewood Cliffs, NJ: Prentice Hall.
Cappelli, P., & Sherer, P.D. (1991). The missing role of context in OB: The need for a meso-level approach. In B.M. Staw, & L.L. Cummings (Eds.), *Research in organizational behavior* (Vol. 13, 55-110). Greenwich, CT: JAI Press.
Carlson, M., Charlin, V., & Miller, N. (1988). Positive mood and helping behavior: A test of six hypotheses. *Journal of Personality and Social Psychology, 55,* 211-229.
Carver, C.S. (1979). A cybernetic model of self-attention processes. *Journal of Personality and Social Psychology, 37,* 1251-1281.
Carver, C.S., & Scheier, M.F. (1981). *Attention and self-regulation: A control-theory approach to human behavior.* New York: Springer-Verlag.
Carver, C.S., & Scheier, M.F. (1990). Origins and functions of positive and negative affect: A control-process view. *Psychological Review, 97,* 19-35.
Catalano, R.A., & Dooley, D. (1977). Economic predictors of depressed mood and stressful life events in a metropolitan community. *Journal of Health and Social Behavior, 18,* 292-307.
Chanowitz, B., & Langer, E.J. (1981). Premature cognitive commitment. *Journal of Personality and Social Psychology, 41,* 1051-1063.
Clark, M.S. (1982). A role for arousal in the link between feeling states, judgments, and behavior. In M.S. Clark & S.T. Fiske (Eds.), *Affect and cognition: the Seventeenth Annual Carnegie Symposium on Cognition* (pp. 263-289). Hillsdale, NJ: Erlbaum.
Clark, M.S., & Isen, A.M. (1982). Towards understanding the relationship between feeling states and social behavior. In A. Hastorf & A.M. Isen (Eds.), *Cognitive social psychology* (pp. 72-108). New York: Elsevier Science.

Clark, L.A., & Watson, D. (1988). Mood and the mundane: Relations between daily life events and self-reported mood. *Journal of Personality and Social Psychology, 54,* 296-308.

Costa, P.T., & McCrae, R.R. (1980). Influence of extraversion and neuroticism on subjective well-being: Happy and unhappy people. *Journal of Personality and Social Psychology, 38,* 668-678.

Cropanzano, R., James, K., & Citera, M. (1993). A goal hierarchy model of personality, motivation, and leadership. In B.M. Staw & L.L. Cummings (Eds.), *Research in organizational behavior* (Vol. 15, pp. 267-322). Greenwich, CT: JAI Press.

Cummings, L.L. (1982). Organizational behavior. *Annual Review of Psychology, 33,* 541-580.

Deci, E.L. (1975). *Intrinsic motivation.* New York: Plenum Press.

Diener, E., Larsen, R.J., Levine, S., & Emmons, R.A. (1985). Intensity and frequency: Dimensions underlying positive and negative affect. *Journal of Personality and Social Psychology, 48,* 1253-1265.

Dubin, R., Hedley, R.A., & Taveggia, T.C. (1976). Attachment to work. In R. Dubin (Ed.), *Handbook of work, organizations, and society* (pp. 281-341). Chicago: Rand McNally.

Dunnette, M.D., & Hough, L.M. (Eds.). (1990). *Handbook of industrial and organizational psychology* (2nd ed., Vol. 1). Palo Alto: Consulting Psychologists Press.

Eden, D., & Leviaton, V. (1974). Farm and factory in the kibbutz: A study of agrico-industrial psychology. *Journal of Applied Psychology, 59,* 596-602.

Ehrlichman, H., & Halpern, J.N. (1988). Affect and memory: Effects of pleasant and unpleasant odors in retrieval of happy and unhappy memories. *Journal of Personality and Social Psychology, 55,* 769-779.

Feather, N.T. (1966). Effects of prior success and failure on expectations of success and subsequent performance. *Journal of Personality and Social Psychology, 3,* 287-298.

Forest, D., Clark, M.S., Mills, J., & Isen, A.M. (1979). Helping as a function of feeling state and nature of the helping behavior. *Motivation and Emotion, 3,* 161-169.

Forgas, J.P., & Bower, G.H. (1987). Mood effects on person perception judgments. *Journal of Personality and Social Psychology, 53,* 53-60.

Forgas, J.P., Bower, G.H., & Moylan, S.J. (1990). Praise or blame? Affective influences on attributions for achievement. *Journal of Personality and Social Psychology, 59,* 809-819.

Forgas, J.P., & Moylan, S. (1987). After the movies: Transient mood and social adjustments. *Personality and Social Psychology Bulletin, 13,* 467-477.

Frijda, N.H. (1988). The laws of emotion. *American Psychologist, 43,* 349-358.

Garber, J., & Hollon, S.D. (1980). Universal versus personal helplessness in depression: Belief in uncontrollability or incompetence? *Journal of Abnormal Psychology, 89,* 56-66.

Gardner, D.G., Dunham, R.B., Cummings, L.L., & Pierce, J.L. (1987). Employee focus of attention and reactions to organizational change. *The Journal of Applied Behavioral Science, 23,* 351-370.

Gardner, D.G., Dunham, R.B., Cummings, L.L., & Pierce, J.L. (1989). Focus of attention at work: Construct definition and empirical validation. *Journal of Occupational Psychology, 62,* 61-77.

George, J.M. (1989). Mood and absence. *Journal of Applied Psychology, 74,* 317-324.

George, J.M. (1990). Personality, affect, and behavior in groups. *Journal of Applied Psychology, 75,* 107-116.

George, J.M. (1992). The role of personality in organizational life: Issues and evidence. *Journal of Management, 18,* 185-213.

George, J.M. (1996). Group affective tone. In M. West (Ed.), *Handbook of work group psychology.* Sussex, England: John Wiley & Sons.

George, J.M., & Brief, A.P. (1992). Feeling good-doing good: A conceptual analysis of the mood at work-organizational spontaneity relationship. *Psychological Bulletin, 112,* 310-329.

Gollwitzer, P.M., & Wicklund, R.A. (1985). The pursuit of self-defining goals. In J. Kuhl, & J. Beckmann (Eds.), *Action control: From cognition to behavior* (pp. 61-85). New York: Springer-Verlag.

Griffitt, W. (1970). Environmental effects on interpersonal behavior: Ambient effective temperature and attraction. *Journal of Personality and Social Psychology, 15,* 240-244.

Hackman, J.R., & Oldham, G.R. (1980). *Work redesign.* Reading, MA: Addison-Wesley.

Hatfield, E., Cacioppo, J.T., & Rapson, R.L. (1994). *Emotional contagion.* Cambridge: Cambridge University Press.

Headey, B., & Wearing, A. (1992). *Understanding happiness.* Melbourne, Australia: Longman Cheshire.

Hersey, R.B. (1932). *Workers' emotions in shop and home.* Philadelphia: University of Pennsylvania Press.

Hochschild, A.R. (1979). Emotion work, feeling rules, and social structure. *American Journal of Sociology, 85,* 551-575.

Hochschild, A.R. (1983). *The managed heart.* Berkeley: University of California Press.

Hyland, M.E. (1988). Motivational control theory: An integrative framework. *Journal of Personality and Social Psychology, 55,* 642-651.

Isen, A.M., & Baron, R.A. (1991). Positive affect as a factor in organizational behavior. In L.L. Cummings & B.M. Staw (Eds.), *Research in organizational behavior* (Vol. 13, pp. 1-53). Greenwich, CT: JAI Press.

Isen, A.M., & Daubman, K.A. (1984). The influence of affect on categorization. *Journal of Personality and Social Psychology, 34,* 385-393.

Isen, A.M., Daubman, K.A., & Nowicki, G.P. (1987). Positive affect facilitates creative problem solving: When we are glad, we feel as if the light has increased. *Journal of Personality and Social Psychology, 51,* 1122-1131.

Isen, A.M., Johnson, M.M.S., Mertz, E., & Robinson, G. (1985). Positive affect and the uniqueness of word associations. *Journal of Personality and Social Psychology, 21,* 384-388.

Isen, A.M., & Shalker, T.E. (1982). The effect of feeling state on evaluation of positive, neutral, and negative stimuli: When you accentuate the positive, do you eliminate the negative? *Social Psychology Quarterly, 45,* 58-63.

Isen, A.M., Shalker, T.E., Clark, M., & Karp, L. (1978). Affect, accessibility of material in memory, and behavior: A cognitive loop? *Journal of Personality and Social Psychology, 36,* 1-12.

Kahn, W.A. (1990). Psychological conditions of personal engagement and disengagement at work. *Academy of Management Journal, 33,* 692-724.

Kahneman, D. (1973). *Attention and effort.* Englewood Cliffs, NJ: Prentice-Hall.

Kanfer, R. (1990). Motivation theory and industrial/organizational psychology. In M.D. Dunnette & L.M. Hough (Eds.), *Handbook of industrial and organizational psychology* (2nd ed., Vol. 1, pp. 75-170). Palo Alto: Consulting Psychologists Press.

Kanfer, R.A., & Ackerman, P.L. (1989). Motivation and cognitive abilities: An integrative/ aptitude-treatment interaction approach to skill acquisition. *Journal of Applied Psychology, 74,* 657-690.

Kavanagh, R., & Bower, G.H. (1985). Mood and self-efficacy: Impact of joy and sadness on perceived capabilities. *Cognitive Therapy and Research, 9,* 507-525.

Klein, H.J. (1989). An integrated control theory model of work motivation. *Academy of Management Review, 14,* 150-172.

Klinger, E. (1975). Consequences of commitment to and disengagement from incentives. *Psychological Review, 82,* 1-25.

Klinger, E. (1982). On the self-management of mood, affect, and behavior. In P. Karoly & F.H. Kanfer (Eds.), *Self-management and behavior change* (pp. 129-164). Elmsford, NY: Pergamon Press.

Kraiger, K., Billings, R.S., & Isen, A.M. (1989). The influence of positive affective states on task perceptions and satisfaction. *Organizational Behavior and Human Decision Processes, 44,* 12-25.

Langer, E.J. (1975). The illusion of control. *Journal of Personality and Social Psychology, 32,* 311-328.

Langer, E.J., Blank, A., & Chanowitz, B. (1978). The mindlessness of ostensibly thoughtful action: The role of "placebic" information in interpersonal interaction. *Journal of Personality and Social Psychology, 36,* 632-635.

Larsen, R.J., & Diener, E. (1985). A multitrait-multimethod examination of affect structure: Hedonic evil and emotional intensity. *Personality and Individual Differences, 6,* 631-636.

Lazarus, R.S. (1991). *Emotion and adaptation.* New York: Oxford University Press.

Little, B. (1983). Personal projects: A rationale and methods for investigation. *Environment and Behavior, 15,* 273-309.

Locke, E.A. (1975). Personnel attitudes and motivation. *Annual Review of Psychology, 26,* 457-480.

Locke, E.A., & Latham, G.P. (1990). *A theory of goal setting and task performance.* Englewood Cliffs, NJ: Prentice-Hall.

Locke, E.A., Shaw, K.N., Saari, L.M., & Latham, G.P. (1981). Goal setting and task performance: 1969-1980). *Psychological Bulletin, 90,* 125-152.

Markus, H., & Nurius, P. (1986). Possible selves. *American Psychologist, 41,* 954-969.

Markus, H., & Ruvolo, A. (1989). Possible selves: Personalized representations of goals. In L.A. Pervin (Ed.), *Goal concepts in personality and social psychology* (pp. 211-241). Hillsdale, NJ: Erlbaum.

Markus, H., & Wurf, E. (1986). The dynamic self-concept: Social psychological perspective. *Annual Review of Psychology, 38,* 299-337.

Maslow, A.H. (1943). A theory of human motivation. *Psychological Review, 50,* 370-396.

Masters, J.C., & Furman, W. (1975). Effects of affect induction in expectancies for serendipitous positive events, success on task performance and beliefs in internal or external control of reinforcement. *Developmental Psychology, 12,* 481-482.

Matsui, T., Kagawa, M., Nagamatsu, J., & Ohtsuka, Y. (1977). Validity of expectancy theory as a within-person behavioral choice model for sales activities. *Journal of Applied Psychology, 62,* 764-767.

Matsui, T., & Ohtsuka, Y. (1978). Within-person expectancy theory predictions of supervisory consideration and structure behavior. *Journal of Applied Psychology, 63,* 128-131.

Meyer, G.J., & Shack, J.R. (1989). Structural convergence of mood and personality: Evidence for old and new directions. *Journal of Personality and Social Psychology, 57,* 691-706.

Mischel, W., Ebbesen, E., & Zeiss, A. (1973). Selective attention to the self: Situational and dispositional determinants. *Journal of Personality and Social Psychology, 27,* 129-142.

Morris, W.N., & Reilly, N.P. (1987). Toward the self-regulation of mood: Theory and research. *Motivation and Emotion, 11,* 215-249.

Mowday, R.T., & Sutton, R.I. (1993). Organizational behavior: Linking individuals and groups to organizational contexts. *Annual Review of Psychology, 44,* 195-229.

Murray, N., Sujan, H., Hirt, E.R., & Sujan, M. (1990). The influence of mood on categorization: A cognitive flexibility interpretation. *Journal of Personality and Social Psychology, 59,* 411-425.

Norman, D.A., & Bobrow, D.B. (1975). On data-limited and resource-limited processes. *Cognitive Psychology, 7,* 44-64.

Nowlis, V. (1970). Mood: Behavior and experience. In M.B. Arnold (Ed.), *Feelings and emotions: The Loyola Symposium* (pp. 261-277). New York: Academic Press.

Nuttin, J. (1984). *Motivation, planning, and action: A relational theory of behavior dynamics.* Hillsdale, NJ: Erlbaum.

O'Reilly, C.A. (1991). Organizational behavior: Where we've been, where we're going. *Annual Review of Psychology, 42,* 427-458.

Oldham, G.R., & Rotchford, N.L. (1983). Relations between office characteristics and employee reactions: A study of the physical environment. *Administrative Science Quarterly, 28,* 542-556.

Parrott, W.G., & Sabini, J. (1990). Mood and memory under natural conditions: Evidence for mood incongruent recall. *Journal of Personality and Social Psychology, 59,* 321-336.

Pekrun, R., & Frese, M. (1992). Emotions in work and achievement. In C.L. Cooper & Robertson, I.T. (Eds.), *International review of industrial and organizational psychology* (Vol. 7). New York: Wiley.

Pervin, L.A., & Lewis, M. (1978). Overview of the internal-external issue. In L.A. Pervin & M. Lewis (Eds.), *Perspectives in interactional psychology* (pp. 1-22). New York: Plenum.

Pfeffer, J. (1982). *Organizations and organization theory.* Marshfield, MA: Pitman.

Pinder, C.C. (1984). *Work motivation: Theory, issues, and applications.* Glenview, IL: Scott, Foresman and Company.

Purcell, A.T. (1982). The structure of activation and emotion. *Multivariate Behavioral Research, 17,* 221-251.

Rafaeli, A., & Sutton, R.I. (1989). The expression of emotion in organizational life. In B.M. Staw & L.L. Cummings (Eds.), *Research in organizational behavior* (Vol. 11, pp. 1-42). Greenwich, CT: JAI Press.

Raynor, J.O., & McFarlin, D.B. (1986). Motivation and the self-system. In R.M. Sorrentino & E.T. Higgins (Eds.), *Handbook of motivation and cognition* (pp. 315-349). New York: Guilford.

Rhodewalt, F. (1986). Self-presentation and the phenomenal self: On the stability and malleability of self-conceptions. In R. Baumeister (Ed.), *Public self and private self.* New York: Springer-Verlag.

Rice, R.W., Near, J.P., & Hunt, R.G. (1980). The job-satisfaction/life-satisfaction relationship: A review of empirical research. *Basic and Applied Social Psychology, 1,* 37-64.

Roberson, L. (1989). Assessing personal work goals in the organizational setting: Development and evaluation of the work concerns inventory. *Organizational Behavior and Human Decision Processes, 44,* 345-367.

Russell, J.A. (1978). Evidence of convergent validity on the dimensions of affect. *Journal of Personality and Social Psychology, 36,* 1152-1168.

Russell, J.A. (1980). A circumplex model of affect. *Journal of Personality and Social Psychology, 39,* 1161-1178.

Ryle, G. (1950). *The concept of mind.* London: Hutchinson.

Schank, R.C., & Abelson, R.P. (1977). *Scripts, plans, goals, and understanding: An inquiry into human knowledge structures.* Hillsdale, NJ: Erlbaum.

Schiffenbauer, A. (1974). Effect of observer's emotional state on judgments of the emotional state of others. *Journal of Personality and Social Psychology, 30,* 31-35.

Schlenker, B.R. (1985). Identity and self-identification. In B.R. Schlenker (Ed.), *The self in social life* (pp. 65-99). New York: McGraw Hill.

Schwarz, N. (1990). Feelings as information. In E.T. Higgins & R.M. Sorrentino (Eds.), *Handbook of motivation and cognition: Foundations of social behavior* (Vol. 2, pp. 527-561). New York: Guilford Press.

Schwarz, N., & Clore, G.L. (1988). How do I feel about it? The informative function of affective states. In K. Fiedler & J. Forgas (Eds.), *Affect, cognition and social behavior* (pp. 44-62). Lewiston, NY: C.J. Hogrefe.

Schwarz, N., Strack, F., Kommer, D., & Wagner, D. (1987). Soccer rooms and the quality of your life: Mood effects on judgments of satisfaction with life in general and with specific life-domains. *European Journal of Social Psychology, 17,* 69-79.

Simon, H.A. (1967). Motivational and emotional controls of cognition. *Psychological Review, 74*, 29-39.

Simon, H.A. (1982). Comments. In M.S. Clark & S.T. Fiske (Eds.), *Affect and cognition: The Seventeenth Annual Carnegie Symposium on Cognition* (pp. 333-342). Hillsdale, NJ: Erlbaum.

Simon, H.A. (1995). The information-processing theory of mind. *American Psychologist, 50*, 507-508.

Sinclair, R.C. (1988). Mood, categorization breadth, and performance appraisal: The effects of order of information acquisition and affective state on halo, accuracy, informational retrieval, and evaluations. *Organizational Behavior and Human Decision Processes, 42*, 22-46.

Staub, E. (1980). Social and prosocial behavior. In E. Staub (Ed.), *Personality: Basic aspects and current research* (pp. 237-294). Englewood Cliffs, NJ: Prentice-Hall.

Staw, B.M., & Barsade, S.G. (1993). Affect and managerial performance: A test of the sadder-but-wiser vs. happier-and-smarter hypotheses. *Administrative Science Quarterly, 38*, 304-331.

Staw, B.M., Sutton, R.I., & Pelled, L.H. (1994). Employee positive emotion and favorable outcomes at the workplace. *Organization Science, 5*, 51-71.

Strack, F., Schwarz, N., & Gschneidinger, E. (1985). Happiness and reminiscing: The role of time perspective, mood, and mode of thinking. *Journal of Personality and Social Psychology, 49*, 1460-1469.

Sullins, E.S. (1991). Emotional contagion revisited: Effects of social comparison and expressive style on mood convergence. *Personality and Social Psychology Bulletin, 17*, 166-174.

Sutton, R.I., & Callahan, A.L. (1987). The stigma of bankruptcy: Spoiled organizational image and its management. *Academy of Management Journal, 30*, 405-436.

Tellegen, A. (1982). *Brief manual for the Differential Personality Questionnaire*. Unpublished manuscript, University of Minnesota.

Tellegen, A. (1985). Structures of mood and personality and their relevance to assessing anxiety, with an emphasis on self report. In A.H. Tuma & J.D. Maser (Eds.), *Anxiety and the anxiety disorders* (pp. 681-706). Hillsdale, NJ: Lawrence Erlbaum.

Thayer, R.E. (1989). *The biopsychology of mood and arousal*. New York: Oxford University Press.

Veitch, R., & Griffitt, W. (1976). Good news-bad news: Affective and interpersonal effects. *Journal of Applied Social Psychology, 6*, 69-75.

Viteles, M.S. (1932). *Industrial psychology*. New York: W.W. Norton & Company.

Vroom, V.H. (1964). *Work and motivation*. New York: John Wiley.

Watson, D., & Clark, L.A. (1984). Negative affectivity: The disposition to experience aversive emotional states. *Psychological Bulletin, 96*, 465-490.

Watson, D., Clark, L.A., & Tellegen, A. (1984). Crosscultural convergence in the structure of mood: A Japanese replication and a comparison with U.S. findings. *Journal of Personality and Social Psychology, 47*, 127-144.

Watson, D., & Pennebaker, J.W. (1989). Health complaints, stress and distress: Exploring the central role of negative affectivity. *Psychological Review, 96*, 234-254.

Watson, D., & Tellegen, A. (1985). Toward a consensual structure of mood. *Psychological Bulletin, 98*, 219-235.

Weiner, B. (1985). An attributional theory of achievement, motivation, and emotion. *Psychological Review, 92*, 548-573.

Wyer, R.S. (1980). The acquisition and use of social knowledge: Basic postulates and representative research. *Personality and Social Psychology Bulletin, 6*, 558-573.

Zevon, M.A., & Tellegen, A. (1982). The structure of mood change: An idiographic/nomothetic analysis. *Journal of Personality and Social Psychology, 43*, 111-122.

WHY DO WORKERS BITE THE HANDS THAT FEED THEM? EMPLOYEE THEFT AS A SOCIAL EXCHANGE PROCESS

Jerald Greenberg and Kimberly S. Scott

ABSTRACT

Employee theft is widespread in scope and extremely costly to organizations. It may be viewed as a nonviolent form of property deviance toward a company committed by an employee of that company for personal gain. A social exchange orientation highlights the roles of social norms and distributive injustice as determinants of employee theft. According to the proposed "cycle of acceptance," societal norms condone employee theft insofar as: (a) people are willing to victimize organizations, (b) employee thieves are only infrequently prosecuted, and (c) guilt over theft is minimal. Supervisors sometimes condone employee theft, such as by serving as models of deviant behavior, and by permitting some theft as an informal source of reward. Social norms within work groups support employee theft and carefully regulate the form it takes. Theft also is conceptualized as an attempt to redress distributive injustice. Theft-induced responses to inequity are motivated by both restitution and retaliation. Experimental studies have demonstrated that these reactions are exacerbated by inequitable conditions in which employees are treated in a socially insensitive manner. The implications for controlling employee theft include: (a) breaking the cycle of acceptance, (b) aligning the interests of employers and employees, and (c) demonstrating interpersonal sensitivity in the treatment of employees.

BACKGROUND

The French call it *le travail noir*, the Russians, *rabotat nalyevo*, and the British, *fiddling*—what Americans commonly refer to as "employee theft." In any language, it is a phenomenon with an ancient history (Mars, 1982). Egyptian papyri over three thousand years old tell us that employee theft from religious facilities was widespread (Henry, 1978). For example, accounts of scribes removing fabric and grain from temple storehouses date back to 1160 B.C. (Peet, 1924). But, modern history provides our clearest insight into this phenomenon.

History and Scope of Employee Theft

Citizens of seventeenth century rural England enjoyed the right to take for their own use a share, carefully regulated by custom, of resources such as wood and hay from the lord's manor (Ditton, 1977a)—a form of in-kind payment enshrined in *Leviticus*:

> And when ye reap the harvest of your land, thou shalt not wholly reap the corners of thy field ... neither shalt you gather the fallen fruit of thy vineyard; thou shalt leave them for the poor and the stranger.

That was, until the aristocracy imposed the Acts of Enclosure, which rescinded common rights, and with them, the material benefits that non-propertied persons had come to expect (Sieh, 1987). Opposition to the Acts was extreme among commoners, who rebelled against the criminalization of practices that were once customary (Thompson, 1975). The result: peasants felt they were unfairly denied property that was traditionally theirs and engaged in widespread poaching to reclaim it despite savage repressive measures to stop them (Hay, 1975). As this occurred, many rural laborers—accustomed to receiving in-kind wages and still stinging from the abrogation of those practices in the countryside—fled to the cities to staff the rapidly growing factories. To the irritation of factory owners, such rural laborers had a "penchant for making off with parts of the workplace or the fruits of their labor there, in addition to their wages" (Ditton, 1977a, p. 43).

Three hundred years later, whether viewed as lingering vestiges of the annexation of customary rights by the ruling class or signs of immorality among the working class, employee theft is still with us. Indeed, although the unreported nature of much employee theft and the questionable basis of some claims precludes the possibility of wholly accurate figures (Murphy, 1993), statistics clearly indicate that theft among employees has reached epic proportions. For example, it has been estimated that approximately three-quarters of all employees steal from their employers at least once (McGurn,

1988), many on a regular basis (Delaney, 1993; London House and Food Marketing Institute, 1993), and that employees at all organizational levels engage in this practice (Coleman, 1985). Theft by employees currently costs American businesses approximately $120 billion annually (Buss, 1993)—a figure expected to grow to $200 billion by the year 2000 (Govoni, 1992; Snyder, Blair, & Arndt, 1990). So extreme is the problem that it has been identified by the U.S. Chamber of Commerce as ten times more costly than the nation's street crime, and responsible for over 30% of all business failures (Bullard & Resnik, 1983), even more—as much as 50%—in some retail businesses (Snyder & Blair, 1989). Not surprisingly, workplace dishonesty has been referred to as the most significant crime problem in American society (Lary, 1988). In the words of one retail industry spokesperson, "shoplifting will steal your profits; employees will steal your business" (Snyder & Blair, 1989, p. 28).

Stealing by employees has certainly come a long way since the peasant uprisings of newly-industrialized England three centuries ago. Employees continue to steal material goods (e.g., supplies, equipment, and finished products) from their employers, to be sure, although these may be high-tech goods with considerable market value ("Ex-employee of IBM," 1993) as well as everyday items (Lipman & McGraw, 1988). However, today's employees also steal valuable intellectual property—such as trade secrets (Solomon, Waldrop, Washington, & Shenitz, 1993; "Two at ULSI System Acquitted," 1991; Yoder, 1993), competitive information ("Two are Sentenced," 1992), and even other employees (Aeppel, 1993). With great regularity they steal other intangibles, as well—notably, time (e.g., taking long breaks, and socializing excessively; Snyder & Blair, 1989; Snyder, Blair, & Arndt, 1990). Theft of cash is, of course, also widely popular in some industries. This behavior ranges from stealing small amounts of change, such as the practice among toll takers of pocketing coins handed to them by drivers (Zeitlin, 1971), to more elaborate corporate embezzlement schemes costing millions (Emshwiller, 1993). In banking, for example, electronic fraud by employees is so easy among those with access to certain computer information that, according to one consultant, "using a gun or stealing cash are really dumb ways to steal from a bank" (Bullard & Resnik, 1983, p. 52).

Some employee theft occurs quite casually, such as when grocery clerks remove items for personal use from store shelves (Boye & Slora, 1993). Other acts are more systematic and deliberate, such as when an employee of an electronics firm stole liquid gold by dipping his spare lunchbox into a vat of it, or when a retail clerk purchased clothing using her discount privileges and returned it at full price at another store in the chain (Bullard & Resnik, 1983). Some enterprising thieves have gone so far as to dig through corporate garbage bins in search of information that may be of value (Howard, 1991; Palmeri, 1994). With increasing frequency, employee theft has been found to occur in groups, or "rings," of employees, such as when the entire parking meter collection staff of San Francisco was caught stealing $3 million over six years (Bullard & Resnik, 1983). Clearly, employee theft is widely prevalent, varied in form, and extremely costly to organizations.

Employee Theft: A Surprisingly Neglected OB Topic

Our goal in presenting these statistics and examples is to make a case for the widespread nature and impact of the problem of employee theft. As obvious as it may be, the importance of this phenomenon appears to have been lost on researchers in the field of organizational behavior (OB). Although the phenomenon has been actively studied by sociologists (e.g., Hollinger & Clark, 1983) and experts in corporate security (e.g., Bintliff, 1994; Bliss & Aoki, 1993; Jamieson, 1994), specialists in OB have all but ignored the issue. In part, this appears to be the result of the widespread fatalistic belief that theft is a byproduct of a rapidly declining level of morality in society about which management can do little except bolster security measures (Jones & Gautschi, 1988). Perceiving employee theft as more of a security and law enforcement problem than a management problem, OB scholars have had little incentive to study it. Curiously, this state exists despite repeated indications by practitioners (e.g., Buss, 1993; Greengard, 1993) that employee theft can be deterred by using appropriate management techniques.

Further, by focusing on only the most sensationalistic, headline-grabbing incidents (e.g., Emshwiller, 1993), organizational scholars generally have considered employee theft a problem involving only a few "bad apples," one that could be adequately addressed by weeding out potential thieves (Carter, 1987). In keeping with this, industrial psychologists dating back to Vitales (1932) have devoted considerable effort to reducing theft by selecting honest employees—research on integrity testing, which has proven controversial at best (Budman, 1993; Dalton, Metzger, & Wimbush, 1994; Ones, Viswesvaran, & Schmidt, 1993; Sackett, 1994). However, as growing evidence indicates that employee theft is prevalent among a large segment of the workforce, and that repeated incidents of seemingly minor theft are even costlier to organizations than the few larger ones that receive attention (Lipman & McGraw, 1988), it has become clear that employee theft is not only a topic deserving of attention by OB scholars, but also that viewing organizational theft as a management issue is extremely worthwhile. As Hollinger (1989) put it, "good management, not necessarily more security equipment, is the route to lower levels of employee theft" (p. 35).

In the face of growing interest in various forms of antisocial behavior in the workplace (e.g., Giacalone & Greenberg, in press; Robinson & Bennett, in press) and evidence linking theft to key organizational variables such as job dissatisfaction and turnover (Ettorre, 1994; Hollinger, 1989), the stage is set for OB-chartered excursions into the largely uncharted waters of employee theft. In the absence of such efforts, there has been a systematic gap in our understanding of the social and situational factors associated with employee theft. Acknowledging this void, Murphy (1993) has noted that this state of affairs "constitutes a major roadblock to understanding and controlling dishonesty in the workplace" (p. 35).

The Social Exchange Heuristic

With an eye toward removing this obstacle, this paper will analyze employee theft from the perspective of *social exchange*, an approach that has for several decades examined the social dynamics of behavior in many settings (Blau, 1964), including organizations (e.g., Hollander, 1980; Nord, 1980). In general, conceptualizations of social exchange (e.g., Homans, 1961; Thibaut & Kelley, 1959) examine the processes by which individuals and groups give resources to other social entities (e.g., other individuals, groups, or organizations) and receive resources from them (Simpson, 1976). The use of a social exchange approach to employee theft is in keeping with the criminologist, von Hentig's (1948) position that explaining crime requires understanding the social dynamics between the criminal and the victim, a break from the tradition of concentrating on the "criminal mind" alone. Similarly, Altheide, Adler, Adler, and Altheide (1978) have argued that employees who steal should not be viewed as thieves, but rather, as parties to a complex set of interactions between themselves and others in the workplace.

Although these theorists' suggestions regarding the benefits of using social exchange as a heuristic to explain employee theft have been voiced some time ago, they have been largely ignored. Today, however, as interest in various forms of deviant, or antisocial, behavior in the workplace is beginning to emerge in the organizational literature (e.g., Giacalone & Greenberg, in press; Robinson & Bennett, in press), the time has come to not only rekindle interest in the social exchange heuristic, but also to update and extend it. Specifically, in examining employee theft as a social exchange process, we will be guided by two major building blocks—norms regulating employee theft, and the motivation to achieve distributive justice (Greenberg, 1984). The literature bearing on these factors will shed light on an important organizational question: "why do employees steal?"

Toward this end, we will begin by formally defining employee theft, identifying its dimensions, and identifying its context relative to other forms of deviant behavior in organizations (Giacalone & Greenberg, in press). We will then describe the role of societal norms, group norms, and supervisory norms in employee theft. Following this, we will examine the role of distributive justice in employee theft. In particular, this analysis will focus on the association between dissatisfaction and theft, the motives underlying inequity-induced theft, and the ameliorative effects of interpersonal treatment. Finally, we will conclude by discussing the practical implications of the social exchange approach, offering suggestions for managing employee theft derived from the present analysis.

THE CONCEPTUAL CONTEXT OF EMPLOYEE THEFT

The first step toward understanding employee theft as a managerial issue is to carefully define it, a task that must begin by distinguishing it from other forms of criminal activity. With this in mind, we draw on the literature to make a series of important distinctions that lead us to the conceptual space for employee theft (see summary in Figure 1).

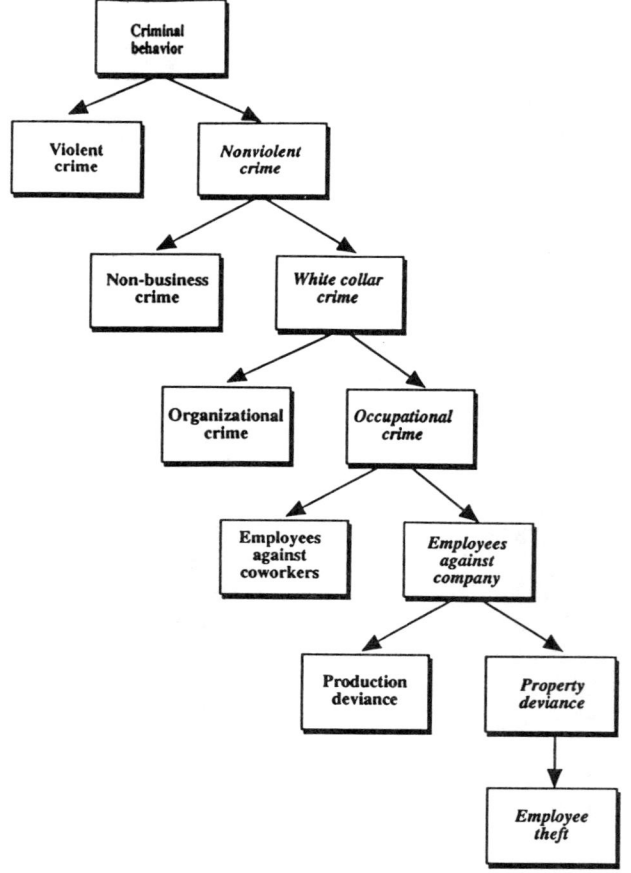

Figure 1. Series of Distinctions between Various Forms of Criminal Activity Leading to the Conceptual Location of Employee Theft

At the broadest level, we follow the lead of criminologists by distinguishing between crime that is violent from that which is nonviolent (Clinard & Quinney, 1973), the category into which employee theft falls. Then, among nonviolent crime, we can distinguish between activity that does not involve business from that which does, commonly referred to as white-collar crime. This term, coined by Sutherland (1940) over fifty years ago, originally referred to criminal activity by a high status person in the course of performing his or her job, although it has come to be used more generally today, focusing on a wide variety of work-related illegal acts by persons at all levels (Braithwaite, 1985; Shapiro, 1990). For example, an analysis of the use of the term "white-collar crime" by twelve different federal agencies revealed that despite differences, there was agreement with respect to the core objectives of white-collar criminal activity: "obtaining or avoiding the payment of money, property, or services through nonviolent and deceitful means in the course of occupational activities" (Yasueda, Middleton, & Kurke, 1978, pp. 3-4).

Two broad categories of white-collar crime have been identified by Coleman (1985). One of these is *organizational crime*: "white collar crimes committed with the support and encouragement of a formal organization and intended in part to advance the goals of that organization" (Coleman, 1985, p. 8). Examples include false advertising, fraud, conspiracies, and tax evasion. Coleman's (1985) second category of white-collar crime is known as *occupational crime*, defined as "white collar crime committed by an individual or a group of individuals exclusively for personal gain" (p. 8). The clearest example of this is employee theft.

Following Turner and Stephenson (1993), it is important to distinguish between occupational crimes perpetrated by employees against their coworkers (e.g., taking credit for another person's sales, stealing cash from a coworker's wallet), and those by employees against their organization. Employee theft falls into this latter category.

Theorists have drawn upon the sociological concept of deviance to help explain the various ways in which employees can act against their employers (e.g., Hollinger & Clark, 1983). Specifically, deviance refers to "behavior which violates the more or less institutionalized expectations for performance of organizational roles set forth by the formal organization" (Kemper, 1966, p. 288). Applying this concept, two major forms of deviance have been identified. The first, termed *production deviance* by Hollinger (1986, 1989; Hollinger & Clark, 1982, 1983) refers to "behaviors which violate the formally proscribed norms delineating the minimal quality and quantity of work to be accomplished" (Hollinger & Clark, 1982, p. 333). These include "withdrawal behaviors" such as turnover, absences, and strikes, all widely studied organizational phenomena (e.g., Lee & Mitchell, 1994). Another, less studied form of deviance has been referred to as *property deviance* (Hollinger, 1986, 1989; Hollinger & Clark, 1982, 1983). This category of deviance focuses on "those instances where employees acquire or damage the tangible property or assets of the work organization without authorization" (Hollinger & Clark, 1982, p. 333). Not only do various forms of employee theft (e.g., pilferage, embezzlement) fit into this category, but also such acts as sabotage (e.g., Giacalone & Rosenfeld, 1987; Sprouse, 1992).

Recently, Robinson and Bennett (1995) used multidimensional scaling to confirm the distinction between deviance based on property and deviance based on production. They found four reliable clusters of deviant workplace behavior by cross-cutting deviance based on organizational and interpersonal targets with a dimension distinguishing the seriousness of the deviant act. Within the quadrant of serious-organizational acts were such actions as "employees stealing company equipment" and "employees stealing money from the cash drawer." In subsequent research these investigators confirmed, using factor analysis, that employee theft could be reliably categorized as organizational deviance (Bennett & Robinson, 1994).

Following the above series of distinctions, we are led to the conceptual space for employee theft: a nonviolent form of property deviance focused on one's company committed by an employee of that company for personal gain. Consistent with this analysis is Merriam's (1977) definition of employee theft: "the unlawful taking, control, or transfer of an employer's property with the purpose of benefiting the employee or another not entitled to the property" (pp. 375-376). Adding to this, Greenberg (1995) noted that employee theft includes, but is not limited to, the removal of products, supplies, materials, funds, data, information, or intellectual property. One common form of theft is *embezzlement*—the destruction or misappropriation of another's money or property entrusted to one's care (Cressy, 1953). Although there are many variants (Merriam, 1977), employee theft is commonly distinguished with respect to the value of the stolen items—anchored at one end by *petty theft* (or, *pilfering*), taking items in small quantities and/or items of limited value, and at the other end by *grand theft*, taking valuable items (Smigel & Ross, 1970).

Despite the dramatic nature of a few large heists, pilferage is far more prevalent, and cumulatively, its potential impact on organizations may be more devastating (Lipman & McGraw, 1988). For this reason, and because much more is known about the social psychology of pilferage than of grand theft, pilferage will be the main form of theft examined in this paper. Having defined employee theft, we will now begin our analysis of this phenomenon from the perspective of social exchange.

SOCIETAL ATTITUDES TOWARD EMPLOYEE THEFT: THE CYCLE OF ACCEPTANCE

Theories of social exchange rest on the assumption that social interaction is guided by a broad umbrella of general rules and attitudes that regulate and

Employee Theft as a Social Exchange Process

direct specific exchange activities (e.g., Simpson, 1976). In this regard, our understanding of employee theft as a social exchange process requires appreciation for the special nature of society's attitudes toward it. Although, strictly speaking, theft of company property by employees constitutes criminal activity, it is generally not considered as serious as other criminal offenses, even theft of the same items by nonemployees (i.e., shoplifting) (Conklin, 1977).

Why is employee theft so widely accepted? Three interrelated dynamics appear to be involved. First, people demonstrate a general willingness to harm organizations. Second, acknowledging that they may be viewed as targets, organizations only infrequently prosecute employees found stealing from them. Third, such inaction tacitly encourages employee theft, leading employees to not feel guilty about stealing from their employers. Not deterred by guilt, the willingness to harm organizations is reinforced, and so the cycle continues (at least until something happens to break it, as we will describe later). We refer to this process, summarized in Figure 2, as the *cycle of acceptance*. Although the cycle has not been tested as a whole, its various components receive support.

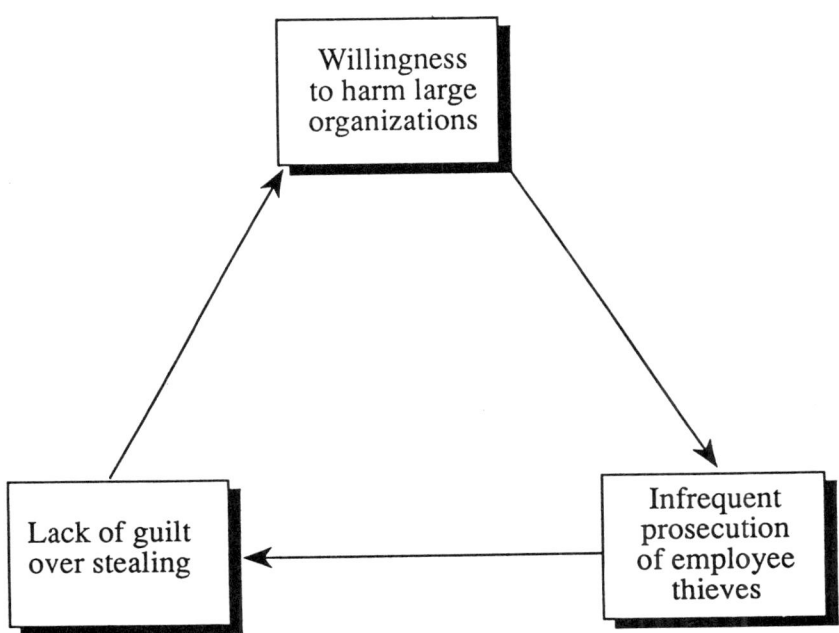

Figure 2. The Cycle of Acceptance Postulated to be Responsible for Societal Acceptance of Employee Theft

Organizations as Victims of Robin Hood

According to legend, Robin Hood and his band of merry men stole from the rich and gave to the poor, but were not timid about helping themselves to some of the loot. To the extent that people perceive organizations as rich, impersonal entities, they may well be expected to be the victims of modern-day Robin Hoods (Willis, 1986). Indeed, "theft appears to be easier to excuse when the victim has larger assets than the criminal" (Smigel & Ross, 1970, p. 7), as is the case among organizations and their employees. Empirical evidence consistent with this premise has been provided by several studies.

For example, Leventhal, Younts, and Lund (1972) had researchers posing as door-to-door salesmen offer rebates to consumers along with their purchases. When the rebates were said to come from the individual salesmen themselves, respondents were significantly less likely to accept them than when they were described as coming from a large company. Extending these findings, Greenberg (1986) found evidence for differential willingness to tolerate underpayment inequity created by individuals and organizations. He deliberately paid only $1 to subjects promised $2 in exchange for completing a brief consumer interest survey. The survey was described as being sponsored by either a large manufacturing company that was soliciting opinions to plan their marketing strategy, or by the researcher himself, to pursue his own academic research interests. Upon leaving, subjects were prompted to acknowledge receipt of the $2 they were supposed to receive, and tape recordings were made of any verbal attempts to redress the inequity. Whereas over 85% of the subjects inquired about the missing dollar when the research was said to be sponsored by an organization, less than 29% did so when the study was described as being paid for by the researcher himself. Greenberg interpreted these findings as evidence of people's greater willingness to tolerate underpayment inequity at the hands of another person, with presumably limited resources, than a large organization, with considerably greater resources.

To the extent that this is true, people would be less accepting of theft from small organizations than large ones. This is precisely what was found in a questionnaire study by Smigel (1970). Whereas only 34% of Smigel's (1970) respondents disapproved of theft from large businesses, significantly more— 50%—disapproved of theft from small businesses. Taken together, the findings of Leventhal et al. (1972), Greenberg (1986), and Smigel (1970) suggest that people are willing to dip into the deep pockets of large organizations if they believe they have a legitimate claim entitling them to do so.

Smigel and Ross (1970) note that it is not only the presumed wealth of large organizations that makes them acceptable targets of theft, but also the fact that organizations are frequently regarded with apathy, at best, or disdain, at worst, by the general public. Specifically, large organizations are often cited as being abusers of power, and bullies of the everyday person. Finding expressions of this attitude over forty years ago, Fisher and Withey (1951) commented, "the bulk of arguments in disfavor [of organizations] can be reduced to the criticism or distaste for big business's power or misuse of power over the worker, the competitor, the consumer, or other societal institutions" (p. 15). Today, although the world of big business is tightly woven into the fabric of Western society, concerns about abuses of corporate power continue to linger in some quarters (Pfeffer, 1992). This too may be responsible for people's seeming insensitivity to victimizing organizations.

Organizational Reluctance to Prosecute Internal Thieves

To the extent that people are more willing to take things from large organizations than from other individuals, it is not surprising that "public reaction to this kind of theft may be weaker than reactions to other kinds of larceny" (Conklin, 1977, p. 27). This attitude is expressed in an interesting combination of statistics: although the average employee steals more than the average shoplifter ($750 compared to $15 during the late 1950s; Taylor, 1958), far more shoplifters than employees are arrested for theft (900,000 compared to 18,000 in 1972; "Employees, Suppliers," 1973). Although these figures are dated, the same general pattern is believed to hold today (Snyder, Broome, Kehoe, McIntyre, & Blair, 1991).

Overall, it has been estimated than fewer than 15% of employees caught stealing are ever brought to criminal prosecution (Kenda, 1982). This is not to say that employee theft goes unpunished. Rather, less extreme forms of internal punishment tend to be used. For example, in Pittsburgh, Food Gallery rarely arrests workers caught stealing. Instead, they suspend the employee for the first offense and fire the person for the second offense ("Labor Report," 1990). This is typical; the vast majority of organizations are more likely to fire employee thieves and have them repay the company for its loss than to seek criminal prosecution (Coleman, 1985). The reliance on organizational sanctions, rather than criminal ones, reflects the notion that thefts among employees are considered "violations of specialized occupational norms" as opposed to attacks on basic societal values (Glaser, 1967, p. 117). Indeed, Ditton (1977b) has argued that employee theft triggers benevolent societal reactions because it represents a subterranean version of a conventional business tradition—maximizing self-interest: "fiddling, like selling, epitomizes the capitalist spirit" (p. 174). Although this assertion is difficult to prove, it is consistent with the tendency for organizations to refrain from criminally prosecuting employee thieves. In fact, some have argued that because many forms of white-collar crime, including theft, are so rarely adjudicated in the criminal courts, that is a misnomer to refer to them as "crimes" at all (Caldwell, 1968).

Lipman and McGraw (1988) note that for several reasons organizations prefer to rely on a "private justice system," their own set of internal rules for dealing with deviant behavior. First, prosecution may be considered unduly harsh treatment for an employee with an otherwise good work record. Second, they may be reluctant to engage the company in a long drawn-out legal battle that might not only require other employees to take time off work to testify in court, but also generate considerable legal expenses. Third, criminal prosecution for employee theft is likely to require a higher quality of evidence than is usually available in companies—typically, reports by security staff. Finally, companies may be reluctant to resort to punishment in a public forum for fear of the bad publicity it will breed. Stories in the popular press of corporate Goliaths going after employee Davids would only reinforce the public's disdain for large organizations noted earlier.

Stealing Without Guilt

Because employees caught stealing from their companies are likely to be penalized less severely than nonemployees engaging in the same behavior, the apparent acceptability of employee theft is reinforced (Carter, 1987). Not surprisingly, employees feel little guilt when they do steal from their companies. Tatham (1974) demonstrated this most clearly in his survey of retail employees' views about theft. Exactly half of Tatham's respondents indicated that they had taken merchandise from their places of employment without paying for it, and even more gave unauthorized discounts to others. Among those taking merchandise, the vast majority (84%) indicated that they felt no guilt for what they did despite acknowledging that it may be considered theft. Surveying a group of specialists in the grocery business, Boye and Slora (1993) found that acts such as taking money, merchandise, or equipment from one's employer without permission were considered extremely serious offenses. Despite this, they also found that 46% of supermarket employees admitted to these very acts, 35% very frequently.

How could it be that so many employees engage in the behaviors that are considered highly deviant by experts in their industry? First, as already noted, employees may interpret their employers' reluctance to prosecute for employee theft as an indication that what they're doing is not completely inappropriate. "After all," they may reason, "if it were truly wrong, the company would do something to prevent it, but because they don't, it must be okay." Thus, whereas theft may be recognized as wrong and worthy of punishment, what they are doing must not be considered theft because it is not punished (Altheide et al., 1978). A second possibility is that employees confront strong norms in their work groups which lead them to rationalize as acceptable ostensible acts of stealing. To the extent that groups have norms that condone (or even encourage) theft and provide collective justifications for engaging in such behavior (Payne, 1989), such behavior is likely to be sustained. Because we will describe these processes in detail later in this paper, we will not elaborate on them here. At this point, suffice it to say that social norms play an important part in dispelling guilt about theft behavior.

Regardless of the underlying process, it appears that employees who engage in theft from their employers tend to feel little, if any, guilt. Not surprisingly, then, organizations become ready targets for employee theft, thereby moving full circle along the cycle of acceptance.

SUPERVISORY NORMS CONDONE EMPLOYEE THEFT

Formally, organizational officials reject employee theft as not only morally inappropriate, but also fiscally irresponsible. Despite this, there is evidence from qualitative research that in some organizations informal norms exist that condone, if not encourage, theft by employees (e.g., Dalton, 1959). Two distinct mechanisms appear to be involved, one involving passive imitation, and another involving active legitimation.

Passive Imitation of Superiors: Parallel Deviance

It has been claimed that some employee theft results when lower-level employees model their superiors' deviant behavior, what Kemper (1966) has referred to as *parallel deviance*. Using Kemper's (1966) example, a secretary who observes his or her boss turn in an obviously padded expense account voucher may be tempted to conclude that some theft on his or her own part may be acceptable. Similarly, Hollinger (1989) recounts an incident in which the housekeeping staff of a hospital complained that they were constantly being accused of thefts although doctors and nurses regularly stole with impunity. As employees scan their environments for appropriate ways to behave, they will likely be influenced by an act, such as theft by superiors, made salient by its apparent incongruence with prevailing societal norms. The message sent may be, "if it's okay for the boss to do it, then it's okay for me to do it too."

The notion that a dual standard of ethics may openly aggravate perceptions of workplace inequity, thereby inviting theft (Hollinger, 1989), is widely accepted among both academicians and practitioners, who maintain that one of the most effective ways to foster ethical organizational behavior is for top executives to "walk the talk," that is, to set the moral tone for their organizations by avoiding deviant behavior themselves (e.g., Adams, 1981; Cherrington & Cherrington, 1985; Hollinger, 1989; Snyder et al., 1991). As Jaspan put it: "Dishonesty starts from the top and works downward.... Show me a half dozen key supervisors who know their business, and I'll show you a thousand honest employees" ("White Collar Crime," 1971, p. 6.).

Although virtuous behavior by superiors may reinforce the ostensible value placed on ethical behavior by a company, contributing to an ethical climate, it does not follow that their apparent misdeeds will automatically trigger unethical behavior among subordinates. There are two reasons for this. First, even if subordinates observe behavior that may be interpreted as theft on the part of superiors, they may come to learn that some such acts are not considered theft by others in the company, but informal "perks" to which certain superiors—but not themselves—are entitled. For example, whereas restaurant managers may be considered entitled to take home some food or wine, servers generally encounter strong prohibitions against doing the same (Hawkins, 1984; Mars, 1973). In other words, they may recognize that their position does not give them the right to make a parallel claim on organizational property. To the extent that a superior's ostensible theft is interpreted as an entitlement linked to his or her high status, lower status individuals may not interpret that activity as a cue for them to behave analogously.

Second, it is difficult to establish that deviant organizational acts, such as employee theft, are uniquely the result of attempts to model similar acts by superiors. Part of the problem lies in the fact that if enough parallel channels of deviance exist, norms may develop that condone this activity, and these norms—not observations of superiors—may have more immediate impact on subordinates' behavior. We are not saying that superiors have no impact on employee theft. Indeed, models of morally appropriate behavior may contribute greatly to the overall ethical climate of an organization. Rather, the existence of norms condoning employee theft make it difficult to trace the unique influence of a particular superior's behavior.

Legitimizing Employee Theft: Controlled Larceny

Although it may be difficult to prove that employees steal because they see their superiors steal, the evidence is clear that employees steal because their superiors allow them, or even encourage them, to do so. Several sociological studies suggest that this may occur. For example, in his interview study of gypsum factory workers Gouldner (1954) described the "indulgency pattern" that existed: supervisors were very lax, allowing the employees to take home for personal use company-owned tools and raw materials. Among garment workers interviewed by Sieh (1987) bosses commonly permitted their subordinates to take for personal use small items (e.g., pins, thread, and zippers) and waste material (e.g., fabric scraps and old patterns). Interviewing an informant employed at a large chain store, Altheide et al. (1978, p. 111) found that a supervisor was quite explicit about his role as an accomplice to an employee's theft:

> Like one time I had cleaned up the entire back room, and there was a lot of damaged merchandise and opened packages, and I put all that to one side. One of the bosses came

in the next day and commented on how nice the stock room looked, and thanks for doing it, and so forth, and I told him where all the damaged stuff was, and among it was some diapers. My sister was expecting a baby and I said gosh, I would sure like to have these diapers... he said, "okay... we'll just charge her ten cents for them, so she has a sales receipt, put them in a bag, and put some tape on it so she can get out the back door."... Now that went on in managing all the time.

Not only do some superiors allow, or help, their subordinates steal, in some cases they make special preparations for it. For example, in his in-depth ethnographic study of employees at a bread bakery in Britain, Ditton (1977b) noted that bakers so strongly expected to be able to take home some bread that 40 extra loaves ("men's bread") were purposely made each day so as to avoid running short. Sometimes superiors even help their subordinates steal items "to order." Dalton (1959) reported this phenomenon when he noted that senior officials of the chemical plant he studied sometimes had items specially fabricated for certain individuals to take. One of Altheide et al.'s (1978) informants explained that employees would sometimes intentionally allow certain merchandise they wanted for themselves to gather dust on stockroom shelves so that they would eventually get to buy it at a reduced price. Although we will probably never know exactly how widespread such practices are, the wealth of sociological evidence attesting to superiors' involvement in their subordinates' theft suggests that we take this phenomenon seriously.

It is important to note that reports of supervisory partnership in employee theft are usually accompanied by specific limits with respect to what may be stolen, and by whom. The result is what has been referred to as a *system of controlled larceny* (Zeitlin, 1971) rather than an open invitation to all company property. For example, among the garment workers studied by Sieh (1987) pilferage of small items was permitted, although there were clear prohibitions against other forms of theft (e.g., using company time, equipment, and materials to make garments to be sold privately). Likewise, Ditton's (1977b) bakery workers were unofficially permitted to take home small quantities of bread, whereas taking other company property (particularly cash) was strictly prohibited. Thus, although some supervisors may allow their subordinates to steal company property, they impose limits on the form it may take. (Later, we make a similar point with respect to restrictions on theft imposed by work group colleagues.)

Some insight into supervisory collusion in employee pilfering is provided by recognizing that managers may use theft instrumentally, as an extra-legal adjunct to the organization's legal reward structure—what has been dubbed the *invisible wage structure* (Ditton, 1977a). In this connection, Henry (1981) noted that an employee's wages should be understood as consisting of legal sources, both formal (such as wages and salaries) and informal (such as perks and tips), and illegal sources, notably "hidden economic rewards" (such as pilfering). Social scientists and managers should be aware of this because many workers certainly are. One British waiter expressed this very colorfully: "Who'd work for £12. 10s. a week for the hours I put in? No one but a bloody nutcase, I can tell you. Fiddles are a part of wages. The whole issue runs on fiddles, it wouldn't work otherwise" (Mars, 1973, p. 202).

By permitting some controlled larceny managers have at their disposal a powerful source of rewards, perhaps even more potent than the legal ones. Several studies reveal that managers utilize hidden economic rewards to supplement workers' overall rewards. For example, Altheide et al. (1978) note that supervisors knowingly expect employees to engage in small amounts of theft in exchange for working undesirable shifts, such as late-night. As they put it, this is "a quasi-institutionalized time for employee theft" and that "working the late hour entitles them to a few more privileges than the day shift" (p. 112). Because late night is a period when business is slow, opportunities to steal without being detected are great. Theft is permitted as a supplemental form of income in exchange for working these undesirable hours.

In another example, Bradford (1976) found that postal supervisors regularly permitted postal carriers to complete their routes within the time allotted although it was well known that it could be done far more efficiently. This practice was justified on the grounds that it made up for the days when mail was heavier and letter carriers had to "really hump" to complete their routes. Because most supervisors were once letter carriers themselves, they embraced this practice as a cherished tradition, and recognized the value it had as a source of reward for a deserving workforce. In fact, when novice substitutes proudly broadcasted that they completed their routes with time to spare they were routinely castigated and given undesirable work assignments to help them "learn their lesson." Theft of time, although explicitly prohibited by postal regulations, was unofficially condoned, if not actively supported.

Three factors appear to be responsible for the considerable impact of supervisory collusion in employee theft. First, the value of theft-based rewards can be sizable, especially among those for whom employee theft is a regularly occurring behavior. For example, when asked how much people earn in this manner, one of the dock workers interviewed by Ditton (1977b) said, "all these extra fiddles pull in about a third of your wages and this is tax free" (p. 92). A second factor that makes employee theft a potent managerial tool is that it is considered "quicker and more convenient to dispense than promotions" (Altheide et al., 1978, p. 97). Dalton (1959), for example, described how chemical factory workers regarded theft of company property as "side-payments," actions of dubious ethical nature that were tolerated by executives insofar as the formal reward system was less flexible and more cumbersome to negotiate. Third, although rather extreme, Zeitlin (1971) has argued that managers should permit reasonable amounts of employee theft because it provides a source of job enrichment, and therefore, helps promote job satisfaction. Indeed, a worker interviewed by Mars (1982) said, "fiddling can be fun...a pleasurable departure from routine and an implicit challenge to authority" (p. 35). To the extent that employees can feel that they have successfully "beaten the system," Zeitlin argues, they may derive satisfaction from their jobs. Therefore, he argues, allowing some employee theft is a potentially useful motivational tool. Although this assertion has yet to be empirically demonstrated, it is worth noting insofar as it relates to our point regarding the managerial power associated with permitting employee theft.

It is important to underscore that instances of managerial acceptance of employee theft are almost always highly informal and unspoken. Publicly, organizations cannot formally condone a practice that is strictly illegal (despite the fact that it is almost never the basis for prosecution) and of dubious ethical nature, although they may privately encourage it. Clearly, there is a high level of duplicity involved. Liebow (1967) articulated this clearly when he said, "The employer knowingly provides the conditions which entice (force) the employee to steal the unpaid value of his labor, but at the same time, he punishes him for theft if he catches him doing it" (pp. 38-39).

Often, this contradiction is clearly expressed within a single communication. For example, there may be a primary negative injunction (i.e., "don't steal") expressed at the literal level, simultaneously accompanied by a metaphoric, secondary and contradictory injunction (e.g., "some theft is okay") (Altheide et al., 1978). The primary socio-linguistic device used by managers in perpetrating this charade is "the wink," a literal or figurative attempt to contradict the primary negative injunction sending the message, "you know I'm supposed to say that." Altheide et al. (1978) give several examples: "Perhaps he [the employee] is told that he can purchase products at 'give away' (wink) prices. Or, that there are always 'cheap' (wink), 'spare' (wink) or 'extra' (wink) goods to be had" (p. 48). To those sufficiently savvy to interpret the communication, the wink effectively eliminates the ambiguity of such altering phrases as "cheap," "spare," and "extra." However, any attempt to open the closed meaning of the wink, such as by overtly questioning its interpretation, would be met with denial (e.g., "I'm not telling you it's okay to steal; you're imagining things"). Such meta-communicative devices appear to play an important role in managers' condoning employee theft (Altheide et al., 1978).

WORK GROUP NORMS SUPPORT AND REGULATE EMPLOYEE THEFT

Organizational scholars have long recognized the profound impact of work group norms on organizational functioning (e.g., Etzioni, 1975; Wilson, 1978; Zander, 1977). In particular, group norms appear to be highly involved with the occurrence of deviant behavior—particularly employee theft. Specifically, it has been found that work group norms sometimes encourage theft, and in a manner that carefully regulates the specific forms it takes.

Group Norms Supporting Employee Theft

Traditionally, studies of socialization within work groups have focused primarily on learning norms of appropriate organizational behavior (Chao, O'Leary-Kelly, Wolf, Klein, & Gardner, 1994). Very little, if any, attention has been devoted to the way groups develop norms of antisocial organizational behavior. However, sociologists and anthropologists recognize that part of what is learned in groups is deviant in nature. In fact, organizations have been referred to as "schools for dishonesty" (Jaspan, 1974, p. 17). Specifically, "Not only does one learn how and what to steal, but one is also expected to participate in the theft directly, or indirectly by not informing on one's friends" (Altheide et al., 1978, p. 109). In this manner, Altheide et al. (1978) also note that employee theft is "ritualistically and symbolically tied to becoming a successful employee, one who gets along well" (p. 101). In fact, group norms about theft on the job have been considered "entrenched...woven into the fabric of people's lives" (Mars, 1982, p. 17), so much so that in many jobs it is considered abnormal *not* to steal.

Moreover, employees recognize the potency of informal group norms in supporting deviant behavior. Specifically, in an ambitious survey study Hollinger and Clark (1982) examined the perceived relative importance of informal norms and formal norms for controlling deviant behavior. The respondents were asked to rate the extent to which various types of formal sanctions (e.g., dismissal) and informal sanctions (e.g., social ostracism) would be effective in deterring theft. Respondents indicated that theft behavior would be more highly constrained by the reactions of one's coworkers than by the threats of formal sanctions imposed by management. Thus, prospective employee thieves are implicitly aware of the potent power of the work group when it comes to regulating deviant behavior.

Group norms frequently dictate the acceptability of employee theft both as an individual activity and a coordinated, group activity. Much research suggests that when employees steal they do so alone. For example, surveying over 1,500 admitted employee thieves who worked in three large department stores Robin (1969) found that 86% stole without involving others. Likewise, employee theft has been found to be a solitary activity among people working in electronic assembly plants (Horning, 1970), restaurants (Hawkins, 1984), and convenience stores (Terris & Jones, 1982). Mars (1982) observed that whether theft occurred alone or in groups depended on the nature of the jobs. Specifically, he found that people in most jobs acted alone whenever they stole from their employers. However, employees in some types of jobs, referred to as "wolves"—including teams of miners, garbage collection crews, and airline flight crews—tended to "steal in packs" (p. 32). The nature of the work performed by these employees is such that high degrees of cooperation are required to succeed, even with respect to coordinating acts of employee theft (in which case, "coordination" may be relabeled "collusion").

A good example of norms of the highly cooperative nature of employee theft is provided by Mars' (1974) observational studies of crews of British dock workers—twenty-six men who worked together loading and unloading cargo ships. Although some crew members had greater access to cargo than others, access alone was insufficient for theft to be carried out without detection; success in this endeavor also required the coordinated support of others. This included checkers, who falsified the paperwork, forklift drivers, who stacked cargo into piles high enough to create visual barriers from superiors, and signalers, who looked out for foremen while doing their normal work. So vital to their theft activities was this careful coordination of roles that new crew members were quickly indoctrinated into the theft ritual. When new members failed to cooperate, crews threatened to engage in work slowdowns until the non-compliant member was reassigned. Viewing this situation as one in which there is a clear distinction between an in-group (the compliant members of the work crew) and an out-group comprising a common enemy (the bosses) it is not surprising that high levels of solidarity existed among dock workers (e.g., Sherif, Harvey, White, Hood, & Sherif, 1961).

When work group norms to cooperate in theft exist, the issue arises of how members divide the outcome of their efforts among themselves. As in many groups, two distributive norms tend to be followed (Homans, 1961). In most cases, the stolen property is divided equally, although in some cases it is divided in proportion to one's status within the group. For example, Mars (1982) described an office in which various employees covered for each other as they made personal phone calls. Norms developed in this group which limited low-ranking employees to making local calls whereas high-ranking employees were permitted regularly to make international calls. Through coordinated effort, higher ranking individuals were granted greater rewards than their lower-ranking colleagues.

Not only does the norm of cooperation support theft within work groups, but also the norm of reciprocity. Sometimes, this takes the form of employees sharing tips about how to steal (Altheide et al., 1978). For example, an informant working at a large department store said:

> Often, we would confer with each other on the best way to steal something. By working together we lessened the possibilities of getting caught and acquired many items which took two people to steal. (Altheide et al., 1978, p. 113)

Reciprocity sometimes takes another form: helping someone steal so as to obligate that person to help oneself steal in the future. One of Altheide et al.'s

(1978) informants, a musician employed at a music store, admitted that a fellow sales clerk gave him a large, unauthorized discount on two cymbals he purchased (charging him less than the price of one for both), and threw in a cymbal stand at no cost. During the transaction, the clerk explicitly mentioned, "I might need your help later in getting something for myself" (Altheide et al., 1978, p. 113).

Evoking the reciprocity norm works not just because of the material rewards gained, but also because of the social rewards provided by fellow group members. Altheide et al. (1978) argue that by stealing, employees demonstrate conformity to a valued group norm, bringing them considerable status within their work groups. Thus, instead of being made to feel guilty about stealing company property, employees are frequently praised by their cohorts for being highly effective in their theft efforts (thereby lending legitimacy to their own thievery) (Jaspan, 1974). In this sense, they assert that employee theft is not purely utilitarian in an economic sense. Rather, people steal for the symbolic rewards received—that is, "because of what it means to do so" (Altheide et al., 1978, p. 107).

The social support received from fellow group members for engaging in deviant behavior is considered an important aspect of employee theft insofar as it allows employees to not have to reconstruct their private selves, acknowledging that they are thieves (Ditton, 1977b). Instead, by supporting the legitimacy of deviant behavior, groups enable employees who steal to enjoy the benefit of continuing to think of themselves as good, honest people who do not do anything wrong (Payne, 1989). In view of this self-reinforcing function, it is not surprising to find that group norms supporting employee theft are especially potent.

These norms are reinforced by the use of a common language that allows for collective rationalization of openly deviant behavior, what Mars (1982) has referred to "vocabularies of adjustment" (p. 27). This form of communication makes it possible for otherwise law-abiding individuals to absolve any feelings of guilt arising from their theft (Payne, 1989). More generally, Sykes and Matza (1957) referred to five so-called "techniques of neutralization"—readily available explanations that can be called upon to psychologically distance oneself from the effects of behaviors that threaten to spoil one's identity. These include:

1. *Denial of responsibility* (e.g., "I shouldn't be held responsible for the theft of property that was left out in the open for anyone to take.")
2. *Denial of injury* (e.g., "I didn't take that much; they'll never miss it.")
3. *Denial of victim* (e.g., "The company is so wealthy that theft won't harm it at all.")
4. *Condemnation of condemner* (e.g., "Given the way this company has treated me they probably expect me to take things.")

5. *Appeal to higher Authorities* (e.g., "The things I'm taking will help pay for medicine for my sick mother.")

Several theorists (e.g., Coleman, 1985; Hollinger, 1989) note that these techniques are not simply post-hoc rationalizations for behavior that employees know is inappropriate, but rather, readily available justifications available to be drawn on *prior* to committing deviant behavior. Although these techniques can be applied individually (Payne, 1989), it is recognized that they are especially effective in neutralizing guilt shared among members of a work group. In this regard, Backman (1985) suggested that moral conduct results from the joint construction of subjective realities that results from social interaction with key members of reference groups. Thus, to the extent that one's group cohorts define their actions as appropriate, so too are new group members likely to share in the collective rationalization. In other words, they become part of the collective reality of the work group that is reinforced through socialization of new group members. As Hollinger (1989, p. 26) put it:

> Justifications for theft are passed from the experienced employees to the newly hired. When substantial numbers of the work force have a reservoir of easily invoked excuses for their dishonesty, we can see how theft can quickly become widespread in an organization.

Group Norms Regulating Employee Theft

Beyond simply conveying that it may be acceptable to steal, group norms frequently regulate the specific parameters of theft behavior. (Recall our earlier discussion noting that theft is similarly regulated by supervisors.) To some degree this occurs because: (a) there often exists a gray area with respect to the property an organization controls, and (b) groups tend to reward acceptable behavior and punish unacceptable behavior among members (Hackman, 1976). Consider, for example, the disposition of spare fabric, zippers, and buttons at a clothing factory, or leftover food at a restaurant. To the extent that group members consider these items to be property of uncertain ownership, norms may develop that support taking these items, but only these items. Group members may collectively define the taking of such property as "wage-pilferage," property to which they perceive they are entitled as a supplement to their wages (Ditton, 1977a), legitimate side-payments typically not regarded as constituting theft (Dalton, 1959). At the same time, they may discourage the out-and-out theft of other items, such as cash (Mars, 1982).

The sociological literature contains several investigations demonstrating the ways in which work groups regulate the theft activities of their members. In one study, Horning (1970) interviewed 88 workers at a midwestern manufacturing plant and found that organizational stories were used as a vehicle to communicate messages about the limits on employee theft that existed within the organizational culture. For example, he tells of one respondent widely known for stealing a great deal:

> They tease him a lot—he really gets it when the line goes down because of a shortage of parts. They all start saying to him, "Hey, how about bringing in some of your parts so we can work tomorrow." (Horning, 1970, p. 61)

Such tales were used to communicate one of the prevailing norms—that pilfering should be limited to only that property needed for personal use. In other words, the taking of items for giving or selling to others was prohibited. Exceeding these limits was viewed as a threat to the entire social system. As a result, violators were denied the support of the work group, and with it, "the right to neutralize one's guilt feelings and deny oneself the definition of one's acts as theft" (p. 62). In the factory studied by Horning (1970) employee theft was strongly controlled, but by the workers themselves more than by management.

Similarly, limits on the quantity of property stolen were also noted by Mars (1974) in his observational studies of British dock workers. Typically, these employees stole material in shipment, but not as much as they could. Rather, they stole only a small percentage of it; more from larger ships and those with valuable cargo, and less from those containing more modest cargo. Such theft was considered their "tax" on the cargo, imposed while they were loading or unloading the ship, what they called "working the value of the boat" (Mars, 1974, p. 213).

Horning (1970) found not only that the *amount* of stolen property was at issue, but also the *nature* of that property. Strictly off-limits was property that was clearly owned either by the company or other employees. Only property of uncertain ownership was permitted for theft by group norms—including: screws, nails, nuts, bolts, and scrap parts. Similar norms limiting theft to items of uncertain ownership were also found among the garment workers interviewed by Sieh (1987): "It was okay to take something of negligible worth but it was not appropriate to take something of value. The work group strongly supported this norm" (p. 187). It was common for these workers to take home zippers, pins, old patterns, scrap fabric, and even "extra" garments, made for purposes of stealing. They would routinely stuff these items into their purses or under the clothes they were wearing. Sometimes they would even throw entire garments out the window and pick them up later. Group norms discouraged workers from using company time to make garments to sell to a competitor. Also frowned upon was the practice of wearing to company social functions any garments that were stolen from the factory inasmuch as doing so would call attention to their practices and flaunt the fruits of their deviant ways in front of management.

Studies in other industries also have found that group norms regulate the nature of employee theft—among them, norms regarding what food items waiters can take from their restaurants (Hawkins, 1984), and what tools gypsum factory workers can take from their plants (Gouldner, 1954). Taken together, these studies make it clear that informal group norms go a long way toward controlling the nature of theft that occurs in the workplace.

THEFT AS A RESPONSE TO DISTRIBUTIVE INJUSTICE

Throughout cultural history taking another's property has been a popular means of redressing grievances (Tucker, 1989). For example, seeking revenge against their owners, slaves in ancient Rome often stole their masters' property (Hopkins, 1978). Today as well, rivalries between various factions sometimes result in the confiscation of property (Bohannan, 1967). In one agricultural village in Lebanon, for example, Witty (1978) found that conflicts between various religious sects, families, and political groups living in the same village were expressed by stealing the opposition's animals. Closer to the hearts of many Americans, disputes between separating marital couples have been known to result in the taking of the other spouse's property, sometimes including their children (Black, 1984).

Despite their differences, these various acts of taking property can all be interpreted as attempts to re-establish distributive justice between the parties involved in a social exchange relationship. Homans' (1961) theory of distributive justice—and its derivative formulation, equity theory (Adams, 1965; Walster, Walster, & Berscheid, 1978)—claims that when people are in a social exchange relationship, they are motivated to maintain a balance between the outcomes they receive from each other and the inputs they contribute to their joint relationship. Unbalanced, inequitable, states cause psychological tension, which the parties are motivated to reduce (Greenberg, 1984). This can be done in several ways, such as reappraising the situation cognitively, and altering the balance of outcomes and inputs behaviorally (for reviews, see Greenberg, 1982, 1987). In this connection, theft can be understood as an attempt to behaviorally redress a perceived inequitable state between parties. For example, among employees who believe they are receiving insufficient outcomes (e.g., pay, recognition) in exchange for their work contributions, stealing from their employers may effectively raise their outcomes, helping to re-establish distributive justice in their exchange relationship.

This idea is implicit within the observations of several corporate security professionals. According to Arnold (1985), for example, "Employees often comment that they feel justified in stealing because their employers had done something to them...[such as being] reprimanded for something that was not their fault" (p. 28). Likewise, Willis (1986) notes that "Employees who feel frustrated or cheated by large, seemingly faceless bureaucracies often will commit crimes against them" (p. 26). The notion that theft can be an attempt to right a wrong in the workplace is not only accepted among security specialists, but as we will review here, is also established in a variety of different studies. The general conceptual model implicitly followed in the literature is straightforward: inequitable treatment leads to dissatisfaction, which leads employees to steal. However, as we will demonstrate, there are complex issues that lie beneath the apparent simplicity of this conceptualization. Specifically, we will examine research focusing on: (1) the link between dissatisfaction and theft, (2) the motives underlying theft as a reaction to distributive injustice, and (3) the ameliorative effects of interpersonal treatment on inequity-induced employee theft.

Association Between Dissatisfaction and Theft

It is widely assumed that employees steal because they are dissatisfied with their jobs. For example, Merriam (1977) has referred to dissatisfaction as "perhaps the most important and least appreciated cause of employee theft" (p. 395). Curiously, however, evidence for a causal link between dissatisfaction and theft is nonexistent. Instead, several studies have shown that the two are significantly correlated. Among the earliest investigations to empirically establish this connection was a survey study by Mangione and Quinn (1975). As part of a larger questionnaire these investigators asked a national sample of over 1,300 workers to rate their job satisfaction (measured on a single item) and self-reports of the frequency with which they stole merchandise or equipment from their employers. A significant negative correlation between these two measures was found among men over 30 years old (although no such association was found among women and younger men).

Extending these findings, Hollinger and Clark (1982) surveyed almost 5,000 people employed in three business sectors—retail, manufacturing, and hospitals. They measured perceptions of eight different dimensions of job satisfaction (e.g., satisfaction with coworkers, the employer, the supervisor, pay, and the like) and self-reports of the frequency of involvement in various forms of theft related to their sector (e.g., taking store merchandise, in the retail sector; taking tools, in the manufacturing sector; and taking drugs and supplies, in the hospital sector). Hollinger and Clark (1982) found significant negative correlations between theft and almost all facets of job satisfaction among retail and hospital employees. Among manufacturing employees only three of the eight job satisfaction dimensions were significantly correlated with job satisfaction in the negative direction. The researchers take this as an indication of the lower social worth of the materials available to steal in a manufacturing plant relative to hospitals and retail stores.

Together, these survey findings demonstrate that employee theft is associated with dissatisfaction: the more dissatisfied employees are, the more they steal from their employers (at least when they can find value in what's available to be stolen). Given the correlational nature of these findings, however, it is important to caution against concluding that dissatisfaction is a direct cause of theft. Although this is a logical possibility, there are two others. First, theft may be a cause of job dissatisfaction. That is, employees who steal must justify their actions. And, finding little satisfaction in the jobs they do may provide such a justification. Their focus on "beating the system" may override any interest they may have in seeking intrinsic rewards from the work itself (cf. Zeitlin, 1971). Second, it is also possible that both high levels of theft and job dissatisfaction are manifestations of a third variable. Evidence suggests several candidates for a third variable that might affect both satisfaction and theft, including: employees' level of interest in the work (Zeitlin, 1971), job commitment (Snyder et al., 1991), and problems of substance abuse (Mangione & Quinn, 1975). In conclusion, although employee theft and job dissatisfaction have been reliably associated with each other, evidence suggesting the existence of any direct causal link between them is lacking at this time.

Motives Underlying the Theft Response to Inequity

Supplementing these survey studies has been observational and interview research in which employees serving as informants describe to sociologists various aspects of their feelings and behaviors related to their theft experiences. Paralleling the questionnaire studies, these investigations also establish a connection between theft and employee dissatisfaction. Specifically, comments from informants suggest that theft as a response to dissatisfaction stems from either or both of two underlying motives. First, theft appears to be the way some employees attempt to "even the score" between themselves and their employer, who is believed to have treated them unfairly (i.e., a *restitution* response). Second, theft also appears to be an attempt by employees to reciprocate some perceived harm done to them by their employers (i.e., a *retaliation* response).

These themes are clearly demonstrated in various statements from employees. For example, the restitution motive was articulated by a clothing store employee interviewed by Zeitlin (1971) who said, "I feel I deserved to get something additional for my work since I was not getting paid enough" (p. 26). Similarly, a copper miner grousing about the difficult conditions under which he worked told Altheide et al. (1978), "I'll take this wrench; I mean they owe it to me" (p. 105). Among the bread delivery drivers interviewed by Altheide et al. (1978), stealing was widely considered a necessary way of compensating for a pay system that penalized them for making mistakes that resulted in under-billing: "When it really hits you hard...is when you come up $8 short...that's when you start saying, 'well shit, I've got to make this up'" (p. 101). These statements suggest that employee theft may be an attempt to rectify inequitable payment ongoing in the workplace. In fact, using theft to achieve an equitable balance between outcomes and contributions was so explicit among the copper mine workers interviewed by Altheide et al. (1978, p. 108) that some felt obligated to steal their quotas:

> Some stupid guy figured out how much workers were taking, something like $300 a year. Some guys said, "I'm behind schedule, hell, there's only three months left in the year and I don't have my $300!"

Extending this notion, it also appears that some theft acts may be understood as a response to a single episode of inequitable treatment. For example, Analoui and Kakabadse (1991) reported an incident in which a barmaid at a night club was denied an opportunity to leave work early enough to catch a bus home. She was not given taxi fare, but believed it was coming to her because other establishments paid for employees' taxis when they worked late. Although she was usually quite honest, she felt entitled to take what she needed to get what she believed she had coming to her. "I'll get a taxi and he'll pay for it" (p. 52) she said, latter admitting pocketing £5 that someone gave her to pay for a round of drinks and using it to pay for her cab fare. This incident was not unusual among the employees Analoui and Kakabadse (1991) interviewed. In fact, they summarize their findings by noting that "Pilferage was thus often resorted to as a means of getting even with employers" (p. 57).

In addition to stealing for purposes of evening the score between themselves and their employers, employees also appear to steal as retaliation against institutions they believe have harmed them. For example, a hotel clerk interviewed by Cressy (1953) made it clear that stealing was his way of redressing a complaint against his company: "I had this fancy grievance against the company, and the owner was not straightening it out fast enough...You might say it [my theft] was in the spirit of retaliation" (p. 59). Getting back at an employer who caused harm was also the theme expressed by one of Altheide et al.'s (1978) informants who worked at a large department store: "after a clean-up boy was lectured on the correct way to mop floors, the boy took several books to show the manager he was not to be belittled" (p. 103). Although the boy referred to did not reveal his theft to the manager directly, he showed them to friends as a chance to belittle the manager in return.

As one would imagine, thefts of this type are most likely to occur among those who are displeased with the treatment they receive from their employers. As an example, consider the remarks of an employee of two record stores as told to Altheide et al. (1978). At one store she believe she was mistreated and disliked the boss. With respect to that store, she said, "I stole there all the time, towards the end I did just because I didn't like him at all" (p. 105). By contrast, she felt very differently about the other record store: "Working for them, you just didn't want to steal; there was no reason to...you liked to work there" (pp. 105-106).

The Ameliorative Effect of Interpersonal Treatment

These findings have an important managerial implication: they suggest that employees are enticed to steal because of the way they are treated (more properly, mistreated) by their employers. An inequitable situation may encourage employees to steal, and poor treatment may fuel any perceived inequity and exacerbate the theft response.

This notion has received considerable attention in a series of recent experimental studies by Greenberg. Participants in the first study (Greenberg, 1990a), were employees of three manufacturing plants owned by the same parent company located in different cities. In response to a financial crisis, company officials reduced all employees' pay in two of the three plants by 15% for 10 weeks. A third plant, serving as the control group (in which identical work was performed by demographically similar employees), suffered no pay cuts. Because the employees in the first two plants received less pay than they had been receiving despite equal performance expectations, there was a naturalistic manipulation of underpayment inequity.

In cooperation with the company, the manner in which the pay cut was explained to the workers was systematically manipulated. Employees at one plant, selected at random, were given a thorough and caring explanation of the need to take this drastic measure (the adequate explanation condition). Specifically, they were given a great deal of information about the need for the pay cut (an elaborate and lengthy presentation involving the use of charts and graphs to detail the nature of the problem and the necessity of taking the action) as well as repeated expressions of remorse over the negative outcomes (e.g., "Will it hurt? Of course! But, it will hurt us all alike...it really hurts me to do this, and the decision didn't come easily"). By contrast, workers in the other plant experiencing the pay cut (the inadequate explanation condition) were given limited information about the need for the pay cut and its justification; the basis for the decision was not described. Only the most superficial expressions of remorse were voiced.

The major dependent measure was the rate of employee theft—the company's standard measure of "shrinkage" (the percentage of inventory unaccounted for by known uses, such as sales and waste). These measures were collected by persons blind to the study on a weekly basis over the 30-week study period—10 weeks before the pay cuts were instituted, 10 weeks during the pay cut period, and 10 weeks after normal pay was reinstated. As expected by equity theory, the workers whose pay was reduced responded to the resulting underpayment inequity by stealing. However, after their pay was returned to

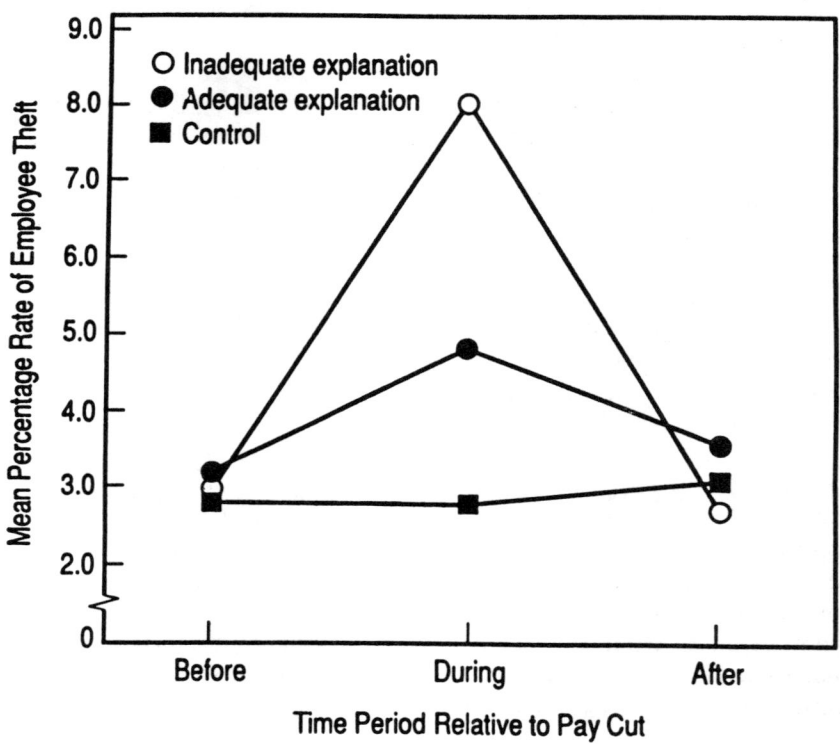

Source: Greenberg (1990a). Reproduced with permission.

Figure 3. Mean Theft Rate as a Function of Time Relative to Pay Cut

its normal level, the theft rate dropped to its lower, pre-pay cut levels (the same low level at which theft occurred in the control group throughout the period of the study) (see Figure 3).

Especially dramatic were the differences in theft rates as a function of the adequacy of the explanation given. Those who received inadequate explanations stole approximately 8% (compared to a base rate of approximately 3%) whereas those who received adequate explanations stole slightly over 4%. This difference was not only statistically significant, but of course also financially significant for the company that bore the cost of the theft. The data provide good evidence that the nature of the interpersonal treatment received by employees may influence their willingness to steal when treated inequitably. In particular, questionnaire results supplementing the theft measure revealed that employees who received adequate explanations felt less unfairly treated than those who received adequate explanations. Thus, to the extent that adequate explanations helped reduce the experienced inequity, it also indirectly lowered the theft behavior.

As dramatic as these findings may be, they are limited by the confounding of two variables that individually may have been responsible for reducing theft—the amount of information presented about the reason underlying the pay cut, and the amount of social sensitivity shown regarding the pay cut. To remedy this limitation, Greenberg (1993a) conducted a follow-up study in the laboratory in which these two factors were independently manipulated. The subjects in this investigation were undergraduates promised $5 per hour (a pay rate established as fair during pretesting) to perform a clerical task. After performing the task half of the participants, selected at random, were told that they would be paid only $3 (i.e., they were underpaid). The remaining participants were told they would be paid the $5 promised them, and were considered equitably paid.

As the experimenter announced the pay rate, he systematically manipulated the quality of the information used as the basis for establishing this rate of pay. The high valid information condition was characterized by the use of information that was: directly acquired, from an expert source, who is identified, and independently double-checked. However, the low valid information condition was characterized by: reliance on hearsay information, from an undisclosed, unidentified, person of unknown expertise, and not independently verified. Specifically, among those who were underpaid, high valid information subjects were told:

> While you were working, I found out from my supervisor that our research sponsor is really only paying $3 instead of the $5 you were promised. As you can see from this document [experimenter shows participant fake budget figures], this is the amount that was planned in the original budget proposal. To make sure, I also called the project's budget officer and was reassured of this figure. Because of a typographical error, some participants did get $5, but this was a mistake. Starting now, you can get only $3.

However, their counterparts in the low valid information condition were told:

> While you were working, I heard from someone in the hall that our research sponsor is really only supposed to be paying $3, instead of the $5 you were promised. As a result, that's what I'll be paying you.

After this information was presented, separate statements were made that systematically manipulated the degree of caring and sensitivity shown subjects with respect to their pay rate. Specifically, high levels of interpersonal concern were created by repeatedly expressing remorse and attempting to dissociate from the outcome. By contrast, low levels of interpersonal concern were created by expressing disinterest with the participants' outcomes. For example, underpaid subjects receiving high levels of interpersonal sensitivity were told:

> You really got a bad deal and I feel very sorry for you. I know it's only a $2 difference, but I feel awful for misleading you. Please recognize that it's not my fault, and that I would pay you more if I could. You seem like such a nice person, I really hate to have to do this to you. I don't want to upset you. It's probably not much consolation, but I feel very badly about this myself.

By contrast, those receiving low levels of interpersonal sensitivity were told:

> That's the way it is; I don't make the rules around here. I really don't care how much you get paid. I don't care too much about how much others get; I'm more concerned about how much I get paid myself.

After making these remarks the experimenter told the subjects that he had to go elsewhere, left them some money, and invited them to take the amount they were supposed to take. Specifically, he reached into his hip pocket and removed a handful of one-dollar bills and some coins, and placed them on a desk. The experimenter's seemingly disorganized state created the impression that he was unaware of the exact amount of money he put on the table. Supporting this message, he said, "I don't know how much is here, but it looks like there's more than enough for you. Just take the $3 you are supposed to be paid and leave the rest on the table." At this point, the experimenter left the room. This procedure made it possible for participants to take as much money as they wanted, believing that the experimenter would be unable to tell how much they took. However, because the amount of money tossed onto the desk was fixed in advance it was possible to determine exactly how much was taken. Amounts in excess of $3 were considered theft.

As summarized in Figure 4, the amount of money taken was dependent upon the manipulations. Among those who were equitably paid, the amount of information about the reason for the pay and the amount of social sensitivity shown about the pay had no impact on theft, which remained almost nonexistent. However, among those responding to the underpayment, the amount of information and the amount of social sensitivity shown had additive effects on theft: each factor contributed somewhat to a reduction in the amount of money taken. That is, among underpaid subjects, theft was reduced when levels of information were high rather than low and when the levels of interpersonal sensitivity shown was high rather than low. In fact, when both factors were high, theft rate was lowest, and when both factors were low, theft rate was highest. Thus, each factor contributed additively and independently to a reduction in theft behavior stimulated by inequitable treatment. These findings suggest that the ameliorative effects of social interaction are contributed to jointly and independently by two factors: information about the inequity and the social sensitivity demonstrated in describing the inequitable situation.

Employee Theft as a Social Exchange Process 141

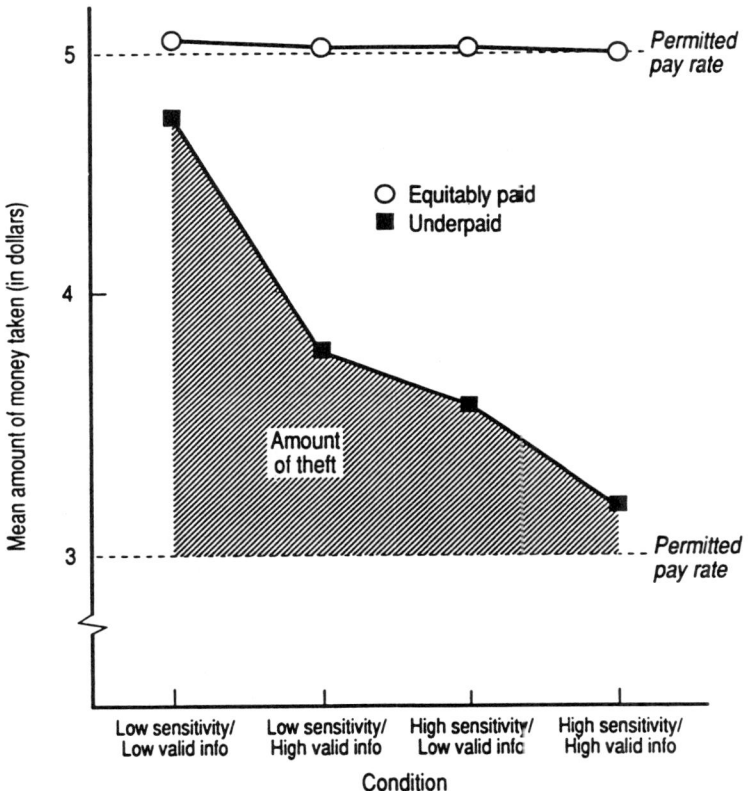

Source: Greenberg (1993a). Reproduced with permission.

Figure 4. Mean Amount of Money Taken in Each Experimental Condition

When Greenberg's (1993a) subjects stole the money they may have been attempting to make up for the underpayment they received at the hands of the investigator, or they may have been attempting to retaliate against the investigator by taking too much money. Indeed, as noted earlier, both restitution and retaliation are possible responses to theft-induced inequities. Because taking more money than one is supposed to simultaneously advantages oneself while disadvantaging the authority figure, it is impossible to distinguish between the restitution and retaliation motives for theft. Acknowledging this limitation, Greenberg (1994a) replicated and extended this study in a manner that made it possible to deduce subjects" underlying motives for stealing.

The task subjects performed consisted of counting small round objects and packaging them into rolls so they could be easily counted. In one condition the objects were 25¢ coins (quarters). In another condition, they were similarly-sized objects—lithium batteries said to be highly valuable experimental prototypes. Subjects performed the task alone in rooms in which buckets of either quarters or batteries were put in front of them. Some subjects encountered an underpayment inequity as they completed the task: they would only be paid $3 for the half-hour's work instead of the $6.00 they were initially promised. After this announcement was made, subjects were given three $1 bills and completed a questionnaire in their work rooms while in the presence of the coins or batteries they were counting. As in the Greenberg (1993a) study, the explanation for this surprising negative turn of events was either thoroughly explained or not thoroughly explained, and in a manner that demonstrated either a high or low level of dignity and personal concern. Because the number of batteries or coins in the bucket was known in advance (although subjects were led to believe otherwise), it was possible to determine if the subjects had stolen anything.

It was reasoned that any theft of the batteries could be interpreted as an act of retaliation insofar as it only would harm the company but be of no value to the subjects themselves. However, theft of the quarters would mutually harm the company while benefiting themselves (making the motive at least retaliation, but also possibly restitution). Thus, in this study, the items stolen were taken as cues to the underlying motives for the theft.

When the subjects were working with quarters, the results replicated those of Greenberg (1993a). That is, both information and sensitivity independently affected theft: when both were high theft was lowest; when both were low, theft was highest; and when one factor was high and the other low, theft was intermediate. However, when the subjects were working with the allegedly valuable lithium batteries the pattern of theft was somewhat different. In this case, the only variable that affected theft was the amount of respect and dignity shown while explaining the inequity. When the level of dignity displayed was high, theft was low or nonexistent. However, when it was low, the level of theft rose considerably. By contrast, the amount of information presented about the reasons for the unexpectedly low pay had no effects on the stealing of batteries; the level of theft observed in this condition was quite low. These results suggest that the combined effects of treating people inequitably while failing to treat them with dignity and respect led them to retaliate against the source of their harm, the authority figure.

Kemper (1966) has referred to this type of retaliative behavior as *reciprocal deviance*—the deviance that results when an authority figure defaults on his or her obligations to an individual. These acts of "striking back" observed here in response to an inequity, are conceptually consistent with the inequitable conditions Kemper (1966) identified as inviting reciprocal deviance. However, it is interesting to note that it was not just the inequity that triggered theft, but the inequity augmented by a lack of personal sensitivity. This combination appears to have added insult to injury, triggering an interest in retaliation. This is not to say that the retaliation response is purely without benefit for he harmdoer. Although acts of reciprocal deviance may fail to redress an inequity financially, they may do so symbolically. That is, if one cannot directly benefit oneself, then at least one can enjoy the satisfaction of knowing that one has given harm to another who has caused harm to oneself.

This idea, that people retaliate against others who have harmed them although there is no direct benefit to themselves, is apparent in research on other forms of deviant social behavior—particularly sabotage (e.g., Giacalone & Rosenfeld, 1987) and workplace violence (e.g., Williams, 1994). Harming one's company by destroying property, both inanimate as well as human (Sprouse, 1992) may restore the balance of justice not by shifting outcomes from one party to another, but by attempting to lower another's outcomes at least to the degree to which one's own outcomes were lowered by that party. This, of course, is in addition to the symbolic value of demonstrating that one is not going to stand by idly as an inequity is perpetrated (Payne, 1989). Although this idea has been expressed in verbal accounts of theft behavior in sociological studies (e.g., Altheide et al., 1978), there has been little research empirically demonstrating that retaliation is a response designed to redress an inequity.

In a notable exception, DeMore, Fisher, and Baron (1988) found that among college students, vandalism on campus was related to perceived inequitable treatment, especially when the students believed they had only limited remedies available to them. Self-reported vandalism was highest among those who felt both inequitably treated by the university and weak control. The frustration the respondents reported under such conditions is consistent with Spector's (1975; Chen & Spector, 1982) finding that frustration (such as with unfair organizational policies) is linked to various forms of deviant behavior in the workplace, such as sabotage, and employee theft.

Taken together, the Greenberg studies (1990a, 1993a, 1994a) call our attention to the idea that it is not only the actual magnitude of the inequity that determines theft, but the *way* that inequity is presented—that is, the treatment of employees. Further illustrating this point Greenberg (1994b) administered a questionnaire to workers assessing their perceptions of various aspects of unfairness they perceived in their workplace. The respondents were approached as they recorded their "punch out" times on a piece of paper as the investigator surreptitiously noted the actual times they left work. (A sign informed the workers that the time clock was being repaired, and directed them to record their names and punch out times on a form provided for that purpose. A large digital clock was stationed at the spot where the time clock usually was.) By comparing the actual punch out times with those recorded, a measure was available of the degree to which the workers engaged in time theft, a common form of theft (Boye & Slora, 1993; Snyder, Blair, & Arndt, 1990)— in this case, the reporting of more hours than actually worked. Although the actual amount of time theft was rather low, variance in this measure was significantly accounted for by responses to several questionnaire items. Notably, two variables, best predicted time theft: the amount of compassion shown by supervisors, and the degree of respect employers show for employees. Interestingly, general measures of pay fairness were weaker predictors of theft. Again, these findings suggest that theft is associated with unfair treatment of an interpersonal nature. Uncaring, inconsiderate supervision is a key determinant of employee theft (Greenberg, 1993b).

In summary, it appears that employee theft is more than simply an attempt to restore a mathematical balance between outcomes and inputs. Such inequities appear to be necessary for theft to occur, but may not always be sufficient. What needs to be added to the formula for employee theft is improper social treatment—variously called social insensitivity, lack of dignity, rudeness, disrespect, or lack of compassion. Although inequitable outcomes may be necessary to instigate employee theft, they may be insufficient to do so. Showing social insensitivity to those outcomes may also be required to trigger the theft response.

PRACTICAL IMPLICATIONS: CONTROLLING EMPLOYEE THEFT

Our analysis of employee theft from the perspective of social exchange has practical implications for the effective management of theft in organizations. These are derived from the two major aspects of social exchange highlighted in this chapter—norms and distributive justice.

Norm-Based Management Practices: Breaking the Cycle of Acceptance and Neutralizing Rationalizations

As we have noted, societal norms condone employee theft in part because organizations are believed to be large, impersonal institutions that can easily afford the loss resulting from pilferage. Therefore, when individual employees feel unfairly cheated by their organizations, theft is readily justified. One practical implication of this notion is that efforts to make salient to employees the losses resulting from employee theft will help employees recognize that theft behavior has a real financial impact on the organization, one they can help reduce by refraining from theft.

At least one published study has shown that this approach is indeed effective in reducing theft. Carter, Holström, Simpanen, and Melin (1988) studied the rates at which three items—candy, hygiene products, and jewelry—were stolen from an independent grocery store in Sweden. Signs graphing the theft rates of these items were posted in the company lunchroom for all employees to see. By comparing theft rates before and after the postings the researchers were able to determine the impact of the information about cost of theft to the company on overall rates of theft. As expected, the mean daily cost of theft dropped significantly for all three items monitored (e.g., from the equivalent of $4.07 per day for jewelry before the posting to only 19¢ per day afterward), saving the company a considerable sum of money in the long run. It is important to note that the theft rate, as measured, made it impossible to distinguish between theft by employees and theft by customers. However, insofar as the feedback about theft was posted someplace where only employees could see it, it is clear that it was employees who were responsible for the reduction in theft. Whether this resulted in their refraining from stealing themselves, or their greater vigilance in stopping shoplifters, is unclear. Still, the results suggest that sharing continuous information about the costs of theft may be effective in reducing it.

These findings are consistent with our claim that theft may be reduced by bringing information about its impact to the attention of employees. Although this is predicated on the assumption that feedback increases employees' awareness of the extent to which they are having a negative impact on their organization, thereby breaking the "cycle of acceptance," direct evidence for this underlying reasoning does not yet exist. Indeed, skeptics may argue that those who wish to retaliate against their organizations and bring them harm may respond in the opposite manner. That is, they actually may use the feedback to reinforce their deviant actions by gauging the negative impact of their theft efforts. For this reason research is needed on the exact nature of the conditions under which feedback about the impact of theft will help reduce it.

Beyond simply sharing information about the financial effects of stealing on the company, our analysis also implies that theft would be effectively managed by neutralizing employees' rationalizations about theft (Snyder et al., 1991). As we have detailed, employees often perceive their theft as completely appropriate and justifiable. Rationalizations for stealing are frequently so deeply entrenched into a work group's culture that employees are not even aware that what they may be doing can be considered theft (Ditton, 1977a). In this connection, consider, the irony of the father who expressed concern over his son's theft of pencils at school. "After all," puzzled the father, "I bring home from work all the pencils he could possibly need" (Hemphill, 1961, p. 40).

Hollinger (1989) recommends that rationalizations be neutralized by helping employees internalize the loss that the company experiences from theft. Specifically, he notes:

> The social prevention of employee theft involves convincing employees that stealing from the company is against their own best interests.... Employees must be helped to recognize the personal benefits derived by protecting the property and assets of their employers. (p. 40)

The underlying rationale is simple: to the extent that work groups provide rewards for conforming to internal pressures to steal, organizations may create counter-pressures by rewarding efforts to help the company financially. Presumably, over time, the financial rewards resulting from stealing would be supplanted by those associated with not stealing, but helping the company. Several methods may be helpful in this regard.

First, using an agency theory perspective Leatherwood and Spector (1991) argue that inducements to refrain from stealing can be provided by pay systems that align the interests of principals (i.e., employers) and agents (i.e., employees). In this regard, they claim:

> Piece rate payments, commissions, and other contingent pay systems motivate agents to take actions that are in the best interests of the principal. Thus, employee misconduct, moral hazard, and shirking should be reduced. (p. 557)

Although these researchers did not measure actual employee theft, they found that MBA students analyzing cases estimated that theft would be low among employees who receive high pay in exchange for their considerable contributions, as would occur in contingency-type pay systems (Heneman, 1992). Under such conditions, subjects frequently expressed concern that theft would be inappropriate insofar as it would unfairly cheat the company.

Another way of aligning the interests of employers and employee is to institute profit sharing (or any of several other "nontraditional reward programs"; O'Dell, 1987) at all organizational levels. By allowing employees to share in their companies' profits, they have an incentive to refrain from jeopardizing those profits. Even stronger incentives discouraging actions that lower profitability, such as theft, may exist in employee-owned companies. In such organizations norms tend to develop to boost profitability (Rosen, Klein, & Young, 1986) because joint outcomes are dependent upon corporate performance. According to an official of the Michigan-based Damman Hardware chain, in which an employee stock ownership program exists, employees widely consider stealing from the company to be inappropriate, viewing it as "stealing from themselves" ("Labor Report," 1990).

In instances in which financial disincentives are not viable options, it is still possible to align the interests of employees and employers. This may be done by developing with employees a psychological contract that discourages them from deviant behavior (Rousseau & Parks, 1993). In this connection, many companies have found it useful to provide explicit codes of corporate conduct to guide employee behavior (Manley, 1991). Although the evidence with respect to the deterrent effects of conduct codes shows them to be limited, at best (Trevino & Nelson, 1995), such efforts may be useful insofar as they provide a mechanism for explicitly countering the usually more potent informal norms that condone theft. To the extent that codes of corporate conduct explicitly prohibit employee theft, efforts to thwart supervisory collusion in theft may be legitimized. Of course, acceptance of the social contract prohibiting employee theft may require equal compliance on both sides. Thus, to the extent that superiors may expect their subordinates to comply with statements prohibiting employee theft, it is critical for them to behave likewise, to exemplify the standard of morality they wish to have emulated (Merriam, 1977).

Justice-Based Management Practices: Clarifying Outcome Fairness and Demonstrating Interpersonal Sensitivity

Our analysis of theft as a reaction to injustice has two major practical implications. The first has to do with the distributive aspects of fairness; the second, with the interpersonal aspects (Greenberg, 1987, 1993b). First, although it may be much easier said than done, theft can be reduced by taking measures to enhance perceptions of payment inequity. The evidence is clear that the more employees believe they are being treated fairly, the less likely they will be to strike out against their employers by stealing from them. For the most part, this has little to do with the absolute level of outcomes received. Indeed, there is considerable agreement that, in general, people do not steal because they need money, but rather because they feel they were denied something they had coming to them (Altheide et al., 1978; Hollinger & Clark, 1983).

With this in mind, it may be useful to take steps to clarify the fairness of compensation systems so as to minimize perceptions of payment inequity. Although a thorough analysis of this issue is the beyond scope of the present paper (the interested reader is referred to Milkovich & Newman, 1991), we take note of a promising innovation in this regard—corporate hotlines. By making available to employees special telephone numbers they can use to address questions about their pay (Taft, 1985), efforts can be made to minimize perceptions of payment inequity. (Similarly, Lawler, 1965, has long noted that public knowledge about pay in the workplace can help minimize feelings of inequity.) Recently, hotlines also have been used to help combat employee theft directly (Addis, 1992), giving employees an opportunity to report it anonymously, without having to face the social pressure imposed by group members. Addis reports that companies such as Georgia-Pacific and Eastern Airlines have found these hotlines to be extremely cost-effective ways of controlling theft and other types of deviant behavior. (Georgia-Pacific's "Business Conduct and Security Hotline" dealt exclusively with employee theft for 10 years before its focus was broadened to all forms of inappropriate behavior in the workplace, including sexual harassment and safety violations.) To the extent that hotlines open avenues of communication between employers (who want to provide opportunities to explain the fairness of their pay policies;

Greenberg, 1990b) and employees (who wish to break away from normative pressures to steal), they may be expected to be effective vehicles for minimizing theft.

Unfortunately, specific recommendations about the elements of satisfaction that may be most closely linked to employee theft cannot be made in the absence of further investigations into the causes of theft behavior. Although models have been proposed linking such variables as equity perceptions, job satisfaction, and organizational commitment to employee theft (e.g., Moretti, 1986; Murphy, 1993), the available evidence does not yet make it possible to fully understand the connections between these variables. Should research along these lines be initiated, it would be most useful to attempt to differentiate between the conditions under which various forms of deviance occur. For example, when will dissatisfied employees be tempted to steal rather than to engage in sabotage or violence? Although initial efforts to answer this question have been taken by Hollinger (1989; Hollinger & Clark, 1983; Hollinger, Slora, & Terris, 1992), we are still far from being able to predict the precise form of deviant behavior that will result in reaction to various types of inequities. Given the obvious practical benefits of such knowledge, research directed at this issue appears to be worthwhile.

A second justice-based practical implication has to do with the interpersonal treatment given employees as they are confronted with the kind of negative outcomes likely to generate perceptions of inequity. Realizing that inequitable outcomes sometimes may be impossible to avoid (such as when economic necessity requires that companies impose pay cuts or layoffs), it is clear that the impact of these situations may be reduced by ostensible demonstrations of interpersonal sensitivity. In other words, if it is not just what happens, but how it is explained that matters, then efforts should be taken to treat employees with the utmost dignity and respect. Indeed, the evidence revealed here suggests that kind, interpersonally sensitive, treatment at the hands of an authority figure may take the "insult" out of the "injury" created by experiencing a negative outcome (for insight into the processes underlying this phenomenon, see Brockner & Wiesenfeld, 1994; Greenberg, 1993b). Practitioners have been implicitly aware of the importance of kind interpersonal treatment as a technique for reducing theft. For example, Taylor (1986, p. 24) has advised managers to, "treat employees with dignity, respect and trust" and to "establish personal, caring, nonadverasrial relationships with employees" because "it's more difficult to steal from a friend than from someone who doesn't care about you." Clearly, this is among the easiest, most effective, and least expensive forms of advice that can be given to help reduce the incidence of employee theft.

Beyond simply "being nice" to employees as a way of controlling theft, it has been recommended that interpersonal sensitivity be demonstrated by giving employees a say in determining how theft will be defined in their workplace—

that is, what may and may not be taken. Specifically, Snyder et al. (1991) have advised that "the process used to define theft should be participatory; that is, employees should be as involved in it as possible" (p. 46). Not only would such a practice be expected to be effective insofar as it dramatizes the company's seriousness about curtailing theft (thereby breaking the cycle of acceptance), but also because it would help make black or white that large gray area in which employees are confused about property ownership (Ditton, 1977a). Just as importantly, this form of involvement would enhance employees' commitment to reducing theft. Again, quoting Snyder et al. (1991): "The more involved they are, the more committed they should be to the decisions made and the more likely they and their fellow employees will not steal from the company" (p. 46). This assertion is completely in keeping with research demonstrating the beneficial effects of "voice" on perceptions of procedural justice (Greenberg & Folger, 1983), and its application to the domain of employee theft is quite logical. However, in the absence of direct empirical support this assertion must be considered tentative—a hypothesis worth testing.

CONCLUSION

Our discussion of employee theft as a social exchange process has been presented as an adjunct to the traditional focus on theft as criminal activity that has dominated the literature (e.g., Clarke, 1990; Clinard & Yeager, 1980; Coleman, 1985). Indeed, we acknowledge that some employee theft is purely criminal in nature, and beyond the scope of a managerial analysis. That is, the primary focus of some employees is on victimizing their employers from within, instead of engaging in productive work (Sutherland, 1983). Our analysis has ignored these "professional thieves" in favor of ordinary employees— individuals whose thievery is more petty and insidious. We believe that although OB scholars may have to defer to criminclogists when it comes to understanding the serious criminal, it has a great deal to contribute to our understanding of pilferage by everyday employees.

We have explained employee theft, and identified ways of controlling it, by examining two social-psychological constructs highlighted by the concept of social exchange—norms and distributive justice. As promising as we believe this perspective may be toward understanding and managing employee theft, we recognize that it is certainly not the only approach that may be taken by OB scholars. For example, we believe that insight into employee theft may be provided by comparing it to behavior at the opposite end of the prosocial-antisocial continuum—namely, organizational citizenship behavior (Organ, 1990). In this connection, it is notable that the effects of justice perceptions also have been identified (Greenberg, 1993c), suggesting that justice may be an important determinant of both prosocial and antisocial organizational behavior. OB scholars also should be encouraged to study the effects of punishment (Trevino & Ball, 1992) and other behavioral "enforcement" techniques (Leatherwood & Spector, 1991) on employee theft. For example, such efforts may focus on the limited effectiveness of security systems as a tool for deterring employee thieves (Karamarsky, 1976; Zeitlin, 1971).

There are most certainly additional areas in which the managerial aspects of organizational theft may be studied by OB scientists. Our intent is not to list them all. Rather, we wish to underscore the point that organizational researchers have a largely untapped vein of valuable theoretical and applied insight to mine in their studies of employee theft. We hope that the present paper has provided the inspiration to pursue this knowledge.

ACKNOWLEDGMENTS

Preparation of this paper was supported by National Science Foundation grant number SBR-9224169. The authors gratefully acknowledge the helpful comments of the following individuals who have commented on earlier versions of this manuscript : Robert J. Bies, Robert A. Giacalone, Kevin Murphy, Stephen L. Payne, Barry M. Staw, and Linda K. Trevino.

REFERENCES

Adams, J.S. (1965). Inequity in social exchange. In L. Berkowitz (Ed.), *Advances in experimental social psychology* (Vol. 2, pp. 267-299). New York: Academic Press.

Adams, V. (1981, November). Hot to keep 'em honest: Honesty as an organizational policy can help prevent employee theft. *Psychology Today*, pp. 50, 53.

Addis, K.K. (1992, July). Company crooks on the line. *Security Management*, pp. 36, 38, 40, 42.

Aeppel, T. (1993, March 27). VW is free to hire 7 GM ex-managers Lopez brought with him, court rules. *Wall Street Journal*, p. A4.

Altheide, D.L., Adler, P.A., Adler, P., & Altheide, D.A. (1978). The social meanings of employee theft. In J.M. Johnson & J.D. Douglas (Eds.), *Crime at the top: Deviance in business and the professions* (pp. 90-124). Philadelphia: J.B. Lippincott.

Analoui, F., & Kakabadse, A. (1991). *Sabotage*. London: Mercury.

Arnold, G. (1985, May). Employee theft: A $40 billion crime. *Management World*, pp. 26-30.

Backman, C.W. (1985). Identity, self-presentation, and the resolution of moral dilemmas: Toward a social psychological theory of moral behavior. In B.R. Schlenker (Ed.), *The self and social life* (pp. 261-289). New York: McGraw-Hill.

Bennett, R.J., & Robinson, S.L. (1994). *The development of a measure of workplace deviance*. Manuscript submitted for publication.

Bintliff, R.L. (1994). *Crime-proofing your business*. New York: McGraw-Hill.

Black, D. (1984). Crime as social control. In D. Black (Ed.), *Toward a general theory of social control* (pp. 1-27). Orlando, FL: Academic Press.

Blau, P.M. (1964). *Exchange and power in social life*. New York: Wiley.

Bliss, E.C., & Aoki, I.S. (1993). *Are your employees stealing you blind?* San Diego, CA: Pfeiffer & Company.
Bohannan, P. (1967). *Law and warfare: Studies in the anthropology of conflict.* Austin, TX: University of Texas Press.
Boye, M.W., & Slora, K.B. (1993). The severity and prevalence of deviant employee activity within supermarkets. *Journal of Business and Psychology, 8,* 245-253.
Bradford, J.A. (1976). *A general perspective on job satisfaction: The relationship between job satisfaction and sociological, psychological, and cultural variables.* Unpublished Doctoral Dissertation, Department of Sociology, University of California, San Diego.
Braithwaite, J. (1985). White collar crime. *Annual Review of Sociology, 11,* 1-25.
Brockner, J., & Wiesenfeld, B.M. (1994). *The interactive impact of procedural fairness and outcome favorability: The effects of what you do depends on how you do it.* Manuscript submitted for publication.
Budman, M. (1993, November-December). The honesty business. *Across the Board,* pp. 34-37.
Bullard, P.D., & Resnik, A.J. (1983). SMR forum: Too many hands in the corporate cookie jar. *Sloan Management Review, 24*[*3*], 51-56.
Buss, D. (1993, April). Ways to curtail employee theft. *Nation's Business,* pp. 36, 38.
Caldwell, R.G. (1968). A reexamination of the concept of white-collar crime. In G. Geis (Ed.), *White-collar criminal* (pp. 376-387). New York: Atherton.
Carter, N., Holström, A., Simpanen, M., & Melin, K. (1988). Theft reduction in a grocery store through product identification and graphing of losses for employees. *Journal of Applied Behavior Analysis, 21,* 385-389.
Carter, R. (1987, July). Employee theft often appears legitimate. *Accountancy,* pp. 75-77.
Chao, G.T., O'Leary-Kelly, A.M., Wolf, S., Klein, H.J., & Gardner, P.D. (1994). Organizational socialization: Its content and consequences. *Journal of Applied Psychology, 79,* 730-743.
Chen, P.Y., & Spector, P.E. (1982). Relationships of work stressors with aggression, withdrawal, theft and substance abuse: An exploratory study. *Journal of Occupational and Organizational Psychology, 65,* 177-184.
Cherrington, D.J., & Cherrington, J.O. (1985). The climate of honesty in retail stores. In W. Terris (Ed.), *Employee theft: Research, theory, and applications* (pp. 27-39). Park Ridge, IL: London House.
Clarke, M. (1990). *Business crime: Its nature and control.* Cambridge, England: Polity Press.
Clinard, M.B., & Quinney, R. (1973). *Criminal behavior systems* (2nd ed.). New York: Holt, Rinehart, & Winston.
Clinard, M.B., & Yeager, P.C. (1980). *Corporate crime.* New York: The Free Press.
Coleman, J.W. (1985). *The criminal elite: The sociology of white collar crime.* New York: St. Martin's Press.
Conklin, J.E. (1977). *"Illegal but not criminal": Business crime in America.* Englewood Cliffs, NJ: Prentice-Hall.
Cressy, D. (1953). *Other people's money.* New York: The Free Press.
Dalton, M. (1959). *Men who manage.* New York: John Wiley & Sons.
Dalton, D.R., Metzger, M.B., & Wimbush, J.C. (1994). Integrity testing for personnel selection: A review and research agenda. In G.R. Ferris (Ed.), *Research in personnel and human resources management* (Vol. 12, pp. 125-160). Greenwich, CT: JAI Press.
Delaney, J. (1993). Handcuffing employee theft. *Small Business Report, 18*[*7*], 29-38.
DeMore, S.W., Fisher, J.D., & Baron, R.M. (1988). The equity-control model as a predictor of vandalism among college students. *Journal of Applied Psychology, 18,* 80-91.
Ditton, J. (1977a). Perks, pilferage, and the fiddle: The historical structure of invisible wages. *Theory and Society, 4,* 39-71.
Ditton, J. (1977b). *Part-time crime: An ethnography of fiddling and pilferage.* London: Macmillan.

Employees, suppliers account for some 75% of stolen merchandise. (1973, November 21). *Wall Street Journal*, p. 30.

Emshwiller, J.R. (1993, December 3). Corruption in bankruptcy system injures firms in need. *Wall Street Journal*, p. B1.

Ettorre, B. (1994, May). Crime and punishment: A hard look at white-collar crime. *Management Review*, pp. 10-16.

Etzioni, A. (1975). *Comparative analysis of complex organizations* (rev. ed.). New York: Free Press.

Ex-employee of IBM charged with theft of computer cards. (1993, March 17). *Wall Street Journal*, p. B7.

Fisher, B.R., & Withey, S.B. (1951). *Big business as the people see it: A study of a socioeconomic institution*. Ann Arbor, MI: Institute for Social Research.

Giacalone, R., & Greenberg, J. (in press). *Antisocial behavior in the workplace*. Thousand Oaks, CA: Sage.

Giacalone, R.A., & Rosenfeld, P. (1987). Reasons for employee sabotage in the workplace. *Journal of Business and Psychology, 1*, 367-378.

Glaser, D. (1967). National goals and indicators for the reduction of crime and delinquency. *Annals of the American Academy of Political and Social Science, 371*, 114-130.

Gouldner, A.W. (1954). *Wildcat strike: A study in worker-management relationships*. New York: Harper and Row.

Govoni, S.J. (1992, February). To catch a thief. *CFO*, pp. 24-32.

Greenberg, J. (1982). Approaching equity and avoiding inequity in groups and organizations. In J. Greenberg & R.L. Cohen (Eds.), *Equity and justice in social behavior* (pp. 389-435). New York: Academic Press.

Greenberg, J. (1984). On the apocryphal nature of inequity distress. In R. Folger (Ed.), *The sense of injustice* (pp. 167-188). New York: Plenum.

Greenberg, J. (1986). Differential intolerance for inequity from organizational and individual agents. *Journal of Applied Social Psychology, 16*, 191-196.

Greenberg, J. (1987). A taxonomy of organizational justice theories. *Academy of Management Review, 12*, 9-22.

Greenberg, J. (1990a). Employee theft as a reaction to underpayment inequity: The hidden cost of pay cuts. *Journal of Applied Psychology, 75*, 561-568.

Greenberg, J. (1990b). Looking fair vs. being fair: Managing impressions of organizational justice. In B.M. Staw & L.L. Cummings (Eds.), *Research in organizational behavior* (Vol. 12, pp. 111-157). Greenwich, CT: JAI Press.

Greenberg, J. (1993a). Stealing in the name of justice: Informational and interpersonal moderators of theft reactions to underpayment inequity. *Organizational Behavior and Human Decision Processes, 54*, 81-103.

Greenberg, J. (1993b). The social side of fairness: Interpersonal and informational classes of organizational justice. In R. Cropanzano (Ed.), *Justice in the workplace* (pp. 79-103). Hillsdale, NJ: Lawrence Erlbaum Associates.

Greenberg, J. (1993c). Justice and organizational citizenship: A commentary on the state of the science. *Employee Responsibilities and Rights Journal, 6*, 222-237.

Greenberg, J. (1994a). *Restitution and retaliation as motives for inequity-induced pilferage*. Unpublished manuscript, the Ohio State University.

Greenberg, J. (1994b). *Interpersonal determinants of time theft in the workplace*. Unpublished manuscript, the Ohio State University.

Greenberg, J. (1995). Employee theft. In N. Nicholson (Ed.), *The Blackwell encyclopedic dictionary of organizational behavior*. Oxford, England: Blackwell.

Greenberg, J., & Folger, R. (1983). Procedural justice, participation, and the fair process effect in groups and organizations. In P.B. Paulus (Ed.), *Basic group processes* (pp. 235-256). New York: Springer-Verlag.

Greengard, S. (1993, April). Theft control starts with HR strategies. *Personnel Journal*, pp. 81-82, 84-86, 88, 90-91.
Hackman, J.R. (1976). Group influences on individuals. In M. Dunnette (Ed.), *Handbook of industrial and organizational psychology* (pp. 1455-1526). Chicago: Rand-McNally.
Hawkins, R. (1984). Employee theft in the restaurant trade: Forms of ripping off waiters at work. *Deviant Behavior, 5*, 47-69.
Hay, D. (1975). Poaching and the game laws on Cannock Chase. In D. Hay, P. Linebaugh, & E.P. Thompson (Eds.), *Albion's fatal tree: Crime and society in eighteenth-century England* (pp. 189-253). London: Allen Lane.
Hemphill, C.F., Jr. (1961, February). Cutting pilferage, petty cash losses. *Administrative Management*, pp. 38-41.
Heneman, R.L. (1992). *Merit pay*. Reading, MA: Addison-Wesley.
Henry, S. (1978). *The hidden economy: The context and control of borderline crime*. Oxford: Martin Robertson.
Henry, S. (1981). *Can I have it in cash? A study of informal institutions and unorthodox ways of doing things*. London: Astragal Books.
Hollander, E.P. (1980). Leadership and social exchange processes. In K.J. Gergen, M.S. Greenberg, & R.H. Willis (Eds.), *Social exchange: Advances in theory and research* (pp. 103-118). New York: Plenum.
Hollinger, R.C. (1986). Acts against the workplace: Social bonding and employee deviance. *Deviant Behavior, 7*, 53-75.
Hollinger, R.C. (1989). *Dishonesty in the workplace: A manager's guide to preventing employee theft*. Park Ridge, IL: London House.
Hollinger, R.C., & Clark, J.P. (1982). Formal and informal social controls of employee deviance. *Sociological Quarterly, 23*, 333-343.
Hollinger, R.C., & Clark, J.P. (1983). *Theft by employees*. Lexington, MA: Lexington Books.
Hollinger, R.C., Slora, K.B., & Terris, W. (1992). Deviance in the fast-food restaurant: Correlates of employee theft, altruism, and counterproductivity. *Deviant Behavior, 13*, 155-184.
Homans, G.C. (1961). *Social behavior: Its elementary forms*. New York: Harcourt Brace, and World.
Hopkins, K. (1978). *Conquerors and slaves: Sociological studies in Roman history* (Vol. 1). Cambridge, England: Cambridge University Press.
Horning, D.N.M. (1970). Blue-collar theft: Conceptions of property, attitudes toward pilfering, and work group norms in a modern industrial plant. In E.O. Smigel & H.L. Ross (Eds.), *Crimes against bureaucracy* (pp. 46-64). New York: Van Nostrand Reinhold.
Howard, J.S. (1991, July-August). Mr. Nice Guy, meet the garbologist. *D&B Reports*, pp. 21-23, 49.
Jamieson, K.M. (1994). *The organization of corporate crime*. Thousand Oaks, CA: Sage.
Jaspan, N. (1974). *Mind your own business*. Englewood Cliffs, NJ: Prentice-Hall.
Jones, T.M., & Gautschi, F.H., III. (1988). Will the ethics of business change: A survey of future executives. *Journal of Business Ethics, 7*, 231-248.
Karamarsky, D. (1976). Surveillance systems: Management's electronic sentries. *Administrative Management, 37*, 4-9.
Kemper, T.D. (1966). Representative roles and the legitimation of deviance. *Social Problems, 13*, 288-298.
Kenda, M. (1982). *Crime prevention manual for business owners and managers*. New York: American Management Association.
Labor report. (1990, February 20). *Wall Street Journal*, p. A1.
Lary, B.K. (1988, May). Thievery on the inside. *Security Management, 32*, 79-84.
Lawler, E.E., III. (1965). Managers' perceptions of their subordinates' pay and of their superiors' pay. *Personnel Psychology, 18*, 413-422.

Leatherwood, M.L., & Spector, L.C. (1991). Enforcements, inducements, expected utility and employee misconduct. *Journal of Management, 17*, 553-569.

Lee, T.W., & Mitchell, T.R. (1994). Organizational attachment: Attitudes and actions. In J. Greenberg (Ed.), *Organizational behavior: The state of the science* (pp. 83-108). Hillsdale, NJ: Lawrence Erlbaum Associates.

Leventhal, G.S., Younts, C.M., & Lund, A.K. (1972). Tolerance for inequity in buyer-seller relationships. *Journal of Applied Social Psychology, 2*, 308-318.

Liebow, E. (1967). *Tally's corner*. Boston: Little, Brown.

Lipman, M., & McGraw, W.R. (1988). Employee theft: A $40 billion industry. *Annals of the American Academy of Political and Social Science, 498*, 51-59.

London House and Food Marketing Institute. (1993). *Fourth annual report on employee theft in the supermarket industry*. Rosemont, IL: London House.

Mangione, T.W., & Quinn, R.P. (1975). Job satisfaction, counterproductive behavior, and drug use at work. *Journal of Applied Psychology, 60*, 114-116.

Manley, W.W., II (1991). *Executive's handbook of model business conduct codes*. Englewood Cliffs, NJ: Prentice-Hall.

Mars, G. (1973). Hotel pilferage: A case study in occupational theft. In M. Warner (Ed.), *The sociology of the workplace* (pp. 200-210). New York: Halsted.

Mars, G. (1974). Dock pilferage: A case study in occupational theft. In P. Rock & M. McIntosh (Eds.), *Deviance and social control* (pp. 209-228). London: Tavistock.

Mars, G. (1982). *Cheats at work: An anthropology of workplace crime*. London: George Allen & Unwin.

McGurn, S. (1988, March 7). Spotting the thieves who work among us. *Wall Street Journal*, p. 16A.

Merriam, D.H. (1977). Employee theft. *Criminal Justice Abstracts, 9*, 375-406.

Milkovich, G.T., & Newman, J.M. (1991). *Compensation* (3rd ed.). Plano, TX: Business Publications.

Moretti, D.M. (1986). The prediction of employee counterproductivity through attitude assessment. *Journal of Business and Psychology, 1*, 134-147.

Murphy, K.R. (1993). *Honesty in the workplace*. Pacific Grove, CA: Brooks/Cole.

Nord, W.R. (1980). The study of organizations through a resource-exchange paradigm. In K.J. Gergen, M.S. Greenberg, & R.H. Willis (Eds.), *Social exchange: Advances in theory and research* (pp. 119-140). New York: Plenum.

O'Dell, C.O. (1987). *Major findings from people, performance and pay*. Scottsdale, AZ: American Productivity Center and American Compensation Association.

Ones, D.S., Viswesvaran, C., & Schmidt, F.L. (1993). Comprehensive meta-analysis of integrity test validities: Findings and implications for personnel selection and theories of job performance. *Journal of Applied Psychology, 78*, 679-703.

Organ, D.W. (1990). The motivational basis of organizational citizenship behavior. In B.M. Staw & L.L. Cummings (Eds.), *Research in organizational behavior* (Vol. 12, pp. 43-72). Greenwich, CT: JAI Press.

Palmeri, C. (1994, September 26). Dumpster diving. *Forbes*, p. 94.

Payne, S.L. (1989). Self-presentational tactics and employee theft. In R.A. Giacalone & P. Rosenfeld (Eds.), *Impression management in the organization* (pp. 397-410). Hillsdale, NJ: Lawrence Erlbaum Associates.

Peet, T.R. (1924). A historical document of Ramesside age. *Journal of Egyptian Archeology, 10*, 116-126.

Pfeffer, J. (1992). *Managing with power*. Boston, MA: Harvard Business School.

Robin, G.D. (1969). Employees as offenders. *Journal of Research on Crime and Delinquency, 6*, 17-33.

Robinson, S.L., & Bennett, R.J. (1995). A typology of deviant workplace behaviors: A multi-dimensional scaling study. *Academy of Management Journal, 38*, 555-572.

Rosen, C., Klein, K. J., & Young, K.M. (1986). *Employee ownership in the United States: The equity solution*. Lexington, MA: Lexington Books.

Rousseau, D. M., & Parks, J.M. (1993). The contracts of individuals and organizations. In L.L. Cummings & B.M. Staw (Eds.), *Research in organizational behavior* (Vol. 15, pp. 1-43). Greenwich, CT: JAI Press.

Sackett, P.R. (1994). Integrity testing for personnel selection. *Current Directions in Psychological Science, 3*, 73-76.

Shapiro, S.P. (1990). Collaring the crime, not the criminal: Reconsidering the concept of white-collar crime. *American Sociological Review, 55*, 346-365.

Sherif, M., Harvey, O.J., White, B.J., Hood, W.R., & Sherif, C.W. (1961). *Intergroup cooperation and competition: The Robbers Cave experiment*. Norman, OK: University Book Exchange.

Sieh, E.W. (1987). Garment workers: Perceptions of inequity and employee theft. *British Journal of Criminology, 27*, 174-190.

Simpson, R.L. (1976). Theories of social exchange. In. J.W. Thibaut, J.T. Spence, & R.C. Carson (Eds.), *Contemporary topics in social psychology* (pp. 79-131). Morristown, NJ: General Learning Press.

Smigel, E.O. (1970). Public attitudes toward stealing as related to the size of the victim organization. In E.O. Smigel & H.L. Ross (Eds.), *Crime against bureaucracy* (pp. 15-28). New York: Van Nostrand Reinhold.

Smigel, E.O., & Ross, H.L. (Eds.). (1970). Introduction. In *Crime against bureaucracy* (pp. 1-14). New York: Van Nostrand Reinhold.

Snyder, N.H., & Blair, K.E. (1989, May-June). Dealing with employee theft. *Business Horizons*, pp. 27-34.

Snyder, N.H., Blair, K.E., & Arndt, T. (1990). Breaking the bad habits behind time theft. *Business, 40*(4), 31-33.

Snyder, N.H., Broome, O.W., Jr., Kehoe, W.J., McIntyre, J.T., Jr., & Blair, K.E. (1991). *Reducing employee theft: A guide to financial and organizational controls*. New York: Quorum Books.

Solomon, J., Waldrop, T., Washington, F., & Shenitz, B. (1993, June 7). The grand pilferer? *Newsweek*, pp. 38-39.

Spector, P.E. (1975). Relationships of organizational frustration with reported behavioral reactions of employees. *Journal of Applied Psychology, 60*, 635-637.

Sprouse, M. (1992). *Sabotage in the American workplace*. San Francisco: Pressure Drop Press.

Sutherland, E.H. (1940). White-collar criminality. *American Sociological Review, 5*, 1-12.

Sutherland, E.H. (1983). *White collar crime*. New Haven, CT: Yale University Press.

Sykes, G.M., & Matza, D. (1957). Techniques of neutralization: A theory of delinquency. *American Journal of Sociology, 22*, 664-670.

Taft, W.F. (1985). Bulletin boards, exhibits, hotlines. In C. Reuss & D. Silvis (Eds.), *Inside organizational communication* (2nd ed., pp. 183-189). New York: Longman.

Tatham, R.L. (1974). Employee views on theft in retailing. *Journal of Retailing, 50*(3), 49-55.

Taylor. F. (1958, April 29). Employee thefts: They rise fast, add to problems of stores plagued by the slump. *Wall Street Journal*, p. A1.

Taylor, R.R. (1986). Your role in the prevention of employee theft. *Management Solutions, 31*, 20-25.

Terris, W., & Jones, J. (1982). Psychological factors related to employees' theft in the convenience store industry. *Psychological Reports, 51*, 1219-1238.

Thompson, E.P. (1975). *Whigs and hunters*. London: Allen Lane.

Thibaut, J.W., & Kelley, H.H. (1959). *The social psychology of groups*. New York: Wiley.

Trevino, L.K., & Ball, G.A. (1992). The social implications of punishing unethical behavior: Observers' cognitive and affective reactions. *Journal of Management, 18*, 751-768.

Trevino, L.K., & Nelson, K. (1995). *Managing business ethics: Straight talk about how to do it right*. New York: John Wiley & Sons.
Tucker, J. (1989). Employee theft as social control. *Deviant Behavior, 10*, 319-334.
Turner, D.L., & Stephenson, R.G. (1993, February). The lure of white-collar crime. *Security Management*, pp. 57-58.
Two are sentenced in scheme to extort money from AT&T. (1992, December 13). *Wall Street Journal*, p. 7A.
Two at ULSI System acquitted of stealing Intel's trade secrets. (1991, June 16). *Wall Street Journal*, p. 8A.
Vitales, M.S. (1932). *Industrial psychology*. New York: W.W. Norton & Co.
von Hentig, H. (1948). *The criminal and his victim*. New Haven, CT: Yale University Press.
Walster, E., Walster, G.W., & Berscheid, E. (1978). *Equity: Theory and research*. Boston: Allyn & Bacon.
White collar crime is greatest among bosses, expert declares. (1971, May 8). *Labor*, p. 6.
Williams, L.C. (1994). *Organizational violence: Creating a prescription for change*. Westport, CT: Quorum Books.
Willis, R. (1986, June). White-collar crime: The threat from within. *Management Review*, pp. 22-32.
Wilson, S. (1978). *Informal groups: An introduction*. Englewood Cliffs, NJ: Prentice-Hall.
Witty, C. (1978). Disputing issues in Sheeman, a multireligious village in Lebanon. In L. Nader & R.F. Todd, Jr. (Eds.), *The disputing process: Law in ten societies* (pp. 281-314). New York: Columbia University Press.
Yasueda, T., Middleton, N., & Kurke, M.I. (1978). White collar crime. In *Comprehensive review of federal law enforcement: Reports for the President's Reorganization Project*. Washington, DC: Executive Office of the President.
Yoder, S.K. (1993, March 5). Grand jury charges Symantic officers with stealing secrets from Borland. *Wall Street Journal*, p. 6B.
Zander, A. (1977). *Groups at work*. San Francisco: Jossey-Bass.
Zeitlin, L.R. (1971, June). A little larceny can do a lot for employee morale. *Psychology Today*, pp. 22, 24, 26, 64.

CULTURE AS SOCIAL CONTROL:
CORPORATIONS, CULTS, AND COMMITMENT

Charles A. O'Reilly and Jennifer A. Chatman

ABSTRACT

The notion of "organizational culture" has attracted a broad base of scholarly interest. While many researchers study culture using an ethnographic approach, we examine it from a functional perspective, viewing culture within groups and organizations as a *social control system* based on shared norms and values. From a psychological perspective, we show how a shared normative order or culture can influence members' focus of attention, shape interpretations of events, and guide attitudes and behavior. Specifically, we explore the psychological mechanisms used to develop social control systems and demonstrate how similar these approaches are across a variety of strong culture settings, ranging from conventional organizations to more extreme examples of cults and religious sects.

INTRODUCTION

Few concepts of the past decade have so captured the attention of scholars and practitioners as that of *organizational culture*. There has been an outpouring of scholarly books (e.g., Frost, Moore, Louis, Lundberg, & Martin, 1985; Hofstede, 1991; Martin, 1992; Ott, 1989; Schein, 1985; Schneider, 1990; Trice & Beyer, 1993), popular books (e.g., Davis, 1984; Deal & Kennedy, 1982; Hampden-Turner & Trompenaars, 1993; Kotter & Heskett, 1992), special issues of academic journals (e.g., *Administrative Science Quarterly*, 1983), articles in both academic and business journals (e.g., Harrison & Carroll, 1991; Schwartz & Davis, 1981) and continual references to the importance of corporate culture in the business press (e.g., Donkin, 1994; Hays, 1994). The topic has been addressed by psychologists (Schneider, 1987), sociologists (e.g., Swidler, 1986), organizational theorists (e.g., Harrison & Carroll, 1991), strategy researchers (e.g., Barney, 1986), management consultants (Pascale, 1990), anthropologists (Brannen, 1992; Van Maanen & Barley, 1984), and even economists are now addressing the subject (e.g., Cremer, 1993; Kreps, 1986; Lazear, 1994). What accounts for this broad-based interest?

The most rational reason for studying culture is the presumed relationship between organizational culture and performance. Saffold (1988, p. 546) notes that part of this interest arises "Because its managerial implications can be readily developed, easily communicated, and illustrated by vivid anecdotes." But, the evidence linking so-called "strong culture" to increased organizational performance is mixed (e.g., Denison, 1990; Gordon & DiTomaso, 1992; Siehl & Martin, 1990). Some recent research suggests that the culture-performance link exists. For example, Kotter and Heskett (1992) hypothesized that strong culture firms would perform better over the long term. They argued that the presence of a strong culture, which they define in terms of the values and norms shared among members of the organization, should be associated with higher goal alignment among organizational members, promote an unusual level of motivation among employees, and provide needed controls without the stifling effects of a bureaucracy. Using a sample of over 200 large public U.S. firms, they surveyed managers to assess the strength of culture in their organizations. They then related culture strength during a recent 10-year period to the firms' economic performance over that same period. They found strong associations between firm culture strength and performance, but only when the strong culture was also strategically appropriate and characterized by norms that permitted the culture to change. They concluded that "even contextually or strategically appropriate cultures will not promote excellent performance over long periods unless they contain norms and values that help firms adapt to a changing environment" (p. 142).[1]

Wilkins and Ouchi (1983) noted that culture may be a more important determinant of performance in certain types of subunits and organizations and less critical in others. Tushman and O'Reilly (1996) provide evidence that different functional units may require different types of cultures. For example, those units that rely heavily on innovation, such as R&D, perform better when their cultures emphasize norms and values that promote creativity and implementation, while other units, like manufacturing, may perform better with cultural norms that emphasize efficiency and speed.

The culture-performance link can be ambiguous, in part, because of the lack of agreement about the definition of the construct of organizational or corporate culture. Some argue that it is simply a resurrection of the earlier notion of organizational climate (Reichers & Schneider, 1990). Questions have been raised about the appropriate level of analysis for the construct; for instance, whether it makes sense to talk about culture at the group, the organization, or industry level (e.g., Chatman & Jehn, 1994; Dansereau & Alutto, 1990; Gordon, 1991; Sackmann, 1992). Others define culture as what an organization *is* while still others argue that it is what an organization *has* (Schein, 1985; Smircich, 1983). Some researchers emphasize its anthropological roots, and argue that culture can be studied and understood only through qualitative ethnomethodological approaches (e.g., Louis, 1985). They believe that culture is an unconscious learned response by a group and encompasses norms, values, rituals, and climate. In this spirit, Trice and Beyer (1993) focus on the taken-for-granted beliefs manifested in symbols, language, and stories. Martin (1992) holds that culture is, by nature, subjective and cannot be described in terms of empirical facts.

Other organizational researchers conceptualize culture in terms of the observable norms and values that characterize a group or organization. They typically stress quantitative measurement schemes and examine behavior rather than phenomenological meaning (e.g., Rousseau, 1990; Thompson & Luthans, 1990). This definition allows for psychometric measurement of attitudes and behavior, either from self-reports or from observers (e.g., Enz, 1988; O'Reilly, Chatman, & Caldwell, 1991).

These differences are more than semantic or methodological. They underlie the basic disagreements and confusion that currently characterize the study of culture. Fundamental questions about what organizational culture is, why it is important, and how to investigate it remain unresolved. As Pettigrew notes (1990), the problem with culture is that it is not just a concept but a family of concepts; not just a variable but a frame of reference for viewing organizations. Like a Rorschach, culture means different things to different people. From an anthropological perspective, Powys concludes that "Culture is what's left over after you forgot what it was that you were originally trying to learn" (1974, p. 5). In the face of this argument and confusion, it is not surprising that, in spite of, or perhaps because of its popularity, the notion of organizational culture has generated more heat than light.

While we acknowledge that differences of opinion exist in defining the construct, we also believe that some of this arcane debate misses a critical function of culture within organizations. Our objective in this paper is to shed light on the importance of organizational as a *social control system* operating within groups and organizations. Culture as a social control system is based on shared norms and values that set expectations about appropriate attitudes and behavior for members of the group. In our view, culture can be thought of as the normative order, operating through informational and social influence, that guides and constrains the behavior of people in collectives. Consistent with other researchers (Kotter & Heskett, 1992; Rousseau, 1990), we define culture as *a system of shared values (that define what is important) and norms that define appropriate attitudes and behaviors for organizational members (how to feel and behave)*.

Culture as a social control mechanism can determine organization members' commitment or intensity of feelings regardless of whether they belong to cults such as the Moonies, religions like the Mormons, or strong culture organizations such as the United States Marine Corps, New United Motors Manufacturing Inc. (NUMMI), or Hewlett-Packard. We take an explicitly psychological view to illustrate how such a system can influence organizational members' focus of attention, behavior, and commitment and, ultimately, the attainment of organizational goals, whether these are in the service of profit, innovation, quality, personal fulfillment, or religious salvation (e.g., Appel, 1983; Foster, 1986; McGaw, 1979: Ofshe, 1992; Weiner, 1988).

We first distinguish culture as *social control* from *formal control*. We also suggest that social control may be a more powerful form of control in modern organizations than traditional formal controls (see the second and third sections). In the fourth section, we explore the social psychological underpinnings of culture. In the fifth section, we illustrate how the psychological mechanisms used to develop social control are similar across a variety of organizations, ranging from the extreme examples of cults and religious sects to more conventional organizations characterized as strong culture firms. Finally, we discuss the boundaries of organizational culture; that is, when culture as social control may be inappropriately applied, as in cases when organizations cause people to harm themselves or others, or ineffective in generating desired behaviors. Both the process of gaining member commitment and the content of the values members commit to may lead, under certain conditions, to high levels of performance through enhanced coordination and motivation to uphold strategically appropriate values and norms. But, under other circumstances these same processes can lead to reduced adaptation, exploitation, and in extreme cases, harmful or unethical behavior.

FORMAL CONTROL IN ORGANIZATIONS

The earliest students of organizations were fundamentally concerned with the issue of control (e.g., Barnard, 1938; Etzioni, 1964; Parsons, 1960). Since these early times, writing on management and organization has focused on ways to control collective activities through the use of formal mechanisms such as supervision, plans, standard operating procedures, structures, budgets, and compensation systems.

Given the wide, and often imprecise usage of the concept of *control*, it is important for us to be clear about our perspective before differentiating formal and social control. Consistent with a more psychological perspective, we focus here on how people *experience* control in organizational settings. In our view: *Control comes from the knowledge that someone who matters to us is paying close attention to what we are doing and will tell us if our behavior is appropriate or inappropriate.* From this perspective, effective control systems, whether they are financial planning systems, budgets, or performance appraisal programs, work when those being monitored are aware that others who matter to them, such as a boss or members of a department, know how and what they are doing. In other words, when one's boss, or members of a department with which one is interdependent has the ability to deliver or withhold valued sanctions for compliance or noncompliance, a control system can be said to exist (e.g., Dornbusch & Scott, 1975).

Typically, formal control systems monitor performance outcomes or behavior, or both (e.g., Ouchi, 1979). The assumptions underlying the presumed effectiveness of formal control are that: (1) calibrating extrinsic rewards (e.g., compensation, benefits) is possible and such rewards are sufficient and timely enough to direct job-relevant behavior; and (2) subordinates perceive organizational authority, or top down influence, as legitimate and worthy of compliance. But, as we discuss below, the effectiveness of formal control systems may be compromised by a variety of sociological and psychological forces.

1. *Calibrating extrinsic rewards is possible, and such rewards are sufficient to direct job-relevant behavior*: Calibrating formal reward systems so that they effectively capture the range and intensity of desired behaviors or performance levels is challenging (Dornbusch & Scott, 1975). It may be difficult to initially identify the desired behaviors due to ambiguous jobs and uncertain future events. For instance, if the job requires initiative and flexibility, how does one specify in advance what behaviors will be required (Staw & Boettger, 1990)? Further, what constitutes high quality or good value in one time period may change as competitors improve, new technology is implemented, or consumer tastes change (e.g., Womack, Jones, & Roos, 1990). Continually updating the reward system may not be feasible under conditions of frequent change.

In addition, uncertainty arises from task complexity. Complex tasks require predictions about whether a set of interdependent tasks will be completed according to plan. But individuals have trouble avoiding the conjunctive and disjunctive events bias (Tversky & Kahneman, 1974); that is, they overestimate the probability of completing conjunctive tasks (tasks or events that must occur in conjunction with one another), and underestimate the probability of completing disjunctive tasks (tasks or events that occur independently). These biases often explain a variety of complex organizational problems including timing problems in projects that require multistage planning (Bazerman, 1994).

Identifying and rewarding the most significant aspects of a job may be further obscured because more tangible tasks (e.g., production output) are often measured and sanctioned, due to ease of observation, while the less readily assessed tasks are often ignored. For example, Scott (1969) found that social workers were evaluated on the basis of the number and timeliness of their visits to clients and the correctness of their calculation of budgets rather than on the quality of their therapeutic casework service. Clearly, numerous examples exist (e.g., Kerr, 1975) that demonstrate the tendency to value a particular outcome but reward a different behavior—which may preclude the fulfillment of an organization's objectives.

Formal control systems typically rely on direct supervision to monitor performance. Yet, direct supervision is one of the most expensive methods by which information on work activities can be acquired due to the large time expenditures required by evaluators (Dornbusch & Scott, 1975). Further, direct observation of some aspects of performance may not even be possible in some jobs, for example, among many of the professions (e.g., Van Maanen & Barley, 1984). The personal scrutiny required to directly observe others may be difficult for evaluators to manage given the potential negative effects on those being supervised (e.g., Harackiewicz & Larson, 1986).

In addition, even if such rewards could be calibrated, it is not clear that people are as motivated by extrinsic rewards, as they are by feedback that highlights the intrinsic value of a tasks. Research has shown that relying solely on extrinsic rewards can reduce performance due to the oversufficient justification effect (e.g., Lepper, Greene, & Nisbett, 1973). This is especially true for performance on tasks which individuals engage in volitionally and from which they derive intrinsic satisfaction. Intrinsic motivation has been conceptualized as the need for a sense of competence and personal determination, derived from individuals' motivation to be the originators of their own behaviors rather than pawns to external forces (Deci & Ryan, 1980). If people believe that tasks are performed exclusively "for the money," they may attribute their behavior to external causes. As a result, the behavior becomes instrumentally linked to the reward and tends not to be performed in the absence of subsequent extrinsic rewards. Research shows that there are important benefits to enhancing intrinsic interest in tasks, especially for enhancing creativity (Cordova & Lepper, 1991), and that creativity declines when it is extrinsically rewarded (Amabile, Hennessey, & Grossman, 1986). Further, material rewards tend to build up members' self-oriented interests as the basis for conforming to organizational values, rather than convincing them that these values are worthy of internalization in their own right (e.g., O'Reilly & Chatman, 1986; Sandelands, Glynn, & Larson, 1991).

2. *Subordinates perceive organizational authority, or top down influence, as legitimate and worthy of compliance.* Historically, most theorizing about control has implicitly been based on the Weberian assumption that legitimate authority is widely accepted; that is, people in organizations will obey orders from their superiors (e.g., Halaby, 1986). While broadly true, psychological theories of reactance (e.g., Brehm, 1972) show that people have a strong desire to maintain their freedom of action. When confronted with influence attempts from others, especially when such appeals take the form of arbitrary orders or commands, individuals experience strong reactance and actually shift their attitudes and behaviors in a direction opposite to those being advocated or demanded (e.g., Worchel & Brehm, 1971). Ironically, so strong is the desire to maintain personal control, and so objectionable are salient attempts to influence others, that individuals sometimes choose to adopt a position they do not really support, or behave in uncharacteristic (e.g., rebellious) ways to avoid accepting the one being urged on them (e.g., Karpf, 1978). People may also act in ways to maintain or restore personal control, for instance through violating or circumventing official rules (e.g., Greenberger & Strasser, 1991).

Formal control systems may exacerbate reactance effects by evaluating supervisors on the basis of their subordinates' performance. Research shows that such judgments increase supervisors' tendencies to provide performance feedback to subordinates in a controlling manner (Harackiewicz & Larson, 1986), potentially increasing feelings of control loss among subordinates. Reactance can be aroused even in the absence of actual influence attempts from others (e.g., Petty & Cacioppo, 1979). For example, Heller, Pallak, and Picek (1973) found that the mere knowledge that a confederate in their experiment intended to exert control over subjects was sufficient to arouse strong feelings of reactance, whether the influence attempt occurred or not. Therefore, paradoxically, managers who have the most influence over subordinates may take steps to reduce members' a priori suspicions about possible influence attempts.

Formal control systems tend to signal that work is bad, because if it were good (fun, enjoyable, or developmental), explicit rewards and rules would be unnecessary, and employees would spontaneously behave and perform appropriately (Bordin, 1979). Psychological research has shown that the mere labeling of a task as work causes people to choose to spend less time performing the task, and report experiencing less enjoyment while they are engaged in the task. But, if the exact same task is called a leisure pastime, people choose to spend more time and are happier while engaged in the task (e.g., Sandelands, 1988; Tang & Baumeister, 1984). Thus organizations walk a fine line between legitimate authority use and the potential for reactance or loss of intrinsic motivation if a member's "zone of acceptance" (Simon, 1976, p. 12) is violated.

In sum, the dominant approaches organizations use to control and motivate employees are formal inducements based on measuring behaviors and outputs relevant to the job. This type of control influences members' behavior as long as members accept the legitimacy of the formal rules and procedures designed to detect deviations in their output. But, as tasks become more unpredictable and uncertain and the need for flexibility and adaptability increases, formal control systems can become less effective and more costly (Caldwell & O'Reilly, 1995). This creates a dilemma: As uncertainty and the need for change increase, traditional control systems become less useful and the specter of loss of control rises. A number of authors note that these trends are increasing and argue for more flexible work arrangements and less formal systems of control (Nemeth & Staw, 1989).

We devote the next section to discussing how, given the inadequacies of formal control discussed above, organizations address the fundamental challenge of persuading their members to contribute to critical objectives. To do this we discuss alternative forms of social control, such as intensive socialization, the use of superordinate goals, and participatory regimes (e.g., Kanter, 1972; Van Maanen, 1991). We show that both the process of socially controlling employees, as well as the content of the norms and values to which members attend to determine whether social control leads to effective organizational performance or, in extreme cases, deviance.

SOCIAL CONTROL IN ORGANIZATIONS

Recall that control comes from the knowledge that someone who matters to us is paying close attention to what we are doing and will tell us when we are behaving appropriately or inappropriately. This notion of control is anchored both in a formal system such as rules, procedures, and organizational hierarchies, but also in personal relationships. Thus, while the principle applies to formal control, it also applies to the notion of *social control*; that is, to the extent that we care about others and have some agreement about what constitutes appropriate behavior, then whenever we are in their presence, we are also potentially under their control. Just as we may comply with a budgeting system less our compensation be affected (formal control), we may also comply with the opinions of our colleagues so that they will think well of us (social control).

In this sense, social control targets values, attitudes, and behaviors that may be relevant to desirable organizational outcomes, such as service, safety, and respect for others. But, of course, social control can also increase undesirable outcomes if the norms and values to which members attend to are not strategically appropriate, or if internalization is so complete that members are unable to even think of alternative ways of doing things. Either way, rather than being based on legitimate or formal authority, social control is based informational and normative influence (e.g., Deutsch & Gerard, 1955).

While formal control mechanisms are usually codified in the form of rules and procedures, social control emerges in the form of values and norms and is regulated through peer influence and the social construction of reality (Berger & Luckmann, 1967). This is an important distinction because, as will be discussed, the reliance on the opinions of valued others implies that social control may be far more extensive and less expensive than formal systems (Van Maanen, 1991). The paradox is that strong social control systems often result in positive feelings of solidarity and a greater sense of autonomy among people, rather than the psychological reactance described earlier. Because the internalization of some organizational values such as helping others and contributing to society can result in a perception of intrinsic value (that is, something that the person believes in rather than something imposed externally and subject to extrinsic justification), it may be accompanied by more positive attitudes and freely chosen behaviors. Below we define norms and values and discuss their role in the social control process. We delay an evaluation of the tradeoffs of using social control until the end of this paper.

Defining Organizational Norms and Values

As suggested earlier, we view culture as a form of social control that operates when members of a group or organization share expectations about values, or what is important, and how these values are to be manifest in norms, that is, in words and actions. Norms and values are closely related, and the distinction between them is one of emphasis. Norms refer to the expected behaviors sanctioned by the system and thus have a specific "ought" or "must" quality, while values provide rationales for these normative requirements (Cialdini, Kallgren, & Reno, 1991). For a value to become an organizational norm it must have a number of qualities: it must have an explicit formulation, it should refer specifically to identifiable behaviors, and its formulation should be systematically linked to behaviors so that it can be enforced (Weiner, 1988).

A second important distinction is that individual norms and values may differ from organizational norms and values. For group norms and values to exist, there must be beliefs about appropriate and required behavior for group members as group members; that is, there must be a commonality of such beliefs such that while not every member of the group must hold the same idea, a majority of active members are in agreement. There should also be an awareness by individuals that there is group support for a given belief (Bettenhausen & Murnighan, 1985). Thus, organization norms and values are a group product, and may or may not be identical to the privately held values of an individual organization member.

A final distinction is between societal and more organizationally relevant values (Hampden-Turner & Trompenaars, 1993). Etzioni (1964) distinguishes between societal values and values which are directly relevant to organizational issues. Societal values, while important, are far more distal and vary across entire societies (e.g., Hofstede, 1991). Organizational values, while potentially equivalent in content, are more bounded in that they are, typically, more relevant to the operations or the stated purpose of organizations.

Organization Culture as Normative Order

If we define organizational values as the beliefs shared by organizational members and norms as the expectations about appropriate attitudes and behaviors derived from these organization values, organizational culture can be viewed as *a system of shared values defining what is important, and norms, defining appropriate attitudes and behaviors, that guide members' attitudes and behaviors.* Jackson (1966) suggests two important dimensions of norms. He argues that norms, whatever their content, can vary: (1) in terms of their intensity, or the approval or disapproval evoked by appropriate or inappropriate behavior; and (2) in the amount of agreement or consensus with which a particular norm is held. A "strong culture" can be said to exist when their are a set of norms and values that are widely shared and strongly held throughout the organization (O'Reilly, 1989).

It is important to note that the operative norms that characterize a group or organization may not necessarily be those espoused by senior management or articulated in the company mission or vision. Repetition by top management of what is important, or the printing of company values on parchment, does not mean that members of the organization accept these as important. With sufficient publicity, espoused values and appropriate behavior may become widely known but not necessarily practiced—a common occurrence when senior management has been talking about a topic, such as quality or customer service, but the values are not internalized by members (e.g., Pascale, 1990). Similarly, norms may exist in one part of the organization but not be widely shared in other parts. For example, the marketing department may value meeting customer's needs through new products while the manufacturing department values stable product designs and long production runs. Variations of this sort may result in strong subcultures (e.g., Sackmann, 1992). However, we use the term "strong culture" to refer to organizational norms that are widely shared and strongly held across the units that comprise an organization. Under these circumstances, it makes sense to talk about an *organizational* culture and to consider its implications as a control system.

The critical feature of these norms and values is that they provide the basis for social control within organizations. When members agree and care about common values, violations of norms that represent these values may be sanctioned by any member, regardless of his or her formal authority or position in the hierarchy. Thus the power of organizational culture—to increase commitment among members—may lie in the power of social control. To the extent that norms emerge in all groups (Bettenhausen & Murnighan, 1991), it is also true that social control systems operate in all organizations. The question is whether these norms are intensely held, whether they enhance commitment or not, and whether they are aligned with environmental demands, that is, whether they enhance organizational performance and permit adaptation to changing circumstances.

We argue below that social control targets a broader range of behaviors, such as contact with nonorganizational members (e.g., Ofshe, 1992; Van Maanen, 1991) than formal control. The punishment for failing to adhere to norms may be exclusion, which becomes more painful for individuals as member affiliations become more multifaceted and intense. Even if an individual should have questions about the wisdom of a given norm, it becomes very difficult to alter because noncompliance may result in sanctions from one's friends. Such questioning is often interpreted as a lack confidence in the group's abilities (e.g., Janis & Mann, 1977) and is considered disloyal.

In this manner, behavior is adapted to and controlled by the situation. As Ofshe points out in discussing how cults manage people (1992, p. 213), "Eliciting the desired verbal and interactive behavior sets up conditions likely to stimulate the development of attitudes consistent with and that function to rationalize new behavior in which the individual is engaging." Over time, behavioral conformance may lead even those with doubts about underlying norms or values to accept the underlying premise of the value; that is, demonstrated behavior may lead to changed belief (Cialdini, 1993; Schlenker, 1982). Even in the face of doubts about the norm or value, individuals are likely to behave in accordance with the desires of their friends. This is a fundamental dilemma of culture as social control; if members accept existing norms and values without question, and the norms and values are or become strategically inappropriate (e.g., emphasize cost over quality when customers care more about quality), then a strong culture can actually become associated with *poor performance.*

THE PSYCHOLOGY OF SOCIAL CONTROL: CONSTRUCTING SOCIAL REALITIES

In this section we develop a framework for understanding both why culture has powerful effects on members' willingness to comply with organizational objectives and the specific mechanisms used to develop and manage demonstrated behaviors through social control. Specifically, we discuss the social psychological factors that enhance member agreement about norms and the intensity with which norms are adhered to. In other words, we address the question of where social control comes from.

Cialdini et al. (1991) have demonstrated that getting people to attend to injunctive norms, or ways people ought to behave, can have a dramatic effect in promoting norm-consistent behavior. If there are important expectations within organizations about attitudes and behaviors that are critical for the attainment of organizational objectives, such as innovation, speed, customer service, quality, adaptability, or safety, then it follows that promoting compliance with these norms will likely be associated with increased performance, as long as the strategic or technological context does not change dramatically. It is clearly the case that if norms exist among group members that run counter to the behaviors needed for effective performance, achieving the organization's objectives will be more difficult. In this regard, the combination of identifying strategically relevant values and norms, as opposed to irrelevant values and norms, *and* promoting agreement, as opposed to chronic conflict among organizational members is critical to creating a strong culture that positively affects organizational performance. If the norms and values chosen are inappropriate but members agree and care about them, the firm could be driven quickly to poor performance. In contrast, if the norms and values chosen are appropriate, but members do not care about them, the norms and values will fail to be implemented behaviorally. Finally, if members care too much about any set of values, their investment in these may prevent them from perceiving a need to shift these values and norms to stay aligned with environmental demands. In the next section, we focus on social control as a mechanism for increasing member commitment. Gaining commitment to the desired set of norms becomes a pivotal managerial task.

Managing Behavior in Organizations: Gaining Member Agreement and Intensity

To ensure that organizational objectives matter to members, an organization might attempt to hire people who are highly motivated and have personalities and interests that already coincide with the organizations'. This rather intuitive reasoning has driven an enormous body of organizational research looking for need and trait-based correlates of performance (e.g., Barrick & Mount, 1991; Maslow, 1943; McClelland & Boyatzis, 1982; Pinder, 1977) and attempting to match individuals to situations (e.g., Caldwell & O'Reilly, 1990). Although research shows that some general characteristics such as conscientiousness, intelligence and ambition contribute to individual performance (e.g., Barrick & Mount, 1991; O'Reilly & Chatman, 1994), the modest correlation between most personality traits or needs and performance may reflect the notion that such characteristics help get people to agree with organizational objectives, but fail to ensure the intensity characteristic of social control. Intensity, or unwavering commitment to norms and values is a factor that ensures peer enforcement of norms.

One reason why this person-centered mentality persists in organizations (and among researchers) is because of the construal process individuals go through in order to understand the relationship between social situations and behavior, and the relationship between behavior and outcomes. The well-known fundamental attribution error describes our tendency to attribute another person's behavior to his or her own dispositional qualities, rather than to situational factors (e.g., Ross, 1977). Instead of acknowledging that situational forces such as social norms can drive behavior, especially under some combinations of personality and situations (e.g., Wright & Mischel, 1987), we generally believe that other individuals freely choose the behaviors they display. Further, these behaviors are viewed as representative of the actor's stable qualities or personality characteristics. The closely related actor-observer bias (e.g., Jones & Nisbett, 1972) is based in part on the inaccessibility, or lack of availability, for observers of relevant situational constraints causing the displayed behaviors.

Given that motivation and personality do not fully predict performance, how do organizations get members to agree with and care intensely about objectives? We argue that they attempt to do so by increasing members' openness to organizational influence, which may include both unfreezing their prior beliefs (e.g., Van Maanen, 1976) and influencing subsequent beliefs and behaviors through shared expectations of valued others. In essence, organizations create a strong situation[2] characterized by norms that are difficult to violate without being sanctioned. Some argue that all organizations have the capacity to become strong situations (Davis-Blake & Pfeffer, 1989), and if this potential is realized, intensity about shared expectations driven by a desire for approval from valued others may further diminish the influence of individual differences on behavior (e.g., Monson, Hesley, & Chernick, 1982).

A variety of psychological mechanisms may be used to clarify expectations and create similar construal of the situation or organizational norms. Some are used to teach people about the norms, and thus to promote agreement. For example, particular information is made more salient than other information (Pfeffer, 1981). Given the ubiquity of ambiguity in organizations (e.g., Cohen & March, 1974), events and causal relationships are often forcefully interpreted by organizational leaders calling attention to the important norms. Further, when people are unsure of themselves and their own judgment, or when the situation is unclear or ambiguous, they are most likely to look to and consider the actions of others as appropriate (Tesser, Campbell, & Mickler, 1983).

Such uncertainty arises from a variety of situational characteristics. Probably the period at which the organizational situation is most ambiguous is when members first join (Louis, 1990; Van Maanen & Schein, 1979). Newcomers are most likely to seek information, given their lack of cues upon entering the firms, and are most open to normative and informational influence (e.g., Morrison, 1993a). Even with relevant past work experience, they may be quite anxious to learn how things are done in this organization in order to establish a secure position in their new setting. Newcomers are not just looking for task related and normative information (Morrison, 1993b), they are also most likely to agree with it when they first join an organization in order to fit in (e.g., Chatman, 1991).

Like agreement, a number of forces combine to create high levels of intensity about organizational norms and values. Indeed, few organizations train recruiters to select candidates systematically on the basis of ability or predicted performance (Rynes & Boudreau, 1986). Rather, recruiters tend to attend to candidates' personality and values rather than their knowledge, skills, and abilities (Jackson, Peacock, & Holden, 1982). Further, people are generally good at discriminating between in-group members (e.g., those who share a set of values) and out-group members, and are attracted to those seen as similar (Moreland, 1985; Wenegrat, 1989). Recruiting procedures, such as interviews, are likely to result in the hiring of someone similar to existing members rather than, necessarily, the best possible performer (e.g., Rothstein & Jackson, 1981). This tendency to hire similar others is augmented by the tendency for job candidates to be more likely to apply to firms that they believe hold similar values to their own (Schneider, 1987; Tom, 1971). Thus, strong culture organizations may be trading-off top level job performance for increased homogeneity and value congruence among recruits.

When people perceive others as similar, they are likely to view them as members of the same group (in-group). Past research has shown that people are significantly more likely to cooperate with those they consider to be part of their in-group (e.g., Brewer, 1979). Social categorization also enhances member's identification with the organization. To the extent that members identify with an organization, they are more likely to support the institution embodying this identity, behaviorally adhere to its values and norms, and ultimately internalize the norms and values (e.g., Ashforth & Mael, 1989). Value internalization represents the strongest form of commitment or attachment and implies that members will not hesitate to go above and beyond the call of duty on the organization's behalf (O'Reilly & Chatman, 1986).

In sum, we argue that behavior in organizations may be partially determined by individual differences, but is also powerfully shaped by the content and process of developing strong norms and values. Organizations can often be characterized as strong situations, developed through informational salience and focus, similarity and liking, and self-categorization and identification processes.

These processes, in turn, may lead members to behave in normatively consistent ways. Then, because individuals seek to justify their own actions to themselves and others whose judgments they care about, they are likely to cognitively reconstruct their values so that they are consistent with their behavior (e.g., Chatman, Bell, & Staw, 1986). A model of performance predicated on individual differences implies that managers spend time becoming experts in selection processes, because personality and cognitive ability do not change easily, or in personality or clinical psychology so that they can understand the unique motivational forces that affect their employees. In contrast, we suggest that a great deal of organizational behavior is influenced by managing informational and normative influence and promoting social control. This implies that influential managers spend time modifying situations and creating conditions that facilitate the desired behaviors. Below we present some of the mechanisms managers may use to leverage culture.

Mechanisms for "Managing" Culture

An individual's values are derived, in part, from stable dispositions (e.g., Staw, Bell, & Clausen, 1986) and, in part, from social contexts. Clearly people use their own experience and preferences to guide numerous important decisions such as what career to choose (Holland, 1976), what organization to join (Chatman, 1991), who they find interpersonally attractive (Tsui & O'Reilly, 1989), or how hard to work (Caldwell, Chatman, & O'Reilly, 1990). But, it is often the case that much of what people accept as "true" or "important" in organizations comes from a consensus of others, particularly others who are in some way important. To know what is important individuals often must rely upon what their peers or group members are doing or telling us is important (e.g., approval or disapproval), and clear signals from management (e.g., what is rewarded and punished). Situations may be even more powerful when individuals have little social support (e.g., when they are new to an organization or away from family and friends), have ambiguous information about the situation (e.g., in a new assignment), are facing problems beyond their control (e.g., a job that has substantial task interdependence with others over whom they have no authority), when previous views have been shown to be ineffective or incorrect (e.g., when performance is declining or the situation is changing), or when experiences undermine self-confidence (e.g., during socialization or when a task is beyond their capabilities) (Kelly, 1967).

These circumstances, a common part of organizational life, can cause individuals to be particularly responsive to existing norms and values. When individuals want to fit in—are subject to formal reward systems and hierarchical authority—the power of the situation may be substantial (e.g., Zucker, 1977). Thus, social learning in organizations is more pronounced the more individuals care about other members, the less familiar individuals are with the setting, or the more old ways of behaving are not working.

Drawing upon the psychological processes we have discussed, four mechanisms are commonly used by strong culture organizations to generate commitment and manage through social control: (1) systems of participation that promote choice and lead people to feel committed; (2) management actions that set goals, focus attention, and help people interpret events in ways that emphasize their intrinsic importance; (3) consistent information from valued others signalling what is and is not important; and (4) comprehensive reward systems that are seen as fair and emphasize recognition, approval, and individual and collective contributions. The power of informational and normative influence is enhanced by consistency and reduced contradictions.

Participation

The literature demonstrating the power of participation to produce commitment is substantial (e.g., Cialdini, 1993; Janis & Mann, 1977). Behavior engaged in without obvious extrinsic justification often results in large and surprising changes in attitudes and subsequent behavior (Ross & Nisbett, 1991). Comer and Laird (1975), for example, used a process of incremental commitment to induce subjects in an experiment to voluntarily eat an earthworm. Similar processes have been employed to increase bone marrow donors (Schwartz, 1970), conserve energy (Pallak, Cook, & Sullivan, 1980), or to secure religious converts (Lang & Lang, 1961). Specifically, Salancik (1977) proposes four characteristics that can accentuate the effects of participation: (1) volitionality or choice, (2) publicity or visibility, (3) explicitness, and (4) irrevocability. Each of these can increase the feeling of personal responsibility and lead to positive sentiments about the choice. Organizations often use these by designing systems that promote participation and choice by members, a common feature of high commitment work practices (e.g., Bowen, Ledford, & Nathan, 1991; Walton, 1985).

Management as Symbolic Action

A second mechanism for developing and managing through social control comes from management in the form of signals about what is important and the intrinsic significance of the work. Pfeffer (1981) describes the influence of language, symbols, and consistency of executive action as a means for cuing organizational members about what is important. He notes that formal power may have large substantive effects on organizational activities, but the attitudinal effect on individuals may be uncertain unless an attempt is made to help employees interpret events in motivationally enhancing ways. Thus, managers may act as signal generators sending messages about what is important through their own behavior, often in mundane ways such as consistently asking certain questions or following up on desired activities. Although particular symbols by themselves are not likely to be effective, when they reflect an important and widely shared value they may shape interpretations and enhance the intrinsic importance attached to specific attitudes and behaviors (Collins & Porras, 1994). In this sense, managers who influence others' interpretation of events and see the intrinsic value of their efforts shape the social control system.

Information from Others

Clear, consistent messages from coworkers also shape an individuals beliefs and behaviors. A large body of social psychological research provides dramatic examples of the power of informational influence (e.g., Latane & Darley, 1968). For instance, Rushton and Campbell (1977) found that face-to-face requests for blood donations were successful 25% of the time. When requests were made in the presence of a model who complied, the rate more than doubled to 67%. Organizations capitalize on the impact of others' behaviors on us in a number of ways. Some emphasize equality among members by reducing distinctions between management and workers (e.g., no special perks such as parking spaces, common titles, open office space, informality, etc.). Others emphasize close relations among members through social activities and family involvement. The very pace of work sometimes acts to isolate workers from others who are not also at the company.

Comprehensive Reward Systems

A final important lever for shaping culture involves the comprehensive use of rewards and recognition for exemplary compliance with the core norms and values. Biggart (1989), for example, describes how direct sales organizations use continual recognition and reinforcement to motivate employees. These may take the form of small gifts, recognition from peers, or even awarding vacations and automobiles. But, as discussed in the second section, tangible rewards must be carefully allocated because they may reduce intrinsic interest and motivation, especially when intrinsic interest is initially high (Harackiewicz & Larson, 1986). For example, providing people with verbal reinforcement and positive feedback, compared with external rewards, increases their intrinsic motivation in tasks (e.g., Deci, 1971). Providing people with small rewards may be more effective in shaping behavior than offering large rewards, especially when the rewards are framed in terms of "appreciation" rather than "control" (Steele, 1988).

These four mechanisms (participation, management as symbolic action, information from others, and informal reward and recognition systems) are the primary levers organizations use to develop culture as a social control system. Each capitalizes on the importance of strong informational and normative influence as a potential determinant of attitudes and behavior. Each acts to provide organizational members with consistent signals about which attitudes and behaviors are important, either from one's own previous behavior or from information provided by valued others. Due to the strong attributional bias and ethics, Western philosophy, or societal norms valuing individualism, the power of these forces to shape behavior is seldom appreciated. Individuals prefer disposition-based predictions, even when confronted with contrary evidence (Pietromonaco & Nisbett, 1982). Ironically, this bias may actually enhance the power of social control systems because observers are less aware of their operation. We present concrete examples below of how these four mechanisms provide the foundation for social control in organizations. Surprisingly these mechanisms are used in organizations as disparate as cults and strong culture corporations.

SOCIAL CONTROL IN ORGANIZATIONS: STRONG CULTURE FIRMS, RELIGIOUS GROUPS, SELF-AWARENESS GROUPS, AND CULTS

The previous section described the psychology of strong situations and individuals' tendencies to underestimate their power. In this section, we review how social control operates in organizations ranging from strong culture corporations to religious organizations and cults. Whether it is a strong culture company such as Hewlett-Packard, a Japanese transplant like New United Motors Manufacturing Inc., or fringe religious groups, the psychological mechanisms used to recruit, socialize, and control members are remarkably similar. In each case, social control is employed to provide members with direction, purpose, and perspective. Of course, cults and cult-like organizations typically exert more control over people and have different intentions than strong culture firms. In cults, leaders want members to internalize their beliefs so that members become loyal deployable agents who will act on the cult's behalf, even if it means violating laws or sacrificing one's friends and family. Strong culture firms typically have less control and a different intent; leaders hope that members will become committed by taking pride in their affiliation with the firm (O'Reilly & Chatman, 1986). But the mechanisms for recruitment and commitment and the psychological processes that underlie these are strikingly similar. Cults and strong culture firms use participation as a means for generating commitment, symbolic action to convey a sense of purpose, consistent information to shape interpretations, and extensive reward and recognition systems to shape behavior (O'Reilly, 1989). In this sense, the underlying psychology of social control is fundamentally the same across these types of organizations. We draw this comparison to show how culture is used as a social control system for both positive and negative ends, and how culture in corporations is developed and managed. The message is not that organizations should be run as cults, but rather that social control can, under some circumstances, be a powerful and productive way to motivate and coordinate collective action.

Social Control in Strong Culture Organizations

Although perceived as more socially acceptable, strong culture organizations often use "cult-like" techniques to generate commitment and social control. To develop the strategically appropriate normative order, three general steps are taken by almost all strong culture organizations: (1) *promoting commitment through participation* by designing processes such as rigorous selection and orientation processes and job designs that require multiple steps; (2) *managing the informational context* through management signalling, often symbolically, that certain goals, attitudes, and behavior are important, minimizing mixed or inconsistent messages to help members develop shared interpretations of events, and continuous emphasis with multiple opportunities for reinforcement; and (3) *developing comprehensive reward systems* that are aligned with the culture and that provide rapid feedback, an emphasis on appropriate attitudes and behavior, and continuous recognition. The focus of these activities is to ensure strong, unambiguous support for the norms and values that define the social control system. The power of the system, as outlined previously, results from the identification and internalization of these norms and values by the members of the organization such that each is willing to live by the values and sanction others for violating the values. When this occurs, the control afforded is extensive and internalized rather that periodic and exogenous.

Japanese organizations, for example, rely heavily on social control developed through elaborate recruitment and socialization procedures, an emphasis on cohorts and work groups, consensual decision making based on participation, a unique company philosophy, and strong evaluation of attitudes and behaviors rather than simple performance (e.g., Brannen, 1993; Clark, 1979). While there may be aspects to Japanese history and society that encourage the use of social control, Abegglen and Stalk (1985, p. 15) observe that the achievement of the Japanese "results not from special diligence, loyalty or other special characteristics of individual Japanese. Rather it results from a total system of employment and governance that combines to produce exceptional results... It is a system whose elements can be introduced into any management system given adequate understanding, conviction and effort." The proof of this can be seen in the success of Japanese manufacturing organizations in Asia, Africa, Europe, and the United States. With appropriate modifications to reflect local cultural norms, these systems, relying on strong cultures that highlight the values of quality, continuous improvement, customer service, and productivity, have been remarkably robust (e.g., Perrucci, 1994; Womak et al., 1990).

New United Motors Manufacturing Inc. (NUMMI), the joint venture between General Motors and Toyota Manufacturing in Fremont, California illustrates these points (Adler, 1994). In 1983 General Motors closed their Fremont Assembly plant. It was one of the worst operations in the GM system with an average daily absenteeism rate of over 18%, exceedingly poor quality, and labor-management relations that resulted in roughly 5,000 grievances per contract. In 1983 Toyota agreed to reopen the plant. Toyota would manufacture cars and GM would handle marketing, distribution, and sales. NUMMI invited back the old GM workers and hired over 85% of those who applied; they agreed to the same UAW representation, and chose not to use the latest technology in their manufacturing process. Studies have shown that NUMMI has some of the lowest absenteeism and highest productivity and quality in the world (Krafcik, 1986). How can this happen? The obvious answers such as a different workforce or new technology do not apply. The answer may lie in the management of the workforce and through the use of culture as a social control system (Pfeffer, 1994). First, the recruitment process required applicants to go through a 3-day assessment program on their own time. The emphasis of this program was on participant's ability to work as a part of a team with clear signals about what norms and values were important. The purpose here was in setting the right expectations as much as it was actually selecting people. After selection, team members (never referred to as "assembly line workers") were continually trained and socialized about the importance of attendance, hard work, and continuous improvement. Semi-autonomous teams are used extensively, including doing the industrial engineering. Training was conducted by other team members and senior managers, signalling that these were important. Rewards and recognition were explicitly designed to enhance teamwork and quality. For example, each team was provided with a budget to support team social functions. The one constraint is that to use these funds *all* team members had to participate, enhancing interdependence and thus social control within the plant. Elaborate private offices or managerial perks that emphasized distinctions rather than similarities among members were avoided. All employees dressed alike. In the Japanese tradition, office design emphasizes open spaces ensuring that people could always observe their colleagues. The goal was to demonstrate that U.S. workers could produce a quality automobile as good or better as the Japanese, and thereby act as a role model for U.S. automobile manufacturers. The emphasis was on the intrinsic worth of their efforts more than profitability.

The three themes of systems of participation, management of the informational context, and comprehensive reward and recognition systems are characteristic of the social control systems in almost all strong culture firms. At Southwest Airlines, Hewlett-Packard, Nordstrom, and other firms the recruitment process involves multiple steps, requiring applicants to escalate their investment in the firm. At Tandem Computer and Cypress Semiconductor, for instance, there is a deliberate attempt *not* to discuss salary before hiring. Instead, candidates are asked to commit to join the firm (i.e., accept the job offer) before discussing the specifics of their salary, a tactic which emphasizes the intrinsic rather than instrumental aspects of belonging. At Southwest, the hiring process, and often the firing process, is based explicitly on whether the individual has the "right attitude." Procedures enable insiders to discern whether candidates fit the culture of the organization, for example Southwest pilots hire other pilots. Similarly, at Worthington Industries, team members vote on whether a probationary employee will be offered a permanent position. From the recruits' perspective, the process is one of incremental and public commitment to subscribe to an explicit set of norms, often conditional on the explicit approval of his or her direct coworkers. (Of course, this process also increases the interdependence among members by making them accountable for new recruits' success in the organization.) Further, some companies that are undergoing major cultural transformations such as British Airways, AT&T, Boeing, ABB and General Electric, use a similar process of re-recruitment and re-socialization to the new norms and values. For example, employees often where people must reapply for their old jobs, publicly sign agreements, and undergo intensive resocialization.[3]

Once an individual has joined a strong culture firm, he or she is continuously socialized to understand the appropriate attitudes and behaviors. For example, all Southwest Airlines employees are brought to corporate headquarters in Dallas for a training session, called a "celebration." At firms like Disney, Arthur Andersen, and Procter and Gamble, these experiences may be highly structured while at other companies like Nordstrom and some investment banks, they may involve total immersion in a group of others who embody the culture, including long hours, off the job socializing, heroic stories, and group celebrations. Collins and Porras (1994, p. 132) report a P&G employee as saying, "P&Gers are expected to socialize primarily with other P&Gers, belong to the same clubs, attend similar churches, and live in the same neighborhoods." Strong signals are continually sent from higher management emphasizing the important norms and values of the company. At Southwest where productivity and teamwork are important, the pilots hold 3 a.m. cook-outs on the flight line to thank the mechanics. They also help flight attendants clean the aircraft during stops (Labich, 1994). At Disney, there is a strong norm that *everyone* is expected to pick up litter, including senior officers. At firms like Federal Express, Mary Kay, and Wal-Mart, constant reinforcement in the form of pictures, stories, parties and celebrations are held to tighten social ties and further illustrate the "correct" attitudes and behavior. Jobs are designed to emphasize teams and peer pressure in almost all such organizations. Stock ownership and profit sharing, requiring members to literally buy-in to the firm, are often found in these firms (Pfeffer, 1994).

Table 1. Designing Social Control Systems

1. "Vision" or purpose which provides intrinsic meaning to work.
2. Select people whose values are similar to the organization's or whose situation is likely to make them willing to change past beliefs and accept new ones (e.g., people without previous experience in the industry).
3. Use multiple recruiting steps requiring escalating commitment on the part of the recruit (e.g., require multiple visits and interviews).
4. Focus on core values that have intrinsic value to the recruit. Be clear and honest about the norms and values of the organization (e.g., explicit descriptions of attitudes and behaviors). Emphasize the affective ties among members and importance of fit.
5. Facilitate a "deselection" process emphasizing "choice." Note that the organization is not for everyone; only certain people can join.
6. Provide extensive exposure to the core values through training, role models, senior management, and participation. These emphasize the specific attitudes and behaviors expected by members. Minimize conflicting signals.
7. Promote strong cohort bonds and social ties among people (e.g., parties, celebrations, and "fun"). Emphasize teamwork and directed autonomy.
8. Offer visible, vivid, and consistent top management support. Management are explicit role models of attitudes and behavior. Set clear, difficult goals. Emphasize the intrinsic importance of the work, not the monetary rewards.
9. Provide frequent reinforcement of the attitudes and behaviors that reflect the core values, especially through recognition, celebration and group approval (e.g., design systems that promote recognition).

What is important to note about these activities is the way in which they draw upon the underlying psychological processes we have described in order to develop strong social control systems. Collins and Porras (1994) note that all organizations have cultures. But the cult-like characteristics serve to ensure the presence of the core ideology and differentiate strong culture firms from their less successful competitors. The common themes linking cults, religious organizations, and strong culture firms are shown in Table 1. These include an emphasis on the intrinsic importance of the effort, participation and incremental commitment, a reliance on clear norms and values, the development of affective ties among members, and continual reinforcement of behavior aligned with the norms and values.

Social Control in Religious Organizations, Self-Help Organizations, and Cults

The previous section described the use of social control in work organizations. In this section we review how the same approach and underlying psychological processes operate in religious organizations, self-help organizations, and cults. Heirich (1977) found that the most powerful predictor of religious conversion was social influence. Long and Hadden (1983, p. 2), compare brainwashing and religious conversion and conclude that, "There are very real differences in content and in emphasis between religious conversion and other forms of socialization, but *the basic process and variables are the same*" (emphasis in the original). Stark (1971, p. 165) reviews the old proposition that there is a positive association between psychopathology and religious commitment and concludes "that the proposition is not simply false, but the opposite of the truth." In cults, leaders want members to internalize their beliefs so that members become loyal, deployable agents who will act on the cult's behalf, even if it means breaking the laws or dying. Strong culture firms have less control and a different intent than these other types of organizations; leaders hope that members will become committed by taking pride in their affiliation with the firm (O'Reilly & Chatman, 1986). But the mechanisms for recruitment and commitment are strikingly similar. Religious organizations, self-help organizations, cults and strong culture firms use participation as a means for generating commitment, symbolic action to convey a sense of purpose, consistent information to shape interpretations, and extensive reward and recognition systems to shape behavior (O'Reilly, 1989). Thus we argue that the underlying psychology of social control is fundamentally the same across these types of organizations. Again, the tendency to account for the fervor of some religious organizations or cults through individual attributes misses the power of social control.

Religious Organizations

Consider the following religion: A century ago it was a small, persecuted religious cult whose leaders were hunted by the U.S. government. Now it is the fastest growing church among the major denominations in the United States, averaging a 6% growth rate per year and with over 75 million members worldwide (Lindsey, 1986). Church membership doubled every 15 years between World War II and 1970, and tripled between 1970 and 1985. It has an estimated $8 billion is assets and an annual revenue of $2 billion, including ownership of insurance companies, radio and television stations, publishing houses, agribusinesses, and real estate (Heinerman & Shupe, 1986).

This religion, the Church of Jesus Christ of Latter-day Saints or Mormons, emphasizes the most American of values: striving, self-reliant, strong families, stable marriages, and close knit families. How has this church managed to grow, prosper and maintain its hold on its members? Aside from its theology, the Mormons use strong social control systems for recruiting new members and managing the flock. Lindsey (1986, p. 34) indicates that, "Any member who violates church directives on doctrine, morality or life style, who challenges the word of the hierarchy, who declines to pay 10 percent of his income to the church, or otherwise fails to pass muster in the eyes of his local lay bishop, faces serious ecclesiastical consequences." This can also include serious interpersonal and economic consequences as well, with those out of favor being deprived of friends and business relationships. Criticism is not appreciated and obedience is expected. Harold Lee (1972), a church leader, stated that each member should "Keep your eye on the President of the Church, and if he ever tells you to do anything, and it is wrong, and you do it, the Lord will bless you for it."

To ensure involvement, membership entails significant participation which can include home visiting and teaching assignments, regular temple attendance, welfare assignments, board meetings, service projects, ward parties, family home evenings and recruiting. For instance, Barker (1987, p. 26) notes that Mormon society, like the old Soviet system, involves "authoritarian systems with extensive programs of education and socialization to promote the values of the institution... In both cases, these values involve doctrinal tenets, ritual and symbolism, and require a high degree of participation within the system by all its members." Barker also points out that there are important differences in means and ends between the two systems, but that both ideologies use similar mechanisms to promote membership and ensure compliance.

Recruiting is particularly targeted at non-Mormons. Members are actively challenged to identify and pursue friendships for the purpose of converting them. Activities are explicitly designed around the interests of a targeted non-Mormon in order to gain his interest (Barker, 1987). The sophistication with which social influence is used is seen most clearly in the 13-step procedure provided in church literature to help Mormons recruit (Eberhard, 1974). Table 2 provides these steps, all directed toward building close interpersonal ties and using these to incrementally commit the subject. The initial focus is on those without close family ties, for instance those who are new to the neighborhood or those who have had a recent death in the family and may be seeking answers. As with the Moonies, the process emphasizes establishing an emotional bond, then involving them in a circle of friends who are Mormons. Gradually, the prospective recruit comes to feel that he or she is among a group of friends with good common values. The instructions proceed to tell the recruiter how to incrementally escalate the target's involvement until the recruit is publicly asked by their new friends to commit to the religion. In a two-year study the recruitment success rate for this procedure was estimated at 50% compared to the less than 0.1% success rate for door-to-door proselytizing (Stark & Bainbridge, 1980).

Self-Help Organizations

Some religious organizations and most cults typically exert almost total control over their members through life-absorbing involvement and isolation, for example, common residences such as dormitories or close-knit communities and extensive church activities (Ebaugh, 1977; Wilson, 1959). Self-help organizations such as Scientology, Lifespring, *est*, and other similar offshoots use the same techniques to generate commitment among members, although

Table 2. Religious Recruitment

1. Select your family. Choose people who are without strong friendship ties (e.g., new to the neighborhood) or who have had a recent death in the family.
2. Learn their names. Be cheerful. Be a good listener. Do a favor for them (e.g., lend them gardening tools).
3. Invite them to your home. Give them a reason not related to the religion.
4. Go out together. Focus on their interests. Let them choose the place or event.
5. Casually mention your religious affiliation. Avoid intensely spiritual subjects.
6. Offer them practical literature such as how to stop smoking. Use discretion.
7. Invite them for a family evening. Emphasize your solid family relationships. Avoid church questions.
8. Introduce them to other church members. For example, invite them to participate in classes. Get your children to help by asking them to invite nonmembers also.
9. Based on their interests, invite them to a church social. Avoid deep religious discussions.
10. Invite them to a church meeting. Carefully select an appropriate event. Let them know what to expect.
11. Share your personal testimony. Keep it simple. Do not include deeply spiritual experiences.
12. Ask the "golden" question; that is, would they be interested in finding out about the religion? Use their interests. Keep trying.
13. Ask them to meet with the missionaries. Set a time and place. Put them at ease. Support them in their decision.

Source: Eberhard (1974).

their control is often less complete. Nevertheless, the process of involvement often leads to reports of secular conversion experiences similar to religious experiences, except the discovery is one of self-enlightenment or "getting it" rather than discovering God (Long & Hadden, 1983). In analyzing the psychology of Alcoholics Anonymous, Galanter (1989, p.185) describes how, "Recruitment into AA occurs in a psychological context that allows communication to be closely controlled, so as to assure that the group's ideology will be sustained in the face of uncommitted drinkers. Most of those attending AA chapter meetings are deeply involved in the group ethos, and the expression of views opposed to the group's model of treatment is subtly or expressly discouraged." AA uses involvement and social control to generate intense personal commitment to the norms and values of not drinking.

Scientology, another self-awareness organization, has an estimated $400 million in foreign bank accounts and 50,000 members (Behar, 1991). They recruit wealthy and respectable members through a network of consulting groups that disguise their ties to the group. Exploiting a recruit's desire for self-awareness, the group uses an escalating commitment process to draw new members into the organization (Bainbridge & Stark, 1980). Both *est* and Lifespring are based on sales motivation courses and use similar approaches involving escalating commitment, strong normative pressure to comply, and processes to reduce critical thinking and overwhelm normal psychological defense mechanisms (Baer & Stolz, 1978; Finkelstein, Wenegrat, & Yalom, 1982). Once in the group, members form new sets of "friends" to whom they are committed. This group acts to ensure social control of the new attitudes and behavior. Recruiting new members becomes an important part of their new roles. As Baer and Stolz (1978, p. 60) conclude, "*est* trainees rarely will complain later; they more often will boast of their exceptional bargain in personal fulfillment, and will be positive that they are now experiencing life rather than being run by others or their past. The alternative to claiming this is to admit that they were conned and didn't even have the courage to walk out in the middle. Very few people will admit to that." The actual evidence for psychological change in *est* graduates is almost nonexistent (Finkelstein et al., 1982). While the intent of these groups is to generate commitment based on the internalization of values (O'Reilly & Chatman, 1986), the evidence suggests that, rather than generating "enlightenment," the mechanism for generating commitment is social control based on informational and normative influence. This approach is typically successful only as long as a person remains a member of the group.

Cults

Cults elicit a certain popular fascination. They often embody the bizarre and are puzzling to try to understand. Before discussing the steps leading to cult membership, it is important to define the common characteristics of a cult. Appel (1983) suggests three defining attributes of cult membership: (1) separation and isolation from friends and family; (2) a conversion experience in which the past life is surrendered or re-interpreted; and (3) a new identity based on the new ideology. While undoubtedly accurate, these attributes could also apply to more conventional religious organizations. Religious leaders in the Catholic church, for instance, are sometimes sequestered from families and take on new names and identities (Ebaugh, 1977). Indeed, further reflection might suggest that the original members of some entrepreneurial start up companies such as Apple or Saturn also meet these characteristics (e.g., working 60-hour weeks can be as isolating as living in a commune).

Marc Galanter (1989), who has studied cults ranging from The Divine Light Mission to the Moonies, suggests a slightly different set of attributes defining a cult: (1) a shared belief system; (2) a high level of social cohesiveness; (3) strong norms defining appropriate attitudes and behaviors; and (4) the imputation of charismatic power to the group or leadership. Again, while this definition fits cults, it may also apply to strong culture organizations such as some military units, corporations with charismatic founders such as Mary Kay and Wal-Mart.

But a fundamental question remains: Why would a rational person join a group such as Jim Jones and the People's Temple in Guyana, the Bhagwan Shree Rajneesh in Oregon, or the Branch Davidians in Waco, Texas? That is, why would an individual sacrifice his or her personal freedom, financial and material wealth, and in some cases, his or her life to be a member of a cult?

When asked "why do people join cults," many offer explanations such as low self-esteem, a high need for structure, being easily influenced, and other person-based explanations; that is, they attempt to explain this apparently irrational act by invoking some dispositional attribute. There is, however, no compelling evidence showing that those who join cults are psychologically different in any important ways from those who do not (e.g., Heirich, 1977; Lynch, 1977; Ofshe, 1992; Stark & Bainbridge, 1980). "The notion that only 'crazies' join cults is misleading. What we are really trying to assert with that assumption is that it can't happen here, it can't happen to you or me. Whether we like it or not, the facts speak otherwise" (Appel, 1983, p. 75).

Research suggests two basic reasons why people join cults. First, vulnerability to cults typically occurs when a person wants to make a difference or do something worthwhile (e.g., Lofland, 1977; Stark & Bainbridge, 1980). Appel (1983, p. 75) quotes a review of *Mein Kampf* by George Orwell who wrote, "Hitler knows that human beings don't only want comfort, safety, short working hours, hygiene, birth control and, in general, common sense; they also, at least intermittently, want struggle and self-sacrifice, not to mention drums, flags, and loyalty parades." Further, many people desire a more collective experience in the modern-day, often alienating world (Bellah, Madsen, Sullivan, Swidler, & Tipton, 1985).

Second, people are more likely to join cults when they are isolated from family and friends (not psychologically alienated but not embedded in their usual social networks). These characteristics are often found among young people, especially those living in college dormitories, foreign students, or travellers, and among retired people, or people facing a major life-change. The parallels between these and the attributes that increase vulnerability to social influence discussed above are clear (e.g., Kelly, 1967). The classic Bennington College study (Newcomb, 1943) offers a dramatic example of the political shift from conservative to active liberal among young women from upper-middle class families. This shift could be explained by the womens' experiences at Bennington, an exciting, cohesive and isolated college led by young politically liberal professors. In a classic study of cult membership, Lofland and Stark (1965) described how these same processes can explain how people enter the Moonies. These processes may also explain membership and conversion in more conventional settings. Table 3 outlines the original Lofland and Stark dimensions and applies them to membership in cults and a very conventional setting, that of a typical MBA program. Remarkably, the underlying logic applies well in both cases.

The Process of Getting Committed to a Cult

Rather than individual personality explaining cult behavior, it is the *process* through which members are recruited and controlled that matters. The history of the Moonies in the United States illustrates this point (e.g., Barker, 1984;

Table 3. Cult Recruitment

Situational Factors	Cults/Religions	MBA Students
1. Perception of a considerable strain or frustration	1. Feeling of inadequacy, unworthiness; desire to contribute to a higher good	1. Frustration in job/career; desire for rewards and challenge
2. Awareness of a religious or ideological rhetoric and problem solving perspective	2. Knowledge of religious tracts; ability to "explain" and solve problems	2. Awareness of methodologies to solve problems (e.g., economics)
3. Self-definition as a "religious seeker"; rejection of traditional solutions to problems	3. Quest for meaning and purpose beyond conventional religious explanations	3. Desire for achievement and advancement; rejection of current career path
4. Turning point reached where the old way is no longer tolerable; contact with cult member begins	4. Invitation to join group for social purposes	4. Contact with representative of school (e.g., alumni); interest in brochures, and so on
5. Development of affective bonds with cult members	5. Intensive involvement and immersion in the group	5. Increasing involvement with students, alumni, recruiters
6. Weak or neutralized ties with old contacts; pre-commitment to convert	6. Escalating commitment with cult members; public identification of association	6. Acceptance to the program; public commitment; sacrifice job; move; financial commitment
7. Intensive, communal interaction with final conversion	7. Full-time involvement; separation from old friends; new identity as deployable agent	7. Heavy course load, new religious perspective (e.g., economics); new group of friends; deployable as MBA

Source: Adapted from Lofland and Stark (1965).

Bromley & Shupe, 1979). The first Moonies in the United States attempted to recruit by proselytizing; that is, they lectured and distributed tapes describing their religious beliefs. This was unsuccessful, and after several years of effort, only a few converts had been made and their motives for joining were suspect. Subsequently, the Moonies developed a recruiting process that, within several years, resulted in hundreds of converts. This process unfolds in five stages, all of which involve incremental and escalating commitment, the development of strong affective ties between the recruit and cult members, and strong informational and normative influence Lofland (1977).

1. *Picking up.* Candidates, who are away from family and friends and at a point in their lives where they want to make a difference, are identified. For instance, recruitment often takes place on college campuses or in airports where people are obviously travelling. Recruiters engage targets in friendly

conversations. Sometimes the contact involves invoking the reciprocity norm, such as giving the person a ride or a small gift (Cialdini, 1993). The subject is then invited to dinner at the local Moonie house.

2. *Hooking-up.* At dinner the subject is surrounded with smiling, talkative hosts. Specific members of the cult are assigned to each guest. The intent is to establish an emotional bond. To do this, an emphasis is placed on similarities, common values, and the use of positive reinforcement. Once established, the target is asked to join the group for the weekend at their camp in Northern California. A promise of a ride to the camp and a return on Sunday is made.

3. *Encapsulating.* Once at the facility there is a modified brainwashing process in which the target is incorporated into the group through a series of collective activities, low protein, disrupted sleep patterns, fatigue, and a diminished ability to cognitively evaluate what they are told. The intent is to logically unfold the ideology in a manner the target will accept.

4. *Loving.* The crux of the weekend is to immerse the target in a caring group of similar others such that the person has the feeling of being loved and accepted by others.

5. *Committing.* Toward the end of this experience, the target is invited to stay on for a continuing week-long workshop. Identification with the new group of friends is promoted and involvement with former family and friends is trivialized. Active screening takes place to eliminate those participants who are seen as not fitting in with the group, including those with psychological problems.

From a social control perspective, the underlying psychology is clear. First, choice and incremental commitment processes are used to promote involvement. Next, affective attachments are developed through the emphasis on similarities, common values, and the use of positive reinforcement. For those who are temporarily isolated, the prospect of a weekend with new friends is not necessarily a burden. Reciprocity, having accepted their hospitality, also may dictate an affirmative response. Once at the camp and subject to more direct pressure, especially in a fatigued state, it becomes progressively more difficult to disagree or see the logical inconsistencies in their choices. Once a potential recruit chooses to stay for the week, leaving becomes increasingly difficult. Over 29% of a group chose to stay on after the weekend experience with the Moonies, and 6% of the original sample of 104 became full-time members (Galanter, 1989). Although of modest size, this 6% represents considerable potential for recruiting subsequent members. The only aspect distinguishing between those who joined and those who did not was that the joiners were less cohesively tied to others outside the cult.

The Moonies recognize that many new converts initially do not agree intellectually with the ideology. As Lofland and Stark (1965, p. 871) note, they also fully appreciate the power of social control, defining conversion as "coming to accept the opinions of one's friends." In studying cults from a sociobiologic perspective, Wenegrat (1989) argues that this tendency has biologic origins and has been evolutionarily adaptive such that "The tendency to agree with one's perceived group appears...to override critical faculties: (1989, p. 200). Thus, once one accepts the similarities between self and group, there may be a natural inclination to also accept the group's consensual views. Once embedded in the group, contacts with outsiders such as family and friends are cut off and strong social pressure is applied to ensure conformity to group norms. Often this involves moving to an isolated location and adopting a communal lifestyle that ensures members are always in the presence of others from the cult. This also ensures the constant enforcement of group norms.

Other cults use similar processes of social control (e.g., Balch & Taylor, 1977). Bainbridge (1978), for instance, provides a fascinating description of the development of a satanic cult. Again, the bizarre obsession with Satan did not result from individual pathology, but from the coupling of affective bonds among cult members with isolation from friends and escalating commitment to the in-group. This resulted over time in the adoption of a satanic theme, the development of symbols and rituals, and strong norms of behavior. A history of Jonestown (Mills, 1979) reveals a similar pattern. Members began spending large amounts of time together in church activities, isolating them from families and friends who were not members. Jim Jones required an escalating series of commitments that made it progressively more difficult to leave, "Soon Jim raised the required commitment to 30 percent of every member's income, and more people were required to go communal or go broke... Most of the people were...so completely controlled that they gave in" (p. 38). Jones also moved his group several times to disrupt stable social networks and ensure isolation and control.

The history of the *Sturm Abteilung* (*SA*) and the *Schutzstaffel* (*SS*) in Nazi Germany have eerie parallels in the use of social control (Sabini & Silver, 1980; Steiner, 1980). Descriptions of the origins of the SA echo the themes of isolation, a sense of making a difference, and the use of social control developed through participation, management as symbolic action, information from others, and clear reward and recognition systems (Merkl, 1980). First, the initial recruits were young men, many of whom had lost their fathers during WWI. They therefore fit the predisposing characteristics of likely cult joiners. Once convinced of the ideal of a proud Germany, they often moved into dormitories with other young men. Here they were socialized into the values and norms of the stormtroopers, provided with symbols, an identity, a charismatic leader, and continual reinforcement and recognition from their peers and superiors. Further isolation from the rest of society and an escalating commitment to an increasingly deviant course of action followed. Again, studies of these recruits and of Nazi leaders do not reveal them to be significantly different psychologically from the larger population. Rather, it appears that well-adjusted people can sometimes find themselves caught in strong situations that determine their behavior (e.g., Milgram, 1964).

Similar processes operated at Synanon (Ofshe, 1980). Membership began with voluntary association (recruitment through a friend or acquaintance). Then isolation was increased as members moved into Synanon dormitories and commitment escalated through acts that were irrevocable or difficult to undo, such as divorce or vasectomy. These further locked participants into the group. Cults rely on intense interpersonal and psychological attachments and guilt to promote compliance. Often this involves the use of a peer group to apply pressure for compliance with group norms. In Synanon, Jonestown, the Branch Davidians, and other cults, this can take the form of marathon meetings, called at any time of day or night, in which members' defense mechanisms are overridden. Guilt, discovered through public confession or counselling, is then used to induce compliance. These lengthy sessions also produce fatigue and make cognitive processing more difficult. Cults often manipulate the totality of a person's environment and use these guilt-inducing processes to ensure compliance similar to the North Korean prisoner of war camps described by Schein (1961).

Whether in strong culture organizations religious organizations, self-help groups, or cults, social control comes from the knowledge that others who are important to us know what we are doing and will tell us when we are out of compliance. The psychological basis for this control is well understood and relies on retrospective rationality and social learning. It operates through processes of choice and participation, incremental commitment, strong informational and normative influence, the use of symbols, emotion, and reward systems, and clear norms and values. In other words, social control characterizes all of these groups.

CONCLUSIONS, LIMITATIONS, AND FUTURE DIRECTIONS

Culture is a prevalent social control system operating in organizations. Based on the psychological mechanisms of participation, management as symbolic action, information from others, and comprehensive reward and recognition systems, managers create strong situations and shape collective action. Culture as social control can, under certain circumstances, be an effective way of meeting legitimate strategic and even socially redeeming organizational objectives. For example, these psychological processes can be used to increase blood donations (Rushton & Campbell, 1977), conserve energy (Pallak et al., 1980) or, as we have shown, promote innovation, high levels of customer service, quality, and a sense of common purpose within organizations (e.g., Collins & Porras, 1994; Tushman & O'Reilly, 1996). But, social control can also result in behavior characterized by deviance and personal and social exploitation. This dark side occurs when beliefs are internalized and critical thinking is constrained to such a degree that individuals can be induced to behave in unethical or harmful ways. Manifestations of this dark side range broadly, from the formation of the *Schutzstaffel* in Nazi Germany (Merkl, 1980), or the delivery of what are believed to be fatal shocks to others (Milgram, 1964), to merely losing sight of relevant changes in the competitive environment leading to reduced organizational performance (Carroll, 1992). Thus, social control can be used to either empower or oppress individuals in groups and organizations, and to achieve constructive or pernicious social and financial ends.

We have emphasized the striking similarities between strong culture firms and organizations as extreme as cults, but it may be the *differences* between organizations and cults that potentially ensure that members are empowered rather than oppressed, and effective rather than ineffective or destructive behaviors emerge. Identifying these differences is a fruitful direction for future research. Some of the information presented in this paper provides clues about key differences between functional versus dysfunctional aspects of social control. Key differences may arise in two forms: (1) from the *content* of the norms and values organizational members are asked to identify with; and (2) from the *intensity of the social control process* to which organizational members are exposed.

On the content side, legitimate organizations may be more likely to be honest about what the group stands for and expects from its members; that is, while cults routinely disguise their real purposes, strong culture firms are typically straightforward about expected norms and values. This honesty can allow potential recruits to make informed choices about the values espoused by the organization, and reduces the chance that individuals will unwittingly join groups that either violate their values, or are judged to be unethical (Chatman, 1991).

A number of process issues must also be considered. In particular, formal control systems, which are often necessary and efficient, may fail to capture people's creativity and emotional commitment. Social control can engage people emotionally and provide them with direction and a sense of purpose. Whereas formal control systems tend to signal to employees that they are cogs in a machine and must conform to established rules and procedures, social control tends to convey a sense of autonomy and individual responsibility, likely precursors to creative thinking. When organizations like Nordstrom and NUMMI design jobs, they often substitute strong social control for formal control. In other organizations, retail clerks and assembly line workers are subject to strong formal controls. The difference in attitudes and performance of workers under the two regimes is often striking.

Further, people's tendency to want to join groups and to distinguish in-groups from out-groups is too strong to discount. This propensity may have sociobiologic origins, and it may be evolutionarily adaptive (Wenegrat, 1989).

To deny or ignore the power of groups to define situations is as dangerous as it is nonsensical. Instead, situations need to be constructed in ways that provide for a common identification while avoiding the total conformity demanded by cult groups. This is a critical difference between the use of social control in cults and strong culture organizations. In the former, the demand for conformity and obedience is usually total. Members are not encouraged to think or challenge the existing order and contact with outsiders is limited or controlled. In the latter, the norms and values often encourage challenge and debate. Members are asked to contribute ideas, and learning from the outside is encouraged. At Intel, for example, constructive conflict is encouraged to ensure that open, honest discussion of all issues takes place. Intel also has a norm of "competitive paranoia" which encourages its members to continually search externally for new ideas, less they be surpassed by unexpected developments. At HP, this tendency is a norm for modesty that encourages looking to other members and organizations for good ideas.

Additionally, the typical characterization of leaders differs between strong culture firms and cults. The leadership of strong culture organizations is typically more balanced in ways that prevent abuse (Pfeffer, 1981). Boards of Directors may provide some check on the tendency for leaders to claim too much power over members. Although exceptions exist, one is more likely to see an openness of process and genuine spirit of equality in strong culture firms than in cults. Cults often have elites that claim inspired or divine privilege (e.g., Chidester, 1988; Gordon, 1987; Ofshe, 1980).

Finally, members' commitment to strong culture firms is more likely to be based on identification or pride of affiliation (O'Reilly & Chatman, 1986), not internalization of beliefs. Once members internalize the values of any organization, such devotion may be used to legitimate actions beyond conventional societal norms, for instance deceiving others for purposes of a "greater good" (e.g., Bainbridge & Stark, 1980; Eberhard, 1974). Cults often use guilt and guilt-producing acts to ensure compliance. Any activity can be justified for the greater good of the cult, even the taking of a life. Strong culture firms often embrace strong codes of ethics and integrity that preclude illegal acts. While the potential for abuse from social control is always there, so too is the opportunity to promote a sense of common purpose and accomplishment of worthwhile or redeeming objectives.

But, while greater openness and honesty reduces the likelihood of people joining and supporting organizations with dangerous or unethical objectives, they do not ensure that the values and norms selected are ones that will contribute to the organization's strategic success. The strategic appropriateness of values and norms requires a consideration both of the content and process aspects of social control. If we apply advice from strategy researchers to the domain of organizational culture (e.g., Hamel & Prahalad, 1994), we suggest that remaining competitive requires that the strategic appropriateness of the values and norms are evaluated continuously in light of changing environmental circumstances. That is, the dynamic capabilities or core competencies of successful organizations may rest, in part, on norms that promote organizational learning and adaptability. Hewlett-Packard, for example, has changed over the past twenty years from an instrument company with over 50 autonomous divisions, to a minicomputer company with significant interorganizational coordination, to a network server and personal computer firm. Cultural norms that encourage autonomy and constant change have permitted HP to enter and withdraw from technologies and markets. Similar norms have also helped Johnson & Johnson reshape itself as the health care market has changed. Silicon Graphics refers to themselves as an "amoeba organization" which is constantly expanding and contracting with shifts in technology and markets. The CEO is explicit in attributing this adaptability to a culture characterized by norms of creativity, risk taking, and a willingness to accept failure.

One interesting question is whether there are conditions under which firms with strong cultures characterized by norms that are no longer strategically relevant will perform *less well* than firms with no agreement or intensity about values and norms. One could argue that the challenge in the former organization is to select appropriate norms and values and re-orient members' focus on these. If successful, this firm may have the potential to outperform the firm with the ambiguous culture, due to increased coordination and motivation among members. But, resistance to change can be considerable in such strong culture firms and introduce substantial lags in the organizations' ability to respond to major environmental shifts. The can be seen in the current plight of organizations as diverse as Sears, IBM, Siemens, and Nissan.

In weak culture organizations major environmental shifts may not reduce their performance as greatly as the misaligned strong culture firm if formal coordinating mechanisms are functioning, or if randomly generated ideas fit with current environmental demands. Future research might, for example, examine comparable firms within industries which vary in terms of the agreement and intensity of values and norms. It may be the case that the stronger the organizational culture, the more extreme performance is over time—that is, strong culture firms may perform either exceptionally well or exceptionally poorly—especially when faced with environmental discontinuities (Tushman & O'Reilly, 1996).

Another consideration is the extent to which adaptation can be built in to the content of norms and values. Strong cultures that embody norms of creativity, innovation, and change may be the most effective mechanisms for promoting organizational adaptability (e.g., Amabile et al., 1986; Caldwell & O'Reilly, 1995). Firms like Intel, 3M, Rubbermaid, and Procter & Gamble deliberately reinforce norms that encourage employees to constantly challenge the status quo. Kotter and Heskett (1992) offer evidence that strong cultures that have as defining norms innovation and change are associated with long-term success. Also, while the tendency is to think of conformity as homogeneity, there can be strong norms encouraging nonconformity. A lack of social control may eventually lead to the predominance of formal control systems, which, as we have shown, can create problems of their own. Thus it seems that complete heterogeneity in attitudes and beliefs is no more of a key to success than is blind conformity.

On the other hand, norms and values for creativity and innovation may not be enough to break through the potential inertia, stagnation, and habitual behavior that can emerge in strong culture firms. The dark side to strong social control is the potential to disempower people through excessive conformity which can characterize a strong normative order. Some authors have worried that these systems may stifle freedom and creativity (e.g. Martin, 1992; Nemeth & Staw, 1989). Others have noted that strong cultures may become inertial and make adaptation and change difficult (e.g., Harrison & Carroll, 1991). As we described, one of the key problems of the social control process is the progressive difficulty members may have in disagreeing or even recognizing logical inconsistencies or sub-optimalities once they have committed to adhere to the organization's values publicly and with the encouragement of valued coworkers. This can lead to arrogance and inertia that sometimes is seen in strong culture firms.

Given the higher level of ideological and social investment members make, one wonders just how far they will stray from characteristic ways of doing things (e.g., the "H-P Way") even when innovation is encouraged. That is, innovation may be encouraged in strong culture firms but stricter norms may exist to differentiate between new ideas characterized as innovative and those characterized as inappropriate due to a lack of alignment with the way things are currently done. These norms may serve to filter out all but the most incremental and non-threatening of innovations. Research may investigate differences in rates of generating innovative products and services between strong culture firms emphasizing innovation, creativity, and being unconventional, strong culture firms which focus on other values, and firms characterized by more disagreement and a lack of intensity about norms and values (implying that everyone is unconventional). For example, strong culture firms may quash potentially viable ideas viewed as inappropriate sooner in the development phase, but support innovations viewed as appropriate at a higher level than firms without strong values for innovation or non-conformity. Further, the magnitude of environmental shifts may moderate the relationship between culture strength and successful innovation. In fairly static industries or periods, strong culture firms may appear most innovative, as members are highly motivated to come up with new solutions to new challenges and opportunities. But in highly dynamic industries or periods, the strong culture firm members may be constrained in their ability to introduce highly divergent ideas. In contrast, in firms with disagreement about values and norms, conflicting groups may be able to come up with widely diverging ideas which reduce (or fail to enhance) performance during stable periods, but may have the potential of adapting to massive environmental shifts.

Organizational researchers and managers would agree that there is merit in developing values and norms which are ethical, redeeming, and strategically appropriate, and applying social control mechanisms which fulfill people's desire to be a part of valuable causes or efforts. But, the mechanisms of social control can also be exploited causing people to become so committed that they loose sight of other ways of doing things. Regardless of whether it is a cult or a firm, more control is often perceived by those under social control as *less*, and this is the ultimate dilemma—social control potentially threatens individual freedom. The challenge for organizations is to maintain the delicate balance between making organizational membership fulfilling, and intensely controlling thoughts and actions. Research that provides greater understanding into the operation of culture as a social control system, and the circumstances in which it is empowering or disempowering, is critical (e.g., Harrison & Carroll, 1991; Lazear, 1994).

NOTES

1. Although having a strong culture and being adaptive may appear contradictory, a firm that has a strong culture consisting of norms such as creativity, trying new things, and paying attention to all constituencies, may allow it to meet changing environmental demands. Later in this paper we discuss the likelihood of and limits to this argument in terms of massive environmental shifts that may disadvantage firms with strong cultures.

2. Strong situations have been defined as those in which everyone construes the situation similarly, uniform expectancies regarding appropriate response patterns are induced, adequate incentives for the performance of that response pattern are provided, and everyone has learned the skills required to perform appropriately (Mischel, 1977).

3. While these examples illustrate the side of social control that can enhance organizational performance, the same process can also lead to the development of a culture that may no longer be strategically appropriate. This can make necessary changes in structure and process more difficult and put the organization at risk, as in the cases of Kodak, IBM, Sears, Philips, and General Motors (Tushman & O'Reilly, 1996).

REFERENCES

Abegglen, J., & Stalk, G. (1985). *Kaisha: The Japanese corporation.* New York: Basic Books.
Adler, P. (1993). The learning bureaucracy: New United Motors Manufacturing, Inc. In B. Staw & L. Cummings (Eds.), *Research in organizational behavior* (Vol. 15, pp. 111-194). Greenwich, CT: JAI Press.
Administrative Science Quarterly. (1983). Special Issue: Organizational culture, *38*(December), p. 28.

Amabile, T., Hennessey, B., & Grossman, B. (1986). Social influence on creativity: The effects of contracted-for reward. *Journal of Personality and Social Psychology, 50*, 14-23.
Appel, W. (1983). *Cults in America: Programmed for paradise*. New York: Holt, Rinehart and Winston.
Ashforth, B., & Mael, F. (1989). Social identity theory and the organization. *Academy of Management Review, 14*, 20-39.
Baer, D., & Stolz, S. (1978). A description of the Erhard Seminar Training (*est*) in terms of behavior analysis. *Behaviorism, 6*, 45-70.
Bainbridge, W. (1978). *Satan's power: A deviant psychotherapy cult*. Berkeley: University of California Press.
Bainbridge, W., & Stark, R. (1980). Scientology: To be perfectly clear. *Sociological Analysis, 41*, 128-136.
Balch, R., & Taylor, D. (1977). Seekers and saucers: The role of the cultic milieu in joining a UFO cult. In J. Richardson (Ed.), *Conversion careers: In and out of new religions* (pp. 43-64). Beverly Hills, CA: Sage.
Barker, E. (1984). *The making of a Moonie: Choice or brainwashing?* Oxford: Basil Blackwell.
Barker, M. (1987, January). The xenophobic Mormon. *Sunstone*, pp. 26-30.
Barnard, C. (1938). *The functions of the executive*. Cambridge, MA: Harvard University Press.
Barney, J. (1986). Organizational culture: Can it be a source of sustained competitive advantage? *Academy of Management Review, 11*, 656-665.
Barrick, M.R., & Mount, M.K. (1991). The Big Five personality dimensions and job performance: A meta-analysis. *Personnel Psychology, 44*, 1-26.
Bazerman, M.H. (1994). *Judgment in managerial decision making* (3rd ed.). New York: John Wiley & Sons Inc.
Behar, R. (1991, May 6). The thriving cult of greed and power. *Time*, pp. 50-57.
Bellah, R., Madsen, R., Sullivan, W., Swidler, A., & Tipton, S. (1985). *Habits of the heart: Individualism and commitment in American life*. Berkeley: University of California Press.
Berger, P. & Luckmann, T. (1967). *The social construction of reality*. New York: Doubleday.
Bettenhausen, K.L., & Murnighan, J.K. (1985). The emergence of norms in competitive decision making groups. *Administrative Science Quarterly, 30*, 350-372.
Bettenhausen, K.L., & Murnighan, J.K. (1991). The development of an intragroup norm and the effects of interpersonal and structural challenges. *Administrative Science Quarterly, 36*, 20-35.
Biggart, N.W. (1989). *Charismatic capitalism: Direct selling organizations in America*. Chicago: University of Chicago Press.
Bordin, E.S. (1979). Fusing work and play: A challenge to theory and research. *Academic Psychology Bulletin, 1*, 5-9.
Bowen, D.E., Ledford, G.E., & Nathan, B.R. (1991). Hiring for the organization, not the job. *Academy of Management Executive, 5*, 22-34.
Bowen, D., & Schneider, B. (1988). Services marketing and management: Implications for organizational behavior. In B.M. Staw & L.L Cummings (Eds.), *Research in organizational behavior* (Vol. 10, pp. 43-80). Greenwich, CT: JAI Press.
Brannen, M.Y. (1992). "Bwana Mickey": Constructing cultural consumption at Tokyo Disneyland. In J.J. Tobin (Ed.), *Re-Made in Japan* (pp. 216-234). New Haven, CT: Yale University Press.
Brannen, M.Y. (1993). *Organizational culture revisited: A theoretical contribution from the Japanese/American organizational experience*. Working paper, School of Business, University of Michigan, Ann Arbor.
Brehm, J.W. (1972). *Responses to loss of freedom: A Theory of psychological reactance*. Morristown, NJ: General Learning Press.
Brewer, M. (1979). In-group bias in the minimal intergroup situation: A cognitive-motivational analysis. *Psychological Bulletin, 86*, 393-400.

Bromley, D., & Shupe, A. (1979). *Moonies in America: Cult, church and crusade.* Beverly Hills, CA: Sage.
Caldwell, D., Chatman, J., & O'Reilly, C. (1990). Building organizational commitment: A multi-firm study. *Journal of Occupational Psychology, 63,* 245-261.
Caldwell, D., & O'Reilly, C. (1990). Measuring person-job fit with a profile comparison process. *Journal of Applied Psychology, 75,* 649-657.
Caldwell, D., & O'Reilly, C. (1995). *Promoting team-based innovation in organizations: The role of normative influence.* Paper presented at the Fifty-Fourth Annual Meetings of the Academy of Management.
Chatman, J.A. (1991). Matching people and organizations: Selection and socialization in public accounting firms. *Administrative Science Quarterly, 36,* 459-484.
Chatman, J.A., Bell, N.E., & Staw, B.M. (1986). The managed thought: The role of self-justification and impression management in organizational settings. In D. Gioia & H. Sims (Eds.), *The thinking organization: Dynamics of social cognition* (pp. 191-214). San Francisco: Jossey-Bass.
Chatman, J.A., & Jehn, K.A. (1994). Assessing the relationship between industry characteristics and organizational culture: How different can you be? *Academy of Management Journal, 37,* 522-553.
Chidester, D. (1988). *Salvation and suicide: An interpretation of Jim Jones, the Peoples Temple, and Jonestown.* Bloomington: University of Indiana Press.
Cialdini, R. (1993). *Influence: Science and practice.* New York: Harper Collins College Publishers.
Cialdini, R., Kallgren, C., & Reno, R. (1991). A focus theory of normative conduct: A theoretical refinement and reevaluation of the role of norms in human behavior. *Advances in Experimental Social Psychology, 24,* 201-234.
Clark, R. (1979). *The Japanese company.* New Haven, CT: Yale University Press.
Cohen, M.D., & March, J.G. (1974). *Leadership and ambiguity* (2nd ed.). Boston, MA: Harvard University Press.
Collins, J., & Porras, J. (1994). *Built to last: Successful habits of visionary companies.* New York: Harper-Business.
Comer, R., & Laird, J. (1975). Choosing to suffer as a consequence of expecting to suffer: Why do people do it? *Journal of Personality and Social Psychology, 32,* 92-101.
Cordova, D., & Lepper, M. (1991). *The effects of intrinsic versus extrinsic rewards on the concept attainment process: An attributional approach.* Unpublished manuscript, Stanford University.
Cremer, J. (1993). Corporate culture and shared knowledge. *Industrial and Corporate Change, 3,* 351-386.
Dansereau, F., & Alutto, J. (1990). Level-of-analysis issues in climate and culture research. In B. Schneider (Ed.), *Organizational climate and culture* (pp. 193-236). San Francisco: Jossey-Bass.
Davis, S. (1984). *Managing corporate culture.* Cambridge, MA: Ballinger.
Davis-Blake, A., & Pfeffer, J. (1989). Just a mirage: The search for dispositional effects in organizational research. *Academy of Management Review, 14,* 385-400.
Deal, T., & Kennedy, A. (1982). *Corporate cultures: The rites and rituals of corporate life.* Reading, MA: Addison-Wesley.
Deci, E.L. (1971). Effects of externally mediated rewards on intrinsic motivation. *Journal of Personality and Social Psychology, 18*(1), 105-115.
Deci, E.L., & Ryan, R.M. (1980). The empirical exploration of intrinsic motivational processes. In L. Berkowitz (Ed.), *Advances in experimental social psychology* (Vol. 13, pp. 39-79). San Diego, CA: Academic Press.
Denison, D. (1990). *Corporate culture and organizational effectiveness.* New York: John Wiley.

Deutsch, M., & Gerard, H. (1955). A study of normative and informational social influences on individual judgment. *Journal of Abnormal and Social Psychology, 51,* 629-636.

Donkin, R. (1994, May 9). Rover's cultural revolution. *Financial Times,* p. 12.

Dornbusch, S., & Scott, W.R. (1975). *Evaluation and the exercise of authority.* San Francisco: Jossey-Bass.

Ebaugh, H. (1977). *Out of the cloister: A study of organizational dilemmas.* Austin: University of Texas Press.

Eberhard, E. (1974, June). How to share the gospel: A step-by-step approach for you and your neighbors. *Ensign,* pp. 6-11.

Enz, C. (1988). The role of value congruity in intraorganizational power. *Administrative Science Quarterly, 33,* 284-304.

Etzioni, A. (1964). *Modern organizations.* Englewood Cliffs, NJ: Prentice-Hall.

Finkelstein, P., Wenegrat, B., & Yalom, I. (1982). Large group awareness training. *Annual Review of Psychology, 33,* 515-539.

Foster, R. (1986). *Innovation: The attacker's advantage.* New York: Summit Books.

Frost, P.J., Moore, L.F., Louis, M.R., Lundberg, C.C., & Martin, J. (1985). *Organizational culture.* Beverly Hills, CA: Sage Publications.

Galanter, M. (1989). *Cults: Faith, healing and coercion.* New York: Oxford University Press.

Gordon, G. (1991). Industry determinants of organizational culture. *Academy of Management Review, 16,* 396-415.

Gordon, G., & DiTomaso, N. (1992). Predicting performance from organizational culture. *Journal of Management Studies, 29,* 783-798.

Gordon, J. (1987). *The golden guru: The strange journey of Bhagwan Shree Rajneesh.* Lexington, MA: Stephen Greene Press.

Greenberger, D.B., & Strasser, S. (1991). The role of situational and dispositional factors in the enhancement of personal control in organizations. In L.L. Cummings & B.M. Staw (Eds.), *Research in organizational behavior* (Vol. 13, pp. 25-51). Greenwich, CT: JAI Press.

Halaby, C.N. (1986). Worker attachment and workplace authority. *American Sociological Review, 51,* 634-649.

Hampden-Turner, C., & Trompenaars, A. (1993). *The seven cultures of capitalism.* New York: Currency Doubleday.

Harackiewicz, J.M., & Larson, J.R. (1986). Managing motivation: The impact of supervisor feedback on subordinate task interest. *Journal of Personality and Social Psychology, 51,* 547-556.

Harrison, J.R., & Carroll, G. (1991). Keeping the faith: A model of cultural transmission in formal organizations. *Administrative Science Quarterly, 36,* 552-582.

Hays, L. (1994, May 13). Gerstner is struggling as he tries to change ingrained IBM culture. *Wall Street Journal,* p. 1.

Heinerman, J., & Shupe, A. (1986). *The Mormon corporate empire.* Boston: Beacon Press.

Heirich, M. (1977). Change of heart: A test of some widely held theories about religious conversion. *American Journal of Sociology, 83,* 653-680.

Heller, J.F., Pallak, M.S., & Picek, J.M. (1973). The interactive effects of intent and threat on boomerang attitude change. *Journal of Personality and Social Psychology, 26,* 273-279.

Hofstede, G. (1991). *Cultures and organizations.* New York: McGraw-Hill.

Holland, J. (1976). Vocational preferences. In M. Dunnette (Ed.), *Handbook of organizational and industrial psychology* (pp. 521-570). Chicago: Rand-McNally.

Jackson, D.N., Peacock, A.C., & Holden, R.R. (1982). Professional interviewers' trait inferential structures for diverse occupational groups. *Organizational Behavior and Human Performance, 29,* 1-20.

Jackson, J. (1966). A conceptual and measurement model for norms and roles. *Pacific Sociological Review, 9,* 35-47.

Janis, I.J., & Mann, L. (1977). *Decision making: A psychological analysis of conflict, choice, and commitment.* New York: Free Press.

Kanter, R.M. (1972). *Commitment and community: Communes and utopias in sociological perspective.* Cambridge, MA: Harvard University Press.

Karpf, R.J. (1978). Altering values via psychological reactance and reversal effects. *Journal of Social Psychology, 106,* 131-134.

Kerr, C. (1975). On the folly of rewarding A while hoping for B. *Academy of Management Journal, 18.*

Kotter, J.P., & Heskett, J.L. (1992) *Corporate culture and performance.* New York: Free Press.

Krafcik, J. (1986). *International motor vehicle program.* Working paper, Sloan School of Management, MIT.

Kreps, D. (1986). Corporate culture and economic theory. In M. Tsuchiya (Ed.), *Technology, innovation, and business strategy.* Tokyo: Nippon Keizai Shumbunsha Press.

Labich, K. (1994, May 2). Is Herb Kelleher America's best CEO? *Fortune,* 44-52.

Lang, K., & Lang, G. (1961). *Collective dynamics.* New York: Crowell.

Latane, B., & Darley, J.M. (1968). Group inhibition of bystander intervention in emergencies. *Journal of Personality and Social Psychology, 10,* 215-221.

Lazear, E. (1994). *Corporate culture and the diffusion of values.* Working paper, Graduate School of Business, Stanford University (April).

Lee, H. (1972). *Ensign,* October.

Lepper, M.R., Greene, D., & Nisbett, R.E. (1973). Undermining children's intrinsic interest with extrinsic rewards: A test of the "overjustification" hypothesis. *Journal of Personality and Social Psychology, 28,* 129-137.

Lindsey, R. (1986, January 12). The Mormons: Growth, prosperity and controversy. *The New York Times Magazine,* pp. 19-46.

Lofland, J. (1977). Becoming a world-saver revisited. *American Behavioral Scientist, 20,* 805-818.

Lofland, J., & Stark, R. (1965). Becoming a world-saver: A theory of conversion to a deviant perspective. *American Sociological Review, 30,* 862-875.

Long, T., & Hadden, J. (1983). Religious conversion and the concept of socialization: Integrating the brainwashing and drift models. *Journal for the Scientific Study of Religion, 22,* 1-14.

Louis, M.R. (1985). An investigator's guide to workplace culture. In P.J. Frost, L.F. Moore, M.R. Louis, C.C. Lundberg, & J. Martin (Eds.), *Organizational culture.* Newbury Park, CA: Sage.

Louis, M.R. (1990). Acculturation in the workplace: Newcomers as lay ethnographers. In B. Schneider (Ed.), *Organizational climate and culture* (pp. 85-129). San Francisco: Jossey-Bass.

Lynch, F. (1977). Toward a theory of conversion and commitment to the occult. *American Behavioral Scientist, 20,* 887-.

Martin, J. (1992). *Cultures in organizations: Three perspectives.* New York: Oxford University Press.

Maslow, A. (1943). A theory of human motivation. *Psychological Review, 50,* 370-396.

McClelland, D.C., & Boyatzis, R.E. (1982). Leadership motive pattern and long term success in management. *Journal of Applied Psychology, 67,* 737-743.

McGaw, D. (1979). Commitment and religious community: A comparison of a charismatic and a mainline congregation. *Journal for the Scientific Study of Religion, 18,* 146-163.

Merkl, P. (1980). *The making of a stormtrooper.* Princeton, NJ: Princeton University Press.

Milgram, S. (1964). *Obedience to authority.* New York: Harper.

Mills, J. (1979). *Six years with god: Life inside Reverend Jim Jones's People's Temple.* New York: Addison & Wesley.

Mischel, W. (1977). The interaction of person and situation. In D. Magnusson & N.S. Endler (Eds.)., *Personality at the crossroads: Current issues in interactional psychology* (pp. 333-352). Hillsdale, NJ: Erlbaum.

Monson, T.C., Hesley, J.W., & Chernick, L. (1982). Specifying when personality traits can and cannot predict behavior: An alternative to abandoning the attempt to predict single-act criteria. *Journal of Personality and Social Psychology, 43,* 385-399.

Moreland, R. (1985). Social categorization and the assimilation of "new" group members. *Journal of Personality and Social Psychology, 48,* 1173-1190.

Morrison, E. (1993a). Longitudinal study of the effects of information seeking on newcomer socialization. *Journal of Applied Psychology, 78,* 173-183.

Morrison, E. (1993b). Newcomer information seeking: Exploring types, modes, sources, and outcomes. *Academy of Management Journal, 36,* 557-589.

Nemeth, C., & Staw, B. (1989). The tradeoff of social control and innovation in groups and organizations. *Advances in Experimental Social Psychology, 22,* 175-210.

Newcomb, T.M. (1943). *Personality and social change.* New York: Dryden.

Ofshe, R. (1980). The social development of the Synanon cult: The managerial strategy of organizational transformation. *Sociological Analysis, 41,* 109-127.

Ofshe, R. (1992). Coercive persuasion and attitude change. In E. Borgatta & M. Borgatta (Eds.). *Encyclopedia of sociology* (pp. 212-224). New York: MacMillan.

O'Reilly, C. (1989). Corporations, culture and commitment: Motivation and social control in organizations. *California Management Review, 31,* 9-25.

O'Reilly, C., & Chatman, J. (1986). Organizational commitment and psychological attachment: The effects of compliance, identification, and internalization on prosocial behavior. *Journal of Applied Psychology, 71,* 492-499.

O'Reilly, C., & Chatman, J. (1994). Working smarter and harder: A longitudinal study of managerial success. *Administrative Science Quarterly, 39,* 603-627.

O'Reilly, C., Chatman, J., & Caldwell, D. (1991). People and organizational culture: A profile comparison approach to assessing person-organization fit. *Academy of Management Journal, 34,* 487-516.

Ott, J.S. (1989) *The organizational culture perspective.* Pacific Grove, CA: Brooks/Cole.

Ouchi, W. (1979). A conceptual framework for the design of organizational control mechanisms. *Management Science, 25,* 833-848.

Pallak, M., Cook, D., & Sullivan, J. (1980). Commitment and energy conservation. *Applied Social Psychology Annual, 1,* 235-253.

Parsons, T. (1960). *Structure and process in modern societies.* Glencoe, IL: Free Press.

Pascale, R. (1990). *Managing on the edge.* New York: Simon and Schuster.

Perrucci, R. (1994). *Japanese auto transplants in the heartland.* New York: Aldine De Gruyter.

Peterson, K.D. (1984). Mechanisms of administrative control over managers in educational organizations. *Administrative Science Quarterly, 29,* 573-597.

Pettigrew, A. (1990). Conclusion: Organizational climate and culture: Two constructs in search of a role. In B. Schneider (Ed.), *Organizational climate and culture* (pp. 413-434). San Francisco: Jossey-Bass.

Petty, R.E., & Cacioppo, J.T. (1979). Effects of forewarning of persuasive intent and involvement on cognitive responses and persuasion. *Personality and Social Psychology Bulletin, 5,* 173-176.

Pfeffer, J. (1981). Management as symbolic action: The creation and maintenance of organizational paradigms. In L.L. Cummings & B.M. Staw (Eds.), *Research in organizational behavior* (Vol. 3, pp. 1-52). Greenwich CT: JAI Press.

Pfeffer, J. (1994). *Competitive advantage through people.* Boston, MA: Harvard Business School Press.

Pietromonaco, P., & Nisbett, R. (1982). Swimming upstream against the fundamental attribution error: Subjects' weak generalizations from the Darley and Batson study. *Social Behavior and Personality, 10,* 1-4.

Pinder, C.C. (1977). Concerning the application of human motivation theories in organizational settings. *Academy of Management Review, 2,* 384-397.
Powys, J.C. (1974). *The meaning of culture.* Westport, CT: Greenwood Press.
Reichers, A., & Schneider, B. (1990). Climate and culture: An evolution of constructs. In B. Schneider (Ed.), *Organizational climate and culture* (pp. 5-39). San Francisco: Jossey-Bass.
Rochford, E. (1982). Recruitment strategies, ideology, and organization in the Hare Krishna movement. *Social Problems, 29.*
Ross, L. (1977). The intuitive psychologist and his shortcomings. In L. Berkowitz (Ed.), *Advances in experimental social psychology* (Vol. 10). New York: Academic Press.
Ross, L., & Nisbett, R. (1991). *The person and the situation: Perspectives of social psychology.* New York: McGraw-Hill.
Rothstein, M., & Jackson, D.N. (1981). Decision-making in the employment interview: An experimental approach. *Journal of Applied Psychology, 65,* 271-283.
Rousseau, D. (1990). Quantitative assessment of organizational culture: The case for multiple measures. In B. Schneider (Ed.), *Organizational climate and culture* (pp. 153-192). San Francisco: Jossey-Bass.
Rushton, J., & Campbell, A. (1977). Modelling vicarious reinforcement and extroversion on blood donating in adults: Immediate and long term results. *European Journal of Social Psychology, 7,* 297-306.
Rynes, S.L., & Boudreau, J.W. (1986). College recruiting in large organizations: Practice, evaluation, and research implications. *Personnel Psychology, 39,* 729-757.
Sabini, J., & Silver, M. (1980). Destroying the innocent with a clear conscience: A sociopsychology of the Holocaust. In J. Dimsdale (Ed.), *Survivors, victims, and perpetrators* (pp. 329-358). New York: Hemisphere Publishing.
Sackmann, S. (1992). Culture and subcultures: An analysis of organizational knowledge. *Administrative Science Quarterly, 37,* 140-161.
Saffold, G. (1988). Culture traits, strength, and organizational performance: Moving beyond "strong" culture. *Academy of Management Review, 13,* 546-558.
Salancik, G. (1977). Commitment and the control of organizational behavior and belief. In B. Staw & G. Salancik (Eds.), *New directions in organizational behavior* (pp. 1-21). Chicago: St. Clair Press.
Sandelands, L.E. (1988). Effects of work and play signals on task evaluation. *Journal of Applied Social Psychology, 18,* 1032-1048.
Sandelands, L.E., Glynn, M.A., & Larson, J.R. Jr. (1991). Control theory and social behavior in the workplace. *Human Relations, 44,* 1107-1130.
Schein, E. (1961). *Coercive persuasion.* New York: Norton.
Schein, E. (1985). *Organizational culture and leadership.* San Francisco: Jossey-Bass.
Schlenker, B. (1982). Translating actions into attitudes: An identity-analytic approach to the explanation of social conduct. In L. Berkowitz (Ed.), *Advances in experimental social psychology* (Vol. 15). Orlando, FL: Academic Press.
Schneider, B. (1987). The people make the place. *Personnel Psychology, 14,* 437-453.
Schneider, B. (Ed). (1990). *Organizational climate and culture.* San Francisco, CA: Jossey-Bass.
Schwartz, H., & Davis, S. (1981). Matching corporate culture and business strategy. *Organizational Dynamics,* 30-48.
Schwartz, S. (1970). Elicitation of moral obligation and self-sacrificing behavior: An experimental study of volunteering to be a bone marrow donor. *Journal of Personality and Social Psychology, 15,* 283-293.
Scott, R. (1969). Professional employees in a bureaucratic structure: Social work. In A. Etzioni (Ed.), *The semi-professions and their organization* (pp. 82-144). New York: Free Press.
Siehl, C., & Martin, J. (1990). Organizational culture: A key to financial performance? In B. Schneider (Ed.), *Organizational climate and culture* (pp. 241-281. San Francisco, CA: Jossey-Bass.

Simon, H.A. (1976). *Administrative behavior* (3rd ed.). New York: The Free Press.

Smircich, L. (1983). Concepts of culture and organizational analysis. *Administrative Science Quarterly, 28,* 339-359.

Stark, R. (1971). Psychopathology and religious commitment. *Review of Religious Research, 12,* 165-175.

Staw, B., Bell, N., & Clausen, J. (1986). The dispositional approach to job attitudes: A lifetime longitudinal test. *Administrative Science Quarterly, 31,* 56-77.

Staw, B.M., & Boettger, R.D. (1990). Task revision: A neglected form of work performance. *Academy of Management Journal, 33,* 534-559.

Steele, C. (1988). The psychology of self-affirmation: Sustaining the integrity of the self. In L. Berkowitz (Ed.), *Advances in experimental social psychology* (Vol. 21). New York: Academic Press.

Steiner, J. (1980). The SS yesterday and today: A sociopsychological view. In J. Dimsdale (Ed.), *Survivors, victims and perpetrators* (pp. 405-445). New York: Hemisphere Publishing.

Swidler, A. (1986). Culture in action: Symbols and strategies. *American Sociological Review, 51,* 273-286.

Tang, T.L., & Baumeister, R.F. (1984). Effects of personal values, perceived surveillance, and task labels on task preference: The ideology of turning play into work. *Journal of Applied Psychology, 69,* 99-105.

Tesser, A., Campbell, J., & Mickler, S. (1983). The role of social pressure, attention to the stimulus, and self-doubt in conformity. *European Journal of Social Psychology, 13,* 217-233.

Thompson, K., & Luthans, F. (1990). Organizational culture: A behavioral perspective. In B. Schneider (Ed.), *Organizational climate and culture* (pp. 319-344). San Francisco: Jossey-Bass.

Tom, V. (1971). The role of personality and organizational images in the recruiting process. *Organizational Behavior and Human Performance, 6,* 573-592.

Trice, H., & Beyer, J. (1993). *The cultures of work organizations.* Englewood Cliffs, NJ: Prentice-Hall.

Tsui, A., & O'Reilly, C. (1989). Beyond simple demographic effects: The importance of relational demography in superior-subordinate dyads. *Academy of Management Journal, 32,* 402-423.

Tushman, M., & O'Reilly, C. (1996). *Staying on top: Managing strategic innovation and change for long-term success.* Boston: Harvard Business School Press.

Tversky, A., & Kahneman, D. (1974). Judgement under uncertainty: Heuristics and biases. *Science, 185,* 1124-1131.

Van Maanen, J. (1976). Breaking-in: Socialization to work. In R. Dubin (Ed.), *Handbook of work, organization, and society* (pp. 67-130). Chicago: Rand McNally & Co.

Van Maanen, J. (1991). The smile factory: Work at Disneyland. In P.J. Frost, L.F. Moore, M.R. Louis, C.C. Lundberg, & J. Martin (Eds.), *Reframing organizational culture.* Newbury Park, CA: Sage.

Van Maanen, J., & Barley, S. (1984). Occupational communities: Culture and control in organizations. In B. Staw & L. Cummings (Eds.), *Research in organizational behavior* (Vol. 6). Greenwich, CT: JAI Press.

Van Maanen, J., & Schein, E. (1979). Toward a theory of organizational socialization. In B. Staw (Ed.) *Research in organizational behavior* (Vol. 1, pp. 75-86). Greenwich, CT: JAI Press.

Walton, R. (1985). From control to commitment in the workplace. *Harvard Business Review, 64,* 77-84.

Weber, M. (1947). *The theory of social economic organization.* A. Henderson & T. Parsons (Eds.). Glencoe, IL: Free Press.

Weiner, Y. (1988). Forms of value systems: A focus on organizational effectiveness and cultural change and maintenance. *Academy of Management Review, 13,* 534-545.

Weiss, H., & Adler, S. (1984). Personality and organizational behavior. In B.M. Staw & L.L. Cummings (Eds.), *Research in organizational behavior* (Vol. 6, pp. 1-50). Greenwich, CT: JAI Press.

Wenegrat, B. (1989). Religious cult membership: A sociobiologic model. In M. Galanter (Ed.), *Cults and new religious movements: A report of the American Psychiatric Association* (pp. 193-208). Washington, DC: American Psychiatric Press.

Wilkins, A., & Ouchi, W. (1983). Efficient cultures: Exploring the relationship between culture and organizational performance. *Administrative Science Quarterly, 28,* 468-481.

Williamson, O. (1975). *Markets and hierarchies.* New York: Free Press.

Wilson, B.R. (1959). An analysis of sect development. *American Sociological Review, 24,* 3-15.

Womak, J., Jones, D., & Roos, D. (1990). *The machine that changed the world.* New York: Harper-Collins.

Worchel, S., & Brehm, J.W. (1971). Direct and implied social restoration of freedom. *Journal of Personality and Social Psychology, 18,* 294-304.

Wright, J., & Mischel, W. (1987). A conditional approach to dispositional constructs: The local predictability of social behavior. *Journal of Personality and Social Psychology, 53,* 1159-1177.

Zucker, L. (1977). The role of institutionalization in cultural persistence. *American Sociological Review, 42,* 726-743.

CONSEQUENCES OF PUBLIC SCRUTINY FOR LEADERS AND THEIR ORGANIZATIONS

Robert I. Sutton and D. Charles Galunic

ABSTRACT

Much research emphasizes that leaders and organizations that are noticed by and please others will be rewarded with power, legitimacy, and resources. This literature implies that leaders, and others in symbolic roles, must work under close scrutiny if they wish to garner such rewards for themselves and their organizations. Yet little theory or research considers the consequences of such scrutiny. This paper lays groundwork for research on public scrutiny by defining it, specifying its consequences, and identifying defenses that may reduce its negative consequences. This intense and intrusive form of attention is characterized by a blend of persistent attention to the leader or organization, close and persistent performance monitoring and evaluation, frequent interruptions, and relentless questions about past, current, and future actions. Consequences for leaders and their organizations include: (1) delays in ongoing tasks; (2) attention and effort devoted toward symbolic activities, away from other kinds of activities; (3) greater adherence to injunctive norms, less adherence to descriptive norms; (4) attention and effort focused on well-rehearsed acts, away from acts that require learning or creativity; and (5) greater perseverance at ongoing and planned activities. We identify interpersonal, procedural, and structural defenses that leaders and organizations use to reduce scrutiny and its negative consequences. We then consider the limitations and drawbacks of such defenses. Finally, we suggest directions that future work on scrutiny might take.

Much research emphasizes that whether leaders and their organizations flourish or fail depends on their ability to attract and manipulate public attention. This scholarly research reflects the popular view that image is crucial to organizational success and that leaders are responsible for "imparting positive spin." But the public spotlight is a double-edged sword. The same public attention that leaders draw on to shape and mold their organizational or personal images can become a harsh and intrusive spotlight with unintended, and often harmful, consequences.

Consider CEO John Mars and his highly successful Mars Company. Reporters, financial analysts, academics, and competitors are constantly trying to break through the wall of secrecy erected by the publicity shy Mr. Mars and other Mars executives, partly to understand why this candy company is so successful (Brenner, 1992). This scrutiny ranges from constant attempts to arrange unwanted press conferences, to conversations with Mars family neighbors, to spying on the Mars home. Organizational research has much to say about the explanations, structures, and procedures that John Mars should use to please various constituencies. But it has little to say about how John Mars, other Mars executives, or the Mars company will be affected by such persistent and intrusive attention. Important questions that are left largely unanswered include: What are the elements of public scrutiny and how are they experienced by leaders and their organizations? What cognitive and emotional responses are triggered by such scrutiny? What are the consequences for leaders and their organizations? What sort of defenses are available against scrutiny?

This paper takes initial steps toward answering these questions. Our review indicates that there has not been a prior attempt to develop such a perspective. Most related literature emphasizes the need for leaders and their organizations to attract and manipulate public attention in order to be successful, not public scrutiny per se. This broad literature has been labeled the symbolic perspective (Pfeffer, 1981). Symbolic research that draws on psychological theory (e.g., Tedeschi, 1981) considers the verbal accounts that leaders use to enhance their organizations' reputations (Ginzel, Kramer, & Sutton, 1993; Staw, McKechnie, & Puffer, 1983). Macro sociological work considers how structures and procedures are used to acquire organizational legitimacy rather than to achieve technical efficiency (Meyer & Rowan, 1977). Recent research has combined these psychological and sociological perspectives to explain how leaders use verbal accounts that refer to organizational structures and procedures (Elsbach, 1994). Other research uses economic theories on agency and signaling to examine stock market reactions to top managers' announcements during accidents, scandals, and product safety incidents (Marcus & Goodman, 1991). Despite varied nuances, these writings all convey that people and organizations that are noticed by, and please, their publics will garner legitimacy, power, and resources.

While symbolic research implies that most leaders, and other people in visible roles, carry out their responsibilities under close public scrutiny, this point is rarely made explicit. Yet observers must devote critical attention before they can be pleased (or offended) by a person or organization. Little research considers the consequences enjoyed or suffered by leaders and organizations that face the bright, and sometimes harsh, spotlight of attention from others. Some aspects of this topic are addressed in the psychological, sociological, and organizational behavior literature, notably in Tetlock's (1985, 1991) work on accountability, Kanter's (1977, 1979) writings on life at the top of organizations, and Kramer's (1994, 1995) research on hostile scrutiny as one of the elements that brings about paranoia in leaders. We draw on this literature. We also draw on popular writings to ground our assertions. Finally, although we draw primarily on existing sources, we also use data from the six months we spent trying (and ultimately failing) to study race relations in a government agency that faced intense scrutiny[1] and from informal interviews with purveyors and targets of public scrutiny.[2]

This paper focuses on intense scrutiny, on defining it, describing its consequences, and identifying the defenses used to reduce its negative consequences. Figure 1 summarizes the preliminary perspective on the consequences of scrutiny developed in this paper. This perspective summarized in Figure 1 is not sufficiently refined to be described as a complete, integrated, or falsifiable theory. Rather, Figure 1, as with the rest of this paper, is an initial effort to sort and weave together what is known about public scrutiny so that complete, integrated, or falsifiable theory can be developed and tested in subsequent work.

This preliminary perspective reflects that, beyond the importance of being noticed and appreciated by others to obtain legitimacy and resources, leaders and organizations benefit in other ways from public scrutiny. We conclude that, on balance, however, unchecked scrutiny has greater negative than positive consequences. We suggest that scrutiny is an intensive and obtrusive form of attention from others, comprising: (1) persistent attention to the leader or his or her organization; (2) close and persistent performance monitoring and evaluation; (3) frequent interruptions; and (4) relentless questions about events that have occurred, are occurring, and will occur, along with requests that the reasons for such actions be explained. Our view is that, although elements of scrutiny have been examined in past empirical and conceptual work, this blend and its consequences have not been the subject of systematic theory development or testing.

We suggest that, if unchecked, these forces cause those under scrutiny to experience constant distraction punctuated by episodes of more pronounced interference with thought and action. These constant and intermittent pressures lead to cognitive overload, with attention focused on how the leader or organization will appear to others and how to explain such appearances. This

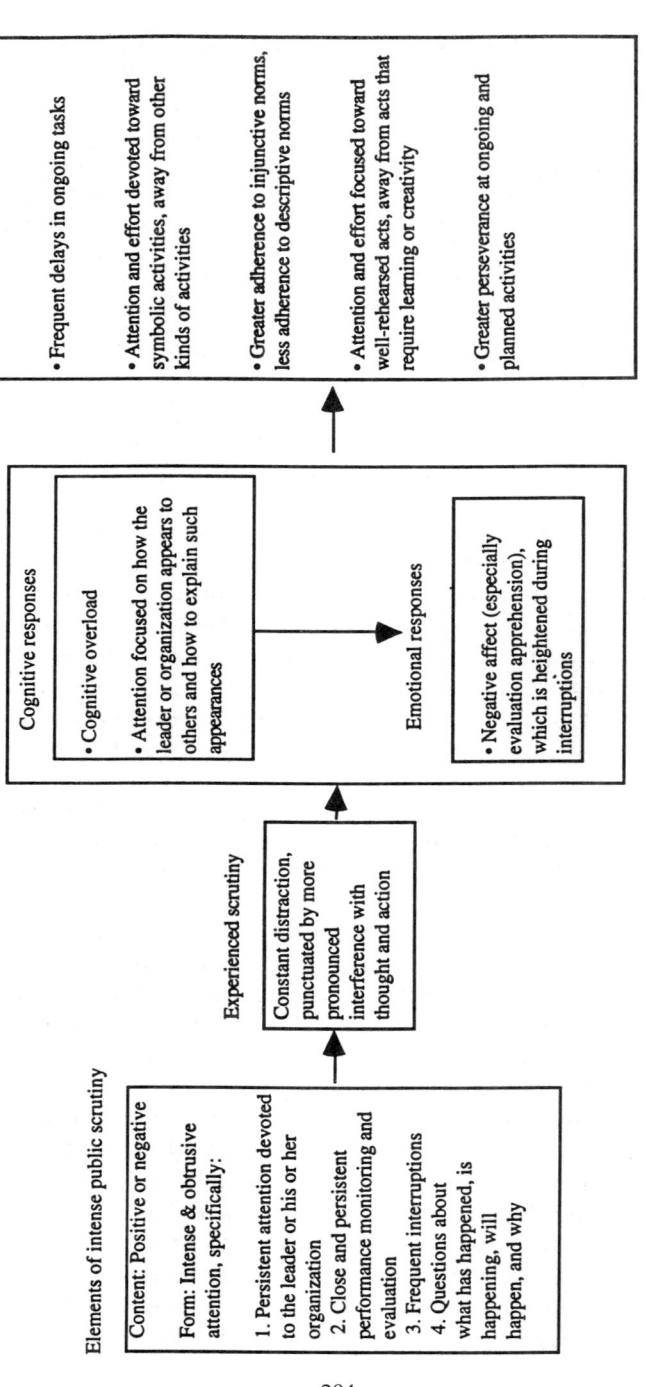

Figure 1. Consequences of Unchecked Public Scrutiny for Leaders and Their Organizations

overload is also proposed to cause negative affect (especially evaluation apprehension), which will be heightened during unwanted interruptions. Figure 1 lists five consequences of these psychological processes for leaders and their organizations that follow from some or all of these proposed intervening forces: (1) delays in ongoing tasks; (2) attention and effort devoted toward symbolic activities, away from other kinds of activities; (3) greater adherence to injunctive norms, less adherence to descriptive norms; (4) attention and effort focused on well-rehearsed acts, away from acts that require learning or creativity; and (5) greater perseverance at ongoing and planned activities.

This paper first explicates the framework outlined in Figure 1. We then identify interpersonal, procedural, and structural defenses against intense scrutiny. Next, we consider the drawbacks of such defenses, focusing on how these methods can create new problems for leaders and organizations. Finally, we discuss directions that future research on scrutiny might take.

ELEMENTS OF INTENSE PUBLIC SCRUTINY

Figure 1 indicates that the content of public scrutiny may be positive or negative from the perspective of a leader or organization. We consider the effects of positive versus negative scrutiny later in this paper. But we are more interested in the similarities than the differences between scrutiny that comes from historically hostile, supportive, or neutral sources, or that is generated by positive or negative features of the leader or organization. We found many important similarities, for example, in the content and the consequences of the scrutiny that leaders of the Wallace Company encountered after winning the prestigious Malcolm Baldridge quality award (Hill, 1993) and the scrutiny that leaders of General Motors encountered when they were accused of making low quality and obsolete cars (Yates, 1983).

As a result, this paper focuses more heavily on the form than the content of public scrutiny. Intense public scrutiny occurs during episodes (from minutes to years in duration) characterized by an intense and obtrusive form of attention from others. These episodes occur when there is something sufficiently novel, interesting, or important about the leader or organization to attract close attention and interference from observers and exchange partners. Various people or groups may help shine the spotlight including friends, enemies, customers, suppliers, stockholders, board members, regulators, internal revenue agents, competitors, superiors, coworkers, subordinates, the press and, in the case of widely recognized public figures such as entertainers, athletes, and politicians, the general public. Scrutiny takes place through numerous human and technological means. Interpersonal settings include one-on-one interactions, interactions with small groups, performances in front of live audiences, or covert observations. A variety of technologies can be used to help shine the spotlight, including tape recorders, cameras, and telephones.

Intense public scrutiny is present when top managers or other organization members face a relentless stream of persistent and curious people who use such interpersonal and technical means of intrusion. Scrutiny is related to but distinct from accountability (Tetlock, 1985, 1991). When a person is accountable, it means that he or she held responsible and is obligated to explain or justify something; when a person is scrutinized it means that he or she is examined closely and methodically, the subject of a "minute inquiry" (*The Random House Dictionary of the English Language*, second edition). Tetlock (1991) implies, but does not explicitly state, that real and imagined close examination by others is a consequence of being accountable, not accountability itself. Moreover, although leaders are often scrutinized closely because they are presumed to be accountable for the actions of their organizations, they may also be scrutinized for other reasons, for example, because they charming, funny, or beautiful.

So public scrutiny, as used here, refers to episodes where leaders and their organizations are examined in a close and obtrusive fashion. Moreover, the diverse evidence from popular and academic sources, as well as pertinent scholarly theory, we reviewed led us to view public scrutiny as a blend of unobtrusive and obtrusive actions that audience members take toward a leader or organization, not a single action. We propose that intense and unchecked public scrutiny is a blend of persistent attention, performance monitoring and evaluation, frequent interruptions, and questions from audience members. We explicate these four elements below.

Persistent Attention Devoted to the Leader or Organization

Leaders (and others in symbolic roles) often report that everything they say, write, and do is watched closely, and that little of what they say, write, or do is likely to stay private despite efforts to keep such information away from watchful constituencies. Leaders face such pressures because, as the people who symbolize what the organization means to both insiders and outsiders, every detail of their lives—both on and off the job—is subject to intense interest and careful observation. Kanter (1979, p. 35) asserts "Life at the top is life in a goldfish bowl, an existence in which all boundaries can be rendered transparent at the twitch of the public's curiosity. The room at the top is all windows."

Top administrators in the public agency we tried to study reported that the press, government officials, the courts, the union of minority employees, the union of (mostly) white employees, lawyers, consultants, and clerical employees watching and dissected their every move. A top administrator said: "We feel like we are under a microscope; every move we make is magnified a hundred times." John Mars, the billionaire CEO of Mars Inc. described earlier, prefers to keep a low profile and routinely refuses (or does not bother to respond to) requests for media interviews. But he continues to be hounded by reporters for interviews, and other Mars family members (who are executives or heirs) are watched closely. A *Washington Post* reporter (Brenner, 1992) who was spying on Mars and his family (and talking to their neighbors) reported, for example, that his house is weathered, his roof sometimes leaks, his shoes are unpolished, and he drives a fourteen-year-old Mercedes. Similarly, A. Bartlett Giamatti described how his life changed after becoming president of Yale University:

> Not that I've been treated unfairly, but you go from being a private person to [everyone] suddenly reading descriptions of your face, your clothes, the way your hands look. (Horton, 1992, pp. 38-39)

High levels of attention may also be devoted to visible organizational decision makers who are not top managers. Pressures for accountability of public officials have resulted in laws that require open records and open meetings (Bok, 1983). These "sunshine laws" often mean that decision makers must use processes in which everything they do and say has the potential to be broadcast to thousands—or millions—of people. McLaughlin and Reisman (1986) conducted a case study of how the University of Florida chose a new president under such laws. Selection committee members found that sunshine laws meant that little evaluation and discussion of candidates was allowed without representatives of diverse constituencies and the press present. The law required that candidate interviews be conducted in public forums. When committee members began an informal group discussion outside of the public spotlight "Vice Chancellor Steve McArthur reminded them that further discussion was inappropriate since the meeting was officially adjourned" (McLaughlin & Reisman, 1986, p. 479).

Especially high levels of public attention are evident when political leaders are involved in alleged scandals. Garment (1991, p. 63) reports that, when President Reagan's national security advisor Richard Allen was suspected of taking a bribe from Japanese journalists in exchange for setting-up an interview with Nancy Reagan, the media began a "death watch," or a stakeout of Allen's home "so they would not miss a single one of his comings and or goings."

Finally, the rise of computerized databases means that close and persistent attention can occur even without any interaction with—or knowledge by—the leader or organization in question. Rothfeder (1992) documents how easy it us to use existing databases to learn numerous details about any person or organization. He describes an advertisement for "Tracers Worldwide," a "superbureau" that sells (often unlawful) information about people and organizations:

Its latest service guide, which I received in the mail, promises to supply telephone records, credit card usage reports, workman's compensation records, earnings reports, names and addresses of employers, Social Security numbers, and reports of bank account searches—"just a few of our more than 100 services." (Rothfeder, 1992, p. 81)

Close and Persistent Performance Monitoring and Evaluation

Intense scrutiny entails more than just close attention from others; it is typically combined with close performance monitoring. Such monitoring is rarely uncritical; people and organizations under the spotlight usually face a constant stream of (often unsolicited) evaluation and advice about what actions they should and should not take. Members of England's Royal family face pronounced public attention, especially Diana Princess of Wales. The introduction to Morton's (1992) book *Diana: Her True Story* thanks Diana's close family, friends, and counselors, and the royal household (especially her brother) for providing revelations about her. Morton reports that members of Princess Diana's social network do more than just observe her; friends, members of her staff, her estranged husband, her estranged husband's staff, Queen Elizabeth, Queen Elizabeth's staff, a diverse set of paid and unpaid personal counselors, and the media industry of "royal watchers" provide persistent evaluation and advice. She is evaluated and advised on seemingly everything, including how she raises her children, how she looks at her husband, which issues she supports and ignores, and her clothes, weight, and posture. Morton reports that the Queen's private secretary, Sir Robert Fellows, criticized Diana for kissing her handsome Italian driver on the cheek and for praising the Prime Minister for his handling of the Gulf War.

Princess Diana faces some of the most relentless evaluation and advice on Earth. Top managers and others in visible roles face similar, if less pronounced, pressures. A CEO told us that he was interviewed by two reporters from the same newspaper at the same time just after he took over a Fortune 50 company. One criticized him for not being confident enough; the other praised him for not being arrogant like other CEOs. Stock prices of publicly held companies are published in the press each day, as are the win-loss records of sports teams. Because the performance of leaders and their organizations are so closely intertwined in the minds of observers (Meindl, 1990), such data are construed as valid evidence about how leaders and their organizations are performing. Quantitative performance data, along with more subjective information, are used by observers to form judgments and shape advice for leaders and organizations. A former Nike manager, who is married to a former top Nike executive and crony of Phil Knight (Nike's CEO), wrote an "unauthorized" account of life inside this multi-billion dollar shoe company (Strasser & Becklund, 1991). It praised Knight and fellow "buttfaces" (the word top managers used to describe themselves) for developing inspired products, aggressive marketing, manufacturing savvy, and being lighthearted and fun. It criticized them, especially Knight, for faults including under-the-table payments for amateur athletes, violating the letter and spirit of other rules governing college athletics, arrogance, meanness, and greed.

Similarly, John Mars, his family, and their privately held company not only are the subject of persistent attention, they also face persistent evaluation and unsolicited praise and criticism from their various publics. The *Washington Post* article mentioned above (Brenner, 1992) is filled with praise and criticism from diverse sources. The family's frugal ways are described in largely positive terms, but the article includes critical remarks by a personal shopper who refused to work for John Mars' sister, Jacqueline Mars, because "She wanted me to shop at Sears, not Saks." The company and the Mars family is praised for its commitment to quality, profits, cleanliness, efficiency, and high paying jobs. They are criticized by past and current employees for being secretive, throwing tantrums, imposing excessively tight control, pressuring employees to work too hard, and doing a poor job of managing the succession to the next generation of Mars children. Alfred Poe, a disgruntled former executive asserted "If they didn't invent it" then "they don't want it." The family is even criticized for giving R. Bruce Murrie (son of a former Hershey president) insufficient credit for developing the hugely successful M&M candy by Mr. Murrie's daughter.

Frequent Interruptions

People who watch, evaluate, and provide advice to those in the spotlight are often not passive, or even polite, observers. Those in the spotlight often face many interruptions. Research indicates that interruptions are a defining feature of the executive role (Bass, 1990). Mintzberg's (1973) widely cited research indicates that the executives are constantly interrupted by phone calls and unscheduled meetings. Thompson's (1967) conceptual work suggests that top managers buffer the organization's technical core from external intrusions of all kinds, including interruptions from people inside and outside of the organization. As Mintzberg (1975) put it, "Someone, only half in jest, once described the manager as that person who sees visitors so that everyone else can get their work done." A related reason that a leader is likely to be interrupted frequently is that, as symbolic head of an organization, he or she will be viewed as responsible for—and in control of—most actions that occur within an organization. Top managers may have only moderate control (Bass, 1990), or even little control (Pfeffer, 1977), over most events associated with the organizations they lead. But work on the romance of leadership suggests that organizational participants and other observers and talk and act as if leaders have great control (Meindl, 1990). As a result, leaders are typically besieged with requests to explain, assist with, or repair a host of (often trivial) details of life within their organizations.

One executive told us that he was "hounded" by interruptions at every turn, via phone messages, e-mail, FAX messages, and people "camping out" in front of both his home and office. Similarly, Bennis (1979, p. 38) described the (largely minor) interruptions that he faced one day during the time he was president of the University of Cincinnati:

> A student complains that we won't give him course credit for acting as assistant to a city councilman. Another was unable to get into the student health center. The teacher at my child's day school, who goes to UC, is dissatisfied with her grades...... An alumnus couldn't get the football seat he wanted. Another wants a coach fired. A teacher just called to tell me the squash court was closed at 7 p.m., when he wanted to use it.

Political leaders face even more pronounced interruptions. Questions about leaders' personal affairs now often arise in places and at times that were once reserved for issues of State. An NBC reporter who was visiting the Oval Office bluntly asked (then President) Bush if he was having an extramarital affair. Bush, clearly angered, retorted that the question only perpetuated sleaze and should not be asked in the Oval office (Sabato, 1993, p. 275). The shocking nature of the question perhaps received more attention in the media than the policy issues faced by the Bush administration.

Questions about What Has Happened, Is Happening, Will Happen, and Why

These interruptions often entail requests for explanations about why events have occurred or have not occurred, or why plans have been made or not been made. Research on information processing indicates that human beings are constantly searching for explanations of their own behavior and of others, that people routinely request causal explanations from others for their behavior, and that they are strongly influenced by such explanations (Fiske & Taylor, 1991).

As a result of this endemic and powerful human tendency, the literature on impression management by leaders and other organizational spokespersons indicates that they devote much energy to answering implicit and explicit questions from real and imagined audiences about why events occurred, will occur, or have not occurred. The notion that leaders spend much of their time and resources answering real and imagined questions is a ubiquitous theme in literature on organizational impression management (Ginzel et al., 1993). Staw, McKechnie, and Puffer (1983), for example, found that much information in letters from CEOs in corporate annual reports focuses on explaining organizational financial performance.

Requests for explanations sometimes come from the press. Reporters are trained to push interviewees to explain past or planned events. Teel and Taylor

(1988, p. 124) exhort aspiring reporters: "You have to ask questions and sometimes you have to irritate your interviewee a trifle. If you are not intrinsically curious and inquisitive, the business of journalism is probably not for you." The reporters surrounding Richard Allen's house during the "death watch" described above shouted questions each time he arrived at or left his house. Garment (1991, p. 64) notes:

> At times during the Allen episode the stakeout of his home consisted of as many as 50 to 60 reporters and their crews, plus the television cameras, sound trucks, and all the cable that goes with them, camped out on the remains of lawn and littering the premises with McDonald's Styrofoam. One group of reporters, Allen complained at the time, had even approached his six-year old daughter, one of his seven children, and tried to interview her. These journalists, when they heard Allen's complaint, protested their innocence. They said that they had merely approached the little girl and asked her nicely "Is your daddy home."

Implicit or explicit requests for top managers to explain events and plans do not, however, come from the press alone. None of the complaints Bennis dealt with in the above example came from the press, but all required him to explain why the various problems he faced had arisen, what he was or was not going to do about each one, and why. Similarly, Sutton and Callahan (1987) found that leaders of computer firms that filed for protection under Chapter 11 of the Federal Bankruptcy Code devoted much time to answering tough questions about why the financial troubles occurred and what was being done to save the company from an array of sources including creditors, board members, lawyers, employees, suppliers, and customers—and only occasionally—from reporters. Existing literature emphasizes how the answers that leaders provide influence the "audiences" who are targets of such explanations. But our perspective turns attention inward. We focus on the consequences for leaders (i.e., thoughts, feelings, and actions) and their organizations of encountering such questions and having to develop such causal explanations.

THE EXPERIENCE OF BEING UNDER PUBLIC SCRUTINY

This blend of attention from others, performance monitoring and evaluation, interruptions, and questions has not been examined in past research. But aspects of scrutiny have been the subject of theory and research, especially in writings by social psychologists. Our reading of this literature, along with our modest original qualitative data, suggests that people experience intense scrutiny as a constant source of distraction punctuated by episodes of more pronounced interference with thought and action.

The social psychological literature suggests three reasons why high levels of sustained attention from others, especially from others who are evaluating performance, will be distracting. First, people who are closely watched and evaluated (or who hold symbolic roles in organizations that are closely watched and evaluated) may devote time and attention to monitoring the reactions of audience members for evidence of approval and disapproval. This search for cues indicating approval and disapproval from others can create further distraction because it is often fraught with apprehension (Geen, 1991). In extreme cases, like former FBI head J. Edgar Hoover (Gentry, 1992) and President Lyndon Johnson (Kramer, 1995), a leader's devotion of time and energy to audience reactions can resemble a paranoid obsession. Kramer illustrates this "hypervigilance" by quoting Herring's (1993, p. 95) description of Johnson as "A compulsive reader, viewer, and listener who took every criticism personally and to heart." "Hypervigilance" has a negative connotation. But devoting close attention to the preferences and evaluations of crucial exchange partners and sources of personal and organizational legitimacy is essential for leaders who seek to be powerful and respected (Pfeffer, 1992). Similarly, recent popular literature on customer satisfaction and quality argues that managers should be relentless in attending to their customers' concerns and criticisms (e.g., Sviokla & Shapiro, 1992).

Second, in addition to devoting attention to audience reactions, Zajonc suggests that people who are watched and evaluated by others will often ruminate about which responses to make. Other people, especially people who are evaluating a person (or an organization that reflects on the person's reputation), may introduce uncertainty about what responses will be needed. The person being attended to and evaluated by others may, as a result, be distracted by ruminations about which responses are appropriate and which are not (Zajonc, 1972, cited in Guerin, 1986, p. 39).

These distractions were evident in the public agency that we attempted to study. Administrators reported that the press, government officials, courts, union of minority employees, union of (mostly) white employees, lawyers, and consultants were watching and dissecting their every move. Even the structure of the top management team was changed so that the former head of the black employees' union and a (hostile) training director could help assure that court-ordered procedures were followed. So it was not possible for top management to meet as a group and be free from outside attention. This scrutiny appeared justified given past racist and sexist actions by this organization; but these administrators were constantly distracted by concerns about how to avoid offending these ever-present outsiders. The former agency head told us "We spent all of our time worrying about how to save our reputations and the reputation of the department." Similarly, Herring (1993, p. 95) reported that Lyndon Johnson was "obsessed with, answering every accusation, responding to every charge."

Third, purveyors of scrutiny may create pleasant as well as unpleasant distractions. Baron (1986) proposes that evaluative others may be fun to interact with or to watch. The president of a real estate company that we interviewed came up with the idea of building an affordable "dream house." He convinced a newspaper and a television station to publicize the contest to design the house, the building of the house, and the reactions from the large crowds of people who visited the house. The president told us that this valuable publicity created an array of pleasant, but time-consuming, distractions he had not anticipated. He was fascinated with newspaper and television reporters and photographers, and would spend precious time watching them work and asking them about their jobs instead of doing his own.

In addition to these ongoing distractions, people under scrutiny face interruptions. Scrutiny results in chronic distraction punctuated by acute interference with ongoing thoughts and actions. Alecia Swasy, a staff reporter from the *Wall Street Journal* who covered Procter & Gamble, and author of a book that was critical of this company (Swasy, 1993), led a barrage of negative publicity about Procter & Gamble's products, practices, and executives. Her efforts were a chronic source of distraction for CEO Ed Artzt and other top executives. Swasy also interrupted these executives in ways that caused acute and pronounced interference with what they were thinking and doing. Once, while Artzt was playing golf in Pebble Beach, California, Swasy left him two phone messages, sent him a FAX, and talked to his wife "who assured me that she'd give her husband the message to call me when she saw him at lunch" (Swasy, 1993, p. 292). Artzt was distracted (and irritated) by this intrusion.

Similar examples of acute interference with thought and action are illustrated by the complaints made by search committee members who selected the president of the University of Florida. The presence of "sunshine laws," which required open meetings and open interviews at all stages in the selection process, meant frequent interruptions. McLaughlin and Reisman (1986, p. 480) found:

> Some committee members had found the audience of reporters a distraction, since reporters scribbled notes throughout the interviews, and flash bulbs went off frequently. One committee member recalled that a reporter had leaned over her shoulder during an interview too see what she had written even though, according to the sunshine law, personal notes that are not entered into committee records can remain private.

The president of the construction firm we interviewed indicated that articles and television stories about the project not only prompted inquires from potential home buyers, it resulted in many unwanted calls and visits. He was interrupted by people who wanted to sell him construction materials he had purchased or would not need. But he admitted that he often found conversations with builders, architects, and others who heard about the project to be more interesting than the boring (but pressing) task that he was working on at the moment. His tendency to answer his cellular phone almost no matter what was doing supports Marshall McLuhan's (1964, p. 238) description of the phone as "an irresistible intruder in time and place."

PSYCHOLOGICAL RESPONSES TRIGGERED BY SCRUTINY

Figure 1 shows that this blend of constant distraction and more pronounced interference with thought and action is proposed to trigger two psychological responses, one cognitive and the other emotional. First, we suggest two closely linked cognitive responses: (a) cognitive overload and (b) a narrowing of attention toward how the leader, or his or her organization, appears to others and how to explain such appearances. The psychological literature helps explain why intense public scrutiny will create cognitive overload. Baron (1986) points out, following work by Kahneman and Cohen, that distractions created by the presence of others, especially evaluative others, may tax cognitive capacity. As a result, a person may only have time to focus on a small number of easily understood aspects of the tasks that he or she faces, especially aspects that seem most important. Furthermore, the interruptions that characterize scrutiny may exacerbate such cognitive overload. Constant requests and questions from people mean that ongoing thoughts and activities are constantly stalled, and so take longer to finish. Most interruptions require time, even just to deny a request or refuse to answer a question, or to simply be added to the pile of tasks. Finally, leaders may find intruders to be interesting to interact with or watch. So both the chronic and acute distractions created by intense scrutiny encourage leaders to focus their narrowed attention on how they, or their organizations, appear to others and how to best explain such appearances.

The content of almost all of these distractions make salient, and so turn attention to, how others view the scrutinized person or his or her organization; so leaders will focus their narrowed attention on symbolic rather than substantive tasks. First, following Tetlock's (1985, 1991) work on accountability, people facing such demands will likely think and act like "intuitive politicians" because their attention is drawn to whether or not they or their organization is viewed favorably. Furthermore, to process information more easily and quickly, people under intense scrutiny—like other intuitive politicians—may use the "acceptability heuristic" to guide the decisions they make. Tetlock (1991, p. 340) described this heuristic:

> The acceptability heuristic allows one to avoid much unnecessary cognitive work ... All one needs to do is to adopt the salient acceptable option. Laboratory and field studies suggest that people frequently do exactly that: they choose the most clearly defensible strategy available to them.

Second, we expect that people under intense scrutiny will devote less attention to factors that they do not believe are relevant to the audiences they seek to please, even if these ignored factors include important aspects like economic efficiency, creativity, or individual well-being. That is, responses will generally mirror the spotlight shined by audiences, focusing more on symbolic and political issues. Few audiences, especially external audiences, have deep knowledge of the inner workings of an organization (e.g., complex technical and creative routines, detailed control and planning systems, and medium- to long-term strategic plans and methods of implementation). So the spotlight will be on symbolic issues, especially on changes that threaten or bolster legitimacy (e.g., "What does your drop in the industry rankings suggest?" or "Why did you get that recent *New York Times* endorsement?").

We propose that scrutiny will also generate negative affect, especially evaluation apprehension. As indicated above, the social facilitation literature suggests that those distractions endemic to intense scrutiny will create apprehension about how to please evaluative others and about what they are thinking. Cognitive overload creates additional negative emotion. Research on role overload suggests anxiety, frustration, and dissatisfaction will be experienced by people who cannot keep pace with demands (Kahn & Byosiere, 1992; Katz & Kahn, 1978). Furthermore, the presence of others can cause anxiety about whether attention should be devoted to the task or to the audience, along with anxiety that the audience will interfere with the ability to perform tasks.

Interruptions are likely to provoke the strongest negative feelings. The questions asked during such interruptions are often requests to explain or predict performance or to describe the methods that the leader or organization is using to improve or maintain performance levels, so the chronic evaluation apprehension is likely to be accentuated by such interruptions. More generally, interruptions can generate negative affect because arousal is mobilized in response to obstruction or interference with organized response sequences (Mandler, 1984). For example, when interruptions (or other distractions) introduce information that clashes with one's life view or slows or impedes progress toward goals, the resulting arousal is likely to intensify or be part of negative emotions like anxiety, frustration, and anger.

The interruptions associated with scrutiny do not always trigger unpleasant feelings; the president of the construction company described above found many of the phone calls he received to be pleasant distractions. And some interruptions carry good news. When interruptions include information that a person is advancing faster than anticipated toward goals, the resulting arousal is likely to intensify or be part of positive emotions like elation and happiness. Nonetheless, as Fiske and Taylor (1991) suggest, many interruptions and distractions are experienced as negative because they interfere with goal accomplishment and overload an individual or system.[3]

The evaluation apprehension, the anxiety from overload, the frustration caused by distractions and interruptions in pleasant and important actions and thoughts, and the anger generated by interruptions, are not always easily contained. Many top managers and other figures in the public spotlight learn to conceal their negative emotions. But the pressures of public scrutiny can cause leaders to lash out at others. Such antics are well-publicized in sports. Bobby Knight, Indiana University Basketball Coach, is infamous for shouting at and swearing at his players and members of the press (Feinstein, 1986). And such flashes of temper are also evident from managers of more traditional organizations. Steve Jobs, co-founder and former CEO of Apple Computer, had numerous well-documented temper tantrums in the presence of employees, often crying and screaming (Young, 1988).

Reporters are infamous for creating distractions and interruptions that provoke negative feelings. A science reporter that we interviewed told us that researchers were sometimes irritated by her request for an interview because it distracted them from their research. Aggressive action by the press can provoke especially strong negative emotions. Procter & Gamble CEO Ed Artzt reacted with pronounced irritation and hostility toward scrutiny from *Wall Street Journal* reporter Swasy (1993, p. 298), who reported that Artzt sometimes called "just to yell at me" and that "During one call in February of 1991 he cursed and screamed about a story on P&G's spending cuts." Charles Lindbergh, the famous aviator, complained bitterly about the constant, rude interruptions that he received from the press. He was especially upset by the way that reporters hounded him during his honeymoon. Seledes (1989, p. 38) quotes a well-known interview in which reporter Marlen Pew interviewed Lindbergh about his honeymoon:

> He felt outraged when some reporters followed him and Mrs. Lindbergh on their honeymoon and "for eight straight hours circled about our boat, at anchor in a New England harbor, in a noisy motorboat and occasionally called across the water to us that if we would pose for one picture they would go away."

CONSEQUENCES OF UNCHECKED SCRUTINY FOR LEADERS AND THEIR ORGANIZATIONS

Figure 1 proposes that these psychological responses lead to five consequences for leaders and organizations: (1) frequent delays in ongoing tasks; (2) attention and effort devoted toward symbolic activities, away from other kinds of activities; (3) greater adherence to injunctive norms, less adherence to descriptive norms; (4) attention and effort focused on well-rehearsed acts, away from acts that require learning or creativity; and (5) greater perseverance at ongoing and planned activities. The remainder of this section explicates how these psychological processes may bring about these consequences and

Frequent Delays in Ongoing Tasks

We asserted above that interruptions mean that ongoing thoughts and activities are stalled. The first outcome of unchecked scrutiny, then, is that regardless of what task a leader is doing, it will take longer to finish. There is controversy about whether the interruptions faced by most executives are functional (Mintzberg, 1973) or dysfunctional (Bennis, 1979). But there is little disagreement that top managers face many interruptions, that unwanted and uncontrolled interruptions can be dysfunctional, and that leaders can be interrupted by others—and themselves—so much that it hampers performance. Mintzberg emphasizes that interruptions are crucial for leaders because they contain current information. He also emphasizes, however, that executives who cannot stop excessive interruptions end up doing many things, but none well.

This dysfunction of unchecked scrutiny was summarized by the owner of the construction company, who was so distracted by, first, the media, and then, the resulting barrage of interruptions from people who had heard media reports, that "Some days, progress on the house just stops because of all the attention we are getting." A related problem was identified by Bennis during his tenure as a university president. He reported that his efforts to develop and implement strategic plans were stalled because he was mired in a constant flow of interruptions about pressing, but less important matters. These interruptions caused Bennis to propose his "Second Law of Academic Pseudodynamics": "Make whatever grand plans you will, you may be sure the unexpected or trivial will disturb or disrupt them" (Bennis, 1979, p. 39). His writings on why leaders cannot lead portray top managers as facing a constant stream of unwanted and irritating distractions and interruptions that make it impossible to engage in long-term planning. Bennis' (1979, p. 38) frustration in this regard was evident when he complained: "Here's a note from a professor, complaining that his classroom temperature is down to 65 degrees. I suppose he wants me to grab a wrench and fix it."

Attention and Effort Devoted toward Symbolic Activities, Away from Other Kinds of Activities

We argued earlier that the narrow focus on how the leader or his or her organization appears to others and how to explain such appearances means that more attention will be devoted to symbolic tasks and less to other tasks. If a leader holds a purely symbolic role, he or she might act solely on the basis of the acceptability heuristic (Tetlock, 1991) and there will be no variance to explain on this dimension. Our perspective suggests, however, that leaders under heavy scrutiny (or who head organizations under scrutiny) and who have both symbolic and substantive responsibilities, will tend to neglect substantive responsibilities.

A newspaper story about Gerhard Casper, Stanford University's president, indicated he was spending so much time on ceremonial and political duties that he had too little time to "worry about academic affairs—the area that I think is most important for the long-term future of Stanford" (Bartholomew, 1993, p. 1). Casper worried "that in trying to perform a full round of both 'Queen Elizabeth' ceremonial duties and 'Margaret Thatcher' governing duties, he might do full justice to neither" (Bartholomew, 1993, p. 6). Similarly, Powell (1987, p. 130) describes how managers at a Boston public television station were often pulled away from substantive tasks because the station faced unchecked scrutiny. Powell found that, because of outside monitoring and evaluation faced by the director of strategic planning, "Not infrequently, she would find herself unable to attend to her work priorities and instead spend days responding to the disgruntled complaints of outsiders." McLaughlin and Reisman concluded that the scrutiny institutionalized by Florida's "sunshine laws" caused search committee members to adopt a decision process that appeared to be fair, careful, and inclusive rather than a process that helped them to select the best university president. McLaughlin and Reisman further asserted that, rather than addressing substantive issues, "the presentations of self in the Florida sunshine [had] the overtones of photo opportunities" (1986, p. 479).

This focus toward symbolic activities and away from other matters was pronounced in the public agency that we attempted to study. The agency head and a consultant told us that so much attention, time, and money had been devoted to dealing with outside attention and intrusions that the agency's ability to accomplish its core task had diminished. Scrutiny that results from favorable news can cause a similar shift. The Wallace Company was the first small manufacturing company to win the prestigious Malcolm Baldridge quality award. After the company won the award, managers from other companies visited for "benchmarking," executives gave speeches at conferences and other companies, and reporters interviewed executives. These flattering distractions helped drive the company into Chapter 11. An executive from the company that acquired Wallace told Hill (1993, p. 79):

> When you do win the Baldridge, there is also an obligation, if not a contractual commitment, to go out and spread the gospel. It takes a lot of time from work for the key people to give talks and spread the gospel. You also have to open up your business to others who want to see your systems and your procedures. That is good, but if you are in the business of trying to survive, it can become a financial problem and defeat your original purpose of being in business.

Similarly, people who have technical roles with few symbolic responsibilities, but who then come under scrutiny, may change activities drastically. A science reporter asserted that once the media "make a professor famous" the distractions are so great that he or she rarely has another original idea. Gleick's (1992, p. 382) biography of physicist Richard Feynman describes how the symbolic distractions that come with winning a Nobel Prize make it hard to do the intensive work that led to this accolade:

> Most scientists knew that not-so-amusing metalaw that the receipt of the Nobel Prize marks the end of one's productive career. For many recipients, of course, the end came long before. For others, the fame and distinction tend to accelerate the waning of a scientist's ability to give his [sic] creative work the time-intensive, fanatical attention that it often requires.

Greater Adherence to Injunctive Norms, Less Adherence to Descriptive Norms

The use of the acceptability heuristic may also lead to more emphasis on following norms about how people and organizations *ought* to act and less emphasis on following norms about how they *typically* act. Cialdini, Kallgren, and Reno's (1991) review indicates that research on norms has not taken sufficient care to distinguish between standards for behavior based on what is commonly approved (i.e., injunctive norms) versus standards for behavior based on what is commonly done (i.e., descriptive norms). They report nine studies on littering to support a "focus theory of normative conduct," which proposes that the relative power of injunctive versus descriptive norms to shape behavior depends on which standard is more salient. Cialdini and his colleagues found that subjects who had attention focused toward possible disapproval from others for littering and away from the amount of littering by others around them were more likely to follow injunctive norms and disregard conflicting descriptive norms.

Leaders facing scrutiny are likely to field questions about whether or not they and their organizations are doing what is commonly approved. Even when they do not face such questions explicitly, leaders may ruminate about how to answer them if asked. We anticipate that such real and imagined questions, along with other pressures to focus on symbolic acts, will encourage leaders to turn attention toward conforming to injunctive norms and away from conforming to descriptive norms. For example, administrators in the public agency we attempted to study asserted that their hiring practices and promotion standards for minorities were similar to comparable agencies in and outside their city. Administrators contended that, as scrutiny increased, they were asked more questions about why they were not meeting idealized and stringent standards about what *ought* to be done to help minorities versus lower standards about what was *actually* being done in most other agencies.

McLaughlin and Reisman (1986) indicated that an effect of Florida's sunshine laws on the search committee they studied was that—compared to searches in the past and at places without sunshine laws—many meetings were scheduled and procedures were adopted that had no purpose other than satisfying idealized norms for fairness and inclusion. Forums were held with interest groups where few people other than the candidate, search committee, and press attended each time. Committee members felt they had no choice but to continue scheduling such sparsely attended gatherings to avoid questions about why they had not conformed to idealized norms about broad-based inclusion in the decision process.

Attention and Effort Focused toward Well-Rehearsed Acts, Away from Acts that Require Learning and Creativity

The cognitive overload associated with scrutiny may not only cause people to rely on the acceptability heuristic (Tetlock, 1991). The vast literature on social facilitation published since Zajonc's (1965) classic paper suggests that the cognitive load and distraction created by the presence of an evaluative audience will facilitate dominant, well-learned responses and inhibit subordinate, less-well rehearsed behaviors (Baron, 1986; Geen, 1991). These robust findings suggest that public scrutiny will be associated with three interrelated outcomes reflecting that, as with the reliance on the acceptability heuristic, people will try to avoid cognitive effort and do what seems immediately functional. First, when scrutiny is intense and unchecked, attention and effort will be focused on carrying out well-rehearsed acts. Second, when scrutiny is intense and unchecked, new approaches and practices should be learned less often and more slowly. Third, when scrutiny is intense and unchecked, the cognitive overload (and associated narrow focus) should mean that leaders and others in symbolic roles will be less creative (Amabile, 1983). An emerging body of experimental research also suggests that the negative affect produced by scrutiny will further fuel this tendency to be less creative (Isen & Baron, 1991).

Staw, Sandelands, and Dutton's (1981) conceptual work and review suggests that these three effects—which are all signs of rigidity—will occur in response to a wide variety of external threats to organizations and leaders. The substantial literature on organizational decline indicates that organizations often respond in this way, at least at first, to decreasing levels of financial resources and to downsizing (Sutton & D'Aunno, 1989). Threat-rigidity effects are also supported by Weick's (1990) analysis of a deadly airplane crash. There is, however, limited evidence that the threat posed by public scrutiny brings about these rigid outcomes in leaders and organizations. Informants in Galunic's (1994) study of a high technology firm indicated that evaluation apprehension and distraction associated with a visible and widely discussed computer product led members of the design team to rely heavily on technologies they had used in the past and to limit their efforts to discover and understand technologies used elsewhere. Although these existing technologies were blended together in imaginative ways, the creative leaps were smaller than if new technologies had been used as well. McLaughlin and Resiman's (1986) study of sunshine laws in Florida suggests that the evaluation apprehension experienced by committee members encouraged them to be less imaginative about the range of candidates that were interviewed. These cases, combined with the substantial literature suggesting that such rigidities occur in response to organizational decline, imply that learning and creativity will be hampered in organizations regardless of whether, for example, they face unchecked scrutiny because they have been dramatically successful or unsuccessful. But more systematic research is needed.

Greater Perseverance at Ongoing and Planned Activities

Staw and Ross' (1987) conceptual perspective suggests that answering questions about what is occurring, what will occur, and why can create commitments that bind organizations and their members to planned and ongoing courses of actions. Their case studies of British Columbia's decision to host the Expo 86 world's fair (Ross & Staw, 1986) and the Long Island Lighting Company's (LILCO) decision to build the Shoreham Nuclear Power Plant (Ross & Staw, 1993) suggest that the public attention to and questions answered by leaders under scrutiny will trigger social binding and norms for consistency, social psychological forces that enhance perseverance at ongoing and planned activities.

First, Staw and Ross' perspective, combined with Salancik's (1977) commitment theory, suggest that scrutiny can create social-psychological binds that are difficult to break. Their case studies support our assertion that, as part of their symbolic roles, leaders and other spokespersons under intense scrutiny are asked to offer a constant stream of justifications for current and planned actions. The need to justify a course of action, despite its possible failing, may result in the leader persevering in the chosen course of action. In the case of the Shoreham plant, as the cost soared from $65 million in 1966 to $5.5 billion in 1989, LILCO leaders repeatedly assured external constituencies that the investment was wise. Ross and Staw (1993) indicate that LILCO's CEO was personally identified with these expressed commitments because he repeatedly spoke in favor of the project when answering questions from the press, shareholders, community groups, and the public utilities commission. So it was difficult to make claims that the CEO was not responsible for his company's commitments unless, as was done before the project was abandoned, a new CEO was hired. Also, the commitment was described by LILCO's top management as their strategic decision, indicating it was voluntary. So the CEO could not make credible claims that he had been forced to make the commitment. Finally, repeated public proclamations of commitment to the project made it difficult to halt because such statements conveyed that these were strongly rather than weakly held beliefs. Thus, as the project's failure became more pronounced, the CEO sought to justify his course of action by increasing commitment to it.

Social norms for consistency reinforced these social-psychological binds. Staw and Ross' (1980) experimental research found that leaders who maintain consistent commitment to a course of action are evaluated more positively than leaders who withdraw from or change their course of action. They point out that our society praises people, especially leaders, who stay the course during difficult times, but win out in the end. In the Shoreham case, commitments were also binding because they were made publicly, so they could not be revoked without leaders being construed as being wrong in the first place, and thus "losing-face." Top management's commitment to the plant was unambiguous. So it could not be revoked by claiming that the audience did not properly interpret it as a tentative or experimental commitment. Ross and Staw report that these presumed virtues of consistent leadership were often mentioned by LILCO leaders. Even after $4 billion had been spent, a LILCO official said "if people just wait until the end, they are going to realize that this is a hell of an investment" (Ross & Staw, 1993, p. 718). Brockner, Rubin, and Lang's (1981) experimental findings provide additional support for our assertion that anxious leaders who face evaluative audiences will persevere at ongoing and planned courses of actions. Brockner and his colleagues found that commitment of resources to a course of action was highest when subjects faced larger audiences and had feelings of higher social anxiety.

The heightened pressures for consistency encountered by leaders do not just lead to escalation of commitment to failing courses of action. These forces can also lead to positive outcomes because perseverance may eventually turn failing projects around, even against long odds. Staw and Ross (1980) suggest that such forces may have led famous leaders including Lincoln, Churchill, and Gandhi to persist and succeed against long odds. The point is that, regardless of whether a course of action will fail or succeed, when a leader makes public, personal, frequently repeated, unambiguous, and voluntary commitment to a course of action, it will be difficult to revoke, both for reasons of self-justification and face-saving. As the owner of the construction firm who built the widely publicized "Dream House" put it, "Once it was in the paper and on TV, I knew I had to go through with it."

In conclusion, these five consequences are proposed to be evident (at least initially) at the individual level because each results from the psychological process portrayed in Figure 1. These processes are psychological because they reflect cognitions and emotions within persons. None of these process concern structural aspects of relationships between persons or institutions, and so are largely outside of the domain of sociological theory. But scrutiny has important consequences at the organizational level. Staw and Sutton's (1992) writings on "macro organizational psychology" indicate that such effects can occur in two ways. First, scrutiny sometimes focuses largely on an individual leader, or a small set of leaders. Leaders' thoughts and feelings may then influence their substantive and symbolic actions, which in turn may sway much or all of the organization. Second, scrutiny is sometimes devoted to the actions of an organization as a whole such as when an investigative reporter tracks down industrial waste that has been dumped unlawfully, or when a reviewer for a computer magazine asserts that a product is one of the year's "ten best" or "ten worst." All or most members may then feel like they are under scrutiny, so their aggregate feelings, thoughts, and behaviors may influence the organization as a whole.

DEFENSES AGAINST SCRUTINY

The five proposed consequences of unchecked scrutiny, on balance, strike us as more negative than positive. These consequences may be positive under some conditions. Interruptions can be advantageous when a leader or follower abandons a less important task and shifts attention to a more important matter. To the extent that a leader has symbolic rather than substantive responsibilities, it may be wise to narrow attention on symbolic acts. Adhering to the (often) higher standards associated with injunctive rather than descriptive norms may lead to more effective or ethical actions. If an organization is in a mature industry with little competition, then it may be most profitable to focus attention and effort on well-rehearsed tasks and, along related lines, to persevere at ongoing and planned activities.

Despite these virtues, there are many times where unchecked scrutiny can harm the reputation and objective performance of leaders and organizations. Unwanted interruptions from people who are not crucial exchange partners or who raise trivial issues can waste attention, time, and money. Leaders, and other visible members, may make poor decisions when they only consider symbolic implications of decisions and ignore technical, financial, or ethical implications. Organizations may waste resources by trying to conform to impractical—and perhaps unattainable—ideals about how they ought to behave. Impaired learning and creativity may hamper the ability to make crucial changes. And perseverance is not wise when it is devoted to a failing course of action.

Leaders and organizations are not helpless victims of unchecked scrutiny. They can and do take steps to defend against scrutiny and its negative consequences. And leaders understand that even the benefits of scrutiny cannot be enjoyed unless efforts are made to defend against certain kinds of scrutiny

Table 1. Defenses Against Intense Public Scrutiny

Rhetorical Defenses
1. Using ambiguous language
2. Being boring
3. Being nasty
4. Raising interesting distractions

Procedural Defenses
5. Hiding
6. Stalling
7. Establishing rules about when, where, and how interactions occur
8. Doing favors for others in exchange for less scrutiny
9. Refusing access to purveyors of "excessive" or "unfair" scrutiny

Structural Defenses
10. Establishing roles to block and absorb scrutiny
11. Decoupling symbolic and substantive leadership roles
12. Using symbolic practices to divert attention from substantive actions

by some people on some occasions. Our review of scholarly writings, case descriptions, and our own bits of data led us to identify 12 defenses that leaders and organizations use to defend against the negative consequences of scrutiny. These 12 strategies are listed in Table 1, where they are grouped into rough categories as rhetorical, procedural, and structural defenses. We discuss how and why defenses may be effective in this section; the drawbacks of using defenses are discussed in the next section.

Rhetorical Defenses

Using Ambiguous Language

Eisenberg (1984) asserts that clarity in organizational communication is overrated. He contends that ambiguity often serves as a useful compromise between total silence, which is often interpreted as sign that one has something to hide, and complete clarity, which can lead some organizational participants to feel excluded and can create obstacles to flexibility and change. Eisenberg proposes that strategic ambiguity promotes unified diversity because, when an organization's goals and values are vague, fewer people will feel excluded. Eisenberg also points out that because strategic ambiguity facilitates organizational change, it is unclear to others what paths the organization has taken, is taking, and will take, the escalation of commitment that occurs when observers know of such courses of action cannot happen. Political leaders in particular are noted for their (often excruciatingly obvious) vagueness. Although lambasted in the press for their inability to take a clear stand on many issues, this vagueness can actually serve the public (and themselves) well when it becomes necessary to alter a failing course of action. In contrast, when there is a lack of vagueness, change becomes more difficult and potentially damaging when attempted. Consider former President Bush's tax increases leading up to the 1992 presidential elections. These measures were necessitated by falling government revenues in the wake of the 1989-1993 recession plus the desire to stem the growth in government debt. Although tax increases seemed prudent, Bush's prior lack of vagueness (i.e., "read my lips, no new taxes") made this decision not only more difficult to make and implement than it might have been but also damaging to the President's credibility as he entered the 1992 race.

Strategic ambiguity may also reduce social facilitation effects because, if purveyors of scrutiny do not know what organization members are thinking, planning, and doing, they cannot serve as evaluative audiences. Using ambiguous language helps maintain "plausible deniability" that an event occurred or was linked to specific organizations or members (Bogen & Lynch, 1989). Such vagueness may protect leaders or organizations from future evaluation for an act or its effects. When little or no information is available about what was done in the past, or a record that contains many vague descriptions is (perhaps intentionally) maintained, it is easier to plausibly deny that the action was taken or linked to a given person or organization (Garfinkel, 1967).

The language used by leaders of financially troubled organizations is often left intentionally vague to obscure what they have done and will do. Terms like "rightsizing," "reorganizing," and "repositioning" provide almost no information about how—or even if—the organization will cut costs. The popular term "downsizing" has been criticized as too vague to facilitate scholarly research on how costs will be cut (Cameron, Sutton, & Whetten, 1988). These vague terms also make it difficult for employees to understand and plan for changes in their jobs and organizations. From management's perspective, however, vague terms can be useful because saying "the organization will experience significant downsizing during the next year" leaves them flexibility. The term downsizing does not convey whether or not, and what mix, of natural attrition, job sharing, pay cuts, reduction in benefits, layoffs, and early retirement incentives will be used. It is so vague that it does not even convey whether labor costs or other kinds of costs will be reduced, let alone how they will be reduced.

Similarly, McLaughlin and Resiman (1986, p. 476) report how members of the search committee for the University of Florida president responded to sunshine laws:

> "Everything said in meetings had to be couched in vague language," one committee member recalled. Several people described the instance when a member of the committee was aware

that a certain candidate had alienated a number of people. Rather than risk being quoted in the press as having said this directly, the committee member said simply, "You might want to look into this man's background. I understand that several people left after he was appointed to his present position." ... More commonly, nothing at all was said, and candidates lost their place on the list due to silence.

Sports figures and their coaches are infamous for using strategic ambiguity to help protect themselves from questions about what they are thinking and what new methods they are trying to learn. Professional athletes play in the public spotlight; social facilitation research suggests that such attention will improve performance when appropriate methods are already well-learned. But when they need to change how they are playing, external attention should hamper learning. In order to maintain flexibility to change in future, and to avoid evaluative attention toward current efforts to change how the game is played, using vague language allows coaches and players to meet expectations that they should talk with reporters and fans about what they are doing, but to avoid some of the harm that these encounters can do to performance.

Being Boring

Leaders and other top managers often are scrutinized because observers find that their actions—or their organization's—to be interesting. It follows that leaders can dim the spotlight of scrutiny by becoming less interesting to others. If done effectively, others will pay less attention to a boring leader or organization, and then devote less energy to monitoring performance, interrupting the leader and other visible members of the organization, and asking questions. Speaking in vague terms can help a person to be construed as boring. Talking about minute details, using colorless language, and talking about dull topics can also make a leader—and by extension the organization—seem boring.

A former CEO of a Fortune 500 company that we interviewed was invited to address a prestigious gathering of the national press. He and a member of his public relations department decided this was a good opportunity to reduce the intense interest that the press had in this organization and its new CEO. They believed that past top managers had been scrutinized too closely by the press and they wanted the organization to be out of the limelight for another year or so until it starting selling some exciting new products that were under development. They decided that the best strategy was—rather than refusing the chance to speak—to give a talk on a boring topic and in a boring manner (with a dry delivery, filled with facts and figures, and sentences written in the passive voice). The CEO told us that the national press seemed to lose interest in him and his company for awhile after giving this boring speech.

Being Nasty

The expression of negative affect to those who shine the spotlight may reduce subsequent scrutiny because those watching or interrupting may not want to repeat such unpleasant interactions. Staw, Sutton, and Pelled (1994, p. 65) contend:

> There also may be costs to conveying positive emotion in interactions with subordinates, peers, and superiors. Employees who respond to interruptions from others by being positive or friendly may reinforce such behavior, and thus be interrupted with increasing frequency. As a result, warm and friendly employees may be unable to get their work done, while negative or hostile employees—whom others may dread interrupting—may be more productive because they work with fewer diversions.

The first author of this paper called a soon-to-be defunct Japanese car dealership to find out if they would like to participate in a study of organizational death (Sutton, 1989). The service manager reacted with anger to this request, telling Sutton that he considered it to be a rude intrusion during a trying time. Sutton was sufficiently discouraged by this hostility that he never called the owner to find out if, despite this employee's angry response, he might be interested in participating. Richard's (1986, p. 327) participant-observation research indicates that administrators at a nursing home tried to reduce her scrutiny of their patient care practices by ridiculing her. Richard reports that administrators responded to a request that her mother get more exercise by sarcastically accusing her of wanting Yoga classes and a swimming pool installed. An administrator also snidely told her that she was known as "the one" who wanted nurses to "roll [disabled] patients around the grass" as a means of exercise. Richard suggests that such nastiness was meant to discourage her from complaining about the facility and to encourage her to move her mother elsewhere.

Raising Interesting Distractions

The final rhetorical strategy entails raising interesting subjects that distract purveyors of scrutiny to avoid intrusion or to avoid subjects that will be time consuming or difficult to address. President Reagan sometimes told jokes and interesting stories about when he worked as an actor or a sports announcer in an apparent effort to distract reporters from asking, or following-up on, tough or intrusive questions (Hertsgaard, 1989). Galunic's (1994) study of business unit strategy included an interview with an R&D manager who was concerned that attention and questions from top managers would distract and constrain a team that was designing a computer peripheral. The R&D manager believed that such scrutiny would hamper the speed, creativity, and quality of the design process. He defended the team by distracting upper management with more visible but—he believed—less important projects. To reduce "hype" about the key project, he always began presentations to top management by talking about other projects and did not leave much time to talk about the one he believed was most crucial. He indicated that, by the time discussion turned to this less visible product, top managers did not have much time left to talk about it and were too distracted and tired to offer strong evaluations. Top managers usually just conveyed a bit of tepid pessimism about the (eventually very successful) product before turning to other matters.

Procedural Defenses

Hiding

A leader or other organization member can avoid scrutiny by being impossible to find or by hiding out temporarily to avoid distraction or interference. These "disappearing acts" can be accomplished through physical means, such as when top managers hold secret meetings away from corporate headquarters, under false personal and corporate names, to decide if organizational units should be closed and which employees should lose jobs (Sutton, 1984). Horton (1992, p. 39) describes how one CEO attempted to construct a physical setting that would preclude intrusion: "a CEO of a Fortune 500 company, exhausted by constant questions from those around him, had his office walled off and a separate building entrance constructed for his private use."

Hiding can also be accomplished by donning physical disguises, as celebrities sometimes do to avoid being recognized. It can also be accomplished by not revealing one's identity. A university provost reported that he needed to get some important papers out of his desk late one evening. He anticipated that doing so would be challenging because his office building was occupied by demonstrators. He was confronted by demonstrators, who asked him if he was an administrator. This (casually dressed) provost said "Sorry, I'm just the janitor." Rather than being explicitly deceptive, people in visible roles can also protect their identities by being vague. Horton (1992, p. 39) reports that AT&T's former CEO responded to a question about what he did for a living by saying "I work for the phone company." There are also some forms of explicit and legitimized hiding. For example, presidential retreats to Camp David are respected by the press as a time for the president, advisors, and sometimes foreign officials to contemplate various policy issues without interruption.

Stalling

Tetlock (1991) suggests that a strategy for avoiding the consequences of accountability is to procrastinate about a decision or action. Similarly, scrutiny might be attenuated through stalling. Decisions or actions that are likely to attract interest and be evaluated, and lead to interruptions and questions, might be delayed. A leader may wait to delay action until a time or place where scrutiny will be more difficult to accomplish or be accomplished by a less strident people. To avoid the scrutiny required by Florida's sunshine laws, selection committee members often waited for private conversations to voice their opinions about candidates. Private conversations between members were not required to be open (McClaughlin & Reisman, 1986).

Electronic or human gatekeepers may be used to delay encounters with purveyors of scrutiny. Such foot dragging can reduce the number of encounters between leaders and purveyors of scrutiny and may discourage future intrusions. A secretary or receptionist may agree, in theory, to set a meeting between a leader and a person who is a source of scrutiny, but it may "need" to be delayed for months because of the leaders' allegedly busy schedule. Or, when electronic or voice mail is used to contact the leader directly, he or she may take a long time to respond. We found that both these forms of stalling were used by administrators in the public agency that we attempted to study. Richard (1986) reports that nursing home administrators used similar delay tactics to reduce scrutiny by family members who complain about the care given to relatives.

Establishing Rules about When, Where, and How Interactions Occur

These tactics limit the amount of time that leaders, spokespersons, or other organization members face scrutiny. These limits on when and in what way scrutiny will occur gives them time to do substantive tasks and to marshal resources so that they can develop ideas about putting their organization—and themselves—in the best light. As Havelock Ellis put it, "To be a leader of men, one must turn one's back on men" (*Columbia Dictionary of Quotations*, 1993). Leaders may simply refuse to talk with members of the press or to representatives of other groups who they find to be distracting or irrelevant. John Mars, the reclusive CEO of Mars Inc., routinely refuses—or ignores—requests for interviews (Brenner, 1992). Similarly, the CEO of a Fortune 50 company told us that he refers all requests for interviews to his public relations staff and refuses to hold a conversation of any kind with reporters. As noted above, Nobel Prize winners often find that, after working in relative obscurity, pressures to engage in symbolic activities after winning the prize distract them from intellectual efforts. Some winners fight against these distractions and interruptions. Gleick (1992, p. 382) reports that Francis Crick used this form letter:

> Dr. Crick thanks you for your letter but regrets that he is unable to accept your kind invitation to:

Send an autograph
provide a photograph
cure your disease
be interviewed
talk on the radio
appear on TV
speak after dinner
give a testimonial
help you in your project
read your manuscript
deliver a lecture
attend a conference
act as a chairman
become an editor
write a book
accept an honorary degree

Athletes like baseball player Ricky Henderson of the Oakland Athletics have a policy of refusing to talk to reporters when injured or in a slump. Henderson said he does so because these intrusions make it difficult to muster the psychological strength needed to recover from such setbacks (Henderson & Shea, 1992). Similarly, San Francisco Giants star Barry Bonds restricts contact with the press during times when, whether he is in a slump or in a hitting streak, he does not want to be distracted from his thoughts about how to play baseball.

A related, but less extreme, set of tactics entails enforcing firm rules about who can interact with or watch the scrutinized person, what questions can be asked, and—in the case of reporters—which topics they can write about. Celebrities often employ publicists to negotiate such arrangements with the press. Natale (1993, p. 18) reports that "Not long ago, when Vanessa Redgrave was in Hollywood promoting a TV movie remake of Whatever Happened to Baby Jane?, journalists were required to sign a release agreeing that they wouldn't ask questions about her controversial political beliefs." Similarly, limits can be set on when aspects of scrutiny occur in order to avoid intrusions that may detract from the quality of decisions made or may waste time. McLaughlin and Reisman (1986, p. 473), report that, although the search committee for the president of the University of Florida held open meetings in accordance with sunshine laws, "committee members decided that noncommittee members would be allowed to address the chair only at the end of each session and that their remarks would be limited in length."

Doing Favors for Others in Exchange for Less Scrutiny

When an organization member, or his or her organization, seeks to avoid or reduce scrutiny, he or she may use the norm of reciprocity (Gouldner, 1960) or what Cialdini called "the old give and take" (1984, p. 29) to eliminate or soften scrutiny. Favors done for purveyors of scrutiny can place explicit or implicit pressure on them to look the other way, to engage in little performance evaluation (or excessively positive evaluation), to interrupt less frequently, or to ask fewer and less difficult questions.

Hertsgaard's (1989) book about the relationship between the press and the administration during Ronald Reagan's presidency contains numerous examples of how small favors were done for reporters as way to gain more favorable and less intrusive media coverage. When Walter Robinson, a *Boston Globe* reporter, broke his thumb while covering a whistle-stop campaign, he discovered that Reagan's aides helped reporters in so many ways that he did not need to take notes because "They gave you, within twenty minutes [Reagan's] remarks, as delivered, with punctuation, pauses, etc. And within in thirty minutes of each train stop, they had sixty phones set up for reporters" (Hertsgaard, 1989, p. 42). A Reagan administration official suggested that such amenities had the desired effect:

> If you give somebody a comfortable place to work, good facilitates, provide food because you know that they can't take time to go to restaurant ten miles away to eat, and in general provide the creature comforts, how then can someone turn around and bite the hand that feeds him? ... I had reporters...tell me. "Jesus Christ, how can I write a nasty story? Every time I need something, somebody is there to provide it for me. I've got two phones right in front of me, food over there, it's really hard to write nasty story." (Hertsgaard, 1989, pp. 41-42).

Refusing Access to Purveyors of "Excessive" or "Unfair" Scrutiny

Leaders or gatekeepers who feel that reporters, "watchdog" groups, clients, or fellow organization members are engaging in excessive or unfair scrutiny may try to avert future scrutiny by ignoring them, ostracizing them, or physically barring or removing them from the premises. Swasy (1993) reports that, in response to her critical stories about Procter & Gamble and her aggressive intrusions in gathering information for these stories, Procter & Gamble's public relations staff ignored her requests for information. When she asked a company spokesperson for "basic information about a Russian venture," his response was "Surely a snooping reporter like you can find out that information," followed by "Why don't call some of your famous sources" (Swasy, 1992, p. 296). Similarly, Natale (1993, p. 14) reported that he was not sure whether to be flattered or insulted when an editor pressured him to interview a movie star because "We're having more and more trouble with these damn publicists wanting to approve our writers, and she has already rejected two of our suggestions. But when I brought up your name she was quite pleased." If successful, efforts to refuse access to the leader or organization not only halt or reduce scrutiny, doing so serves as a warning to others that they may be removed or ostracized if they are too critical, intrusive, or zealous.

Structural Defenses

Establishing Roles to Block and Absorb Scrutiny

Thompson's (1967) classic *Organizations in Action* describes strategies that organizations use to buffer or seal-off their core technical activities from environmental influences. As Scott (1992, p. 194) put it, such strategies "close the system artificially to enhance the possibilities of rational action." For example, "coding" of inputs is used to screen-out inappropriate clients and defective materials to avoid introducing unnecessary delays and confusion into the performance of technical activities. Similarly, leaders and other members may try to buffer or screen out unwanted intrusions from people within and outside their organizations.

Gatekeepers screen-out unwanted encounters and schedule and set priorities among desired encounters and so are a primary structural means that leaders use to buffer themselves from unwanted intrusion. Gatekeepers accomplish such "blocking" by using many of the rhetorical and procedural defenses described above. They may, for example, use vague language or be nasty to unwanted intruders, help leaders hide by refusing to connect calls, or lie that the boss is "out of the office." They may also enforce restrictions on interactions with a leader or tell purveyors of "excessive" scrutiny that access to a leader has been revoked. Secretaries and receptionists often hold such buffering roles. Sutton (1989) found that people in these roles often blocked his attempts to talk to leaders of dying organizations. They sometimes refused to transfer calls to a leader because he or she was "too busy" or "too upset." They also often deflected Sutton's calls to public relations personnel rather than top managers. Sutton found, for example, that his request to interview leaders who were closing a department store was foiled when the receptionist (without warning) transferred his phone call to a public relations manager. This manager was enthusiastic when being interviewed, but told Sutton he could not interview other managers.

Tom Wolfe's (1970) essay "Mau-Mauing the Flak Catchers" presents a stylized example of buffering by bureaucrats at the San Francisco's Office of Economic Opportunity in the late 1960s. When representatives of minority groups came in the office to lobby decision makers for funds, Wolfe tells how they were blocked, at least at first, by career, lower-level, gatekeepers they called "flak-catchers." Wolfe described how a flak-catcher responded to a request to see the "The man:"

"I'm sorry that Mr. Johnson isn't here today," he says, "but he is not in the city. He's back in Washington meeting some project deadlines. He's very concerned and would want to meet with you people right now if he were here, but right now I know that you'll understand that the most important thing that he can do for you is to push these projects through in Washington".... "Now I'm here to answer any questions I can," he says, "but you have to understand that I'm only speaking as an individual, and so naturally none of my comments are binding." (1970, pp. 109-110)

People in gatekeeper roles do more than just block scrutiny, they also absorb it. By doing so they, they further buffer leaders from intrusion and distraction. These bureaucrats were called "flak-catchers" because they absorbed angry questions and demands so that decision-makers did not have to face such intrusions. Wolfe describes how representatives of minority groups that were seeking funds construed encounters with these bureaucrats:

And then it dawns on you, you wonder why it took so long to realize it. The man is the flak catcher. His job is to catch flak for the No. 1 man. He's like the professional mourners you can hire in Chinatown. They have certified wailers, professional mourners, in Chinatown, and when your loved one dies, you can hire the professional mourners to wail at the funeral and show what a great loss to the community the departed is. In the same way this lifer is ready to catch whatever flak you are sending up. It doesn't matter what bureau they put him in. It's all the same. Poverty, Japanese imports, valley fever tomato-crop parity, partial disability... whatever you're angry about, it doesn't matter, he's there to catch the flak.

Decoupling Symbolic and Substantive Leadership Roles

Meyer and Rowan (1977) proposed that organizations separate—or decouple—symbolic structures and practices from substantive ones, in part, to reduce inspection and evaluation from external and internal audiences. Scott (1992) describes this as a strategy for buffering the technical core because it diverts attention toward ceremonial and presumably more normatively acceptable symbolic structures and actions. By doing so, technical structures and actions are constrained less by external intrusions. One way to reduce inspection, evaluation, and interruption is to establish distinct symbolic and substantive leaders so that scrutiny will be directed toward the symbolic leader, while the substantive leader will be left unfettered. This way, the substantive leader can deal with technical matters like resource allocation, planning, and decision making more efficiently. The English government, with the king and queen versus the prime minister and parliament illustrates such decoupling. It is an imperfect example because, although English royalty have no substantive responsibilities, the prime minister and parliament have much symbolic work because they are elected politicians.

Many corporations split symbolic and substantive leadership, at least to some degree. In the early years of Apple Computer, Steve Jobs played a large symbolic role, marketing the product, making speeches, talking to reporters, and securing venture capital funds, while co-founder Steven Wozniak developed Apple's early products, especially the wildly successful Apple II (Young, 1988). Similarly, while Hewlett-Packard CEO John Young was the official head of this Palo Alto-based corporation during most of the 1980s, Richard Hackborn, an executive who worked much of the time in relative obscurity in an office tucked in a modest shopping center in Boise, Idaho, was the firm's most influential technology and marketing strategist. Hackborn was largely responsible for imagining and then implementing the corporation's current dominance of the laser printing industry. Young played important roles in strategic decisions about the printer business. But our conversations with Hewlett-Packard executives suggest the most important role that Young played was taking heat from internal and external constituencies so that Hackborn could develop and implement his ideas relatively free from evaluation and interruption.

Using Symbolic Practices to Divert Attention from Substantive Actions

Meyer and Rowan (1977) propose that, beyond enhancing their technical performance, organizations adopt structures and practices for symbolic or ceremonial reasons. Organizations may help buffer their activities—including managerial action—by adopting widely used, endorsed, and visible structures and practices. Such structures and practices can reduce the scrutiny that leaders and organizations face because, when present, these ceremonial responses distract observers from—and may help mask—less visible and more controversial structures and practices.

Scott and Meyer (1991) propose that employee training, beyond helping organizations control employees and as a means of conveying knowledge, is often adopted for such institutional reasons. Training programs can be used as symbolic responses that are decoupled from the other organizational activities. Organizations that are criticized for racial and gender discrimination, sexual harassment, or ethical violations sometimes try to please (and distract) critics by "training" employees to "learn" to avoid these unsavory behaviors. Training can be used—and is used—without changing policies for hiring, disciplining, firing, compensating, or promoting employees. A history of racial discrimination and tension between black and white employees plagued the public agency that we attempted to study. Some changes were made in hiring and promotion practices. But much time and money were also devoted to "diversity training." Leaders appeared to speak with great sincerity about the importance of such training during public appearances. Nonetheless, leaders, other employees, and even some of those who did the training privately described it as a waste of time and money and as having no impact on day-to-day race relations. But leaders believed that diversity training was needed to convince external and internal constituencies to leave them alone so they could do their work.

LIMITATIONS AND DRAWBACKS OF DEFENSES

Leaders and organizations that use these defenses may enjoy benefits including fewer delays in crucial tasks, not wasting time and attention on symbolic tasks, not being bound by unrealistic injunctive norms, learning more easily, being creative, and avoiding perseverance at failing courses of action. These virtues are reflected in "shy billionaire" and executive vice-president Forest Mars' assertion that much of his company's success is due to the privacy that they work so hard to maintain, which he contended "allows us to do the very best we can, the best we know how, without being concerned about self-aggrandizement" (Brenner, 1992).

Nonetheless, it is difficult to protect leaders and organizations from scrutiny if they are pursued by sufficiently large numbers of persistent and imaginative people. No matter which defenses are used or how vigorously implemented, intruders may be able to circumvent these impediments. Teel and Taylor's (1988, p. 120) text teaches aspiring journalists techniques for obtaining interviews with recalcitrant subjects, including "the face-off" (barging in his or her hideout), "the sit-in" (camping-out until the subject consents to the interview), "the assault" (running along side the subject and making "your appeal as quickly and strongly as possible"), and "beg." Bok (1983) describes reporters who lie about their identities and motives to get around defenses. She describes how a German reporter, Gunter Wallraff, disguised himself as a guard to learn about an insurance company, as a right-wing emissary to learn about a planned coup in Portugal, and as a reporter to learn about the sleazy practices used by a German tabloid.[4]

Beyond the fact that even the most carefully designed defenses can be overcome by people who are sufficiently curious and persistent, we identified four other ways that defenses can be ineffective, backfire, or have unintended negative consequences.

Defenses Consume Valuable Resources

Implementing many of the defenses listed in Table 1 can be expensive. Writing well-crafted ambiguous and boring language takes time for executives, public relations staff, and other gatekeepers. Establishing procedures and paying gatekeepers to block and absorb scrutiny is expensive, as are symbolic structures and programs like training. Managing an organization's image is something that can and should occupy the time of skilled people; all organizations need to obtain and protect legitimacy. As Tetlock's (1991) work on accountability suggests, however, such defenses may be used so much that not enough resources are devoted to substantive tasks. This drawback was especially apparent in the public agency that we attempted to study. Vast amounts of time and money were spent on defenses like limiting interaction with purveyors of scrutiny, hiring gatekeepers to reduce scrutiny, hiring lawyers and other outsiders to help respond to scrutiny, and conducting symbolic training programs. Leaders, employees, and consultants all expressed concerns that the organization's ability to carry out its core mission, which involved protecting the public, had suffered. Similarly, Stanford University hired Hill & Knowlton, the largest public relations firm in the country, to help leaders answer charges of misuse of federal funds (Gottlieb, 1991). Stanford paid for hundreds of hours of such consulting—at a rate of $200 to $300 per hour—during a period when substantial cost cutting, including layoffs, was occurring throughout the university.

Defenses May Make the Leader or Organization More Interesting to Observers

The defenses listed in Table 1 are used in efforts to reduce scrutiny. As the reclusive billionaire Howard Hughes discovered, however, when people or organizations go through great trouble to defend against intrusions from outsiders, it may lead to even greater scrutiny because outsiders may construe that there is something interesting, and perhaps unsavory, to hide (Bok, 1983; Eisenberg, 1984). Brenner (1992) wrote two long stories in the *Washington Post Magazine* about Mars Candy largely because the members of the Mars family were so secretive. Swasy (1993) became increasingly interested in covering Procter & Gamble, in part, because they used defenses like hiding, stalling, establishing rules about interactions with the press, doing favors for local journalists, and ostracizing "biased" reporters. She found these defenses interesting to write about and wondered what the company had to hide. Swasy reported that Procter & Gamble did such a severe "Ivory Snow Job" that its public relations department sometimes refused to confirm that products were on the market even when they could be found on store shelves. She also reported that a former chief financial officer was proud of being told by a financial analyst that he gave a new meaning to the word "stonewall." These and other defenses helped protect Procter & Gamble executives and their company in the short term. Ultimately, however, the defenses themselves attracted scrutiny from publications like the *New York Times* and *Wall Street Journal*.

Similarly, Paul Biddle, an auditor from the Office of Naval Research who asserted that Stanford University overcharged taxpayers million of dollars, contended he became suspicious partly because Stanford officials avoided meeting with him, gave him incomplete information, did favors for his superiors in exchange for softer scrutiny, and tried to get him removed as an auditor because he was overzealous and biased. He asserted that these and other defensive actions led him to examine Stanford's accounting practices more closely, actions which resulted in a costly and embarrassing episode for Stanford (Cooper, 1991).

Defenses May Be Poor Impression Management

It is ironic that leaders and organizations use many of the defenses in Table 1 to protect their reputations, but using some defenses can harm such reputations. Use of these tactics may be interpreted as a sign that a leader or organization has something to hide, is directing his or her attention toward how actions look instead of toward more substantive actions, or that funds are being wasted. Any or all of these impressions can undermine the legitimacy of a leader or organization. For example, Stanford's use of a public relations firm to help defend against charges of federal funds misuse was criticized as wasteful and an attempt to refuse blame (Whetzel, 1991). When Procter & Gamble used defenses like hiding, stalling, and ignoring and ostracizing reporters to reduce scrutiny, these defenses did harm to Procter & Gamble's reputation beyond the information that was uncovered about unsafe products and environmental pollution. Swasy (1993, p. 300) reports:

> The *Washington Post* editorial read: "In this affair P&G has suffered a certain loss of dignity as well as abrasions to its reputation for common sense." Even the usually friendly *Cincinnati Post* editorial page blasted P&G: "After years of working to improve its reputation as a corporate bully and impenetrable fortress, this incident paints that picture all over again." …. For *The Dayton Daily News*, [cartoonist] Mike Peters drew a lone cleaning woman in a KGB office telling a caller "Sorry Comrade… the agents are gone. They all went to work for Procter and Gamble."

Defenses that enhance a leader's or organization's reputation under some conditions can damage reputations under other conditions. For example, being boring can fuel negative scrutiny if the leader is expected to be charismatic. French prime minister Edouard Balladur was applauded in the past for his no nonsense and pragmatic approach to, and conduct in, government. As the candidate for the much more powerful and visible role of French president, however, being boring drew him more criticism and attention than any of his past failures as prime minister. *The Economist* wrote (1995, p. 29):

> Although content with the phlegmatic and pragmatic Mr. Balladur as prime minister, the French want something more from a president. Mr. Balladur's manifesto, trumpeted on February 13, was a disappointment. It read more like a government programme for the coming year than a future president's vision for the next seven. It was competent, moderate, boring-like the man himself.

Defenses May Seal-Off Leaders and Organizations from Key People and Data

Many of the defenses listed in Table 1 seal-off leaders and other people in symbolic roles from important information that is needed to take sound substantive and symbolic action. Leaders who are boring and nasty may drive away exchange partners who can provide valuable information. Procedural defenses like hiding and limiting interaction with outsiders limits the flow of such information into top management's purview. Gatekeepers block and absorb incoming information; in particular, they are likely to screen-out unpleasant visitors with "unpleasant" information who will upset their superiors. Moreover, Crozier (1964, p. 45) describes how, in interactions with their superiors, subunit heads are likely to "bias the information they give in order get the maximum of material resources and personal favors."

The blend of defenses against scrutiny and incentives mean that, especially for top managers of large organizations, information that they need—especially negative information—often never gets to them. Brock Yates (1983) asserted that this blend helped insulate General Motors executives from warning signs that they needed to build smaller and higher quality cars in the late 1970s and early 1980s. As John De Lorean, a General Motors executive at the time, put it: "The system quickly shut top management off from the real world because it surrounded itself in many cases with 'yes' men. There soon became no real vehicle for input" (Wright, 1979, p. 47). Swasy (1993, p. 305) quotes a stockholder who described the long-term effects of such screening on Proctor & Gamble executives: "People at the top of big companies get out of touch sometimes. They have so many people kissing their ass, they don't know right from wrong."

The defenses that organizations use against scrutiny may create arrogant leaders because negative information and people who have negative views of the organization or the leader are kept away from leaders. This is a role theory view of arrogance (Hallmark & Curtis, 1994) because it suggests that, while arrogance may be fueled by personality characteristics like high self-esteem, leaders often claim excessive status because of the information they do and do not receive about personal and organizational performance. Regardless of whether evaluations of the leader or organization are generally positive or negative, the defenses used when scrutiny is high may screen out a disproportionately large amount of negative information and let in a disproportionately large amount of positive information. The long run effect may be that leaders begin to develop self-aggrandized views of their importance and how well they and their organizations are performing and will perform. In turn, they may make excessive claims about their own virtues and those of their organizations. Schwartz (1990) provides a compelling example of such an excessive claim by a NASA administrator. Nobel-Prize winner Richard

Feynman served on the Rogers Commission, which investigated the explosion of the space shuttle Challenger. Feynman asked a group of engineers to estimate the chances that the shuttle's main engine would fail. Their estimates ranged from 1 in 200 to 1 in 300. When Feynman asked their boss for the same estimate, he proposed a failure rate of 1 in 100,000. Feynman asserted that this was just one of many illustrations that managerial isolation from reality was rampant throughout NASA (Schwartz, 1990, p. 89).

DISCUSSION

This paper proposed that, in carrying out their symbolic roles, leaders and other visible organization members must operate in the bright and often harsh spotlight of public scrutiny. Our perspective was grounded in a combination of scholarly theory and research and less systematic data from the popular media, failed efforts to study a public agency, and informal interviews with leaders who had faced and conveyed public scrutiny. We anticipate that future work in this area will refine, expand, refute, and replace our preliminary ideas about the definition of intense scrutiny, its consequences for leaders and their organizations, defenses against scrutiny, and the drawbacks of defenses. Our efforts to review pertinent literature and to write this paper suggested several fundamental issues that might be developed in subsequent work.

We portrayed scrutiny as an unavoidable experience for people in symbolic roles in organizations, especially for leaders. Our preliminary hunch, after examining the psychological literature, the organizational studies literature, and case examples is that the consequences of scrutiny (and the unintended side effects of defending against it) are, on balance, more negative than positive. We acknowledged that delays in ongoing tasks, devoting attention and effort to symbolic rather than substantive acts, following injunctive rather than descriptive norms, reduced learning and creativity, and perseverance at ongoing and planned action can be sometimes desirable. More often, however, we portrayed these consequences as costs that leaders and their organizations had to pay if they wished to promote images that would bring legitimacy, resources, and power. This view that scrutiny is often a necessary evil for people who hold symbolic roles needs to be tested. Boundary conditions under which scrutiny has negative versus positive effects also need to be identified. For example, we proposed that scrutiny causes people to work harder at what they know how to do well. Perhaps, despite the setbacks caused by interruptions, scrutiny may have a positive impact as long as creativity and learning are not crucial.

We do not mean to imply that public scrutiny is always harmful and should be avoided. We believe that business, political, religious and academic leaders should all be held responsible for performing in a competent and ethical fashion. This paper recognizes, however, that in our frenzy to place these people and their organizations under the spotlight of public attention, we may be creating dysfunctional consequences, including driving talented people out important positions or discouraging them from ever seeking such positions. As Sabato writes of U.S. political leaders and the price of power (1993, p. 206):

> Simply put, the price of power has been raised dramatically, far too high for many outstanding potential officeholders. An individual contemplating a run for office must now accept the possibility of almost unlimited intrusion into his or her financial and personal life. Every investment made, every affair conducted, every private sin committed from college years to the present may one day wind up in a headline or on television... American society today is losing the services of many exceptionally talented individuals who could make outstanding contributions to the commonweal, but who understandably will not subject themselves and their loved ones to abusive, intrusive press coverage.

We devoted little attention to the differences between positive and negative scrutiny. We proposed that attention, performance monitoring, interruptions, and questions can be provoked by successes or failures or can come from friends or enemies. There may, however, be systematic differences between the mechanisms of positive versus negative scrutiny. Persistent and unchecked positive scrutiny may lead to arrogance by leaders. We already proposed that arrogance may result when defenses screen out disproportionate amounts of negative information. There are also times when leaders face unchecked scrutiny that is largely or wholly positive. Leaders of wildly successful organizations, for example, may encounter praise at every turn. The combination of great success and constant praise may cause leaders to believe that they can do little or no wrong, even in spheres where they have little or no competence. John Scully followed Steve Jobs as Apple Computer's CEO and, eventually, played a central role in firing Jobs. Scully contended that the press and many Apple employees treated Jobs like he was a "Messiah." Scully asserted that such praise, in combination with Apple's early financial success, caused Jobs to believe that he was free from adhering to binding legal obligations, to overestimate how strongly members of the Apples board of directors supported him, and to overestimate his technical ability (Scully & Byrne, 1987).

In contrast, Kramer's (1994, 1995) work on paranoia suggests that relentless hostile scrutiny threatens a person's self-esteem, security, and identity. When a person faces criticism at every turn, has no other meaningful positive identity to turn to, and efforts to reduce hostile scrutiny seem to have further alienated others, Kramer shows that exaggerated distrust or suspicion of others' intentions and motives occurs. Kramer's (1995) case study of U.S. President Lyndon Johnson during the Vietnam War shows that the relentless criticism he faced (and his failure to halt it) meant "every expression of doubt and criticism, even from close friends and even when clearly intended as constructive, was transformed into a personal assault on his claim on the nation's leadership." Arrogance and paranoia are extreme responses to extreme scrutiny. The day-to-day praise and criticism that all visible leaders receive may lead to milder episodes of overconfidence and unwarranted suspicion. Extreme responses to extreme scrutiny make interesting reading. But it might be more useful to focus research attention on the more moderate levels of scrutiny and associated responses that are typical of larger numbers of settings.

Subsequent work on scrutiny might also consider the potential negative effects of "explaining why" on leaders' information processing and decision making. A defining feature of scrutiny is that leaders face, and routinely answer, an onslaught of questions about what has happened, is happening, is planned to happen, and why. Theory and research by Wilson and his colleagues suggests that answering such questions may reduce the quality of subsequent decision making. Wilson and Schooler's (1991) overview of the vast normative theory and research on decision making and decision analysis indicates that—beginning with assertions by Benjamin Franklin—many scholars have argued that developing a set of prior justifications will lead to superior decision making. This work suggests there are benefits to developing a systematic "balance sheet" of reasons why past successes or failures occurred or of the pros and cons associated with making a current decision (e.g., Janis & Mann, 1977; Raiffa, 1968). It suggests that, by decomposing a complex problem into simpler elements, the problem as a whole can be better understood.

Despite the intuitive appeal of these rational perspectives, research by Wilson and his colleagues suggests that people who first develop a list of careful justifications may subsequently make worse rather than better decisions. A study reported by Wilson and Schooler (1991), for example, describes the preferences subjects had for different brands of strawberry jams. It compared the preferences of subjects who provided detailed justifications before ranking brands of strawberry jam to subjects who simply tasted and then immediately ranked brands. Preferences of subjects who first developed detailed justifications were not significantly correlated with experts' rankings ($r = .11.$); but preferences of students who were not asked to first develop reasons for their rankings were significantly and highly correlated ($r = .55$) with experts' rankings. Wilson and Schooler report similar findings for course evaluations by college students.

Wilson and Schooler explain these findings as a dysfunction of "thinking too much." They argue that much experimental research suggests that people often have limited information about the forces that determine their attitudes and behaviors (see Nisbett & Wilson, 1977; Wilson, Dunn, Kraft, & Lisle, 1989). When people are asked to reflect on what causes their preferences and actions, they typically report plausible and salient causes rather than actual causes. As Nisbett and Wilson (1977) put it, people tell more than they know. Wilson and Schooler propose that making such inaccurate reports can shape subsequent preferences or actions, specifically that doing so can reduce the quality of subsequent judgments because people come to believe their espoused criteria and then try to apply those (typically) flawed and incomplete criteria to subsequent decisions.

This theory and the associated findings have intriguing, and unexamined, implications for future research on the effects of public scrutiny and symbolic leadership. They imply that when a leader faces and answers an unchecked flow of requests to justify past, current, and planned actions, he or she is espousing a constant stream of plausible (but likely inaccurate) explanations for individual and organizational decisions. These criteria are likely to be inaccurate partly because all humans have trouble discovering the real criteria guiding their actions (and, we would add, partly because leaders tend to only report criteria that put them or their organizations in a positive light). Leaders may use these inaccurate criteria to guide their own decisions and to impose decision-making criteria on subordinates. Or subordinates may imitate the criteria espoused (rather than used) by their superiors as a way of garnering praise or to put themselves in a more defensible position should a poor outcome occur. As a result, a first hypothesis might be to the degree a leader provides detailed justifications and explanations for personal or organizational actions, the quality of subsequent decisions will decay. A second hypothesis might be that the quality of the decisions made by his or her subordinates will decay as well. These hypotheses could be motivated and refined in inductive field research and then, building on the methods developed by Wilson and his colleagues, could be tested with experimental methods.

We also encourage researchers to devote less attention to how scrutiny is conveyed and described by the popular media than we did in this paper. We did not intend to give intrusions by the press or reactions to the press any special status in our conceptual perspective. We were careful to provide examples of how unchecked scrutiny can be conveyed by other "audiences" or "publics" like stockholders, clients, subordinates, and suppliers. Nonetheless, a substantial proportion of the examples presented here concern intrusions by the press or were derived from reports in the popular media. We used reports by and about the press so much because they were often available when evidence about scrutiny from other sources—especially scholarly publications—was not available. The performance criteria imposed, intrusions made, and questions asked by the press do, to some extent, serve as an avenue through which other internal and external constituencies scrutinize leaders and their organizations. But leaders are often scrutinized directly by such constituencies rather than indirectly through observation by and interactions with the press. The way in which scrutiny is conveyed by the press may differ in important ways from how it is conveyed by other groups and individuals. And mass media reports of how scrutiny is conveyed by other groups may omit key consequences and defenses that should have been included in our perspective. As a result, our perspective may have been shaped excessively by how leaders respond to and defend against scrutiny by the press and the way that the press reports about scrutiny.

Finally, future work might also examine why blatant misrepresentations appear to be used so much when scrutiny is present, along with and the effects of such misrepresentations on the targets and purveyors of scrutiny. We were surprised by how much dishonesty we encountered in writings about scrutiny, especially in writings about defenses against scrutiny. Leaders seem to routinely provide vague and inaccurate information to avoid intrusion. The apparent purpose of maintaining plausible deniability, for example, is so that a person can lie without getting caught later. It seems that gatekeepers routinely lie about the whereabouts of leaders and that organizations will sometimes establish symbolic programs like diversity training and mislead external constituencies about the impact that leaders believe it will have on life within their organization. We even encountered an example of high ranking government officials who bragged about a deceitful trick that they used. Frost, Mitchell, and Nord (1986, p. 421) reprinted an Associated Press story about a prank that White House officials used to distract and punish a reporter who routinely read and reported about documents from officials' desks without their permission:

> Tired of reporters stealing glances at White House memos, presidential spokesman Larry Speakes got his revenge when two reporters "bit like snakes" at fake memos planted on a press aide's desk. One of the fake documents contained a proposal to move the press corps from the White House next door to the Old Executive Office Building. .... "They both made calls all over this White House about relocating the press," Speakes said. "We held the line on it for two days here, and we wouldn't tell them anything."

Perhaps this deceit was justified given the reporter's unauthorized scrutiny. More generally, perhaps as Nyberg (1993) asserts, lying to others is sometimes a more moral act than telling the truth. He argues that lying may be necessary to protect the mental health of others because telling them the truth will lead to unnecessary and destructive pain and suffering. And lying to protect a leader might be morally justifiable if it is necessary to help him or her do important work without intrusion. Nonetheless, we are not convinced that misrepresenting the facts to avoid scrutiny is a means that always justifies the end.

People who misrepresent facts about themselves or their organizations may not always be engaging in conscious deceit. Leaders and their gatekeepers may, like other human beings, make false statements because they are engaging in wishful thinking or deceiving themselves (Ashforth & Lee, 1990; Snyder & Higgins, 1988). Lazarus (1985) suggests that there are times when denial of reality facilitates well-being and decision making. Denial of facts is sometimes destructive, as when a cancer victim delays treatment. But Lazarus proposes that denial can be healthy when it helps a person divert attention away from a source of distress that he or she cannot change; in such cases, focusing attention on and worrying only saps the person's ability to cope with other matters that he or she has the power to change. In the case of public scrutiny, Lazarus' perspective suggests that, when rhetorical, procedural, and structural defenses against scrutiny fail or are not feasible, it may be in the best interest of leaders to try some denial of these elements. The term "denial" implies that the leader does not believe that such scrutiny has occurred. But Lazarus suggests that people may benefit from using some milder, denial-like processes, to avoid attending to irrelevant or uncontrollable threats. The CEO of one Fortune 50 company that we spoke to indicated that he never read, listened to, or viewed media reports about him or his corporation. He asserted that it was easier to please key constituencies directly rather than through the mass media and that he could not learn useful new information about his corporation from the media, in part because such reports usually contained so many errors. As a result, he said that such reports—whether they were positive or negative—were a useless distraction from his duties as CEO.

CONCLUSION

We began this paper by asserting that a broad range of research in psychology, sociology, economics, and organizational behavior emphasizes that people and organizations that are noticed by and please others will be rewarded with power, legitimacy, and resources. We asserted that although this literature implies that leaders, and others in symbolic roles, must work under close scrutiny if they wish to garner such rewards for themselves and their organizations, little theory or research considers other consequences of such scrutiny. Our perspective suggests that occupying a role that has a mix of symbolic and substantive responsibilities creates difficulties because, beyond the problem of allocating limited resources to two sets of responsibilities, doing symbolic tasks may make it difficult to do substantive tasks at all, and when they are done, to do them well. These conclusions are based on thin data and tentative theory. Future research may refute them or show that these drawbacks occur under rare conditions.

Suppose, however, that these troublesome conclusions do prove to be true, at least when scrutiny is greatest. Suppose that when we devote more attention to leaders and others who make crucial decisions, they work more slowly, learn more slowly, are less creative, focus on doing what looks best rather than doing their best, and persist even when it is almost certain they will fail. Also suppose, to the extent that leaders try to defend against scrutiny, these problems are accentuated and new problems are created as well. If so, this admittedly pessimistic interpretation suggests we cannot always rely on the leaders and organizations we care about to defend against scrutiny; and we should not always blame them when they fail to defend against or are distracted by scrutiny. It might be better to stop scrutiny from occurring in the first place or to halt scrutiny quickly once it begins. In order to understand how to stop it from occurring, future work might devote as much attention to the purveyors of scrutiny as to the targets of scrutiny. A promising place to start such research might be to focus on settings where averting scrutiny of a leader or organization is in the audience's best interest. A challenging but important question for such work will be how—and if—audiences can learn to ignore the leaders and organizations they are most interested in and care about most.

ACKNOWLEDGMENTS

We wish to thank Blake Ashforth, Thomas D'Aunno, Jane Dutton, Kimberly Elsbach, Gary Alan Fine, Daniel Julius, Roderick Kramer, and W. Richard Scott for their contributions to this paper, which was prepared while the first author was a Fellow at the Center for Advanced Study in the Behavioral Sciences. The second author wishes to the thank the Social Sciences Research Council of Canada for their support. We are grateful for financial assistance provided by Hewlett-Packard and the National Science Foundation (SBR-9022192).

NOTES

1. The two authors of this paper attempted to study how the transition to a more diverse workforce affected a large public agency. This organization was characterized by 20 years of often severe legal and interpersonal conflicts between white and black employees, and had been subject to severe criticism from a wide variety of sources. We devoted considerable effort to starting a study of this organization because an initial meeting between the top manager and the third member of our research team (who had a long-term consulting relationship with top management) indicated that they were willing to participate despite its controversial nature. Our efforts to begin this study included over 50 (often unreturned) phone calls to members of the organization, approximately 20 phone conversations and meetings between the authors and the consultant in which we discussed the public agency, three meetings with head of the agency in which the study was discussed, two meetings (including a lengthy interview) with the former head of the black employees union who had become a member of top management, an attempted interview with the second highest ranking manager in which he declined to participate because he feared that we would leak our findings to the media, and gathering hundreds of pages of documents about the organization including newspaper stories, consultant reports, and court records. As it became clear that our efforts to study this organization would fail, we began to realize that we were not learning much about race relations and what we were learning was already well-documented in psychology, sociology, and political science. But we also realized that we were learning a great deal about the impact of public scrutiny on people and organizations, and that there was much less scholarly literature on this subject.

2. We spoke with three members of the media and six leaders of large organizations about scrutiny. The reporters included a business writer, an editor who specialized in stories about Washington, DC politics, and a science reporter. The leaders we spoke to were the president of

a real estate firm, a former CEO of a Fortune 50 company, a current CEO of a Fortune 50 company, two former university administrators, and a current university administrator. Furthermore, about a year after our efforts to study the public agency failed, we spoke with the (recently fired) head of the agency. These conversations focused on how scrutiny is presented to and experienced by people in the public eye, how such people defend against and take the best advantage of scrutiny, and the costs and benefits of scrutiny for leaders and their organizations.

3. Carver and Scheier (1990) make a similar argument, suggesting that emotions are part of a process of feedback and self-regulation in which positive emotion is felt to the extent that one exceeds goals and negative emotion is felt to the extent that one falls short of goals.

4. Reporters can be imaginative at getting past animal as well human defenses. Oliver North reports in "Under Fire" (1991), that his dog "Max" responded to reporters camping outside his house by barking furiously, which sent them scurrying away. North goes on to say, however, that the reporters soon learned that they could calm Max by giving him "a 7-Eleven doughnut" and that "over the next few months that dog must have gained 20 pounds" (North, 1991, p. 394).

REFERENCES

Amabile, T.M. (1983). *The social psychology of creativity*. New York: Springer-Verlag.

Ashforth, B.E., & Lee, R.T. (1990) Defensive behavior in organizations: A preliminary model. *Human Relations, 43*, 621-648.

Baron, R.S. (1986). Distraction-conflict theory: Progress and problems. In L. Berkowitz (Ed.), *Advances in experimental social psychology* (Vol. 19, pp. 1-40). Orlando, FL: Academic Press.

Bartholomew, K. (1993, January 20). A matter of time: Casper does his thinking on the run. *Stanford University Campus Report* (Vol. 25), pp. 1, 6, 8.

Bass, B.M. (1990). *Bass & Stogdill's handbook of leadership*. New York: Free Press.

Bennis, W. (1979). Why leaders can't lead. In R.M. Kanter & B.A. Stein (Eds.), *Life in organizations* (pp. 36-48). New York: Basic Books.

Bogen, D., & Lynch, M. (1989). Taking account of the hostile native: Plausible deniability and the production of conventional history in the Iran-Contra Hearings. *Social Problems, 36*, 197-224.

Bok, S. (1983). *Secrets: On the ethics of concealment and revelation*. New York: Pantheon

Brenner, J.G. (1992, April 12). The shy billionaires. *The Washington Post Magazine*, p. W14.

Brockner, J., Rubin, J.Z., & Lang, E. (1981). Face-saving and entrapment. *Journal of Experimental Social Psychology, 17*, 68-79.

Carver, C.S., & Scheier, M.F. (1990). Origins and functions of positive and negative affect: A control-process view. *Psychological Review, 97*, 19-35.

Cameron, K.S., Sutton, R.I., & Whetten, D.A. (1988). *Readings in organizational decline: Frameworks, research, and prescriptions*. Boston: Ballinger.

Cialdini, R.B. (1984). *Influence: The new psychology of modern persuasion*. New York: Quill.

Cialdini, R.B., Kallgren, C.A., & Reno, R.R. (1991). A focus theory of normative conduct: A theoretical refinement and reevaluation of the role of norms in human behavior. In *Advances in experimental social psychology* (Vol. 24, pp. 201-234).

The Columbia Dictionary of Quotations. (1993). Newark: Columbia University Press.

Cooper, K.J. (1991, September 30). Navy to honor Biddle's Campus Crusade: Accountant unearthed research billing excesses at Stanford. *The Washington Post*, p. A9.

Crozier, M. (1964). *The bureaucratic phenomenon*. Chicago: University of Chicago Press.

The Economist. (1995, March 11-17). "France, Unpredictable afterall," pp. 29-30.

Eisenberg, E.M. (1984). Ambiguity as a strategy in organizational communication. *Communication Monographs, 51*, 227-242.

Elsbach, K.D. (1994). Managing organizational legitimacy in the California Cattle Industry: The construction and effectiveness of verbal accounts. *Administrative Science Quarterly, 39,* 57-88.
Feinstein, J. (1986). *A season on the brink.* New York: Simon & Schuster.
Fiske, S.T., & Taylor, S.E. (1991). *Social cognition* (2nd ed.). New York: McGraw-Hill.
Frost, P.J., Mitchell, V.F., & Nord, W.R. (1986). *Organizational reality: Reports from the firing line.* New York: Harper-Collins.
Galunic, C.D. (1994). *The evolution of intracorporate domains: Divisional charter losses in high technology, multidivisional corporations.* Doctoral dissertation, Stanford University, School of Engineering.
Garfinkel, H. (1967). *Studies in ethnomethodology.* Englewood Cliffs, NJ: Prentice-Hall.
Garment, S. (1991). *Scandal: The crisis of mistrust in American politics.* New York: Times Books.
Geen, R.G. (1991). Social motivation. *Annual Review of Psychology, 42,* 377-400.
Gentry, C. (1992). *J. Edgar Hoover: The man and his secrets.* New York: Norton.
Ginzel, L.E., Kramer, R.M., & Sutton, R.I. (1993). Organizational impression management as a reciprocal influence process: The neglected role of the organizational audience. In B.M. Staw & L.L. Cummings (Eds.), *Research in organizational behavior* (Vo. 15, pp. 227-266). Greenwich, CT: JAI Press.
Gleick, J. (1992). *Genius: The life and science of Richard Feynman.* New York: Pantheon.
Gottleib, J. (1991, February 2). Heavyweight joins Stanford defense team. *San Jose Mercury News,* p. 1B.
Gouldner, A. W. (1960). The norm of reciprocity: A preliminary statement. *American Sociological Review, 25,* 161-178.
Guerin, B. (1986). Mere presence effects in humans: A review. *Journal of Experimental Social Psychology, 22,* 37-77.
Hallmark, S.W., & Curtis, R.C. (1994). *Arrogance: The public interaction of role claims and role performance.* Paper presented at the Society for the Study of Social Problems.
Henderson, R., & Shea, J. (1992). *Off base: Confessions of a thief.* New York: Harper.
Herring, G.C. (1993). The reluctant warrior: Lyndon Johnson as Commander in Chief. In D.L. Anderson (Ed.), *Shadow on the White House: Presidents and the Vietnam War, 1945-1975* (pp. 87-112). Kansas: University of Kansas Press.
Hertsgaard, M. (1989). *On bended knee: The press and the Reagan presidency.* New York: Schocken Books
Hill, R.C. (1993). When the going gets tough: A Baldrige Award winner the line. *Academy of Management Executive, 7*(3), 75-79.
Horton, T.R. (1992). *The CEO paradox: The privilege and accountability of leadership.* New York: AMACOM.
Isen, A.M., & Baron, R.A. (1991). Positive affect as a factor in organizational behavior. In L.L. Cummings & B.M. Staw (Eds.), *Research in organizational behavior* (Vol. 13, pp. 1-53). Greenwich, CT: JAI Press.
Janis, I.L., & Mann, L. (1977). *Decision making.* New York: Free Press.
Kahn, R.L., & Byosiere, P. (1992). Stress in organizations. In M.D. Dunnette & L.M. Hough (Eds.), *Handbook of industrial & organizational psychology* (2nd ed., Vol. 3, pp. 571-650). Palo Alto, CA: Consulting Psychologists Press.
Kanter, R.M. (1977). *Men and women of the corporation.* New York: Basic Books.
Kanter, R.M. (1979). How the top is different. In R.M. Kanter & B.A. Stein (Eds.), *Life in organizations* (pp. 20-35). New York: Basic Books.
Katz, D., & R.L. Kahn. (1978). *The social psychology of organizations.* New York: John Wiley & Sons.
Kramer, R.M. (1994). Distrust and suspicion in nasty social dilemmas: The role of paranoid cognitions. *Motivation and Emotion,* in press.

Kramer, R.M. (1995). Power, paranoia and distrust in organizations: The distorted view from the top. In R.J. Bies, R.J. Lewicki, & B.H. Sheppard (Eds.), *Research in negotiation in organizations* (Vol. 5, pp. 119-154). Greenwich, CT: JAI Press.

Lazarus, R.S. (1985). The costs and benefits of denial. In A. Monat & R.S. Lacers (Eds.), *Stress and coping: An anthology* (pp. 154-173). New York: Columbia University Press.

Mandler, G. (1984). *Mind and body: Psychology of emotion and stress*. New York: Norton.

Marcus, A.A., & Goodman, R.S. (1991). Victims and shareholders: The dilemmas of presenting corporate policy during a crisis. *Academy of Management Journal, 34*, 281-305.

McLaughlin, J.B., & Reisman, D. (1986). The shady side of sunshine. *Teachers College Record, 87*, 472-494.

McLuhan, M. (1964). *Understanding media: The extensions of man*. New York: Penguin.

Meindl, J.R. (1990). On leadership: An alternative to conventional wisdom. In B.M. Staw & L.L. Cummings (Eds.), *Research in organizational behavior* (Vol. 12, pp. 159-204). Greenwich, CT: JAI Press.

Meyer, J.W., & Rowan, B. (1977). Institutionalized organizations: Formal structure as myth and ceremony. *American Journal of Sociology, 83*, 340-363.

Mintzberg, H. (1973). *The nature of managerial work*. New York: Harper & Row.

Mintzberg, H. (1975). The manager's job: Folklore and fact. *Harvard Business Review, 4*, 49-61.

Morton, A. (1992). *Diana: Her true story*. New York: Simon & Schuster.

Natale, R. (1993, January). The guardians of the glitz. *San Francisco Examiner Image*, pp. 14-18.

Nisbett, R.E., & Wilson, T.D. (1977). Telling more than we can know: Verbal reports on mental processes. *Psychological Review, 84*, 231-259.

North, O.L. (1991). *Under fire: An American story*. New York: Harper.

Nyberg, D. (1993). *The vanished truth*. Chicago, IL: The University of Chicago Press.

Pfeffer, J. (1977). The ambiguity of leadership. *Academy of Management Review, 2*, 104-112.

Pfeffer, J. (1981). Management as symbolic action. In L.L. Cummings & B.M. Staw (Eds.), *Research in organizational behavior* (Vol. 3, pp. 1-52). Greenwich, CT: JAI Press.

Pfeffer, J. (1992). *Managing with power*. Boston: Harvard Business School Press.

Powell, W.W. (1987). Institutional effects on organizational structure and performance. In L.G. Zucker (Ed.), *Institutional patterns and organizations: Culture and environment* (pp. 115-136). Cambridge, MA: Ballinger.

Raiffa, H. (1968). *Decision analysis*. Reading, MA: Addison-Wesley.

Richard, M.P. (1986). Goffman revisited: Relatives vs. administrators in nursing homes. *Qualitative Sociology, 9*, 321-338.

Ross, J., & Staw, B.M. (1993). Organizational escalation and exit: Lessons from the Shoreham Nuclear Power Plant. *Academy of Management Journal, 36*, 701-732.

Ross, J., & Staw, B.M. (1986). Expo '86: An escalation prototype. *Administrative Science Quarterly, 31*, 274-297.

Rothfeder, J. (1992). *Privacy for sale*. New York: Simon & Schuster.

Sabato, L.J. (1993). *Feeding frenzy: How attack journalism has transformed American politics*. New York: The Free Press.

Salancik, G.R. (1977). Commitment and the control of organizational behavior and belief. In B.M. Staw & G.R. Salancik (Eds.), *New directions in organizational behavior* (pp. 1-54). Chicago: St. Clair Press.

Schwartz, H.S. (1990). *Narcissistic process and corporate decay*. New York: New York University Press.

Scott, W.R. (1992). *Organizations: Rational, natural and open systems* (3rd ed.). Englewood Cliffs, NJ: Prentice-Hall.

Scott, W.R., & Meyer, J.W. (1991). The rise of training programs in firms and agencies: An institutional perspective. In L.L. Cummings & B.M. Staw (Eds.), *Research in organizational behavior* (Vol. 13, pp. 297-326). Greenwich, CT: JAI Press.

Scully, J., & Byrne, J.A. (1987). *Odyssey.* New York: Harper & Row.

Seldes, G. (1989). The press and the individual. In T. Goldstein (Ed.), *Killing the messenger: 100 years of media criticism* (pp. 30-50). New York: Columbia University Press. (Originally published in 1935)

Snyder, C.R., & Higgins, R.L. (1988). Excuses: Their effective role in the negotiation of reality. *Psychological Bulletin, 104,* 23-35.

Staw B.M., & Ross, J. (1980). Commitment in an experimenting society: An experiment on the attribution of leadership from administrative scenarios. *Journal of Applied Psychology, 65,* 249-260.

Staw, B.M., & Ross, J. (1987). Behavior in escalation situations: Antecedents, prototypes, and solutions. In L.L. Cummings & B.M. Staw (Eds.), *Research in organizational behavior* (Vol. 9, pp. 39-78). Greenwich, CT: JAI Press.

Staw, B.M., & Sutton, R.I. (1992). Macro organizational psychology. In J.K. Murnighan (Ed.), *Social psychology in organizations: Advances in theory and research* (pp. 350-384). Englewood Cliffs, NJ: Prentice-Hall.

Staw, B.M., McKechnie, P.I., & Puffer, S.M. (1983). The justification of organizational performance. *Administrative Science Quarterly, 28,* 582-600.

Staw, B.M., Sandelands, L.E., & Dutton, J.E. (1981). Threat-rigidity effects in organizational behavior: A multilevel analysis. *Administrative Science Quarterly, 26,* 501-524.

Staw, B.M., Sutton, R.I., & Pelled, L.H. (1994). Employee positive emotion and favorable outcomes at the workplace. *Organization Science, 5,* 51-71.

Strasser, J.B., & Becklund, L. (1991). *Swoosh: The unauthorized story of Nike and the men who played there.* New York: Harcourt, Brace, Jovanovich.

Sutton, R.I. (1984). *Organizational death.* Doctoral dissertation, The University of Michigan, Department of Psychology.

Sutton, R.I. (1989). Reactions of nonparticipants as additional rather than missing data: Opportunities for organizational research. *Human Relations, 42,* 423-429.

Sutton, R.I., & Callahan, A.L. (1987). The stigma of bankruptcy: Spoiled organizational image and its management. *Academy of Management Journal, 30,* 405-436.

Sutton, R.I., & D'Aunno, T. (1989). Decreasing organizational size: Untangling the effects of people and money. *Academy of Management Review, 14,* 194-212.

Sviokla, J.J., & Shapiro, B.P. (1992). *Keeping customers.* Boston: Harvard Business Review.

Swasy, A. (1993). *Soap opera: The inside story of Procter & Gamble.* New York: Random House.

Tedeschi, J.T. (Ed.). (1981). *Impression management theory and social psychological research.* New York: Academic Press.

Teel, L., & Taylor, R. (1988). *Into the newsroom: An introduction to journalism.* Chester, CT: The Globe Pequot Press.

Tetlock, P.E. (1985). Accountability: the neglected social context of judgment and choice. In L.L. Cummings & B.M. Staw (Eds.), *Research in organizational behavior* (Vol. 7, pp. 297-332). Greenwich, CT: JAI Press.

Tetlock, P.E. (1991). The impact of accountability on judgment and choice: Toward a social contingency model. *Advances in Experimental Social Psychology, 25,* 331-376.

Thompson, J.D. (1967). *Organizations in action.* New York: McGraw-Hill.

Weick, K.E. (1990). The vulnerable system: An analysis of the Tenerife air disaster. *Journal of Management, 16,* 571-593.

Whetzel, O. (1991, March 27). Why Great America P.R. beats Stanford approach. *San Jose Mercury News,* Extra 2, p. 1.

Wilson, T.D., & Schooler, J.W. (1991). Thinking too much: Introspection can reduce the quality of preferences and decisions. *Journal of Personality and Social Psychology, 60,* 181-192.

Wilson, T.D., Dunn, D.S., Kraft, D., & Lisle, D.J. (1989). Introspection, attitude change and attitude-behavior consistency: The disruptive effects of explaining why we feel the way we do. In L. Berkowitz (Ed.), *Advances in experimental social psychology* (Vol. 22, pp. 287-343). San Diego: Academic Press.

Wolfe, T. (1970). *Radical chic and mau-mauing the flak catchers.* Noonday Press: New York.

Wright, J.P. (1979). *On a clear day you can see General Motors: John Z. De Lorean's look inside the automobile giant.* New York: Avon.

Yates, B. (1983). *The decline and fall of the American Automobile industry.* New York: Empire Books.

Young, J.S. (1988). *Steve Jobs: The journey is the reward.* Glenview, IL: Scott-Foresman.

Zajonc, R. (1965). Social facilitation. *Science, 149,* 269-274.

ENTRAINMENT:
PACE, CYCLE, AND RHYTHM IN ORGANIZATIONAL BEHAVIOR

Deborah Ancona and Chee-Leong Chong

ABSTRACT

This paper applies the concept of entrainment from the natural sciences to organizational behavior. Entrainment is defined as the adjustment of the pace or cycle of one activity to match or synchronize with that of another. The entrainment lens focuses on dominant macro cycles that "capture" the pace and cycle of organizational activities. Examples include the fiscal year in public firms and the semester cycle in academic institutions. The paper provides examples of the various types of entrainment and shows how the concept of entrainment can augment current theories of organizational behavior. The paper then addresses the mechanisms by which entrainment occurs, the functions that it serves, and the types of analyses it suggests. Entrainment presents organizational life as cyclical and rhythmic, where there is an active interplay among paces, cycles, and rhythms of different activities at different levels of analysis, where windows of opportunity come and go, and where speed and timing are critical to understanding the nature of organizational life.

INTRODUCTION

With few exceptions (Gersick, 1988, 1989; McGrath & Kelly, 1986), time and timing have not played a significant nor explicit role in organizational behavior research. This is surprising because there are numerous references to time in organizations such as windows of opportunity (Tyre & Orlikowski 1994), time to market (Clark & Fujimoto, 1987), sequence of activities (Wicker & King, 1988), and organizational life cycles (Cameron & Whetten, 1988). In addition, there exist specific time concepts of velocity (Eisenhardt, 1990), clocks (Keck & Tushman, 1993), cycles (Homans, 1950), and coordination within time constraints (Thompson, 1967). It is indeed a paradox that while time plays a key role in identifying many organizational phenomena and concepts, it has seldom been isolated as a key variable, compared across theoretical frames, or melded into general organizational theory (see Albert, 1994 for an exception).

Most of the work that has been done on time and timing results from a recent surge in interest among organizational researchers (Bluedorn & Denhardt, 1988; Gersick, 1991, 1994). The issues of how long, how fast, and when activities do and should occur within organizations have recently gained prominence as competitive pressures grow and speed and timing are seen as prerequisites for corporate success (Clark & Fujimoto, 1987). Perhaps this change has been inspired by managers who are obsessed with shifting their organizations' temporal patterns with initiatives to decrease time to market, shorten product development cycles, achieve just-in-time manufacturing, and time strategic initiatives to fit the "window of opportunity" (Haveman, Meyer, & Russo, 1993; Tyre & Orlikowsky, 1994). Perhaps researchers too have been influenced by the mass media and its message that we not only have to work better, we also have to work faster, get it done sooner, and have it out before the competition.

As organizational theorists begin to wrestle with issues of time and timing, their work has taken two main thrusts. One thrust is to identify existing work processes in organizations (e.g., product development and decision making), to catalogue their phases or component parts, and time taken to execute them. The intent is to understand how to speed up those processes in order to achieve competitive advantage (Clark, 1989; Eisenhardt, 1989). The second, and related, thrust has been to examine the timing of events (e.g., different types of changes) in groups and organizations. In this second arena there are two broad categories of thought (Sastry & Chong, 1995): (1) deterministic, closed-system views in which an entity shifts along predictable stages or internal clocks, irrespective of its environment; and (2) nondeterministic, open-systems perspectives in which an entity shifts in relation to environmental change.

Paradoxically, while these different perspectives offer unique contributions, each is missing part of what the others have to offer. Those examining the acceleration of work processes and those examining deterministic change fail to capture the influence of the environment and the interdependence of multiple paces, cycles, stages, and clocks throughout the organization. These researchers tend to ignore the system in which the work process or event resides.

On the other side, those who view the timing of events like team and organizational change as following the unpredictable pattern of environmental events (e.g., Tushman & Romanelli, 1985), fail to notice the periodicity of these events and the fact that they are occurring synchronously with other events across other levels of analysis. In other words these events can take place in bundles—many of them at once rather than events at one level following another—that are predictably timed. These researchers fail to notice patterns in the timing of events across levels of analysis. The concept of entrainment fills in some of the gaps left by the deterministic and the open-systems views, while providing some insight into the difficulties of accelerating existing cycles.

We define entrainment, a term borrowed from biology, as the adjustment of the pace or cycle of an activity to match or synchronize with that of another activity. The adjustment could be in the phase, periodicity, or magnitude of the activity. Pace refers to the speed at which an activity takes place. A cycle is a single complete execution of a periodically repeated phenomenon (Ancona & Chong, 1992; McGrath & Rotchford, 1983). Over time a rhythm develops based on the nature of the repetition of the cycle.

For example, entrainment of pace occurs when management speeds up product development to match the accelerated innovation cycle set by the competition. Entrainment of cycle occurs as multiple activities and processes shift predictably throughout the year in conjunction with the quarters laid out by the fiscal year. A rhythm develops as salespeople and customers act in unison and create sales figures that follow a flat pattern followed by high growth at the end of every quarter, with the fourth quarter always showing more dramatic rise at the end. Thus pace or *tempo* entrainment examines the change and alignment of speed, while phase entrainment examines the synchronization of cycles.

The fundamental idea behind entrainment in organizational theory is that endogenous cycles exist within individuals, groups, organizations, and environments. These endogenous cycles are often influenced by other cycles within the system or outside the system so as to occur in synchrony; in entrainment language the cycles are "captured" by an external pacer so as to have the same phase, periodicity, or magnitude. These external pacers are often signaled by cues in the environment called zeitgebers (Aschoff, 1979). The "captured" cycles establish an entrained rhythm that then "pulls" many other cycles into synchrony. The rhythm creates a dominant temporal ordering that serves as a powerful coordination mechanism for that entity. As more and more cycles entrain to this rhythm it becomes inertial. The fiscal year in public firms and the semester in academic institutions are two examples of pacers that create entrained organizational rhythms which dominate and "capture" many organizational activities.

If we shift to an entrainment lens, then the focus of research on time and timing will also shift. Rather than simply monitoring the phases or periodicities of ongoing processes and trying to accelerate them, researchers will examine those processes in the context of external paces and cycles to determine whether faster really is better. Rather than viewing change as either a function of internal clocks or pacing mechanisms, or as a response to environmental jolts, it may also be seen as part of a bundle of changes across levels of analysis that are all tied to a given cycle. Rather than assuming that organizational behavior is linear and steady, researchers must also view behavior as cyclic and rhythmic. Rather than viewing time as an objective entity, entrainment suggests that time may be subjectively determined via a temporal reference framework that provides organizational members with a sense of time. Rather than considering the levers of success in organizational change to be *what* is changed and *how* is change is implemented, entrainment suggests that *when* change takes place is critical to its success. Finally, rather than achieving coordination through an analysis of information processing requirements and activity, coordination can also be achieved through timing.

We argue that entrainment complements existing organization theory by providing a new theoretical lens that focuses on the existence and effects of pace, cycle, and rhythm on the behavior and performance of individuals, groups, and organizations. The entrainment concept illustrates the need to examine cycles of behavior over time at multiple levels of analysis rather than doing cross-sectional studies of static behavior at a particular level of analysis. Entrainment allows us to better understand the speed, timing, and coordination of various aspects of organizational behavior.

This paper goes on to present some background on the entrainment concept, further specification of terms and definitions with examples in the organizational arena, an outline of how entrainment shifts our focus of research and understanding of organizational phenomena, and some speculation on why entrainment does or does not occur, what functions it serves and how it can hamper organizational functioning. The paper concludes with some ideas for a future research agenda mapped out by the entrainment concept.

BACKGROUND OF THE ENTRAINMENT CONCEPT

Huygens, a great Dutch physicist, was the first to write about entrainment in the seventeenth century (Minorsky, 1962). He observed that two pendulum clocks that he had built were swinging in perfect synchrony. When he disturbed one of them, within a half hour they regained synchrony. He suspected that the two were influencing one another via tiny vibrations in their common support. Sure enough, when moved to opposite sides of the room, the clocks fell out of step. Such began the subbranch of mathematics known as the theory of coupled oscillations or entrainment (Strogatz & Stewart, 1993).

Since then, numerous examples of entrainment have been found throughout the natural world. Within human beings coupled oscillations have been found in pacemaker cells in the heart, and neutral networks in the brain and spinal cord that control such rhythmic behaviors as breathing, running, and chewing. Entrainment also occurs across organisms such as crickets that chirp in unison and synchronously flashing fireflies—each of which has its own rhythm but is brought into harmony with those around it by the sight of its neighbors' lights (Strogatz & Stewart, 1993). Other examples showing how rhythms are meshed include the simultaneous flowering across large geographic expanses of trees and plants such as the Pinot pine and bamboo, with periods ranging from several years to a century; and the synchronized emergence and irruption of insect species like the Gypsy moth and locust.

Scientists also speculate that the moon did not always have the same day as the earth. Through entrainment, however, the orbital pattern of the moon became synchronized with its rotational period causing the moon to present the same face to the earth at all times (Sterman & Mosekilde, 1993).

The term entrainment is most commonly used in biology, where researchers argue that most behavioral processes are rhythmic or cyclical in nature (Oatley & Goodwin, 1971). Entrainment refers to the process whereby an endogenous biological rhythm is modified in its phase and periodicity by powerful exogenous influences called external pacers. Entrainment is thought to govern many processes that move at various temporal orders (microseconds, minutes, hours, months, years) in the human body. The synchronization of these numerous processes via their mutual entrainment to each other, and external entrainment to the environment is thought to be necessary to achieve the requisite temporal organization of the human system (Aschoff, 1979; McGrath, Kelly, & Machatka, 1984; Pittendrigh, 1972).

A common biological example of entrainment is the circadian (meaning about a day) rhythm, where most bodily cycles are entrained to the external light-dark 24-hour cycle of the earth. In studies that isolate individuals away from natural light for several weeks, many bodily cycles (e.g., temperature and urinary cortisol excretion), free-run and resume their "natural" periodicities that are usually more than 24 hours (Aschoff, 1979; McGrath et al., 1984). The new internal ordering of these free-running cycles is very different from that of a system entrained to a 24-hour cycle. For example, during entrained conditions maximum temperature occurs during the late afternoon. When free-running, the maximum temperature occurs several hours later in relation to the sleep-wake cycle. Thus, entrainment of these bodily cycles to one another, and together to the light-dark circadian rhythm shifts the timing of these cycles so that we follow the rhythm of the sun.

Jet lag illustrates how a disturbance to the 24-hour cycle impacts those cycles. During travel to a different time zone, the timing of the external light-dark cycle shifts and causes a reordering of the entrained system of bodily cycles. However, different physiological and behavioral cycles reentrain at different rates which inadvertently result in the various cycles being out of phase with each other. Thus, we experience performance decrements after flights not only due to sleep deprivation, but also because psychological processes are not entrained to each other or to the new external cycle. The fact that most of these cycles free-run at periodicities longer than 24 hours helps to explain why reentrainment takes longer following an eastbound flight than a westbound flight. The observation that reentrainment is enhanced in people who go outdoors compared to those who stay in their hotel rooms demonstrates the importance of external cues that signal the periodicity of the new cycle (Aschoff, 1979; Mackie, 1977).

Entrainment has been used to explain phenomena in economics. The macroeconomy generates multiple cyclic modes such as the business cycle, construction cycle, and long wave, which may then entrain to one another such that they tend to peak simultaneously from time to time. The roughly 20-year construction cycle in the oil tanker industry seems to be entrained at about a 4:1 ratio with the business cycle in oil demands, leading to periods of deep depression in shipbuilding. Similar dynamics exist in the real estate, mining and mining equipment, and paper and pulp industries (Sterman & Mosekilde, 1993).

ENTRAINMENT IN ORGANIZATIONAL BEHAVIOR AND CONCEPT CLARIFICATION

Organizations, with their multiple cycles, seem ripe for similar analyses. They are subject to multiple variant cycles, such as the quarterly and annual accounting cycles, the seasonal cycles of demand, and the roughly four-year business cycle, and contain processes with intrinsic response times that vary substantially (order fulfillment may take seconds while capacity expansion may take years). Organizations are filled with individuals going through various career and life cycles, and teams pace themselves to temporal milestones (Gersick, 1994). Organizations exist in environments with technological, market, and business cycles in which pace seems to be ever quickening; forcing organizations to reentrain to new external pacers while having to maintain the coordination among internal cycles. These characteristics call for analysis through the entrainment lens.

McGrath and Rotchford (1983) were the first to use the term entrainment to explain processes in social and organizational behavior. They define social entrainment as the "capturing and modification of human activity cycles by

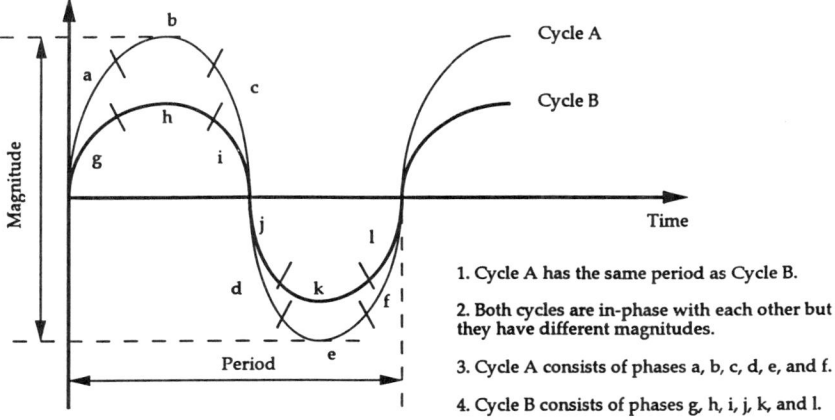

Figure 1a. Features of a Cycle and Two In-Phase Cycles

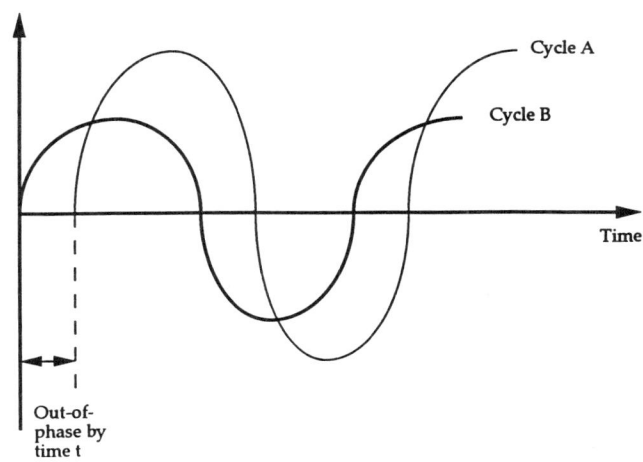

Figure 1b. Two Out-of-Phase Cycles

various social customs, norms, and institutions" (1983, p. 78). They catalogued the existence of shared social cycles at various levels (e.g., weekly cycles such as workdays and weekends, and organizational cycles like slack periods and inventory times), and then provided evidence that individual activity entrains to these cycles. They presented a salient example of the shift worker whose behavior is primarily entrained to the work organization and how the family also becomes entrained by shifting eating and leisure activity to fit the particular shift. They further discuss various issues regarding the implications and consequences of social entrainment (e.g., the macro effect of daily rush hours and long lines in the cafeteria at lunch time).

We have built on, and elaborated, the work done by McGrath and Rotchford (1983). As stated earlier, we now define entrainment as the adjustment of the pace or cycle of an activity to match or synchronize with that of another activity. Under entrained conditions endogenous paces and cycles that exist within individuals, groups, organizations, and environments are somehow "captured" by (or capture) other paces and cycles within the system or outside the system so as to have the same pace, phase, or periodicity (see Figure 1 on cycles).

The impact of these enmeshed cycles is that the level of organizational activity is not stable over time. There are periods of speeded up activity and periods of slowed activity. In other words, organizations have rhythm. The rhythm of the organization depends on the pattern mapped by these cycles. Cycles may repeat themselves at regular intervals or frequencies such as those associated with the fiscal year, or irregularly such as is the case with technology cycles. Cycles may repeat themselves with the same magnitudes or different magnitudes. For example, the first three quarters may all show levels of sales and manufacturing activity and individual stress rise dramatically as the quarter comes to a close, but this pattern is especially strong in the fourth quarter.

In addition to the notion of dominant pacers that capture and organize activity into temporal patterns and zeitgebers, the cues that signal those pacers, is the idea that there may be a need to adapt to a new pacer or to a change in the period of an existing cycle (as in the case of shorter product development cycles in the computer or automobile industries). When the period of an existing cycle is shortened any entity that entrains to that cycle has to speed up while a lengthening of the cycle's period creates a slow down. Thus, changes in the period of a cycle are related to changes in pace. Tempo entrainment or the entraining of pace is thus related to the period of the cycle.

Phase entrainment, however, is related to the phase of the cycle rather than to its periodicity. Phase entrainment can be either synchronic or asynchronic. Synchronic phase entrainment implies having two activities (a and b) whose cycles come to have an in-phase pattern; that is, they are at a similar phase state at the same time, when a is high b is high and when a wanes b wanes. Asynchronic phase entrainment implies having two activities in an out-of-phase pattern. In this case b follows a by some amount. In the most extreme case, a is high when b is low and vice versa.

Each type of entrainment, tempo or phase, can be internal or external. When entrainment involves only the activities of the subsystems within a system, it is internal with respect to that specific system. External environment involves adjusting bundles of internal paces and cycles to external ones.

Entrainment must also be differentiated from related concepts. Pseudo entrainment, a term we have coined, mimics entrainment but is not entrainment because there is no adjustment of any periodicity or phase. Pseudo entrainment simply involves two activities whose pacers happen to be matched or whose cycles are coincidentally synchronized. A mentor-mentee relationship is an example of pseudo entrainment. There seems to be asynchronic entrainment because the cycles of the mentor and the mentee are out of phase, and yet they go together due to the complementarity of those phases.

The mentor knows the ropes, has a good sense of personal strengths and weaknesses, is eager to pass on individual learning, and to guide the next generation. The mentee is anxious to learn the ropes, discover the best career route to take, and desires to learn from others (Erikson, 1963; Graves, Dalton, & Thompson, 1980). These two individuals are in distinctly different stages of career and personal development, yet, for a brief time their interests mesh. The relationship exhibits pseudo entrainment because neither the mentor nor the mentee adjust their cycles, each just happens to be at a phase that meshes with the other person. As each person develops, the two can move in and out of phase complementarity (Kram, 1985). The mentee may move out of the dependency stage, while the mentor maintains a protective stance. Again, however, the cycles are not mutually adjusted, they simply evolve.

Entrainment must also be differentiated from adaptation. Firm change in response to environmental jolts or discontinuities would signal adaptation. This adaptation would be considered entrainment if the firm were regularly coupling its pace or cycle to an ongoing pace or cycle in the environment. In other words, entrainment involves repetition over time and requires some form of periodicity or pace change in the environment. For example, Berkeley's decision to get an outside business Dean to help raise money in a lean time is adaptation, but if operations were to change periodically to cater to economic business cycles then that would be entrainment.

Analysis through the entrainment lens becomes quite complex. Within an organization there may be a dominant cycle set by the fiscal year and numerous other cycles such as the product development cycle, team cycles and individual career cycles. On top of that are external cycles that involve the technological, market, and legal environments as well as the economic cycles that may vary over 5, 10, or 20 years. Customers and suppliers may be operating at different paces, cycles, and rhythms as well. Before dealing with the complexity, however, it might be useful to present some examples and evidence of tempo and phase entrainment in the organizational arena. The examples to be presented occur at multiple levels of analysis, showing how the entrainment concept can be used to develop multilevel and cross-level theory (Rousseau, 1985).

Tempo Entrainment

Tempo entrainment can be illustrated at the individual, group, and organizational level of analysis. At the individual and group level, studies have shown that work is done at the pace that matches a given time limit. In a series of studies, Kelly and McGrath (1985) showed that individuals and groups who are given 5, 10, and 20 minutes respectively to solve anagrams learn to work at decreasing rates of speed. The shorter the time limit, the higher the rate at which anagrams are solved. McGrath, Kelly, and Machatka (1984) argue "that individuals and groups 'attune' their rates of work to fit the temporal conditions of their work situations." When time frames were changed such that groups subsequently had 20, 10, and 5 minutes respectively to do their work, they continued to work at the pace set by their original time limit, illustrating tempo entrainment to the initial pacer.

At the organizational level Eisenhardt (1989) illustrates that entrainment to the pace of environmental change can occur. In a study of five companies in "high velocity environments" some top management teams were able to match their pace of strategic decision making to the accelerated pace of technological and market change. These teams did not sacrifice thoroughness nor the number of alternatives considered, yet through frequent meetings, up-to-date operational data, mechanisms for conflict management, and simultaneous consideration of multiple alternatives, they were able to accelerate decision making to match the pace of the environment. Other top management teams were not able to speed up decision-making processes.

Phase Entrainment

Phase entrainment involves a meshing of cycles. Perhaps the pattern of phase entrainment within organizations that most closely resembles the circadian rhythm within the individual is the aggregate rhythm that is mapped by a set of intertwined organizational activities. Whereas individuals match their internal biological processes to the light-dark cycle of the earth, organizational processes are matched to the fiscal year. At the end of the fiscal year performance data must be reported, accounts closed, and annual reports written. While the organization founders usually set the date of this event, once it is created organizational activities entrain to this pacer. For example, while there is no inherent reason that planning cycles, performance reviews, sales account closings, or revenue accounting should be yearly events that occur at the same point in time every year, all these activities center around the quarterly calendar established by the fiscal year. Performance reviews are set so that salaries and bonuses can be calculated and fed into the numbers that must be computed at the end of the fiscal year. Sales account closings peak at the end of each quarter, and particularly at the end of the fourth quarter in time to be counted in end-of-year bonuses. Division managers with profit and loss responsibilities attempt to pass off costs before the fiscal year ends so that their end-of-year performance is enhanced. The enduring regularity and timing of these behaviors suggests that synchronic phase entrainment is constantly occurring within organizations at multiple levels and across a multitude of activities.

Phase entrainment, such as that which occurs during entrainment to the circadian rhythm, basically organizes processes that would ordinarily follow their own cycles into an interwoven pattern with a common aggregate rhythm. One example of this type of entrainment occurred at a Norwegian hospital (Leenders, 1994) that was engaged in a change effort aimed at improving the motivation, turnover, working environment, and work pressure of the nursing staff. As a set of consultants analyzed the problems faced by the nursing staff they found that many issues stemmed from the interaction among various hospital disciplines (e.g., medical services, dietary services, and technical services). For example, many services were offered at the same time creating work pressure for the nurses and discomfort for the patients. Linens were being changed at the same time that food came for the patient at the same time that medical tests had to be conducted. If the food was not eaten in the hour after it was delivered, it was taken away. If the patient was busy getting tests taken, she might miss out on lunch.

The solution to these problems was to identify the appropriate pacer and create a "new day rhythm" that was entrained to it. Thus, rather than having each group operating at its own schedule, all groups got together to create a schedule that would revolve around the needs of the patient. The staff created "critical care moments" that could not be touched by certain functions, and specific time slots for other activities. Thus, doctor visits and linen changes could not occur during meal times, while room cleaning was synchronized with patient social activities in the common room. Medical staff changed their working hours and the timing of medical and nursing care, paramedic care, nutritional services, laundry, and recreational activities all came to be determined by the new day rhythm. The result was less overlap of functions, less stress on the staff, and a more orderly day for the patients.

Thus, in order to understand phase entrainment it becomes necessary to study ongoing cycles of activity, the periodicity and timing of those cycles, and the interaction of those cycles. The key unit of analysis is the aggregate pattern that repeats itself over time and that consists of bundles of highly enmeshed cycles of activity. While these examples have shown some of the positive aspects of entrainment, this is not always the case. The entrainment of behaviors to the fiscal year provides the organization with a uniform pacer which unifies action within the organization. On the other hand, the irregular sales pattern of peaks and troughs may not optimize customer service or employee stress. Also, entrainment to a yearly cycle may reinforce a short-term orientation that puts the United States at a disadvantage vis-à-vis the long-term orientation of the Japanese (Hatvany & Pucik, 1981).

Theoretical Implications of Entrainment

While the previous sections have attempted to articulate the concept and properties of entrainment, its background, and some illustrative examples, we now move to the theoretical implications of entrainment. What is the contribution of the concept and how does it shift the way we examine organizational behavior? We organize this section by examining six assumptions that entrainment changes.

1. Rather than simply monitoring the phases or components of ongoing processes and trying to accelerate them, researchers will examine those processes in the context of external paces and cycles to determine whether faster really is better.

Given the current competitive environment a great deal of current research is focused on how to accelerate ongoing organizational processes, such as decision making (Eisenhardt, 1989, 1990; Wally & Baum, 1994), and shorten organizational cycles, such as product development (Clark & Fujimoto, 1987, 1991). In the latter area there is a growing stream of research around how to achieve concurrent engineering by moving from sequential activity to overlapping of upstream and downstream design activity (Imai, Takeuchi, & Nonaka, 1985; Krishnan, Eppinger, & Whitney, 1994; Takeuchi & Nonaka, 1986). Central to this work is a careful examination of the tasks to be carried out and a reworking of the engineering and industrial design to speed up information exchange. The underlying assumption here is that faster is better and will improve competitive advantage. Two examples speak to problems in this assumption due to the fact that the product development cycle is often entrained to other cycles. Accelerating one cycle alone can cause it to go out of synchrony with the other cycles and creates havoc in the system.

A recent *New York Times* article focused on Japanese computer companies that actually had to slow down product introductions. These companies were all trying to outpace one another with their product introductions and they managed to introduce products at ever-decreasing time intervals. This success, however, led to problems. Profits suffered as customers kept putting off their buying decisions in order to wait for the "next best" model, which would be out shortly. Other parts of the organization could not keep up as salespeople could not keep track of all the new models, and there were inventory problems. Sales and coordination suffered because the new, shorter periodicity interfered with the entrained cycles of other groups within the organization.

In a second example, a new set of learning techniques were applied to a team creating a new car model (Learning Center Case History, 1995). The techniques were so successful that the model was actually designed and manufactured on time. Deliveries were made and dealerships had full stocks of the new model. The dealers were very angry, however, because there was no advertising going on. Advertising had been planned, as it always had been, following assumed delays in the product development process. In the existing product development cycle each related product development activity was enmeshed to create a set periodicity for the cycle. This in turn defined the time and timing for each individual activity. When one of these activities became entrained to a new pacer, the temporal ordering went awry. Thus, entrainment calls into question the notion that speeding up a particular process or cycle is good. Concern for the context of enmeshed paces and cycles that are entrained to a given pacer and periodicity is needed.

2. Rather than viewing the timing of change as a function of internal stages or clocks, the timing of change may be seen as more tightly linked to external events.

Some of the research on the timing of individual, group, and organizational change follows a deterministic, closed-system view in which an entity shifts along predictable stages or internal clocks, irrespective of its environment (Sastry & Chong, 1995). Both stage and pacing models fall into this view of change.

Stage models of individual, group, and organizational transition follow a long tradition of metamorphosis models in psychology and organization theory. Such theories argue that transformations occur when an entity completes a given stage or somehow outgrows its old form and mode of operation. Examples of stage models include career stages (exploring, establishing, maintaining, and declining; Graves, Dalton, & Thompson, 1980) and life stages for individuals (Levinson, 1978), product development (exploration, exploitation, and exportation; Ancona & Caldwell, 1988) and life stages for groups (forming, norming, storming, performing; Tuckman, 1965), and managerial (promotor, consolidator, and administrator; Starbuck, 1965) and life stages for organizations (creativity, direction, delegation, coordination, and collaboration; Greiner, 1972).

Current research at the group level suggests that these stage models may not hold for all groups and that a pacing model may be a more accurate model of change. In a series of studies, Gersick (1988, 1989) found that groups did not follow a universal sequence of stages, but rather followed a punctuated pattern of change. The first pattern that Gersick found was that teams quickly settled in on a mode of operation and stayed in that mode until the midpoint of the project. Even if members were unhappy with the way in which the group operated, they waited until halfway between their starting date and its expected deadline to adopt new perspectives, change their mode of work, and engage outside stakeholders. Work then continued in the same mode until a final push at the end of the project. Gersick (1994) explained, "Transitions are triggered by a pacing device. Sometimes consciously, sometimes not, groups select the midpoint (or occasionally another time) as a heuristic milestone and use it like an alarm clock, to help insure they will move fast enough to finish by their deadlines" (p. 12).

In both the stage and the temporal pacing models of change the team is viewed as a closed-system that initiates change on its own through internal mechanisms. In these models interaction with the external environment occurs when the team is ready (e.g., at its midpoint) and the team sets its deadlines according to the task at hand (e.g., it will take six weeks to develop a prototype). Yet later worked by Gersick and others shows that this closed-system approach does not hold for teams that are entrained to the external environment.

In a study of a new venture, Gersick (1994) discovered that pacing is not simply based on internal mechanisms and on the task at hand. Instead, teams entrain to "consequential time limits and schedules originating in its strategic environment" (Gersick, 1994, p. 37).

> For example, the ten-year limit for the development of the business, which triggered a major assessment at the five-year mark, seems to reflect a widespread convention of the venture capital community .... The midsummer occurrence of M-Tech's strategic planning meetings was chosen explicitly to bisect its fiscal and evaluation year, but mid-summer also placed M-Tech's planning conveniently before important annual industry meetings and poised it for the yearly Labor Day surge back to work in the U.S. culture at large. Such synchrony is probably not a coincidence, but the result of a nested complex of economic rhythms. M-Tech was entrained to its investors' schedule of evaluation, which, it could be hypothesized, was entrained to annual national patterns, along with businesses all over the country. (Gersick, 1994, p. 38)

In another study of temporal pacing, this one in software development teams, Chong (1995) found that teams that were buffered from their external environment paced themselves through internal mechanisms and the task at hand. A buffered team set its deadlines based on estimates of the complexity of the product and when it completed a given set of tasks it transitioned to another mode of operation. Even when people were unhappy, change was saved for the transition periods that were set by task demands. Teams that were not buffered from the external environment, however, exhibited entrainment to external rhythms. Entrained teams would set deadlines not by how long it would take to finish a set of tasks, but by pacing to the organizational budgeting cycle and quarterly paced layoffs. Team members might even spend days or weeks without working, or days or weeks working at a frantic pace to mesh with these organizational rhythms.

Thus, entrainment shifts our notion of pacing. In an entrained system internal clocks are set to link to external cycles. The deadlines that determine the endpoints from which a given midpoint is selected are not based solely on task demands but on organizational rhythms. The events upon which event-based pacing takes place are not solely internal but also regularly occurring external events such as budgeting decisions. We might also speculate that individuals, groups, and organizations that are entrained to external cycles move through sequential stage models not solely due to the mechanisms of development and growth, but also according to linkages to those outside rhythms. Here the notion of closed-system change needs to be augmented by one of open-systems linking to ongoing external patterns.

3. Rather than viewing adaptation as simply a reaction to external environment jolts, it should also be seen as a periodic phenomenon that results from entrainment to external rhythms.

In contrast to the closed-system view of change described above, researchers studying adaptation often take on an open-systems view which focuses on the organization's interaction with its environment (Sastry & Chong, 1995). Contingency theories and resource dependence views show organizations adapting to external changes. According to many of the researchers in this area (see Galbraith, 1977; Nadler & Tushman, 1988), top management teams must engage in careful monitoring of the external environment to be sure to identify the irregular environmental changes that shift the information processing needs of the task or shift the resource configuration in the environment and therefore require organizational actions or change. Missing from these theories is the notion that change and adaptation also take place regularly and systematically due to entrainment to ongoing environmental cycles. Two examples follow.

Pettigrew (1985) chronicles and episodic pattern of change at a Fortune 100 company, ICI, that is entrained to the external business cycle.

> The periods of high levels of change activity have tended to occur around every decade, and are associated with the second low point of the 4.5 year business cycle. Thus there were concentrations of organization and manpower changes involving the reshaping and relabeling of divisional boundaries during and immediately after the business downturns of 1961, 1971, and 1981.... It is in the context of this episodic and environmentally driven change response, where in each case the formulation of the strategic changes was in the hands of a small group of very senior executives. (p. 429)

Another example of entrainment at the macro level is a study of the growth in city bureaucracies and its relation to economic cycles. Stevenson (1985) describes a 3- to 5-year cycle of change in size across three cities: Chicago,

Philadelphia, and Detroit. His data illustrate "the wave-like undulation in the rate of growth in the data...which might be attributed largely to changes in the national economy" (p. 288).

The key issue of adaptation illustrated here is that it may be more orderly and regular than the contingency and resource dependence models specify. For entrained organizations we may see frequencies of change that match with economic, technological, or market cycles, seasonal shifts in demand, or even political cycles. We might even speculate that organizations hold off on adapting to perceived changes until the external cycle signals a change is due. This would explain why organizations are reacting to some jolts and not others.

4. Rather than viewing organizational life as linear and steady, we view it as cyclic and rhythmic.

Whether following the closed-system models of change or the open-systems models, a key assumption is that organizational life is usually linear and steady. Individuals, teams, and organizations are viewed as following one mode of operation, one mode of thinking, one pace, and one world view until such time as another developmental stage is reached, or until a temporal milestone is reached, or until the environment creates the need for change. Consistent with this view of organizations are our research methods, which assume linearity or discontinuity. We do not question whether observations done in February are different from other done in April, or whether our data better fit quadratic rather than linear patterns. Under entrained conditions, however, change may be a regular part of organizational life, even within developmental stages and between environmental discontinuities.

Entrainment suggests that everyday life in organizations is rhythmic—frantic and fast paced at one moment and quiet and slow the next. Much as we are attuned to the four seasons, so too do organizations shift as they move from the "budgeting season" to the "summer lull." Nuclear power plants shift personnel and management as they regularly move from ongoing operations to the "shut-down phase" (Carroll & Perin, 1994). Political organizations move on a four-year cycle moving from election time craze to post-election analysis and planning. Academic organizations move from September orientation and socialization of new students to graduation and summer research and executive program activity. In a study of hospitals Zerubavel (1979) found that five major social cycles—the year, the rotation, the week, the day, and the duty period—force both routine and nonroutine activities into regular temporal patterns that had their own rhythmic structure. The pattern of the administration of medicine showed that even purely medical activities were forced into rhythmic patterns which were dictated by nonmedical schedules. For example, medicine was administered when it fit into the schedule of the duty period of the nurse, not when it was most needed by the patient.

While studying a hundred sales teams in a telecommunications company (Gladstein, 1984), the differences between selling at the start of the quarter and the end of the quarter became very apparent. At the start of the quarter sales activity was slow, customer visits were spread throughout the weeks, and a lot of time was spent finishing up the paper work from the last quarter and strategizing about the future. As the quarter progressed customer calls increased, the pace became frantic, and strategizing was replace by actual selling and struggling to install the system "on time." As quarterly deadlines approached, people worked harder and faster, especially in the fourth quarter so that salespeople could make their quarterly and yearly targets and bonuses. In addition, the company offered large discounts at the end of the quarter and the fiscal year that were not provided at other junctures. Customers "learned" that they could get better deals toward the end of the quarter, so they often waited until that period to buy. The result was a set of intertwined behaviors that created the well-documented "hockey stick" pattern for the quarter, and an uneven saw pattern throughout the year (see Figure 2). The entrained cycles created uneven rhythms, not smooth patterns of activity. Thus, the current models of smooth activity punctuated by revolutionary change (Tushman & Romanelli, 1985) due to developmental or environmental change are not thoroughly accurate. Our research lenses seem to be assuming minimal change punctuated by major change while missing the ongoing tumult that is part of everyday life.

5. Rather than assuming that time is an objective reality we should also assume that time is subjectively determined.

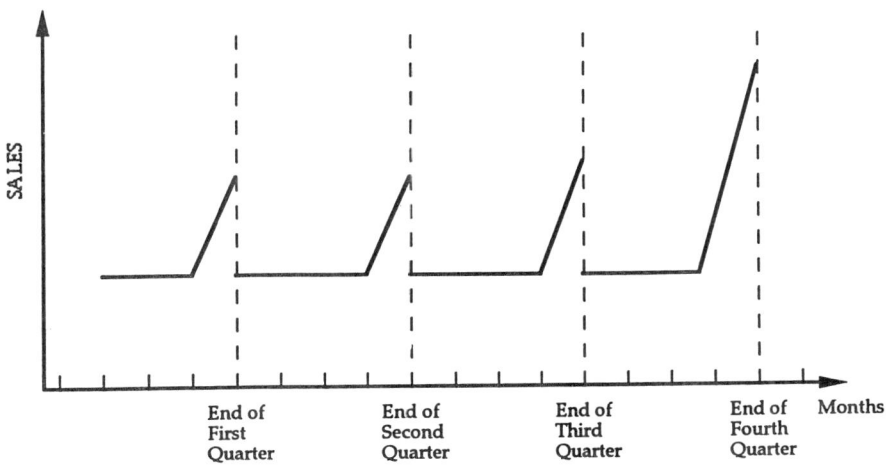

Figure 2. "Hockey Stick" Pattern in Organizations

Time can be so accurately measured now that we assume its objective reality. After all, a second is a second anywhere in the world and a minute does not change from one moment to the next. Thus, it is reasonable to assume that time means the same thing from one organization to the next. Under entrained conditions, however, a "temporal reference framework" (Zerubavel, 1979) is created that differentiates the understanding and experience of time from one moment to the next and from one organization to the next.

Take for example the experience of an executive who moved from a high-technology company in a competitive market with short product life cycles to a monopolistic company with long product life cycles. The executive was brought in to help the company become more competitive as its monopoly was being taken away. When the executive asked a member of his staff whether a particular product was going to come out on time, the answer was "yes." When the product turned out to be three months late the executive confronted the staff member about why he had said that the product was going to be on time. The staff member replied that it was on time. The issue here was not semantics, but rather the meaning of early and late. If your product cycles are eight years, then three months is on time. If your cycle is nine months then three months is very late. Thus, entrainment to different kinds of cycles creates different meanings to the same time interval. Levine (1988, p. 39) describes this phenomenon when he said that "If man does not keep pace with his companions, perhaps it is because he hears a different drummer."

The meaning of time could even switch as one moved from entrainment to an internal organization cycle (if the report is a week late that is fine) to an external customer cycle (quality standards are only maintained if we meet our deadlines precisely), or from a work cycle (our staff meetings always start fifteen minutes late) to a school cycle (picking up a child from nursery school fifteen minutes late could result in a fine and a lonely, frightened child). Even the major shift involved from entrainment to a work schedule to entrainment to a vacation schedule, shows how these schedules determine our subjective meaning of time. So the notion that an hour is an hour is an hour does not hold. An hour when entrained to a tight deadline has a different meaning, a different feel, and a different sense of elapsed time, than does an hour on vacation. Thus, entrainment shifts our notion of time as objective and measurable to subjectively determined.

6. Rather than the levers to successful change resulting solely from what is changed and how change is brought about, we are also concerned with when change takes place.

Ever since Lewin created the model of change consisting of unfreezing, moving, and refreezing, organizational researchers have been interested in the process of change. The bulk of the myriad studies that have been done in this area focus on what needs to be changed in organizations (e.g., the structure, the power relationships, or the underlying cultural assumptions), and how to go about making change (e.g., top down, in a participative manner, all at once, etc.). Entrainment suggests that the timing of change has a big impact on the nature and outcome of the change process.

While entrainment suggests that the choice of which cycles to align is key to determining how successful a change intervention will be, it also suggests that ongoing paces and cycles will create windows of opportunity in which change will be more easily accomplished and other periods in which there will be more inertia and resistance. Take for example a change process in a state department of education (Ancona, 1990). The educational consultants within the organization were to be reorganized into cross-functional teams that would provide educational services to specific geographical areas. Although teams were formed in the early fall, they did not really start work until January because that was when many organizational projects finished and personnel had the time and opportunity to begin team initiatives. Because the project send-off occurred in September with a big three-day, off-site meeting, but little actual work was done until late January, the project lost momentum and people wondered whether or not it would succeed. The lull in January would have been the best window to start the change effort.

Work was further delayed because the school districts to which the teams were consulting had already been through the planning process for the academic year and were locked into programs until the following fall. Teams progressed with whatever initiatives they could get through at the time, but the real impact in the school districts was delayed causing frustration on the part of the consultants. Later the teams entrained to the cycles of the school districts, and planned their interventions so as to be able to have input into the schools' curriculum. Ultimately the change effort was successful, despite the initial lack of entrainment. The evaluation cycle within the department of education also came to align with the external cycle.

It seems clear that attention to both the internal organization cycles and the external client cycles would have facilitated the change process. Starting the project when consultants were freed up from other commitments would have meant a faster start to the change effort and momentum might have built up more quickly. Also, planning early team assignments to better match client readiness for help might have lessened frustration. Thus, according to entrainment change will be facilitated when the change process takes into account ongoing paces and cycles within and external to the system being changed.

Albert (1994) also argues that external cycles can determine policy and the nature of change. In a study of the Persian Gulf War he found that:

> Timing dictated policy rather than the reverse: the limited window for military action influenced whether action would be taken at all: "when" helped decide "whether." That is not to say that the decision to go to war was completely influenced by factors such as

the weather, the date of pilgrimage to Mecca, the timetable for congressional elections, etc., but that it should be at all is difficult to accept. (p. 80)

Despite these entrainment examples and indications of how entrainment can make its contribution to current theoretical debates, the major argument of this paper is that we have spent too little time examining the interrelated paces, cycles, and rhythms within and across organizations. We do not know very much about the dominant cycles and their effects, the extent to which lesser cycles are entrained, and how these patterns change over time with what effect. We now turn our attention to the research questions that are spurred by the notion of entrainment and begin to speculate on answers to those questions.

WHAT MECHANISMS CAUSE ENTRAINMENT?

Entrainment is a process involving interaction between an entity and its environment. While Huygens could look to the transfer of vibrations in that environment and astronomers can look at gravitational pulls, social science researchers must seek other mechanisms for entrainment. Entrainment depends on the presence of zeitgebers so that the pacer can be identified and adjustments to pace, cycle, or rhythm can be carried out. There is evidence that dominant and regular macro cycles provide many vivid and salient cues to their existence. For example, as one enters the academic system there are so many cues indicating that meetings, decision making, teaching and general academic business goes on from September to December and from February to June, that one just gets caught up in that pattern.

In this day and age consultants, the media, and organizational press releases also serve as cues about product development, technology, market, and business cycles. Just as the fireflies signal to one another their light patterns, so too do organizations and those who report on them signal the pace and timing of their activities. Isomorphic and modeling processes that create similarity across behavior and structure at the organizational and group levels (see DiMaggio & Powell, 1983) may also create similarity of pace, cycle, and rhythm. We not only learn *what* to do from others, we also learn *when, how fast,* and *how long* to do it. For example, computer companies often set their product development cycles to match those of their best competitor.

While the existence of vivid and salient zeitgebers are important to entrainment, so too are other characteristics associated with permeable boundaries. Like the jet lagged traveler who more quickly adjusts to a new time zone by going outside and receiving zeitgebers signaling the new cycle, we argue that individuals, groups, and organizations that are more open to their environment will be more likely to entrain to that environment than those with impermeable boundaries. Borrowing from Kurt Lewin (1936, 1951) we hypothesize that an entity's ability to entrain is related to its permeability. Biological receptor cells that link systems within the body respond more readily, and change more easily, when they come into contact with chemical stimuli than do other cells. Within organizations these characteristics could include a greater ability to change cognition and behavior and to incorporate new information (Lewin, 1936; Polster, 1983). Thus, in a study of consulting teams (Ancona, 1990) the teams that were best able to entrain to organizational and client rhythms were those that both had extensive interaction with their environment and an ability to use the information they had gained to flexibly and creatively shift in response to it.

Yet the presence of external cues and openness to the environment still do not entirely account for an entrainment response. The underlying mechanism of entrainment may be what Amburgey and Miner (1992) refer to as repetitive momentum. Repetitive momentum occurs when "organizations repeat previous strategic actions." For example, if an organization changed its CEO during a regulatory jolt, this response may be captured and codified in the form of "modification routines" (Nelson & Winter, 1982; Haveman et al., 1993) or "meta-norms" (Gersick & Hackman, 1990). Momentum reinforces earlier solutions and trajectories of change thereby further institutionalizing them.

While repetitive momentum alone does not indicate entrainment, it suggests a way that the organization can store information about the relevant cues that signal a key pacer and the circumstances under which to entrain to that pacer. This pairing and timing element that includes rules identifying which pacers are relevant and which changes should synchronize with their appearance, becomes part of the routine that is institutionalized and repeated over time. So for entrainment, it is the information about pairing and timing that is important, not the content of the changes that will take place.

Taking this mechanism to other levels of analysis, we might speculate that entrainment becomes an automatic response because it is built into the schema of individuals and the norms of groups. Under entrained conditions individuals and groups are proposed to develop change schema and norms that contain rules for the periodical coupling of particular internal and external rhythms. Furthermore, the activation of these rules would be more apparent under conditions of permeable boundaries and vivid external cues.

Finally, entrainment can also be seen as a conscious, rational decision to achieve economic efficiencies. For example, as a movie maker I might decide to release one movie at Christmas time each year in order to take advantage of people being at home, people being in a spending mood, other movies coming out, and so forth. In this case entrainment is intentional and economically advantageous.

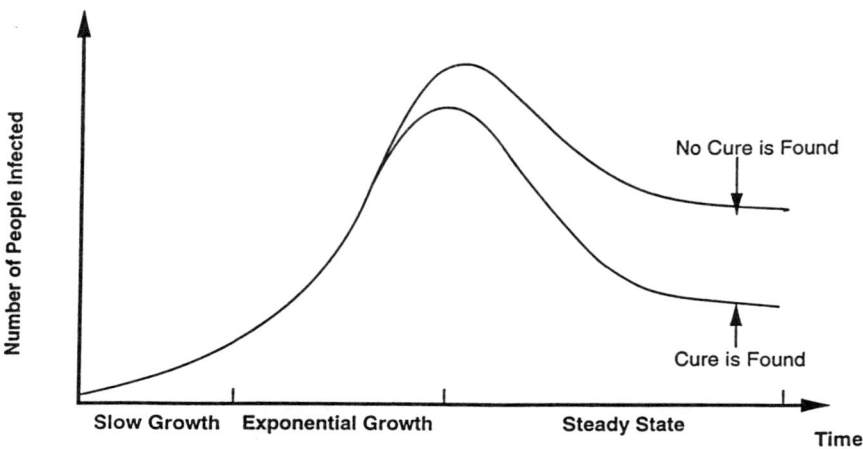

Figure 3. Epidemic Cycle of AIDS

WHY ENTRAINMENT MAY NOT OCCUR?

Related to the mechanisms that create entrainment are those that hamper it. There are numerous instances when entrainment does not occur. For example, the link (or lack of link) between external environmental cycles and internal decision-making cycles seems particularly interesting. Why is it that some firms or agencies can act when an external cycle shifts while others are always too late? Take legislative activity and the AIDS epidemic. The progression of AIDS has been nonlinear and has followed the typical epidemic cycle (see Figure 3). This cycle begins with a period of slow growth and spread of the disease, followed by exponential growth to peak, followed by a steady state, or elimination of the disease if a cure is found (Rosenberg, 1990). The cycle is repeated again, and again, as it spreads to different population groups. The cyclical behavior of the epidemic makes different intervention strategies more successful and less costly at different points in time. In other words, there are phase-optimal interventions. During the period of slow growth the best intervention appears to be one of containment of the infection through encouragement of behavior change in the infected. Later the intervention must shift to damage control and work with susceptible groups as well as the infected group. This cycle needs to repeat itself such that the phases of the epidemic and interventions corresponds across the multiple groups that are affected.

The problem is that legislation and funding follow their own entrained rhythms. Often programs are just getting underway when they are ceasing to

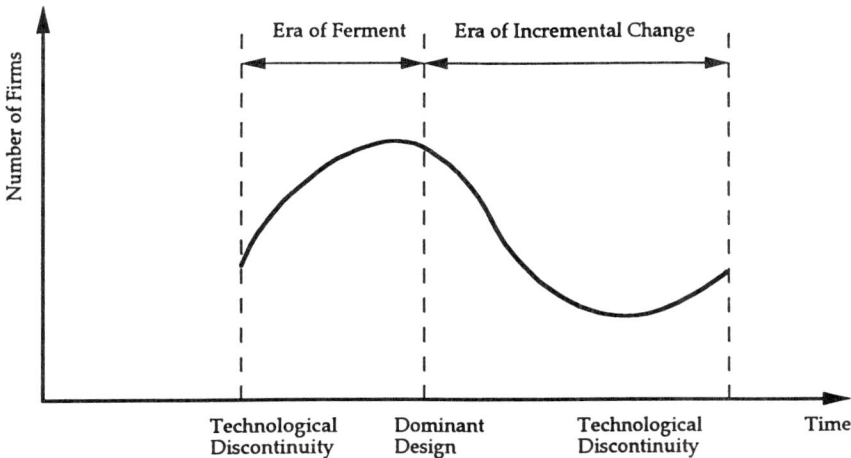

Figure 4. Technology Cycle

be most effective. Such programs are obsolete almost from the start due to a lack of entrainment of the epidemic and the legislation. The same issue occurs with legislative efforts to help the economy out of recession—success is limited due to the inability of the legislative cycle to mesh with the business cycle.

Similarly, each repetition of a technological discontinuity follows a particular pattern (Anderson & Tushman, 1990). The cycle begins with an era of ferment where many firms and entrepreneurs compete to take advantage of the opportunity provided by a new technology. The era of ferment is punctuated by the choice within the market of a dominant design, which signals the exit of many of the competitors. Those that are left enter the era of incremental change characterized by elaboration of the dominant design, and retention of technological and organizational knowledge (see Figure 4). The strategy needed to enter the market when a new technology has been discovered (market leader) is very different from that of later periods (e.g., price leader). If there is a lack of entrainment between the phase of the market and the matched strategy, the economic consequences for a firm can be enormous. Thus, the question of why entrainment does not occur is of central interest.

In trying to answer this question we might speculate as to why some CEOs and top management teams do not entrain organizational change to ongoing environmental cycles such as the business cycle.

First, entrainment represents a shift in pace or cycle for the CEO, team, or organization. Entrainment may be difficult, however, because each level may currently be entrained to a different pacer. That is, CEO succession often follows a pattern that is more a function of the CEO's age, experience, accomplishments, and career aspirations (Ancona & Nadler, 1989) than of changes in the environment. The top management team and organization may also follow dynamics of their own and may be more entrained to internal dynamics than external contingencies at a given point in time (Ancona, 1990; D'Aveni & MacMillan, 1990; Gersick, 1988). Thus, the CEO, the top team, and the organization may all be strongly entrained to different pacers; with the consequence that they are not able to shift to particular external paces and cycles.

A second reason that entrainment may not occur is that the zeitgeber that signals a periodic environmental change is not perceived. For individuals, groups, and organizations environmental scanning and external interactions come to follow established patterns and decrease over time (Hambrick & Fukutomi, 1991; Katz, 1982; Tushman & Romanelli, 1985). Furthermore certain phases of developmental, task, and change cycles tend to stress internal rather than external focus. In the absence of attention to external signals in the environment an entity does not have the cues necessary to entrain.

A third reason that entrainment to external pace and cycle may not occur is that the cycle may have shifted and yet formerly entrained cycles are inertial. In a study by Kelly and McGrath (1985) groups retained the rates at which they originally learned to work even when the time they were subsequently given to carry out a task increased or decreased. Academia still follows the pattern of summers off even though this pattern originated when students needed time off to work in the fields. Furthermore, once an entrained rhythm is established many other cycles and rhythms entrain to it. Once there is a set of interrelated rhythms that involve multiple actors and activities they are even harder to change. Thus, it is not surprising that pace and cycle become entrenched and require meta change schema, norms, or routines in the presence of very vivid and powerful external zeitgebers in order to re-entrain to a new pace or cycle.

Finally, it may be the case that organizations learn that entrainment is not beneficial (Sastry, 1995). For example, if external cycles have a very short periodicity but there are lags in accomplishing organizational change, then change comes too late and the organization remains out of phase with the external cycle. Conversely, if external cycles have very long periodicities then organizations may not be able to sustain the skills necessary for successful change. That is, over time the skills needed for successful change erode from lack of use.

WHAT FUNCTIONS DOES ENTRAINMENT SERVE?

We argue that entrainment serves two major functions: coordination and clock resetting. Coordination is most often thought of as a way to managing dependencies among activities (Malone & Crowston, 1991; Thompson, 1967). Coordination calls for identifying interdependent activities, analyzing their interdependencies (e.g., pooled, sequential, reciprocal), and information processing requirements), and then designing a structure and process to meet those requirements.

Entrainment offers a different way to think about coordination: coordination by time rather than by activity. Like the biological studies of human beings where processes are coordinated so as to all fit together in a 24-hour period, so too do organizations coordinate by mapping to time frames. Like a dance program where varied activities come together on particular beats, organizations coordinate by having various subsections all simultaneously following the temporal patterns laid out by macro cycles such as the fiscal and calendar year. Similarly, like a family that is coordinated by a pattern of shared time together (e.g., people convene in the morning before work and school, in the evening after work and school, and on weekends), organizations provide people with opportunities to work together by having them be at the same place at the same times over the course of the day, week, and year.

Take as an example the university setting. People all go about their separate activities until a certain day in September when students, faculty, administration, recruiters, and so on come together. Then there is a two-year period (in the business school setting) to get the product out the door. Coordination by professors is accomplished by giving each a certain amount of time, on certain days, for three-month intervals. If someone tries to deviate from that program there are inevitable conflicts, confusion, and lack of coordination around the school. Career services knows when to do its work—not during class time and before the recruiters show up on campus. Recruiters know they can come to campus only during certain intervals and they can have the students only when the students are not in school. Building facilities are "leased" to other parts of the university when the majority of students are away. Thus, huge amounts of coordination take place among large numbers of disparate activities through the entrainment to the academic calendar.

Today's changes in organizational design through interventions such as just-in-time manufacturing may really be a shift from coordination by activity to coordination by time, and from entrainment to internal manufacturing and administrative cycles to entrainment to external customer and market cycles. These designs specify fitting activities to deadlines. People are not only told what to do with whom, they are told to flexibly reconfigure themselves to meet deadlines, and periods that are shifting over time.

Coordination by time already goes on in firms. Everybody pulls hard at the end of the fiscal year. Manufacturing ramps up anticipating that the sales force will be speeding up their work at that time. Technical services schedules its seminars at the start of the quarter because they know they will get better attendance than they do at the end, when other activity takes precedence. The rhythm is a mechanism to have people working in unison on disparate activities that come together to create products and services. There is also economic utility to having everyone in the organization engaged in activities like budgeting and planning at the same time.

A second function of entrainment is to enable all activities that entrain to the same cycle to align their phases to begin on their new cycles at the same time. In other words, the clocks for all the activities are reset to zero simultaneously. To illustrate the dynamics of this process we use the example of entrainment to environmental discontinuities, even though these discontinuities do not represent regular, predictable repetitions of a cycle. One could argue that entrainment occurs if internal organizational cycles regularly change in conjunction with external cycles that have irregular frequencies such as environmental discontinuities.

Virany, Tushman, and Romanelli (1992) propose that some firms (those that are more successful) show entrainment of CEO succession and/or top management team replacement, and major change within the firm to technological discontinuities. Havemen et al. (1993) also show this adjustment of CEO succession to align with regulatory discontinuities. This entrainment may serve the important function of simultaneously aligning multiple levels (the top team and the CEO) within the firm by having each cycle starting at the same time. To illustrate this process we look at the cycle of each level separately (teams, the CEO, and environmental discontinuities) and then together.

When teams are first forming they are establishing norms, performance strategies, and external patterns of interaction (Ancona, 1990; Bettenhausen & Murnighan, 1985; Gersick, 1988). At this point they are open to new information from diverse sources and their work cycles are getting established (Hambrick, 1994). Similarly, the CEO at the beginning of his or her term is open to new information and able to make changes that are later frowned upon (Hambrick & Fukutomi, 1991). Thus, if CEO and top management team change are both linked to each environmental discontinuity—clocks at all levels are reset to zero at once—then this provides a mechanism to have the individual and group open to change at precisely the time when it is needed to shift the organization in response to new regulatory and technological imperatives. Furthermore, with the introduction of a new external pacer these multiple levels all have the same guide directing the pattern of a new bundling. Thus, entrainment is a useful device for resetting all clocks to zero when entities are most open to change, and for providing a common guide for recalibration.

HOW DOES ENTRAINMENT HAMPER ORGANIZATIONAL FUNCTIONING?

While entrainment clearly serves important coordination and adaptation functions for organizations, there do appear to be problems associated with it. First is the issue of paces, cycles, or rhythms that become dysfunctional when entrained to a dominant pacer. Take for example our university's policy of evaluating secretaries at the start of the second semester. The time of the evaluation is set by entrainment to the semester rhythm. This is the point at which the professors are most dependent on their secretaries, work load and stress are very high for professor and secretary alike, and thus the faculty avoids negative evaluations. At some point this inability to provide accurate feedback becomes dysfunctional for the system.

Second, entrainment can be planned (e.g., firms attempt to shorten the product development cycle) or it can be unplanned. The problem is that one does not always know the appropriate pacer to choose for planned entrainment or whether to try to interfere with unplanned entrainment. Should CEO succession be tied to every jolt? Only regulatory and technological jolts? Only jolts above a certain level? Should the fiscal year coincide with the calendar year? Should macro dominant cycles continue to rule for their coordination and adaptive value, or should some cycles be uncoupled? Which ones? Should organizations be entrained to customers, suppliers, distributors, or all three? These are questions which will need to be answered if entrainment is to be useful to managers and researchers alike.

Third, entrainment to one external pacer may wreck havoc on other entrained cycles. For example, an increased work week in the United States has resulted from massive downsizing in many organizations. The increased work week is resulting in fatigue and inadequate time for leisure and family activity, which is asynchronously entrained to work. Also, as previously mentioned, speeding product development if advertising, manufacturing, and distribution cannot also speed up produces problems.

Fourth, if the system is weakly entrained, the meshed cycles can easily go out of synchronization with one another. They either entrain to new pacers or revert back to their endogenous state. The temporal ordering is no longer binding system together. On the other hand, if a system is strongly entrained the behavior is entrenched and there is little chance of adjustment to external pacers even when the need arises. The strength of the entrainment is therefore important. Theoretically, a system should be sufficiently entrained so that the synchronization holds under most conditions, yet not so strong as to bind it indefinitely to a certain temporal structure. This balance is delicate and difficult to attain.

Fifth, as McGrath and Rotchford (1983) point out, bundles of entrained paces, cycles, and rhythms may create macro problems through their aggregated effects. For example, because all faculty teach at the same times and have the same start dates, secretaries, reproduction departments, and computer centers all face work overload in the first two weeks of September and January followed by work lulls. In economics, the large impact of the business cycle on multiple arenas often causes the lows to be lower and the highs to be higher. The impact of everyone buying or selling at the same time is to exaggerate ongoing swings in the system. Thus, bundled entrainment of multiple people and processes can create negative aggregate effects.

Finally, entrainment can hamper creativity. Entrainment represents repeated patterns of activity, hence by its very definition there is an emphasis on repetition not innovation. If a course is always given in twelve weeks, a product always designed in two years, and a team always evaluated every three months, then there are limits to the way we teach, design, and work. If entrainment sets the time parameter at some constant, it hinders the possibilities created by expanding or delimiting deadlines. Perhaps some courses would be better taught for three full days, some products better created by people living together for a week and some teams more productive by doing their major work in the fourth month. These options are less likely under a scenario of entrainment to a fixed pace, period or rhythm. Thus, entrainment may lessen the probability of searching for, and finding, creative solutions and new modes of operation. For all of its usefulness in providing order, coordination, and adaptive capability, entrainment also may have negative consequences.

SETTING A RESEARCH AGENDA

The entrainment concept lays out a new research agenda. The first step in that agenda calls for identifying the paces, cycles, and rhythms of dominant activities. Entrainment calls for a focus, not just on what is being done, but on how fast, following what phases and patterns, and according to what repetition, activities are taking place.

A great deal of work has already been done in this first step of research. There have been studies of the pace of strategic decision making (Eisenhardt 1989, 1990; Wally & Baum, 1994), product development (Clark & Fujimoto, 1991), business cycles (Sterman & Mosekilde, 1993), and technology cycles (Anderson & Tushman, 1990). There has been work done on career phases (Bailyn, 1992; Katz & Tushman, 1979), life phases (Erikson, 1963), team development (Gersick, 1989; Tuckman, 1965), and organizational development (Greiner, 1972; Miles & Snow, 1978). There has even been some work on the nature of the repetition of environmental cycles with research showing that technological discontinuities are less frequent in stable industries (Anderson & Tushman, 1990).

Some of the major gaps come in a lack of attention to the pace, cycle, and rhythm associated with the dominant temporal patterns that punctuate organizational life. This would include understanding the patterning and impact of the fiscal year, the semester cycle, the four-year political cycle, the military calendar, and the farming season to name a few.

The essence of entrainment, however, is in its focus on the interaction among paces, cycles, and rhythms. Step two in the research process is therefore to begin to document when and where entrainment of pace, cycle, and rhythm occur, and perhaps more interestingly, when and where it does not occur. How is it that some real estate firms manage staff to match the boom/bust of the real estate cycle, while others retain their bloated staffs even when the market falls and subsequently go bankrupt? Through these kinds of studies we can begin to learn more about the mechanisms of entrainment and its impact.

Instances of entrainment and lack of entrainment can be examined within firms as well as across firms. How a given company handles its interactions with clients, the government, its competitors, the market, and suppliers, each of which may be operating at a different pace and on a different cycle would help to illuminate how to balance entrainment to multiple external cycles while maintaining an internal ordering.

A third step in research would be to compare similar processes and tasks under both entrained and unentrained conditions (e.g., product development teams that must compete and match the development cycles of other companies versus those with a committed client), and to monitor when change occurs in both. If unentrained and buffered conditions result in stage change or pacing to temporal milestones set by internal events, then how does change occur under entrained conditions? Does pacing seem more forced when it is set to external clocks? Is readiness for change the same under both conditions? Also, one would use different methods from those currently used in most organizational research. As entrainment calls for cyclical rather than linear thinking, one should contemplate using systems dynamics to construct simulation models that allow systems to play out over time and include responses to external influences and feedback.

A fourth step in research would be to examine new coordination mechanisms and organizational forms suggested by entrainment. Perhaps a firm could be configured with groupings by time frame rather than by client or geography or function. In this scenario customer-oriented functions would be working on the same schedule as customers, while others would be oriented to time frames set by product design or manufacturing cycles. In each "time division" the clock-setting process would occur at a different time, but each would synchronize with its particular environmental rhythm.

Simultaneously, teams or projects could differ by pace or by rhythm. Some projects could move at a very fast pace and others could be slow. Some could require long hours and some could fit a 35-hour week. These projects could be matched to both client and employee needs. Those clients that needed work done tomorrow would get a different grouping than one with a long-term project. Employees could rotate. If someone was feeling burnt out after a fast-paced, long-hour work schedule, he/she could shift pace for the next assignment. Similarly, employees with shifting family needs (see Bailyn, 1992) could be accommodated. Employees could work at one pace when single, another when young children were around, and a third when children were older.

CONCLUSION

Entrainment should be apparent to all of us as it pervades our daily lives. Any babyboomer struggling with the demands of working, having children, caring for elderly parents, and trying to "speed up" to get it all done (Hochschild & Machung, 1989) knows that work cycles and life cycles do not always entrain in an optimal fashion. Even though it is apparent to us that social and organizational life are temporarily structured and regulated, we did not have the vocabulary and framework to address temporal patterns explicitly. The entrainment lens provides a possible tool. It is one that focuses on pace, cycle, and rhythm, and their interaction over time. It pushes us to take into account speed, the impact of interlocking cycles, and the timing of activities. It also pushes us to collect different kinds of data and to ask a different set of research questions.

While many researchers concentrate their work at a single level of analysis or at one point in time, entrainment argues for a multilevel and longitudinal approach. While most of our methodologies, statistics, and theory assume a linear world, entrainment pushes us to map out cycles and rhythms. Finally, while most of our literature focuses on activity, entrainment focuses on the timing and the temporal patterning of that activity.

At a basic level entrainment focuses on how patterns of activity repeat themselves in cycles over time, how long each cycle takes, how fast the activity moves, how the phases of different cycles interlock, with what effect. We become interested in the properties of those paces, cycles, and rhythms, such as inertia and change, and the mechanisms by which those paces, cycles, and rhythms synchronize. Rather than treating time as a control variable, we adopt a mindset that explicitly focuses on time as depicted by pace, cycle, and rhythm both within and between systems.

Through an understanding of entrainment processes we can understand that faster is not always better. Before shifting a pace or cycle it becomes necessary to see how that cycle fits in to a system of entwined cycles that has coordination and adaptation benefits associated with it. The entrainment lens highlights change as a process that is linked to external cycles as well as internal clocks, that can be regular as well as random, and that can be better managed by taking associated cycles into account. It highlights the rhythmic nature of organizational life and the subjective nature of our sense of time. It provides a new view of coordination and an appreciation of how much of our activity is already coordinated through timing mechanisms.

The organizational arena is filled with references to time, where practitioners, journalists, and theorists alike point to an ever increasing pace of change, to closing windows of opportunity, and to the scarcity of time. Yet those of us in the organizational realm have been slow to incorporate these ideas into theory. Entrainment is a research lens that can help us to understand a broad array of phenomena, from the survival value of mutual entrainment of biological subsystems within the human body to the coordination of individuals, groups, and organizations. It is now time to implement research that models tempo, and phase entrainment. From there we may find better ways to conceptualize and cope with the many meanings and effects of time.

ACKNOWLEDGMENT

We would like to thank Lotte Bailyn, Jean Bartunek, John Carroll, Connie Gersick, Neal Mitra, William Ocasio, Julio Rotemberg, Barry Staw, John Sterman, Bob Sutton, and John Van Maanen for their helpful comments and support.

REFERENCES

Amburgey, T.L., & Miner, A.A. (1992). Strategic momentum: The effects of repetitive, positional, and contextual momentum on merger activity. *Strategic Management Journal, 13*, 335-348.
Ancona, D.G. (1990). Outward bound: Strategies for team survival in the organization. *Academy of Management Journal, 33*, 334-365.
Ancona, D.G., & Caldwell, D.F. (1988). Beyond task and maintenance: Defining external functions in groups. *Group and Organization Studies, 13*, 468-494.
Ancona, D.G., & Chong, C. (1992). *Entrainment: Cycle and synergy in organizational behavior.* Working paper 3443-92-BPS, Sloan School of Management, MIT.
Ancona, D.G., & Nadler, D.A. (1989). Top hats and executive tales: Designing the senior team. *Sloan Management Review, 31*, 19-28.
Anderson, P.C., & Tushman, M.L. (1990). Technological discontinuities and dominant designs: A cyclical model of technological change. *Administrative Science Quarterly, 35*, 604-633.
Aschoff, J. (1979). Circadian rhythms: General features and endocrinological aspects. In D. Krieger (Ed.), *Endocrine rhythms* (pp. 1-61). New York: Raven Press.
Bailyn, L. (1992, Fall). Issues of work and family in different national contexts: How the United States, Britain, and Sweden respond. *Human Resource Management*, 201-208.
Bettenhausen, K., & Murnighan, J.K. (1985). The emergence of norms in competitive decision-making groups. *Administrative Science Quarterly, 30*, 350-372.
Bluedorn, A.C., & Denhardt, R.B. (1988). Time and organizations.*Journal of Management, 14*, 299-320.
Cameron, K.S., & Whetten, D.A. (1988). Models of organizational life cycle: Applications to higher education. In K.S. Cameron, R.I. Sutton, & D.A. Whetten (Eds.), *Readings in organizational decline* (pp. 45-62). Cambridge, MA: Ballinger.
Carroll, J., & Perin, C. 1994). *Organization and management of nuclear power plants for safe performance.* Annual Report. Cambridge, MA: MIT Sloan School.
Chong, C. (1995). *Temporal patterns of chnage in groups.* Unpublished Ph.D. dissertation, Sloan School of Management, MIT.
Clark, K.B. (1989). Project scope and project performance: The effects of parts strategy and supplier involvement on product development. *Management Science, 75*, 1247-1263.
Clark, K.B., & Fujimoto, T. (1987). *Overlapping problem solving in product development.* Working paper 87-048, Harvard University Graduate School of Business Administration, Cambridge, MA.

Clark, K.B., & Fujimoto, T. (1991). *Product development performance: Strategy, organization, and management in the world auto industry*. Boston, MA: Harvard Business School Press.

D'Aveni, R.A., & MacMillan, I.C. (1990). Crisis and the content of managerial communications: A study of the focus of attention of top managers in surviving and failing firms. *Administrative Science Quarterly, 36*, 634-657.

DiMaggio, P.J., & Powell, W.W. (1983). The iron cage revisited: institutional isomorphism and collective rationality in organizational fields. *American Sociological Review, 48*, 147-160.

Eisenhardt, K.M. (1989). Making fast strategic decisions in high-velocity environments. *Academy of Managment Journal, 32*, 543-576.

Eisenhardt, K.M. (1990). Speed and strategic choice: How managers accelerate decision making. *Academy of Management Journal, 32*, 543-576.

Erikson, E. (1963). *Childhood and society*. W.W. Norton.

Galbraith, J.R. (1977). *Organization design*. Reading, MA: Addison-Wesley.

Gersick, C.J.C. (1988). Time and transition in work teams: Towards a new model of group development. *Academy of Management Journal, 31*, 9-41.

Gersick, C.J.C. (1989). Marking time: Predictable transitions in task groups. *Academy of Management Journal, 32*, 274-309.

Gersick, C.J.C. (1991). Revolutionary change theories: A multilevel exploration of the punctuated equilibrium paradigm. *Academy of Managment Review, 16*, 10-36.

Gersick, C.J.C. (1994). Pacing strategic change: The case of a new venture. *Academy of Management Journal, 37*, 9-45.

Gersick, C.J.C., & Hackman, J.R. (1990). Habitual routines in task-performing groups. *Organizational Behavior and Human Decision Processes, 47*, 65-97.

Gladstein, D. (1984). Groups in context: A model of task group effectiveness. *Administrative Science Quarterly, 29*, 499-518.

Graves, J.P., Dalton, G.W., & Thompson, P.H. (1980). Career stages in organizations. In C.B. Derr (Ed.), *Work, family, and the career* (pp. 18-50). New York: Praeger.

Greiner, L.E. (1972). Evolution and revolution as organizations grow. *Harvard Business Review, 50*(4), 37-46.

Hambrick, D.C. (1994). Top management groups: A conceptual integration and reconsideration of the "team" label. In L.L. Cummings & B.M. Staw (Eds.), *Research in organizational behavior* (Vol. 16). Greenwich, CT: JAI Press.

Hambrick, D.C., & Fukutomi, G.D.S. (1991). The seasons of a CEO's tenure. *Academy of Management Review, 16*, 719-742.

Hatvany, N., & Pucik, V. (1981, Spring). Japanese management practices and productivity. *Organization Dynamics*, 5-21.

Haveman, H.A., Meyer, A.D., & Russo, M.V. (1993). *Institutional environments in flux: The impact of regulatory change on CEO succession and firm performance*. Unpublished manuscript.

Hochschild, A.R., & Machung, A. (1989). *The second shift: Working parents and the revolution at home*. New York: Viking.

Homans, G.C. (1950). *The human group*. New York: Harcourt, Brace.

Imai, K., Takeuchi, H., & Nonaka, I. (1985). Managing the new product development process: How Japanese companies learn and unlearn. In K.B. Clark, R.H. Hayes, & C. Lorenz (Eds.), *The uneasy alliance: Managing the productivity-technology dilemma*. Boston, MA: Harvard University School Press.

Katz, R. (1982). The effects of group longevity on project communication and performance. *Administrative Science Quarterly, 27*, 81-104.

Katz, R., & Tushman, M.L. (1979). Communication patterns, project performance, and task characteristics: An empirical evaluation and integration in an R&D setting. *Organizational Behavior and Human Performance, 23*, 139-162.

Keck, S.L., & Tushman, M.L. (1993). Environmental and organizational context and executive team structure. *Academy of Management Journal, 36*, 1314-1344.

Kelly, J.R., & McGrath, J.E. (1985). Effects of time limits and task types on task performance and interaction of four-person groups. *Journal of Personality and Social Psychology, 49*, 395-407.

Kram, K.E. (1985). *Mentoring at work: Developmental relationships in organizational life.* Glenview: Scott Foresman.

Krishnan, V., Eppinger, S.D., & Whitney, D.E. (1994). *A model-based framework to overlap product development activities.* Working Paper 3635-93--MS, Sloan School of Management, MIT.

Learning Center Case History. (1995). Organizational Learning Center, Sloan School of Management, MIT.

Leenders, M. (1994). *Nursing Home 'Oudshoorn', Alphen AID Rijn, The Netherlands: Project 'Day Rhythm.'* Term papers written at Boston College for Professor Creed.

Levine, R.V. (1988). The pace of life across cultures. In J.E. McGrath (Ed.), *The social psychology of time: New perspectives*, pp. 39-60). Beverly Hills, CA: Sage.

Levinson, D.J. (1978). *The seasons of a man's life.* New York: Knopf.

Lewin, K. (1936). *Principles of topological psychology.* Translated by Fritz Heider. New York: McGraw-Hill.

Lewin, K. (1951). *Field theory in social science: Selected theoretical papers.* New York: Harper.

Mackie, R.R. (1977). *Vagilance: Theory, operational performance and physiological correlates.* New York: Plenum Press.

Malone, T., & Crowston, K. (1991). *Toward an interdisciplinary theory of coordination.* Working paper CCSTR#120, Center for Coordination Science, Sloan School of Management, MIT.

McGrath, J.E., & Kelly, J.R. (1986). *Time and human interaction: Toward a social psychology of time.* New York: Guilford.

McGrath, J.E., Kelly, J.R. & Machatka, D.E. (1984). The social psychology of time: Entrainment of behavior in social and organizational settings. In S. Iskamp (Ed.,), *Applied social psychology annual* (Vol. 5, pp. 21-44). Beverly Hills, CA: Sage Publications.

McGrath, J.E., & Rotchford, N.L. (1983). Time and behavior in organizations. In L.L. Cummings & B.M. Staw (Eds.), *Research in organizational behavior* (Vol. 5, pp. 57-101). Greenwich, CT: JAI Press.

Miles, R.E., & Snow, C.C. (1978). *Organizational strategy, structure, and processes.* New York: McGraw-Hill.

Minosky, N. (1962). *Nonlinear oscillations.* Princeton, NJ: Van Nostrand.

Nadler, D.A., & Tushman, M.L. (1988). *Strategic organization design: Concepts, tools and processes.* Glenview, IL: Scott, Foresman.

Nelson, R., & Winter, S. (1982). *An evolutionary theory of economic change.* Cambridge: Harvard University Press.

Oatley, K., & Goodwin, B.C. (1971). Explanation and investigation of biological rhythms. In W.P. Colquhain (Ed.), *Biological rhythms and human performance.* New York: Academic Press.

Pettigrew, A.M. (1985). *The awakening giant: Continuity and change in Imperial Chemical Industries.* New York: Blackwell.

Pittendrigh, C.S. (1972). On temporal organization in living systems. In H. Yaker, H. Osmond, & F. Cheek (Eds.), *The future of time.* new York: Anchor Books.

Polster, S. (1983). Ego boundary as process: A systemic-contextual approach. *Psychiatry, 46*, 247-258.

Rosenberg, C.E. (1990). What is an epidemic? AIDS in historical perspective. In S.R. Granbard (Ed.), *Living with AIDS.* Cambridge, MA: MIT Press.

Rousseau, D. (1985). Issues of level in organizational research: Multi-level and cross-level perspective. In L.L. Cummings & B.M. Staw (Eds.), *Research in organizational behavior* (vol. 7, pp. 1-37). Greenwich, CT: JAI Press.

Sastry, M.A. (1995). *Time and tide in organizations simulating change processes in adaptive punctuated and ecological theories of organizational evolution.* Ph.D. dissertation, Sloan School of Management, MIT.

Sastry, M.A., & Chong. C. (1905). *Time for a change? A dual-method study of timing in organizational transformation.* Unpublished manuscript, Sloan School of Management, MIT.

Starbuck, W.H. (1965). Organizational growth and development. In J.G. March (Ed.), *Handbook of organizations.* Chicago: Rand McNally.

Sterman, J.D., & Mosekilde, E. (1993). *Business cycles and long waves: A behavioral disequilibrium perspective.* Working paper No. 3528-93-MSA, Sloan School of Management, MIT.

Stevenson, W.B. (1985). Organizatioal growth and hierarchical change in formal structure. *Journal of Mathematical Sociology, 11,* 287-306.

Strogatz, S.H., & Stewart, I. (1993). Coupled oscillators and biological synchronization. *Scientific American, 269*(4), 102-109.

Takeuchi, H., & Nonaka, I. (1986, January-February). The new product development game *Harward Business Review,* 137-146.

Thomson, J.D. (1967). *Organizations in action: Social science bases of administrative therapy.* New York: McGraw-Hill.

Tuckman, B. (1965). Developmental sequence in small groups. *Psychological Bulletin, 63,* 384-399.

Tushman, M., & Romanelli, E. (1985). Organizational evolution: A metamorphosis model of convergence and reorientation. In L.L. Cummings & B.M. Staw (Eds.), *Research in organizatioal behavior* (Vol. 7, pp. 171-222). Greenwich, CT: JAI Press.

Tyre, M.J., & Orlikowski, W.J. (1994). Windows of opportunity: Temporal patterns of technological adaptation in organizations. *Organization Science, 5,* 98-118.

Virany, B.B., Tushman, M.L., & Romanelli, E. (1992). Executive succession and organizational learning approach. *Organization Science, 3,* 72-91.

Wally, S., & Baum, J.R. (194). Personal and structural determinants of the pace of strategic decision making. *Academy of Management Journal, 37,* 932-956.

Wicker, A.W., & King, J.E. (1988). Life cycles of behavior settings. In J.E. McGrath (Ed.), *The social psychology of time: New Perspectives* (pp. 182-200). Beverly Hills, CA: Sage.

Zarubavel, E. (1979). *Patterns of time in hospital life: A sociological perspective.* Chicago: University of Chicago Press.

CUSTOMER-SUPPLIER TIES IN INTERORGANIZATIONAL RELATIONS

Mark Fichman and Paul Goodman

ABSTRACT

This paper presents a multilevel view of the relationships between customers and suppliers in industrial markets. The paper focuses on transactions between customers and suppliers at three levels: the individual's evaluation of transactions between firms, the dyadic relationship between a customer and supplier, and the network of relationships in which transactions and customer-supplier relationships are embedded. At the individual level, we consider how actors initiate, evaluate, and respond to transactions. At the dyadic level, we consider the forms a relationship can take and how these relationship forms influence the nature of transactions and the processing of transactions between customer and supplier. At the network level, we identify the structure of the interorganizational network, composed of a buying center, a selling center, and the network of relations tying the two parties together. We then consider how this network structure affects the transactions between buyer and supplier. The critical point raised in the paper is that one must consider all three levels simultaneously if a fuller understanding of the dynamics of ties between customers and suppliers is to be developed in organizational science.

INTRODUCTION AND MOTIVATION

Our goal for this paper is to identify research needs and opportunities in the study of customer-supplier linkages. We focus on the transactions between the customer organization and the supplier organization. How do individuals cognitively represent these transactions? How does the nature of the relationships between customers and suppliers influence their responses to these transactions? Does the network of social relationships between organizations influence the quality of customer-supplier ties?

Rationale

There are a number of trends which make analysis of customer-supplier transactions timely. First, customer-supplier relationships have changed dramatically in the past decade. The boundaries between customers and suppliers are becoming more transparent. Customers are involved in organizational activities such as designing new products and services. Customer evaluations of service quality are becoming an important component in managerial reward systems. Customer satisfaction with the organization is a new, emerging indicator of organizational effectiveness. Given these and other dramatic changes, we should examine our existing intellectual tools and empirical findings for understanding customer-supplier relationships and point to the development of new tools.

There is surprisingly little organizational research on customer-supplier transactions. The predominant literature on customer evaluations of these transactions appears in the marketing literature. Recently, there has been a call from marketing researchers (Iacobucci, Grayson, & Ostrom, 1994; Webster, 1992) to build organizational perspectives in order to better understand the relationships between buying and selling organizations (Anderson & Weitz, 1992). The organizational perspective work by Schneider and his colleagues (Schneider & Bowen, 1985, 1995) on customer service has demonstrated that internal organizational relationships of the supplier affect how customers evaluate transactions with suppliers. While this work demonstrates the importance of an organizational perspective on customer-supplier transactions, there are relatively few research programs in this tradition. One goal of this paper is to provide a new organizational framework for approaching the study of customer-supplier relationships.

A third rationale for this paper is that we adopt a multilevel perspective—individual, relational, and network—to explore the complex transactions between customer and supplier. The existing literature has primarily focused on the individual level and sometimes at the relational level. Our analysis explores all three units of analysis and their interrelationships. This focus is consistent with the recent movement in organizational research toward a more multilevel perspective (House, Rousseau, & Thomas-Hunt, 1995).

After reading this paper, our hope is that you see exciting research opportunities in customer-supplier relationships. This paper provides a picture of important areas for explorations for both theory and practice. At another level, you will be exposed to problems and related intellectual controversies which should also be considered the focus for new research activities.

Scope

Our analysis will focus on customer-supplier relationships. While there are many interesting new forms of interorganizational partnerships which have emerged in the last decade, such as joint ventures or service alliances (Kanter, 1989), our attention is on customer-supplier exchanges. The recent invasion of total quality management practices in organizations has made us sensitive to "internal" and "external" customers. While this distinction is useful, we focus on "external" customers here.

The distinction between industrial and customer markets is another way to further characterize customer-supplier relationships. We have chosen industrial markets as the focal point in our investigation. These markets deal with exchanges between organizations as compared with exchanges between organizations and individuals. Automotive manufacturers buy parts worldwide from other manufacturers for automobile assembly. Telephone companies buy fiber optic cable from cable manufacturers. We selected industrial markets because we want to analyze exchanges among organizations.

A MULTILEVEL ANALYSIS OF CUSTOMER-SUPPLIER RELATIONSHIPS

Our analysis of customer-supplier relationships is organized around three themes:

1. Individual Evaluations of Customer-Supplier Transactions,
2. Modeling Customer-Supplier Relationships, and
3. A Network View of the Interorganizational Structure.

In each theme we identify and explore some problem areas. Our goals are: to frame these problem areas so they are tractable, to delineate some of the theoretical mechanisms in these problem areas, and to identify areas for research.

The three themes focus on different levels of analysis. These three levels of analysis are illustrated in Figure 1 and discussed below.

1. The individual transaction level (Theme I) focuses on how individual actors initiate, evaluate, and respond to transactions between customers and suppliers. How do individuals represent these transactions? What are the critical mechanisms affecting such representations? What are the consequences of these representations?

2. The dyadic level (Theme II) focuses on the relationship between customer and supplier. What are different forms of these relationships (e.g., economic versus relational)? How does the relationship form affect the nature of the transactions and the basic underlying processes between customer and supplier organizations?

3. The network level (Theme III) focuses on the structure and processes of the interorganizational relationship between the customer and supplier. There are three interconnected social systems we will consider: first, the buying center, which is the network of individuals in the customer firm involved in the ongoing transactions with the supplier; second, the selling center, which we define as the network of individuals in the supplier firm involved in ongoing transactions with the customer firm; and third, the interorganizational relationship, which develops a structure of ties between firms.

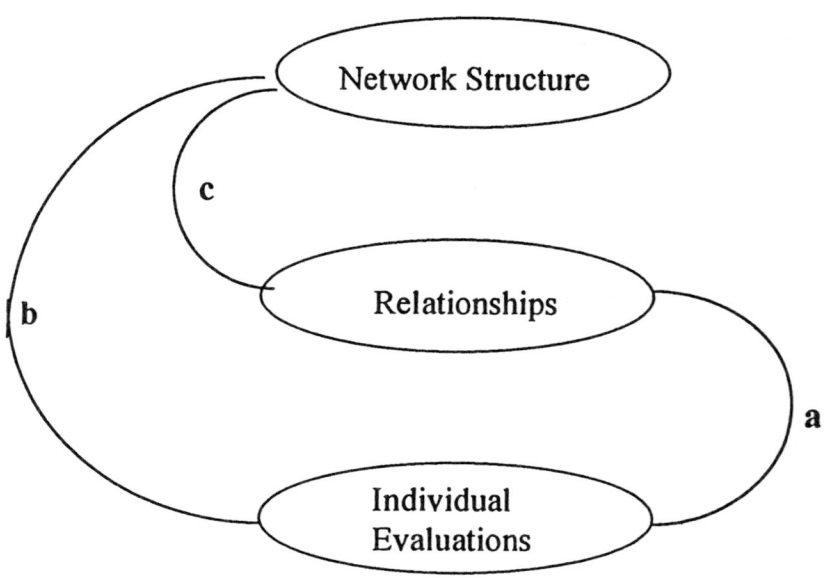

Figure 1. Multilevel Analysis of Customer-Supplier Relationships

We have framed these three themes because they are critical parts of the customer-supplier relationship. To develop a new organizational perspective on customers and suppliers, one needs to focus on each theme and their interrelationships.

In Figure 1, why should we consider arc a, linking the relationship level to the individual? The quality of the relationship can influence how carefully the customer monitors the transaction. If there is a high level of trust, monitoring may be reduced. On the other hand if there is a high level of trust *and* involvement, negative outcomes may be very surprising, strongly violating expectations and leading to stronger evaluative reactions (Goodman, Fichman, Lerch, & Snyder, 1995). The customer-supplier relationship and its qualities can influence the monitoring and evaluation process at the individual level. Arc a allows the influence of evaluations of the individual experience to affect the quality and dynamics of the relationship. A negative outcome may change the evaluation of the relationship itself, or change its dynamics. We see causal processes working in both directions on arc a.

Let us turn to the impact of network position on this individual evaluation process as suggested by arc b. Information about the transaction travels along certain social networks. Transaction information may only be available if one is in a particular social network position. We believe network position will affect the ensemble of information available for evaluation. Can individual action influence a social network such as that created in an industrial market? Turnover in key actors can influence the continuity and quality of customer-supplier ties. Seabright, Levinthal, and Fichman (1992) showed that turnover of key actors in the customer side increased the probability that customer-supplier ties would be broken.

Arc c suggests that network structure and relationship qualities will influence each other. Networks can influence the information that may be available to customer-supplier relationships, which should affect the nature of the transactions. Similarly, changes in the relationship between customers and suppliers can change networks. For example, as Supplier A's downstream customers change their requirements, the kinds of transactions and requirements placed on a supplier will change. We review below work by Florida and Kenney (1991) showing that American suppliers to Japanese auto assemblers located in the United States (transplants) changed their work practices and networks as a result of their interaction with the Japanese transplants.

The brief outline of arcs a, b, and c in Figure 1 illustrates the value of this multilevel analysis. It provides a distinctive, new perspective for analyzing customer-supplier relationships. We now turn to our discussion of the three themes.

Theme I: Individual Evaluations of Customer-Supplier Transactions

Our first theme focuses on the individual level of analysis. How do individual members of the buying (or selling) center evaluate transactions? How do they make sense of or assign meaning to transactions? To provide the reader a real context for these questions, we have provided sample responses from interviews we conducted with major business customers of the United States Postal Service (USPS) (see Goodman et al., 1995, for a description of this study.)

Table 1 includes respondents' satisfaction or dissatisfaction with first-class mail and their rationale for selecting a particular response. Respondents are members of a customer organization who interact with USPS.

The interview quotes represent one dimension (i.e., overall satisfaction with first-class mail) that customers may consider when evaluating transactions with a supplier. It is interesting to note (1) that the two very satisfied respondents discuss different attributes, one discussing pickup and the other discussing timeliness, and (2) there is variation in the level of differentiation in the rationales. Some are sparse; others are fairly differentiated. The quotes are presented to stimulate the reader to think about how customers may evaluate transactions as we explore aspects of the evaluation process.

Theme I, then, is about how people make these evaluations. This process is critical to understanding evaluations. This process is critical to understanding customer-supplier relationships. Whether relationships grow, become stagnant, or dissolve is, in part, based on how the relevant players view the

Table 1. Responses to Satisfaction with First-Class Mail

Satisfaction with First-Class Mail	Rationale
Satisfied	It's something that I don't really have any complaints on. No news is good news. I only hear if there are complaints. Nobody calls up and says that their mail got delivered in one day; they only call about problems.
Very Satisfied	We mail to Erie quite often. They usually get it the next day; Harrisburg, second day. Usually don't have any complaints. Not guaranteed to be there, but it usually does get there, no real problems.
Very Satisfied	The mail service picks up off of our dock twice a day. I'm very positive. USPS waits for me to meter out a couple pieces of important mail. I have no complaints on delivery. As long as I don't hear complaints, that makes me happy. I've only had two lost packages the whole five years I've been here.
Slightly Satisfied	We have loan customers in Cleveland—15-day grace period. If the customer does not get their bill for 5-7 days, they complain that they don't have enough of a grace period to pay their bill. In the Pittsburgh area, I am satisfied; Cleveland is where we have had problems.

relevant players view the relationship. Our analysis will focus more on process issues than the content of specific evaluation categories (e.g., product quality, responsiveness). Also, while there are clear differences in the literature between customer satisfaction and service quality, again our focus is more on how the evaluations are made. Most of our discussion and examples will be from the perspective of the customer. That is where the literature resides.[1] We will close this section by looking at evaluations from the supplier firm's perspective.

Current Models

Gap/discrepancy models have been frequently used in the literature on evaluating service quality or customer satisfaction (Churchill & Suprenant, 1982; Zeithaml, Parasuraman, & Berry, 1985). We introduce these models more to illustrate some of the basic features of how customers evaluate transactions rather than to focus on the validity of these models.[2] These models hold that customers have expectations about a transaction and have perceptions about actual experiences (or performances) with the transaction. Expectations and experiences are compared, and lead to the confirmation or disconfirmation of expectations, (i.e., a gap) which, in turn, affects positive or negative evaluations. For example, if a customer expects a product to be delivered in two weeks but it takes four weeks, a negative evaluation of responsiveness follows. If the product was delivered in two weeks, expectations are met and positive evaluations should follow. If delivery occurs before the promised date, the evaluations probably remain positive. Our understanding about the effects of positive discrepancies is probably not as refined as in the case of negative discrepancies, a point we will cover later.

Given the prominence of this model for customer evaluations, there, of course, have been many elaborations. Some researchers have examined the role of ex ante and ex post expectations (McGill & Iacobucci, 1992). Others have focused on the difference between "should" and "will" expectations (Boulding, Staelin, Kalra, & Zeithaml, 1993). Still other researchers have been interested in whether the gap or the individual elements in the model affect evaluations. For example, do expectations or perceptions of performance drive the evaluation process independent of any gaps or disconfirmations (Fornell, 1992; Tse & Wilton, 1988)?

Some Criticisms

Despite the predominance of these models in the literature on how people judge service quality or customer satisfaction, there have been criticisms (Iacobucci et al., 1994) which raise some fundamental questions about the evaluation process. One question has been whether expectations actually exist. If there is a first time transaction, there may not be a basis to form an expectation. Or the object to be exchanged may be very novel. Another factor may be the explicitness of the transaction. In some customer-supplier transactions, there may be explicit offers and acceptances. For example, I will deliver you a product in three days, and you agree to pay "X" dollars. In this case, the expectations are explicitly formed in the contract. In other cases, there may be no contract. Some empirical studies (McGill & Iacobucci, 1992; Woodruff, Cadotte, & Jenkins, 1983) also suggest that post-experience-based norms may be better predictors of customer satisfaction than expectations. These findings question the role of prior expectations in the evaluation of quality or satisfaction.

A second question is whether perceptions of the experiences can be formed. In many cases the transactions between customer and supplier are visible. For example, I buy office equipment, and it appears in my office, and it is used. However, not all transactions are visible. In Table 1, we provide evaluations from major customers of USPS. Think about what this major mailer knows. In most cases the delivery of their mail by the USPS is not directly visible. A utility company does not directly know if its bills are delivered. Only if some other act occurs (e.g., customer calls to say they received the wrong bill) would there be any knowledge of the delivery event. A related point is that even if all transactions flow between the customer and supplier, the nature of some of the transactions may not be visible to all members of the buying center. One individual may make the decision to buy a work station, but may not be the user. Unless there is direct communication between the user and the buyer, the buyer would have no "experiences" with the machine.

The third question concerns the comparison mechanisms in the gap or disconfirmation paradigms. The idea that expectations are compared to experiences seems fairly straightforward. However, there may be multiple standards (e.g., ideal product, industry standards) used in evaluating customer-supplier transactions (Cadotte, Woodruff, & Jenkins, 1987; Iacobucci et al., 1994), and how these standards may be combined is not well understood. Also, standards can be absolute or relative. A product, for example, may be delivered 10 days late. Consider two cases—one where the promised delivery time was 10 days, and another where the time was 100 days. Is the meaning of 10 days late the same in both cases? This issue of whether people use relative or absolute standards is not well specified (Goodman & Garber, 1994; Iacobucci et al., 1994). In this example, the person may have considered 10 days absolutely, in which case the two experiences are identical, or they may consider it relatively, in which case 10 days late/10 days promised is different from 10 days late/100 days promised. Another aspect of the comparison process is when performance exceeds expectations. As the reliability of the product exceeds expectations, do positive evaluations increase as a linear or nonlinear function? Again, both the theory and empirical literature are unclear about this point.

The reason for exploring these issues is not to critique the gap or disconfirmation paradigms. Rather, it is to indicate to the reader the complexities in evaluating customer-supplier transactions. Perhaps we need to stop and rethink how these evaluations occur and develop a new approach. In the next section we present an approach for thinking about the evaluation process. It is based in part on the premise that we need to (1) acknowledge the differences in what is being evaluated, and (2) relate the evaluation processes to these differences.

Different Objects for Evaluation

The customer-supplier relationship is characterized by a large number of transactions. The transactions may be acts (e.g., delivery of a product) or requests for information (e.g., price). These acts or requests for information can be characterized by different criteria. For example, we could evaluate delivery time in terms of reliability or responsiveness. Or we could talk about the level of empathy exhibited by a customer service agent. In this analysis, objects for evaluation are the acts or information exchanges specified by some criteria. The responsiveness of delivering a product is an object for evaluation.

Our first argument is that there are inherent differences among objects which are important for understanding the evaluation process. Our classification of objects is a function of the inherent characteristics of the object and the availability of information about the object. Objects for evaluation can be embedded in physical or social reality (Festinger, 1954). Objects in physical reality are measurable by common agreed upon standards. For example, I promise to deliver you our product in five days. Delivery time is an objective, concrete dimension. It is easily understood and interpretable. When confronted with an evaluation task in physical reality, we expect that individuals will utilize the commonly understood metrics versus relying on opinions of others. Objects in social reality are not easily measurable. They are more difficult to interpret. What do we mean by the level of empathy exhibited by a customer service representative? Evaluating levels of empathy is a complex task and one where opinions of others are often sought. The basic argument here is that there is a fundamental difference among objects that might be evaluated in customer-supplier transactions. Our focus is on (1) the process individuals use to code and form expectations or to interpret experiences, and (2) how the objects for evaluation may change how evaluations are done.

Another way to characterize objects is in terms of how explicitly they are enunciated in customer-supplier transactions. Fundamentally, transactions represent offers and acceptances to do certain activities for some level of consideration. The explicitness and formalization of these transactions shape the evaluation process. For example, I offer to sell you a product for "X" dollars and deliver it in "Y" days. You accept the offer and the obligation to pay for the transaction. This transaction can be made more explicit by formalizing the transaction through written documents. Other transactions may be very implicit. That is, objects of evaluation such as responsiveness, courtesy, or empathy in interactions may not be included in any formal or informal agreement and never discussed.

An explicit scenario provides some clear standards for evaluations. There are explicit promises which can signal the supplier's intentions (Goodman & Garber, 1994) or which can be used to assess performance. In the implicit scenario, there are no easily accessible expectations or standards. In evaluating an object which has been implicit in customer-supplier transactions, the customer must construct some meanings. One option may be to create a standard ex ante. Another strategy is to create "post experience" standards. In Table 1 customers express satisfaction with USPS without evoking any standard. (Note USPS has explicit standards, but they were unknown by most of our respondents.) The basic point is that the process of evaluation in the implicit case is different from the explicit case.

Table 2 combines the two ideas of physical versus social reality and explicit versus implicit transactions to highlight the different types of evaluations. In Cell 1 the customer has a promise or a clear set of expectations about an object which is easily measured and verified. Matching expectations (standards) and experiences should be fairly straightforward. In Cell 2 the supplier has promised that its representatives interacting with the customer will be courteous and friendly. While this promise may make these dimensions salient and subject to scrutiny by the customer, the objects are not easily operationalized as expectations or perceived performance. What does the supplier mean by friendly? The problem of matching expectations and performances is clearly more difficult as compared to Cell 1.

In Cell 3 the supplier says nothing about the object, but the object is easily measured and interpreted. For example, suppose the supplier does proactive,

Table 2. Objects for Evaluation in Customer-Firm Transactions

	Physical Reality	*Social Reality*
Explicit Contract	Delivery Time 1	Promised Courteous Transactions 2
Implicit Contract	Post-delivery Service Calls 3	Friendly Customer Service Agents 4

post-delivery service calls. The supplier can anticipate potential problems and provide service before the problem arises. Let us assume the supplier provides one, three, or five of these calls in a year. The number of calls is a clearly measurable act. But is five calls better than three? Would it lead to more positive or negative evaluations of post-delivery service? The problem in this case is that there is no a priori standard. It could be in this context that a standard is derived after the service encounter (Iacobucci et al., 1994). Or the customer may construct an evaluation based on some other specific event with the supplier. It is also possible that one could use another firm's performance as a benchmark or evoke some generalized norm about post delivery service.

In the last cell there are no explicit promises, and the object is difficult to measure and interpret. For example, the friendliness of a customer service agent may not be particularly salient for the customer. It was not made explicit in the transactions. It is difficult to put friendliness into a form where one can compare more or less friendliness.

Processes in Evaluation

There are different types of evaluations in customer-supplier relationships. While there are discussions in the literature about the differences between service quality and satisfaction (Iacobucci et al., 1994) or between tangible and intangible items, we are proposing that the features of both the object and the evaluation processes are necessary to provide a more differentiated view. We now turn to some of the processes involved in evaluating objects in customer-supplier relationships. We start by identifying some of the critical processes, and then apply them to the different types in Table 2.

We begin with three meta processes and frame these processes in terms of questions.

1. *What initiates the evaluation processes?* We assume people make evaluations occasionally and in certain settings. Many factors initiating evaluations are probably external. A supplier's communication to a customer may initiate evaluation. Creating changes in the relationship or violating or exceeding promises in the relationship may initiate the evaluation. If the supplier firm surveys customers, this will initiate some evaluation. A competitor of the focal organization may initiate the evaluation by promising better products or services. An interesting first step here would be to describe how often customers make evaluations and on what dimensions. In certain relationships and on certain objects, there may be very infrequent evaluations. A related question would be the interrelationship of evaluations. What is the impact, for example, of frequent surveys on customer expectations and subsequent evaluations? How does priming at time t_1 affect evaluations at time t_2 (Salancik & Pfeffer, 1978).

Most of the literature on service quality or customer satisfaction does not ask the initiation question. Some work by Zeithaml et al. (1985) indicates that external communications from the supplier may stimulate the formulation of expectations. Literature on equity evaluations on pay (Goodman, 1974) suggests that external events can initiate evaluation processes. Thus, external events which change the perception of equity in the customer-firm transaction may stimulate the evaluation process. Research on psychological contracts between employers and employees suggests people do attend to violations (Robinson, Kraatz, & Rousseau, 1994). Violations of expectations may initiate evaluation.

While there is some support for external factors as initiators of the evaluation process, we need descriptions of how often external factors initiate evaluations and what types of evaluations do occur.

2. *What affects the availability of information for the evaluation process?* In Table 2, we noted that standards may be explicitly stated in the contract between the supplier firm and the customer. Without these explicit standards, the customer can construct a standard after a service encounter. These "experienced-based" norms (Woodruff et al., 1983) have been good predictors of customer satisfaction. The idea is that the evaluator retrieves from memory a series of similar incidents, and retains some exemplars to evaluate a specific recent experience (Iacobucci et al., 1994). Another process to construct standards may be to generalize to a more abstract set of norms or standards (Corfman, 1991) and use these to evaluate a specific transaction. For example, we may have some general standards of courtesy which we apply to a specific transaction (e.g., customer service representative and customer).

Another factor in the evaluation process is the availability of information about the actual transaction. Sometimes, many of the transactions are not visible to the customer. In the USPS example (Table 1) major mailers do not see their mail being delivered to their customers. They only learn about inaccurate or delayed deliveries by setting up special tests or waiting for customer complaints. In other cases, only certain roles in the buying center interact with the focal organization, so some roles will have information about transactions but others may not. For example, a service representative may interact with the user of office equipment but not with the buyer of that equipment. The structure of the buying center, a topic we will elaborate on later, then can determine the flow (and availability) of information.

The frequency and nature of the transactions also can influence information availability in memory. If an evaluation object appears in a few transactions, the individual may attempt to evaluate all the transactions. If there are many transactions, limits on individual memory and ability to process information (Simon, 1957) will constrain the information an individual can consider. For example, if there is a large number of transactions, the individual may be only able to attend to recent events or outlier events. In some preliminary field work we did for a study on organizational responsiveness (Goodman & Garber, 1994), one striking observation was the existence of "outlier stories" in customer organizations. Outlier stories refer to extreme examples of poor service. Stories about poor service events (e.g., five to ten years ago) were still circulated among organizational members and used by customers in evaluating the supplier's responsiveness.

The basic theme is that the information available will shape the evaluations. Some information emerges from actual transactions, other information is constructed. How standards and experiences are generated is not well explored (Iacobucci et al., 1994). We have suggested some of the processes that might evoke standards, and features (e.g., roles) that may provide information on experiences.

3. *How do people select standards and evaluate transactions?* Computational ease should drive the initial selection of standards. Computational ease means individuals select referents to make comparisons which minimizes cognitive effort (Kiesler & Sproull, 1982). Consider the following example. The supplier promises to deliver a product in four weeks and the offer is accepted. The product is delivered in five weeks. In this example, the promised date is most likely to be used as a standard. It is in the same metric (time) as the event. It comes from the same transaction as the experienced event. There, obviously, are other possible standards. There have been other deliveries in the past by the same vendor. There are experiences with other firms or possible industry standards that could be used. However, all of these cases require more complex processing. Because the products, organizational contexts, and people involved are likely to be different from the particular transaction or experience we want to evaluate, adjusting or equating these standards to the evaluation event is much more complex and requires much more effort.

There is some theoretical and empirical support for the role of computational ease in selecting referents (Goodman, 1977) and the role of minimizing cognitive effort (Kiesler & Sproull, 1982). It should be noted that cognitive ease does not always imply that people select specific standards (e.g., promised delivery time) that match the event being evaluated (e.g., actual delivery time). As we have noted, explicit standards may not be available and the individual might have to construct the standard. If the individual has some well rehearsed general standards, these might be applied to evaluate the specific transactional event. In this case it might require less cognitive effort to evoke a general standard (e.g., about courtesy between people) than to construct different standards from different events.

Implicit in any discussion of selecting standards is a relativistic perspective on evaluation processes. That is, one compares objects relative to standards in order to determine evaluations. We believe that the absolute levels of standards, in addition, can shape the evaluation process independent of any comparison. Standards or expectations can have signalling value in their own right. For example, a supplier could offer a delivery time for a product well beyond the modal time period for delivery from this supplier in the past or compared to other suppliers' delivery practices. In this case the promised time, even if accepted, signals low responsiveness. That is, regardless of whether the actual delivery time matches the promised delivery time, we would expect lower ratings of responsiveness. A series of studies reviewed by Iacobucci et al. (1994) and a recent study by Goodman and Garber (1994) support this role of standards on the evaluation process.

Research Opportunities

We conclude our discussion of this theme by pointing to some research opportunities. We frame these by relating the three process questions (cited above) to Table 2.

1. How do the evaluation processes get initiated across these four types of evaluations? Do different types of initiation events evoke different evaluation processes and outcomes across the four categories? For example, a customer satisfaction survey and the violation of a customer's expectation may evoke different evaluations. Wilson, Dunn, Kraft, and Lisle (1991) have shown that the very survey process can change evaluations, initiating evaluations when the questions are asked. The violation could evoke more negative incidents than a survey and perhaps lead to lower evaluations. In this case the process and outcome would be different. A related issue is whether violations would evoke different processes and outcomes across cells. For example, violations are probably more easily coded and assessed in Cell 1 as compared to Cell 4. This would suggest that the process of evaluation is different.

2. Will the information availability affect the evaluation process? We have argued the nature of roles and the networks for the customer or supplier will filter information that is available. The frequency and complexities of transactions also can affect availability. When there are many transactions, people may attend only to recent events or outliers. When there is no information on standards, one strategy is to construct standards. When people construct standards, are they used again in similar evaluations or does the individual initiate a new construction process? What are the implications of this restructuring on the consistency of the evaluations over time? How does the reconstruction process differ if one is dealing with objects in physical reality (Cell 3) as opposed to social reality (Cell 4)?

There may be other heuristics that are used in the absence of information. For example, some of the respondents in Table 1 do not express any standards although the supplier does publish national standards about delivery time and geographical distance. It appears that the judgment process for these individuals is based on the absence of negative information. That is, "I do not have any complaints; therefore, I am satisfied." Is this absence of complaints "rule" usable in all four cells? Are there other rules which are utilized in the absence of information?

3. The third set of opportunities revolves around how people select standards and evaluate transactions. Do the selection and evaluation processes vary across cells? For Cell 1 we argued that the standards are embedded in offers and acceptances. In Cell 1 we also would expect the standards to serve as a signal of the supplier's services, and at the same time serve as a benchmark for evaluating the object in question. We would not expect standards used in Cells 3 and 4 to have signalling functions because these standards are not derived directly from the supplier's offers.

We need to learn more about the evaluation process for objects in social versus physical reality. To evaluate the courtesy or friendliness of a customer representative, one might consider the friendliness of past representatives from this supplier or representatives from other firms. Selecting a past representative simplifies comparing across different firms and products. One also could evoke general norms of friendliness. How would the evaluation outcomes differ if one evoked general norms or specific others seems like an obvious question.

In addition, we need to learn more about the evaluation process for "delighted" customers. In this case the supplier exceeds all customer expectations. How does the evaluation of delight occur in the different categories in Table 1?

We have taken the point of view of the customer because the literature is focused almost entirely on how customers evaluate the supplier and not how the supplier views the customer. The alternative, of course, would create a whole new area of investigation. How does the supplier evaluate these transactions? How satisfied or dissatisfied is the supplier with the customer? We think the underlying processes of initiation, availability, and selection of standards for evaluations are the same and should guide investigations of how the supplier evaluates transactions with the customers. In the following theme on relationships we will focus more on the supplier's role in these transactions.

Theme II: Modeling Customer-Supplier Relationships

The second theme focuses on the interactions and transactions between the customer and the supplier. How can we characterize the relationship between customer and supplier? What are the underlying processes which drive this relationship? The unit of analysis in Theme II is the relationship or dyad. In Theme I we examined how the individual evaluates or makes sense of transactions in the relationship.

Current Relationship Models

There is interesting research which focuses on understanding relationships from the perspectives of the customer and supplier (see Heide, 1994, for a review of different approaches to this subject). We will examine studies in the industrial marketing context (Anderson & Narus, 1984, 1990; Anderson & Weitz, 1992; Heide, 1994). Many of these studies specify, measure, and estimate the relationship among a set of social-psychological variables (e.g., trust and communication) which can explain the relationship between firms and their customers.

A study by Anderson and Narus (1990) illustrates this perspective. They developed a model of manufacturer and distributor working partnerships. The basic arguments captured in the model are: (1) perceived relative dependence in the relationship affects the relative influence of the supplier and partner over each other and in turn, on other variables such as conflict and satisfaction; (2) communication levels are positively related to levels of trust which enhances cooperation and satisfaction; and (3) outcomes such as comparison levels among alternatives, derived from Thibaut and Kelley (1959), are related to levels of communication and relative dependence. These models were estimated from measures collected from matched manufacturers and distributors. The basic findings support many constructs in the models.

The research is part of a growing body of work on "relationship marketing." This research has several strengths. First, there is a clear attempt to specify theoretical models grounded in social-psychological (Thibaut & Kelley, 1959) or organizational theory (Williamson, 1975, 1985). Second, these models are tested in the field with matched pairs of customers and suppliers with multiple informants per firm. Third, sophisticated analytic techniques are utilized to test the complicated relationships specified in the models. Fourth, the design and findings permit identifying the commonalities and differences among factors which affect satisfaction and commitment for the suppliers and their customers. Some of these substantive findings have been specified above.

Limitations of Current Literature

While this literature on "relationship marketing" has many desirable features, there are several limitations that should be noted. First, there is a strong reliance on perceptual data to test these models. Given a within-subject and cross-sectional design, it is difficult to identify common method effects and direction of causality when information on trust, cooperation, and communication is collected from the same individuals at the same time. It would be useful to anchor some of the subjective measures (perceived communication) with some objective counterpart and examine these relationships over time.

Second, while these studies acknowledge the role of process in customer-supplier relationships, there is a tendency to focus on a single process (e.g., selecting a comparison relationship). We think it is important to delineate more comprehensively the critical processes underlying customer-firm transactions.

Third, and perhaps most importantly, many of the organizational parameters are not included in the proposed models. For example, the level of involvement between supplier and customer may affect the nature of the transactions and evaluations of those transactions. Level of involvement refers to the scope of activities between these two parties. It could vary from simple economic transactions to a situation where the customer may be involved in designing the supplier's product and where the supplier is involved in many of the customer's ceremonies (e.g., a retirement party). In high involvement settings, the number of activities and the nature of the boundaries are different from low involvement situations.

Another organizational component that may shed light on the customer-supplier relationship is the nature of the market segment of the customer's business. Customers operating in different segments may attend to different dimensions of the transactions and, therefore, evaluate and behave differently in the relationships (Goodman & Garber, 1994; Iacobucci et al., 1994).

There is a growing useful literature on relationship marketing. We feel that understanding customer-supplier relationships can be enhanced by attending more to organizational contextual factors. We begin by looking at different forms of customer-supplier relationships, and then explore in more detail some of the underlying processes.

Different Dimensions of Customer-Supplier Relationships

In the organizational literature (Rousseau & Parks, 1993), distinctions between economic and relational contracts are sometimes used to characterize relationships. In the recent social-psychological literature (Clark & Reis, 1988), degrees of interdependence and closeness are used to characterize interpersonal relationships. The strategy literature (Kanter, 1989) distinguishes among service alliances, opportunistic alliances, and stakeholder alliances. Webster (1992) discusses a range of marketing relationships that begin with a single transaction and evolve to long-term relationships, partnerships, alliances, and network organizations.

The basic assumption is that different forms of customer-supplier relationships have different types of transactions and underlying processes. If one were to study these relationships, an initial step might be to characterize the customer-supplier relationships in terms of four dimensions, thus permitting a multidimensional characterization, as shown in Table 3 and discussed below.

Table 3. Dimensions of Customer-Supplier Relationship

Dimension	Form of Dimension		
1. Scope of Involvement	Single Core Activity	Multiple Core and Peripheral Activities	Multiple Core Peripheral and Extra Transactional Activities
2. Goals	Economic Goals (Short/Long run)	Economic and Strategic (Cooperative/Competitive)	Economic, Strategic Expressive
3. Level of Institutionalization	No Culture		Strong Private Culture Between Customer and Supplier
4. Network Relationships	Single Dyad		Complex Network for Customer and Supplier

1. *Scope of Involvement.* We describe scope of involvement in terms of participation in core, peripheral, and extra transactional activities. Core transactions are the fundamental basis for all customer-supplier relationships. However, there also may be peripheral activities tied to the core activities. For example, in one of our research sites the core activities are selling office equipment. However, the supplier provides other related services such as training and services that are peripheral activities in this relationship. Both core and peripheral activities can affect the level of satisfaction with the relationship (Iacobucci et al., 1994).

There also is a class of extra-transactional activities that represent points of involvement. These extra-transactional activities are not tied directly to the core or peripheral transactions. Some of these extra transactions are instrumental in nature and are designed to improve effectiveness. For example, the office equipment manufacturer may help the customer by providing assistance in process re-engineering. This activity is designed to improve the effectiveness of the customer and is not directly related to selling any product or service by the focal organization. Another type of extra-transactional activity may be non-instrumental. Attendance by the supplier in social or ceremonial activities initiated by the customer represents involvement in more personal or social activities.

We can characterize customer-supplier relationships by their level of involvement across core, peripheral, and extra-transactional activities. The frequency and duration of these activities across the three categories provide a supplier involvement profile. Different levels of involvement in these different activities may affect both the transactions and outcomes of customer-supplier relationships. For example, a recent study of the United States Postal Service (USPS) by Goodman et al. (1995) examined the relationships among involvement, satisfaction with core activities, and overall satisfaction with the relationship. They report that when industrial customers are highly involved in USPS and when they are dissatisfied with the core product (first-class mail), they express greater levels of dissatisfaction in the overall relationship than customers who are dissatisfied with the core product but are not highly involved.

2. *Goals.* Goals can drive or motivate the relationship. We expect that in any relationship there are multiple goals, some are more salient than others. The relative salience of the goals may change over time, and there may be asymmetries between suppliers and their customers. In addition, we would expect that different classes of goals may be operating at the same time.

There are several classes of goals. Economic goals are the most obvious driver of customer-firm exchanges. Optimizing some value in the exchange motivates both parties. The focus may be on short-term exchanges or securing longer term stable suppliers. Another motivation in entering a relationship may be to learn or acquire strategic information from the partner about products, processes, and markets. This strategic information may be used to enhance the relationship or to terminate the relationship as the information permits one partner to perform activities provided by the other.

Expressive goals represent motivators derived from the inherent nature of the relationships. If there are a lot of positive exchanges, the transactions themselves may acquire some value. Other sources of expressive goals may be tied to personal relationships. Valued personal relationships may be a motivator of transactions between the customer and the supplier, quite independent of any economic exchange. In relationships where expressive goals are important, both parties may evaluate exchanges differently from a relationship based solely on economic exchanges.

3. *Institutionalization of the Relationship.* Relationships between customers and suppliers may vary in terms of whether there is a shared set of beliefs and values unique to that relationship. All customer-supplier relationships are guided by statutory and common law and rules of business. Institutionalization refers to a specific set of norms and values that create a culture between the customer and supplier. At one extreme there may be no unique norms or values, and transactions are guided by general economic rules. On the other hand there may be a culture unique to the relationship. This culture would contain interactional habits, norms, roles, and shared worldviews (Blumstein & Kollock, 1988).

The culture is shared by members of the customer and supplier organizations. It provides guidance and social meaning to both organizations, and it exists independently of any member of the customer-supplier organizations. One implication of a positive, supportive culture is that many monitoring activities found in customer-supplier relationships may be absent.

4. *Single or Multiple Organizational Networks.* Our characterization of the customer-supplier relationship has been in terms of the single dyad. Some customer-supplier relationships are embedded in more complex forms. Service

alliances where multiple suppliers (e.g., regional telephone companies) join together to create another organization (e.g., Bellcore) represent a more complicated customer-supplier relationship. Here, multiple customers are coordinating their efforts with a single provider. Other examples of more complicated forms include joint ventures, stakeholder alliances (Kanter, 1989), and networked organizations (Webster, 1992). We introduce this dimension because customer-supplier relationships could be embedded in complex networks or exist as a stand-alone relationship. The nature of this relationship (the focus of Theme III) should affect both the evaluations and viability of the ties between customer and firm.

Table 3 summarizes the major dimensions for characterizing customer-supplier relationships. We argue that it is important to acknowledge some of the basic structural differences in supplier-customer relationships. These differences shape some of the processes underlying these relationships and, in turn, are shaped by the processes. The intersection between these dimensions and the processes identify new research opportunities.

Processes

There are several critical processes driving the relationships between the customer and supplier. These processes account for variation in satisfaction, commitment, and performance of members in the relationships, which can be considered measures of effectiveness in customer-supplier relationships. In addition, these processes drive the basic dynamic properties in relationships such as development and dissolution.

While there are many possible processes to consider, we focus on three—monitoring, interpretation, and redesign. Monitoring focuses on the collection of data on the customer-supplier transactions by the respective parties. Interpretation deals with assigning meaning to the data collected about the relationship. Redesign involves modifying or adjusting the structure or basic processes in the customer-supplier relationship rather than "fixing" a specific transaction. We selected these three processes because they can account for dynamic changes in customer-supplier relationships over time.

Monitoring

There has been a variety of different theoretical perspectives on monitoring behavior (Williamson, 1975). We want to highlight some basic questions about monitoring in customer-supplier relationships and use the questions as a way to frame some new research opportunities. We focus on four questions.

1. *Why does monitoring occur?* One reason is that customer-supplier relationships are contractual in nature. Offers, acceptances, and considerations

are presented, and goods and services of value are exchanged. Even in long-term, highly involved, institutionalized relationships, there are underlying contractual arrangements about the exchanges that need to be verified. Another reason is that it may be difficult to specify contract terms in advance. This may be so because of the inherent nature of the exchange or because new activities enter into the relationship after the basic contract has been established. Monitoring serves as a control mechanism for unplanned activities, and adjustment serves to redefine the relationship over time. Motivational and power considerations also may initiate monitoring behavior. In relationships motivated by integration versus competition, one might see less monitoring. Also, when power and dependence among the partners are more symmetrical rather than asymmetrical, there may be less monitoring activity. Lastly, there may be tendencies for contracts to "drift" over time (Rousseau & Parks, 1993). The drift may occur because one party in the relationship may change their beliefs about their own obligations relative to their partner's obligations to the relationship over time (Robinson et al., 1994).

2. *What are the counter forces for monitoring?* While we think monitoring is an important process in customer-supplier relationships, there are many forces working against these processes. First, and quite important, is the competition for focus of attention. Customer-supplier relationships are complex. All parties are involved in multiple relationships. People are busy, easily distracted, showered with lots of information, and confronted with many competing stimuli (Berscheid, 1994). While factors such as unexpected or unfamiliar stimuli or events that are important to one's well being may be more salient than other stimuli, the process by which attention (an initial step in monitoring) is evoked in complex natural settings is not well specified.

Another factor potentially inhibiting monitoring is the extent to which cognitive processes in the relationship are automatic versus controlled (Berscheid, 1994). Many of the models describing customer-supplier relationships suggest controlled processing. This means that experiences between customer and supplier involve cognitive processes that are explicit, conscious, effortful, capable of being verbalized, and controllable. An alternative view is that many of the transactions between customer and supplier are unconscious, not verbalized, and uncontrollable (Fletcher & Fincham, 1991). An automatic process develops through repetition and routinization, and the processing of many events, particularly in long-term relationships, may be automatic (Berscheid, 1994, p. 16). One implication is that the shift to automatic processing may reduce monitoring activity. An interesting research problem is to understand the role of automatic processing in customer-supplier relationships on two dimensions. First, how does automatic processing affect monitoring? Second, does it contribute to biases or errors (e.g., the fundamental attribution error) in the processing of customer-supplier transactions (Fletcher & Fincham, 1991).

3. *What types of monitoring mechanisms might be used?* Formal measurement of performance indicators is one form of monitoring. The monitoring would be of output measures that are core or central to the relationship. If output measures are not available or operational, we could select interim measures. Or one could select external standards (e.g., benchmarking) to assess quality of outputs.

An interesting issue is to explore the effect of possible asymmetries in forms of monitoring activities. There seems to be a growing use of measurement strategies by the customer to assess their supplier's performance. Similar extensive use of customer satisfaction surveys by the suppliers is another way to assess their own performance (supplier). Who monitors the customer's performance? What behaviors or performance by the customer should be monitored?

4. *What are the substitutes for formal monitoring?* That is, it may not be possible to initiate formal monitoring because the output is not operational or not accessible. Or the parties might want to create a "relational" contract (Rousseau & Parks, 1993) built on trust and cooperation and a long-term proposed relationship. In either scenario the parties might generate alternatives to monitoring. These may come in the form of incentive systems focused on specific behaviors or on the display of relationship attitudes and behavior (Heide, 1994). Learning systems which generate norms and values governing the relationship represent other substitutes for monitoring. In just-in-time systems, suppliers are often certified, at which point parts are not inspected. However, often in such systems, defective parts will show up quickly (due to low inventories) and be readily attributable to the supplier (because low or zero inventories require delivery of parts close to the point of production). In such a case, monitoring stops but the system of production can quickly detect problems as well, so detection capability is maintained.

Interpretation

How do suppliers or customers make sense of the data captured in day-to-day transactions and in the monitoring process? This is a broad and complicated question. There are many perspectives such as social construction and sense making (Weick, 1979), social exchange theory (Cook & Emerson, 1978), and transaction costs (Williamson, 1985) which bear on this question. Our focus is more limited. We want to illustrate that ascribing social meaning to transactions in the customer-supplier relationship is difficult and needs to be better understood. Two illustrations are offered, one on interpreting signals and the other on making sense of the value of a transaction.

Customers and suppliers are involved in a series of transactions about core and peripheral activities as well as strategic decisions. These activities, and particularly the decisions, may signal intentions of one party concerning their commitment to the relationship.

A study by Anderson and Weitz (1992) illustrates this point. They studied antecedents of commitment between pairs of manufacturers and distributors. Commitment refers to the desire for a stable relationship. Idiosyncratic investments represent one form of antecedent to commitment. These investments are specific to a relationship and are difficult to deploy to another relationship. Some examples include dedicating personnel to servicing a specific manufacturer's product, adopting a common order system, and a distributor building facilities for a manufacturer. These idiosyncratic investments are potentially powerful signals. They represent observable acts that can be monitored, not just words. They both limit the degrees of freedom of the provider, but also signal their commitment to the relationship.

Anderson and Weitz (1992) find that when distributors believe manufacturers have made idiosyncratic investments, they perceive manufacturers as more committed. Distributors' commitment to a relationship is affected by their perception of the manufacturer's commitments. On the other hand, some investments or pledges do not seem to affect commitment. For example, if the manufacturer agrees to a contract clause that limits its freedom to terminate a relationship with a distributor, this act does not affect the distributor's perception of the manufacturer's commitment.

While these findings support the signalling process, there are still many unanswered questions. Some forms of unique investments, such as pledges of exclusivity, do not lead to improvements in commitments. Why are some investments by partner A, which increase A's dependence on B, more likely to signal commitment? If the investments are primarily unilateral versus bilateral, how will levels of commitment change? We have limited our discussion of signalling to idiosyncratic acts or decisions. How does the signalling process work in day-to-day performance of core or peripheral activities?

The social construction of value in customer-supplier transactions represents a second illustration of interpretation. The initiation of customer-supplier relationships is based on the exchange of value. Both customer and supplier receive outcomes for certain costs or inputs. The evaluation of the value of the transaction is an important determinant of the termination of a relationship. The question is how is value socially constructed? In a review of the customer satisfaction literature, Iacobucci et al. (1994) point to the lack of studies on price and value.

There are a number of interesting issues in understanding value in this context. They serve as new research opportunities.

First, value in customer-supplier exchanges can be framed in equity terms. That is, the value of goods or services can be assessed by relating outcomes (i.e., attributes of a product or service) to inputs (i.e., price paid) compared to other outcome/input ratios. Do customers and suppliers evoke these relatively complex models? Research (Clark & Reis, 1988) in examining equity in interpersonal relations (e.g., friendship) indicates the evaluation of total benefit received may be more important than equity evaluations. This research also indicates that social context is important. That is, in a more communal setting, need-based rules may be more important than equity rules in evaluating the relationship. Translating this finding to our context, customer-firm relationships high in involvement may not use equity-based rules to evaluate relationships as compared to low involvement, short-term, economic-based relationships. Time in the relationship may also affect the use of equity rules. Early in a relationship equity rules may be frequently evoked to provide meaning to the overall relationship. Once global impressions of equity have been formed, new transactions may not evoke this comparison process.

Second, value in customer-supplier transactions can be framed in procedural terms. That is, the process of providing the outcomes not the distribution of outcomes creates perceptions of value. In the customer satisfaction literature, for example, Zeithaml, Parasuraman, and Berry (1990) have provided evidence that dimensions such as reliability, responsiveness, assurance, and empathy affect perceptions of service quality. These dimensions characterize the exchange process between customer and supplier. Schneider and Bowen (1985) and Bowen and Folger (1994) also have focused on procedural issues as important frames for how customers and suppliers evaluate exchanges in their relationship.

The procedural perspective can provide some interesting research opportunities. One starting point is to examine procedural justice issues at different points in the product or transaction life cycle. One can specify the transaction life cycle, including pre-order activities (e.g., collecting information on price), ordering, check order status, delivery, and post-delivery service. How do procedural justice issues vary across this cycle? The context in ordering a product may be different from the context in managing an inoperable product in a post-delivery service encounter. How would assessments of procedural justice vary as a function of points in the transaction cycles?

A third issue is whether there are spillover effects between procedural evaluations and other evaluations. That is, do evaluations of procedural issues affect evaluations of the core product? In a study of customer-supplier relationships, Goodman et al. (1995) found that customer perceptions of the focal organization's responsiveness affected overall customer satisfaction, but this procedural variable also seemed to impact evaluations of the core product. So there is some evidence for spillover.

Redesign

While one can link monitoring, interpretation, and redesign as a process, it is reasonable to consider redesign mechanisms in their own right. How do customer-supplier relationships become redesigned? A proactive strategy for redesign is to build contingencies into the initial contract. If one can anticipate changes, the contract can guide redesign processes. Planning is another proactive strategy to respond to environmental uncertainty. Heide (1994) discusses different types of planning activities for customer-supplier relationships in bilateral or unilateral governance modes. In contrast one can initiate formal or informal reactive adjustment mechanisms. The parties may simply acknowledge the need for adjustments and renegotiate when internal or external changes occur.

An interesting problem would be to understand the relative effectiveness of different redesign mechanisms and the antecedents of effective redesign. Heide (1994) illustrates potential research opportunities in this area by examining the relationship between level and form of dependence in the relationship and the flexibility of the redesign or adjustment process. He reports that symmetric and high dependence in a relationship leads to flexible adjustment processes. There are many unexplored issues about the form and effectiveness of adjustment processes.

Research Opportunities

We can conclude our discussion of this theme by noting some research opportunities. In discussing each of the processes, we have indicated some interesting questions for investigation. For example, what are the conditions when monitoring will and will not occur? What are the conditions when equity versus procedural frames will affect how customers and firms evaluate the transactions? Why do certain customer-supplier relationships have greater capacity for redesign?

A different class of research opportunities can emerge if one looks at the intersection between the processes and the different descriptors discussed at the beginning of this section. We argued that customer-supplier relationships may vary on dimensions such as the level of involvement or the degree of institutionalization. One needs to understand these differences in customer-supplier relationships in the light of the processes discussed above.

We can illustrate this intellectual task of linking the processes and existing dimensional structure of customer-supplier relationships with some examples and some questions. Consider a customer-supplier relationship where there is a high degree of involvement and institutionalization. What would be the rates and types of monitoring in this environment as compared to a low involvement, low institutionalized environment? What would be the effects of idiosyncratic investments as a signalling device in this setting? What are the conditions when equity or procedural frames would be used in this type of customer-supplier relationship? These are interesting questions suggested by linking processes and structure descriptions. One can study such questions in many different ways. Suppose we want to study the impact of idiosyncratic investments as signalling devices. One could build scenario studies varying the level of idiosyncratic investment, and present these choice problems in the different environments (e.g., high or low customer-supplier involvement). We could then examine how levels of involvement may moderate how customers or suppliers interpret the investments and recommit themselves to this relationship.

The basic argument is that the context of the customer-supplier relationship makes a difference. Researchers need first to describe the contextual differences and then ask how these differences influence the processes enumerated in this section, and finally how these effects bear on the outcomes and the growth or dissolution of customer-supplier relationships.

Theme III: A Network View of the Interorganizational Structure

The structure of the customer-supplier relationship is captured in three components: a buying center, a selling center, and the ties across the organizational boundary. Such a network may be highly elaborated and complex, or it may be little more than an arm's length economic relation between two parties governed by a formal contract. Individual behaviors and interpersonal relations are conditioned by this network. Relationships between customers and suppliers are affected by the interorganizational network social structure. We have chosen a network view because it fits the many observations suggesting that noncontractual, often informal, relations are critical in interorganizational transactions (Anderson, Håkansson, & Johanson, 1994; Burt, 1992; Galaskiewicz, 1985) and how practices diffuse across organizations (e.g., Galaskiewicz & Burt, 1991; Galaskiewicz & Wasserman, 1989). In this section, the network, not the dyadic relation, is the unit of analysis. This view is illustrated in Figure 2.

We first consider network effects which occur independent of tie strength, arguing that exposure to information from others in the network influences evaluations. We will then consider the value of distinguishing strong and weak ties (Granovetter, 1973) when we explore embeddedness in the context of the customer-supplier network.

The Buying and Selling Centers

Buying and selling centers (see Figure 2) are the key components in studying interorganizational relationships between buyers and sellers. The concept of the buying center in industrial buying was developed in the mid-1960s in marketing (Johnston & Bonoma, 1981), and has received more attention in recent years.

The buying center is the network of individuals in the customer organization involved in transactions with the supplier firm. These individuals may be involved in the purchase, use, maintenance, payments for a product or service,

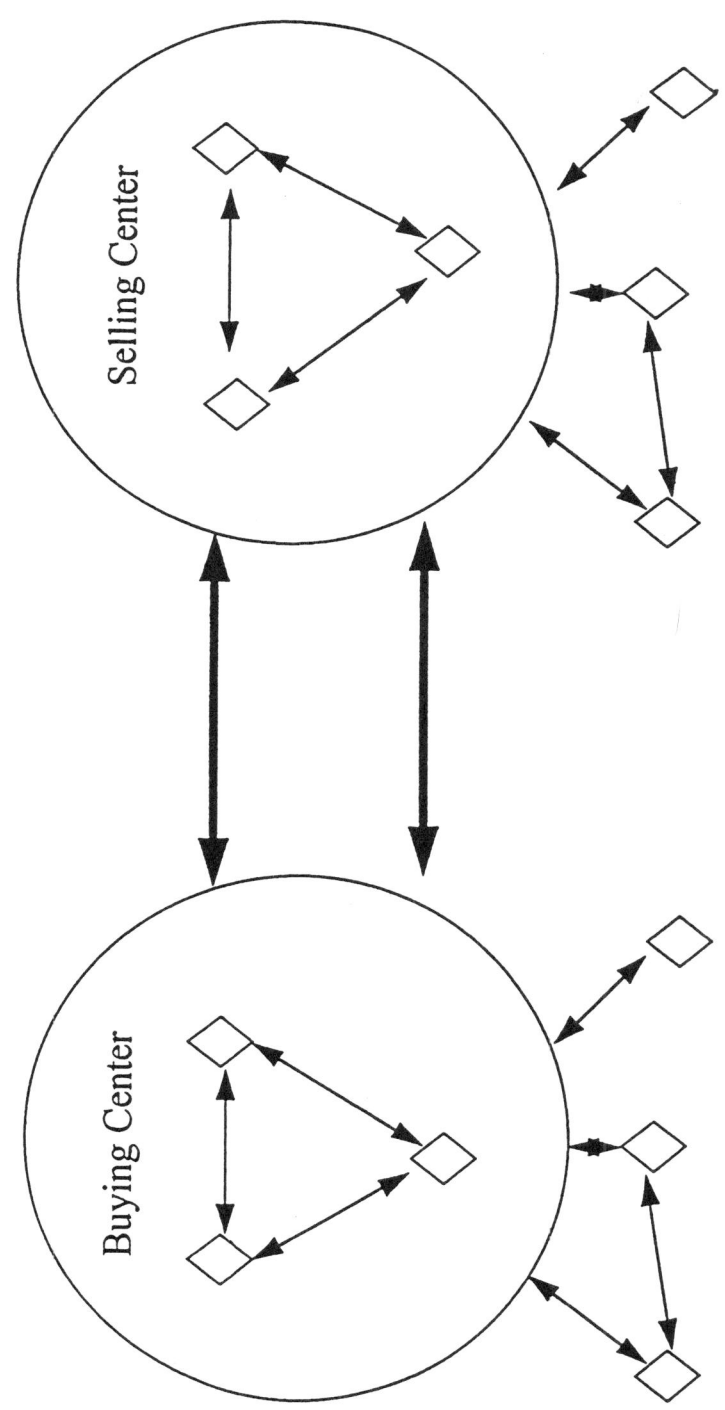

Figure 2. Inter- and Intraorganizational Network Structure

and so on. For example, we worked with an office products firm that sold complex mechanical and electronic machines and associated services for an office-related environment. They defined the buying center of their customers as composed of users of their machines, managers of the customers' offices where the machines were deployed, and the individuals who had the authority to purchase their machines. For very large customers, there were many users and managers, and in most cases, one principal buyer. In very small firms, the manager and buyer roles could be the same. In Figure 2, we see that the buying center has certain permanent members (within the circle), such as a purchasing agent and some primary users. These permanent members may interact with others in the firm outside the buying center, gathering information which influences the purchase or repurchase decision. Sometimes outsiders will be drawn into the purchase decision, enlarging the size of the center. At other times, outsiders will be drawn in when there need to be modifications in the agreements between the two sides. The key idea is that people in these buying center roles engage in transactions with the supplier throughout the product's life cycle, with the number of players varying during the life of the customer-supplier relationship.

The selling center is the network of individuals in the supplier organization involved in transactions with the customer organization. In our office equipment example, this would be sales personnel, product engineers, and service personnel, as well as financial people involved in financing and billing activities. As was true with the buying center, the selling center may vary considerably in terms of size, depending on the customer. Also, the members of the selling center may work in close proximity to each other or may be geographically distributed to meet customer needs. Again, Figure 2 illustrates that participation in the selling center can vary, with actors outside the selling center interacting with selling center members.

Both the buying and selling centers are dynamic entities. As the buying center reviews product offerings, the demands on sales and product engineers may be the greatest. Once the product has been purchased, more transactions may occur between the selling centers' service personnel and the users in the buying center. If you examine the provision of office services such as telecommunication, computing, and duplicating in your own organization, you will undoubtedly find the same level of dynamism and complexity.

Early research, influenced by Cyert, Simon, and Trow (1956), used a problem-solving information processing approach to understand the buying center. Subsequent research examined phases in the buying process and influence processes in the buying center (e.g., Kohli, 1989; Ronchetto, Hutt, & Reingen, 1989). Fundamental problems such as *who is the buyer* are persistent issues in industrial markets (Johnston & Spekman, 1987). For example, Silk and Kalwani (1982) report low levels of agreement among buying group members about the influence exerted on the buying decision. This suggests that the buying center is not a well-articulated structure for the customer, and is probably quite fluid over time and buying decisions. Both early and more recent research in marketing on buying centers has a very organizational flavor. This is not surprising given that organizational buying is viewed predominantly as an organizational decision. Only in the last few years has the level of analysis issue been clearly identified.

> Since most of the purchasing situations encountered by organizations involve more than a single individual, it is necessary to understand the functioning of the multiperson process from a group perspective. Indeed, most of the empirical and conceptual studies ignore this requirement and ... focus on the individual who invariably is the purchasing agent. (Johnston & Spekman, 1987, p. 99)

We see in the marketing literature that there are some very basic problems which require attention (Dwyer, Schurr, & Oh, 1987; Heide, 1994; Johnston & Spekman, 1987; Silk & Kalwani, 1982; Spekman & Johnston, 1986) if our understanding of the buying system is to grow. We need to develop a clearer conceptual definition of the buying system which allows us to clearly identify and measure the *members* and *structures* in the buying system. This will help us explore critical processes in the buying system.

Membership. Who are the members of the buying system? How does membership in the system change over time? What impact does changing membership have on the quality of the relationships between network members? Such questions have been explored in other areas of interorganizational relations but not systematically in the buying system. Such questions address whether the relationships between firms are embedded in the social ties which develop, or whether the ties are sufficiently robust that changing membership does not affect the functioning of the interorganizational system. Under what conditions will turnover influence customer-supplier ties? For example, Seabright et al. (1992) studied ties between auditors and their clients. Auditors and clients remain in relatively durable relationships, often lasting decades (Levinthal & Fichman, 1988). The primary reasons for enduring ties are specialized auditor skills developed in the relationship, the competitive cost and knowledge advantages of the auditor who is already in place, and the industry expertise of the current auditor. Such features are clearly strategic and are not necessarily linked to network structures and relations. Seabright et al. (1992) looked at whether senior officers, who should be part of an interorganizational linkage between auditor and client, influence the relationship. They found that when senior officers in the client firm who were responsible for auditor monitoring and supervision left the client firm (officers such as CFOs or the head of the audit committee of the board of directors), the probability of the client engaging a new auditor increased significantly. This suggests that network links between the auditor and client do influence the customer-supplier relationship in the most basic way, influencing its continued existence.

Structures. What are the advantages and disadvantages of different approaches to characterizing the structure of the interorganizational system? We are arguing that a social network view will be most useful, but other perspectives looking at more traditional organizational structure concepts like formalization and number of exceptions which must be handled may also prove quite useful for certain applications. For example, the notion of formalization and the handling of exceptions shows up in a recent study of EDI (electronic data interchange)—an electronic network linking buyer and supplier to facilitate transaction processing. The findings suggest that whether the EDI network is handling standard transactions or exceptions has an enormous impact on EDI processing and effectiveness (Srinivasan, Kekre, & Mukhopadhyay, 1994). This result suggests that other types of typologies or structural characterizations may prove useful in analyzing an interorganizational structure (in this case, one which may involve an investment in physical capital in the form of an EDI system).

The social network perspective allows for ways of examining the buying center structure in Figure 2 and its impact on transactions which concepts like formalization and standardization do not capture. The density of interactions and the flow of information within the buying center and with other actors in the customer firm can significantly affect transactions and the experience of the customer. Where there is a high density of information flow, changes in customer requirements may be communicated rapidly and accurately in the buying center, allowing for more rapid communication to the supplier. Links between the buying center and the customer's production of goods or services can enhance how well transactions are done. If the customer's transactions are widely dispersed and experiences are not communicated in the customer organization, you may find that learning in one part of the customer organization may not diffuse to other parts of the customer firm, creating greater variability in customer requirements and making the task of managing the relationship more difficult.

The selling center, the network of relations in the supplier firm which links to the customer, also can affect the quality and duration of the ties between the two firms. This is particularly true given the closer and more varied interpenetration of buyers and sellers in recent years (Powell, 1990). For example, research on professional organizations such as Eccles' and Crane's (1988) on investment banking or Heinz's and Laumann's (1982) work in Chicago law firms strongly suggests that the organization of activities and the quality of network ties with the supplier (in this case of professional services) are critical to understanding the linkages between the customer and supplier.

As suppliers take a more direct, closer role in codesigning and coproducing products and services, we will have to consider the organization of the supplier and how effectively the supplier organizes to initiate and sustain the relationship with the client. Florida and Kenney (1991) provide an interesting example of this in their analysis of the automotive transplants. They find that not only do Japanese auto assemblers like Mazda, Honda, and Toyota successfully bring their industrial practices to the United States, but that these practices must become part of the suppliers' method of operation. In fact, they find that American suppliers increase the use of work teams, quality processes, and multiskilling.

When examining network structure, we must appreciate that it is not static but dynamic. Iacobucci and Hopkins (1992) suggest that we attend to network dynamics. The network and changes in the network represent critical units of analysis. An example from the office products firm we studied illustrates this point. Early in the life of the network and the relationship, sales personnel and key decision makers are central. In terms of Figure 2, sales personnel reside in the selling center, key decision makers in the buying center, and they develop links between them. Once the customer has committed to the seller, service personnel in the supplier link with sales in the selling center, as service takes over the primary management of day-to-day relations with the buyer. The buyer is now the end user. Periodically, billing enters the network in the selling center, linking not with end users or key decision makers, but with purchasing or accounting in the buying center. Billing and administrative practices now take on a more important role, while service and end user satisfaction dominate the relationship after its initiation. As one service manager told us, "Service owns customer satisfaction." From this description, you can see that the buying center may change players and link with new players within the firm. A similar process occurs in the selling center. These players in each center create different linkages with their counterparts on the other side; service personnel with end users, billing personnel with accounting, and so on. The original players (sales and key decision makers on the buying side) may have different and less active roles now as the factors that influence satisfaction with the relationship shift. With reference to Figure 2, over time, new players within the firm outside the centers become involved, and play important roles in shaping and structuring the interorganizational network as it evolves.

This dynamic portrayal of network structures means that the information flows within the organization will be changing and differentially available to members of the buying and selling centers. How the individual evaluates products or services will be conditioned by the information flows between and linkages within the buying and selling centers.

Network Ties and Individual Evaluation Processes

We want to pose two questions:

1. How do networks influence expectations, standards, and evaluations? and
2. How do these evaluations and expectations influence behavior?

We suggest that both processes are affected by the networks in which these processes unfold. In Theme I, evaluation and attitude formation processes were examined, highlighting issues of standards, information availability, and the difficulties people have attending to and processing information with respect to their experience with transactions. In this analysis, intra-individual processes are the primary focus. We suggest that one must also consider the social network and its influence on individual experiences with transactions (Erickson, 1988). In this analysis, we ignore tie strength, focusing on how network structures mediate information flows. Such an analysis links Themes I and III.

Network, Standards, and Expectations

Network position and available information should significantly influence the derivation of standards. When we do not have explicit standards, and many transactions do not have explicit standards, a good source of standards are those around us (Festinger, 1954). We use others for multiple comparison purposes, as has been found in studies of equity and fairness, where people choose comparison others to evaluate outcomes.

How do social networks influence the expectations of individuals in the interorganizational network about the transactions that occur between the customer and supplier? Standards help generate expectations. We observed in our own field work that some customer expectations are influenced by network interactions outside the traditional industrial market. Note that these are interorganizational ties outside the buying or selling center. Most discussions of standards and expectations focus on expectations set in the communication between buyer and seller, and are often intra-organizational. Often times, traditional market benchmarks can be generated by industry associations and industry analysts. With the advent of TQM (total quality management), customers and suppliers are benchmarking across industries, developing expectations based on suppliers in other industries rather than the industry they are in. Furthermore, key executives meet with executives in other industries, developing different expectations of themselves and others based on what they learned about other industries than their own. Consultants are another source of expectations.

Consultants are often asked about what is happening in other industries given their unique ability to see the inner workings of numbers of firms in different markets. Without considering the networks of information flows of individuals outside standard industrial market channels, the sources for such expectations and attitudes would not be identified. For example, a customer might ask in billing whether the billing processes are as timely and accurate as those of American Express, rather than just the standard in their industry. These are examples of how expectations and standards are influenced by network ties and information flows outside the buying and selling centers, as suggested in Figure 2.

Network, Evaluations, and Customer Behaviors

We think that explicitly considering the linkage between evaluations and customer behaviors can be very useful for looking at whether continuity is a function of preferences (which reflect attitudes and attitude change), inertia or some other process. Most studies of interorganizational and network relations between firms make similar assumptions, which follow the Thibaut and Kelley (1959) hypothesis about relationship choice being a function of CL-alt (comparison level to alternatives). These views assume that there is a strong link of evaluations, consideration of alternatives, and customer behavior. In organizational and social-psychological work, we have learned that assuming there is a strong relation between behavior and attitudes is risky. Is this true in the industrial marketplace as well? To answer this question depends, in part, on the dynamic nature of the network structure. For example, in the study of the U.S. mail service to industrial customers, we found substantial variation between firms in how information was distributed across members of the buying center (Goodman et al., 1995). In some firms, only one person in the buying center had knowledge of day-to-day events, while in other buying centers, members were linked and shared evaluations of the mail service. One interesting issue is whether in buying centers with high consensus in evaluations there are closer connections to choice behaviors (e.g., stay, leave, or modify the relationship) than in centers with diffuse understanding.

Another issue concerns the players in the network and the objects of evaluation. We have argued there is a lot of flux in the membership in the buying and selling centers. At any point in time, some of the players (e.g., major decision maker) may be more central than others (billing administrator) to the viability of the relationship. To some extent, the link between evaluations and behavior may depend on the nature of the principal actors and the objects under consideration.

There are, of course, many factors that affect the link between evaluations and behavior. Some other ideas will be presented later in the "research opportunity" section. The key idea is that the network structure within and between the buying and selling centers introduces a different level of complexity than appears in the job attitude-behavior discussion.

Embeddedness, Networks, and Dyadic Relationships

We have looked at how flows of information across network ties and observations of others made by network members can influence network members' experiences and evaluations. We turn now to how relations are initiated and sustained and the impact of strong ties.

The initiation of transactions and exchanges is constrained by the network of relations in which the individual is embedded. For example, Macaulay's (1963) analysis of noncontractual relations in interfirm analysis and Geertz's (1992) analysis of information search in the bazaar showed that markets and market relations have social components. Williamson (1985) extends these types of insights, showing how "private" orderings of relations may often replace contractual relations. In all these cases, individual transaction-related behavior is influenced by factors such as trust, private knowledge, anticipations about the future with respect to the behavior of others (Heide & Miner, 1992), and so on. These arguments and results suggest that the quality of social relations and embeddedness exert an impact on such economic transactions. We are extending the proposal that transactions are constrained by the network structure (Baker, 1984; Granovetter, 1985; White, 1980) into the industrial market.

Granovetter (1985) argues that individual action is embedded in social systems, and cannot be analyzed without regard to concrete social contexts and forces. For example, even in highly efficient markets like publicly regulated commodity markets where prices offered should dominate choice of exchange partners, Baker (1984) has shown that social networks play a significant role in the flow of transactions. For example, traders tend to make trades within a social network on the exchange floor, rather than making trades with anyone in the exchange market. The traditional approach to customer evaluation of products and services also assumes price and product features dominate exchange partner choice (reflecting the undersocialized, individualistic conception in marketing derived from *both* psychology and economics) where evaluation relies solely on the consumer's tastes and preferences.

Embeddedness and Customer-Firm Relationships

We now want to look at how embeddedness in the network influences the quality of relationships and interpersonal interactions. First we ask, "How does the nature of the interorganizational structure and network spanning the buying and selling systems influence the relationships in the network?" The relationships between individuals in the customer-supplier relationship, particularly across organizational boundaries, should reflect some of these processes. We want to extend the analysis beyond the evaluations which we addressed above.

Frenzen presents an interesting set of results illustrating some implications of the embeddedness concept for marketing transactions. Frenzen and his colleagues (Frenzen & Davis, 1990; Frenzen & Nakamoto, 1993) suggest that consumer behavior is embedded in social networks. They expect word-of-mouth to flow along social network ties and that the willingness of people to transmit information is influenced by the strength of network ties such that when the moral hazard associated with transmitting information is high, information will only flow along strong ties (Frenzen & Nakamoto, 1993). In this context, moral hazard means the risk that if A gives B a piece of useful information, B may use that information but not provide something of equal utility in return to A (i.e., B free rides on A). Frenzen and Nakamoto (1993) do find that when moral hazard is high, information *only* flows along strong ties. When moral hazard is low, information flows across strong or weak ties (Granovetter, 1973).

For example, suppose a potential customer asks for information on future product offerings so they can gauge how a current commitment to a supplier will unfold over the next five years. This is a common concern in many industrial settings and is frequently done for customers. Moral hazard would be high here if the potential customer can use this information about future product offerings to extract a concession from a competing supplier, or use that information in some way while not committing to the relationship. In this context, strong ties or trust may be critical to the supplier's willingness to reveal their future product plans to the potential customer, as there is moral hazard. Moral hazard would be lower if the customer has no conceivable way to use the information or if the potential customer provided something of equal value to the supplier (e.g., some hostage or other sort of information to guarantee the potential customer's good behavior). This issue is most critical if there are real asymmetries in power between the supplier and customer. Many industries have the conditions which create such moral hazards. For example, suppliers in an industry may supply multiple customers (if they have a critical resource valued by all) and customers may have leverage with suppliers over revealing information about rivals. (This can occur in industries such as software, autos, and other durable industrial products.)

Analysis of industrial markets has been strongly influenced by the Thibaut and Kelley (1959) analysis of interpersonal relationships. Such analysis is similar to the game-theoretic strategic analysis one can apply to industrial market relations, such as might be seen in industrial organizational or contract analysis in economics. Both an economic/strategic analysis or a Thibaut and Kelley-oriented analysis portray multiple actors with diverging interests and information sets (which may or may not be identical). Given these conditions, actors in the industrial market act so as to best meet their interests.

How does an embeddedness framework and the results reported by Frenzen and colleagues enrich this game-theoretic, quasi-rational analysis shared by both social psychologists and economists? If strong ties exist in the network, the embeddedness argument suggests that transactions across such ties will show different characteristics and qualities. If trust is high (e.g., concerns about moral hazard are minimized), communication is considerably eased. Boundary spanners can send and receive information with less concern about strategically self-interested behavior by those with whom they are tied. There is less need for policing transactions, thereby lowering the costs of exchange. Suppliers are more willing to invest in special purpose technologies, and buyers are more willing to increase their dependence on suppliers. The social capital embodied in these ties provides real value to both parties, value that can only be realized jointly by the two parties. This can further bind the two parties to each other. Do other considerations such as competitor behaviors and the CL-alt disappear? Certainly not. If an alternative supplier can provide superior service or has a distinctive capability which a current supplier does not have, the competitive advantage which can be provided by the alternative supplier can not be ignored. However, much that suppliers have to offer in industrial markets requires customer specific capabilities and commitments. Strong ties should enhance the probability of making such commitments and developing such capabilities, because the higher level of trust in a strong tie increases the willingness of both parties to commit to each other. That increased willingness alone is sufficient to sustain both parties, as long as neither party reneges. If the strong tie facilitates communication and eases transaction costs, neither side (barring some exogenous shock) will have an incentive to leave.

Recently, GM had engaged in a wholesale renegotiation of supplier contracts, often cancelling multiyear agreements with suppliers to achieve large unit price reductions. This was done often with brutal speed. When suppliers at GM were asked about their willingness to invest in future technologies for GM or its competitors, the suppliers indicated an unwillingness to make investments on GM product lines, with far greater willingness to invest for GM's competitors. This is precisely the problem of moral hazard when strong ties do not exist. We argue that suppliers who are more strongly tied to their customer should show greater willingness to share designs and have designs shared with them by auto makers, reducing both sides' costs and easing transactions between them. Much of this social capital's value is realized in the ease of communication, the ability of each side to "know what the other is thinking," and the trust they have in this judgment.

Our Theme II discussion of relationships can be linked to network structures. The embeddedness argument suggests that there is a continuum from atomistic market relations to the internalization of social norms. Theme II provides a way of characterizing that continuum in a compact way, using the scope of involvement, goals, and institutionalization of behaviors to characterize relationships. Variation in involvement, goals, and institutionalization of behaviors can influence the impact of social network structures. Studying such variations in relationships will help us understand the conditions under which network ties affect relationship qualities. We expect that when a relationship has a broad scope, the network structure will get more elaborate and complex, tying more individuals into the relationship. This will increase the levels of involvement of both the buying and selling center with each other. More weak ties and relations for information flows will develop.

Goal differentiation (how many goals are pursued by each side in the relationship) and network structure can be expected to mutually influence the other. Multiple goals may create more bases for interaction between people within and across the buying and selling centers. Increased bases for interactions may increase the volume of interactions and the chances of strong ties forming. Furthermore, as more goals are pursued via the network, more opportunities arise for interaction, increasing the possibility of strengthening ties. A second possible outcome is that if multiple goals are attained via these network relations, there may be fewer needs for other relations, cutting off the network from weak ties with other networks. This would lead to insulation and isolation of the interorganizational network.

The third relationship dimension, institutionalization, also will affect the impact of network relations. As practices in the network are institutionalized, they are becoming internalized by actors. That is, practices that were supported by instrumental needs and network influences are now seen as the only appropriate behavior. We expect as the practices are institutionalized and become a "natural" way to do business, the demands on the network participants decline and the behaviors are supported now because they seem like "the right way to do things."

Research Opportunities

We have argued that a network view of customer-supplier relationships can enrich our understanding of the ties between firms and how those ties are composed and change over time. This suggests a number of interesting research questions which the study of customer-supplier relations can address.

Who is tied to whom in customer-supplier relations? One very interesting question which can be addressed in this context is: when there are ties between two organizations, what forces and constraints affect those ties? Are ties between customers and suppliers a function of the interdependence between the two firms, driven primarily by the availability of critical resources? This argument can be derived from a resource dependency perspective. In this context, the tie will hold across people and network affiliations, as the resource constraints of the two parties dominate their choices of partners. This implies that the appropriate level of analysis is at the firm level. This certainly happens. In our own work in auditing, we found that when the customer outgrows the capabilities of its supplier of audit services, it will change suppliers (Levinthal & Fichman, 1988). Others have found similar results.

Might the ties between firms be mediated by individuals? Eccles' and Crane's (1988) description of investment banking identified the "relationship" manager, whose role it was to manage the relationship with a client. Relationship managers oversaw the numerous activities engaged in by the bank, and coordinated them so as to fit the needs of the client. In that industry, the movement of critical players could frequently lead to clients going with these managers. The critical issue in such a switch is whether the investment bank has resources unique to it which it can offer the client. If so, then the client would be less willing to move. This more complex scenario suggests that when there are strong interpersonal ties and there are not a great deal of client specific assets in the supplier firm, the role of interpersonal networks is stronger. In particular, if the client-specific assets such as knowledge of client needs and personnel is embodied in the relationship manager, then the resource moves with the relationship manager (i.e., clients move with the manager). This brief set of scenarios suggests that we need to give careful thought to the roles of both critical resources and interpersonal networks. This question has also arisen in the literature on interorganizational networks. Cook and Whitmeyer (1992) suggest that much network research views the organization as an actor. Further, they assume "that the same model of the actor can be used for organizations ... and for individual humans." There are two separable questions here which can be addressed in the customer-supplier context:

1. Do we need to consider an individual level of analysis in understanding interorganizational ties such as customer-supplier exchanges? That is, if we identify at the organizational level the critical needs of the firms and their motives and constraints to engage in exchange, will that be sufficient to explain the matching of customers and suppliers? Do we also need to consider events such as ties at an individual level? Organizations can be viewed as coalitions of interests. If so, then the assumption of the organization as an actor may be a useful analytic fiction to make this problem tractable, but it may not reflect the internal political processes in the firm.
2. Is the organizational level of analysis sufficient to explain pairings of customers and suppliers? Are individual ties necessary but not sufficient to match two firms? That is, one could argue that who the players are fulfilling organizational roles is irrelevant to determine a pairing of two firms (organizational level sufficient and individual level is not

necessary). Another possibility is that interpersonal ties are necessary but not sufficient, such that individual ties may be required, but if the organization's resource needs and capabilities do not motivate a match, the match will not be realized. Larson (1992) suggests that the success and durability of the relationship may be realized if, and only if, the interpersonal networks are effective. This implies that interpersonal ties may not be necessary nor sufficient to motivate a tie, but may be necessary to sustain a tie between two firms. This question of the causal force and causal ordering of individual network and organizational level variables requires further exploration.

How are evaluative responses to products and services formed at the organizational level? That is, when thinking about customer satisfaction, you can ask, "Whose satisfaction is it anyway?" We think it is reasonable to assume that customers respond to product and service experiences. Many supplier firms hope that they are listening to their customers. Who is being satisfied or dissatisfied? Who is listening to the customer? How are the experiences of customers and suppliers at the points of contact with each other communicated and transformed into evaluations by others? As suggested above, maybe the rules by which decision makers operate are decoupled from day-to-day operational experiences. If the president of the company does not hear anything bad, then everything must be okay. This is a simple rule, and suggests that how evaluations are formed are not linked to products and experiences, except in a very minimal way. We expect that in many customer-supplier situations there are no links, and if there are links, they are very noisy.

Should we expect product and service experiences and evaluations to be tightly coupled to buying decisions and decisions about continuity in the relationship? We suggested that an individual's experience with a product or service from a supplier may be loosely coupled to the evaluations and experiences of others, including those in the buying center. If this is true, then how should individual customer responses like customer satisfaction map onto customer behavior like rebuying, modified rebuying or exiting from the relationship? This is an important and exceedingly complex question.

To address this question, we first have to consider how evaluations are formed in a network. Sometimes a firm has bought a piece of equipment used by one person, and that person is fully knowledgeable about that machine and its performance. In that case, with clear performance information, that person could analyze the relevant information and conclude whether or not the machine is effective. As one moves from this situation to one where there are multiple users with poor information about competitive alternatives, varying training, and varying interest in the product under consideration, then the evaluations become noisier, and how one should aggregate them becomes much less obvious. If performance is multidimensional and users have different preferences for machine performance, aggregating individual evaluations to form a collective choice is much more difficult.

Suppose we can determine that one product or service is more attractive (more satisfying) than another to an individual or a set of individuals. Do we expect that behaviors will fall in line with evaluations? Research on attitudes and behaviors in organizational behavior and social psychology suggests that the linkage of attitudes and behaviors may be quite weak. The operation of factors like constraints on behavior, individual and organizational inertia, and the costs of switching may reduce the impact of attitudes towards the product or service like customer satisfaction. We believe that linking evaluations and customer satisfaction to customer actions addresses an interesting and fundamental question about organizational action. What drives organizational action? Several types of answers can be considered. It may be forces of institutionalized beliefs and conformity (institutionalization theory), inertia and initial conditions (Freeman, Carroll, & Hannan, 1983; Stinchcombe, 1965), or adaptive responses to resource constraints (Salancik & Pfeffer, 1978) or some combination that influences organization actions and choices. This question, how are individual processes in the supplier or customer firm translated into collective action, is very close to the heart of organizational behavior and theory. This question can be looked at in a very focused way in customer-supplier relationships. This would be very useful.

We think that addressing this issue requires attention to Theme I (how customers evaluate transactions), Theme II (how customer-supplier relationships are formed, sustained, and dissolved), and Theme III (how flows of information and experience are mediated by the networks of the interorganization structure). It is only by linking such microprocesses in the customer firm as transaction evaluations to more macro structures like relationships and networks that we can link macro behaviors like interorganizational transactions to micro behavioral events in the organization. For us, the customer-supplier relationship presents an excellent setting for examining these fundamental questions of evaluation and action.

CONCLUSION

We have tried to cover a great deal of ground in this paper, considering customer-supplier relationships at several levels of analysis. Our view of customer-supplier relationships is intended to complement the work of others. We think there are several potential contributions we can make.

First, we hope to promote greater dialogue between organizational and marketing researchers. There is much that we can learn from each other. For example, in our analysis of evaluation processes, we do not think the marketing analysis of customer evaluation that focuses on customer satisfaction as a function of expectations and outcomes is wrong. There is much about it that is right. We believe our perspective enriches how one views customer evaluation by beginning to clarify the sources of standards and information, and trying to characterize how expectations are influenced by organizational processes.

Second, we join with recent researchers like J.C. Anderson, E. Anderson, Heide, and Frenzen in trying to more fully understand industrial markets as interorganizational networks. Again, we believe an organizational perspective has much to offer a marketing analyst of industrial markets and channels. By the same token, the greater concern and analytic attention to evaluations of transactions by marketing scholars can enrich the organizational theorists analysis of interorganizational relations, networks, and exchanges. In organizational work, we assume the evaluation process is operational, with organizational actors responding in a self-interested way to outcomes. There is concern about noise, uncertain information, information impactedness and so on, but within those constraints, evaluation is viewed as a reasonable mapping of experience onto some set of evaluative criteria. We think the richer customer satisfaction perspective in marketing and elaborated in this paper can help the analyst of interorganizational exchange better understand the responses of both parties to an exchange to the transactions between them.

Most importantly, we think a multilevel analysis as illustrated in Figure 1 is required to fully understand the experiences of individuals and organizations in customer-supplier relationships. We tried to suggest, for example, that dyadic relations can best be analyzed with consideration both for network structures which condition them and individual evaluation processes of actors who are in these dyadic relationships. It is this general strategy of viewing customer-supplier relations at multiple levels that we hope will be the lasting contribution of our analysis.

ACKNOWLEDGMENTS

Thanks to David Krackhardt, Dan Levinthal, Fernando Olivera, Rangaraj Ramunajam, Denise Rousseau, and Laurie Weingart for their comments on and suggestions for earlier versions of this paper.

NOTES

1. Most of the literature treats the seller as a self-interested party who has chosen to sell to the customer. Given this choice, we assume the seller will continue selling as long as self-interest is met. This self-interest is usually viewed as realization of expected outcomes, principally exchanged resources. While we do not explicitly treat this here, we do think this may be too narrow a view to take of sellers. Sellers may voluntarily opt out of a transaction if the conditions are unacceptable, such as abusive customers, unacceptably high costs of sustaining the relationship, and so on. This type of issue is rarely acknowledged or treated in the literature we examined.

2. Organization researchers studying job satisfaction have noted the many problems with gap models. Because these problems are well understood and are not central to our concerns in this paper, we will not reiterate them here.

REFERENCES

Anderson, J.C., & Narus, J.A. (1984, Fall). A model of the distributor's perspective of distributor-manufacturer working relationships. *Journal of Marketing, 48*, 62-74.

Anderson, J.C., & Narus, J.A. (1990, January). A model of distributor firm and manufacturer firm working Partnerships. *Journal of Marketing, 54*, 42-58.

Anderson E., & Weitz, B. (1992). The use of pledges to build and sustain commiment in distribution channels. *Journal of Marketing Research, 29*(1), 28-34.

Anderson, J.C., Håkansson, H., & Johanson, J. (1994). *Dyadic business relationships within a business network context.* Unpublished manuscript, Kellogg School, Northwestern University.

Baker, E.W. (1984). The social structure of a national securities market. *American Journal of Sociology, 89*(4), 775-811.

Berscheid, E. (1994). *Interpersonal relationships.* Unpublished manuscript, Psychology Department, University of Minnesota.

Blumstein, P., & Kollock, P. (1988). Personal relationships. *Annual Review of Sociology, 14*, 467-490.

Boulding, W., Staelin, R., Kalra, A., & Zeithaml, V.A. (1993, February). A dynamic process model of service quality: From expectations to behavioral intentions. *Journal of Marketing Research, 30*, 7-27.

Bowen, D.E., & Folger, R.G. (1994, April). *Justice in employee-customer exchange.* Paper presented at Ninth Annual Conference of the Society for Industrial and Organizational Psychology, Nashville, TN.

Burt, R.S. (1992). *Structural holes: The social structure of competition.* Cambridge, MA: Harvard University Press.

Cadotte, E.R., Woodruff, R.B., & Jenkins, R.L. (1987). Expectations and norms in models of consumer satisfaction. *Journal of Marketing Research, 24*, 305-314.

Churchill, G., & Suprenant, C. (1982). An investigation into the determinants of consumer satisfaction. *Journal of Marketing Research, 19*, 491-504.

Clark, M.S., & Reis, H.T. (1988). Interpersonal processes in close relationships. *Annual Review of Psychology, 39*, 609-672.

Cook, K., & Emerson, R. (1978, October). Power, equity, and commitment in exchange networks. *American Sociological Review, 43*, 721-739.

Cook, K.S., & Whitmeyer, J.M. (1992). Two approaches to social structure: Exchange theory and network analysis. *Annual Review of Sociology, 18*, 109-127.

Corfman, K.P. (1991). Comparability and comparison levels used in choices among consumer products. *Journal of Marketing Research, 28*, 368-374.

Cyert, R.M., Simon, H.A., & Trow, D.B. (1956, October). Observation of a business decision. *Journal of Business, 29*, 237-248.

Dwyer, F.R., Schurr, P.H., & Oh, S. (1987, April). Developing buyer-seller relationships. *Journal of Marketing, 51*, 11-27.

Eccles, R.G., & Crane, D.B. (1988). *Doing deals: Investment banks at work.* Boston, MA: Harvard University Press.

Emerson, R. (1962). Power dependence relations. *American Sociological Review, 27*, 31-41.

Erickson, B. (1988). The relational basis of attitudes. In B. Wellman & S. Berkowitz (Eds.), *Social structures: A network approach* (pp. 83-98). New York: Cambridge University Press.

Festinger, L. (1954). A theory of social comparisons. *Human Relations, 7,* 117-140.
Fletcher, G.J., & Fincham, F.D. (1991). Attribution processes in close relationships. In G.J. Fletcher & F.D. Fincham (Eds.), *Cognition in close relationships.* Hillsdale, NJ: Lawrence Erlbaum Associates.
Florida, R., & Kenney, M. (1991, June). Transplanted organizations: The transfer of Japanese industrial organization to the U.S. *American Sociological Review, 56,* 381-398.
Fornell, C. (1992). A national customer satisfaction barometer: The Swedish experience. *Journal of Marketing, 56,* 6-21.
Freeman, J., Carroll, G.R., & Hannan, M.T. (1983). The liability of newness: Age dependence in organizational death rates. *American Sociology Review, 48,* 692-710.
Frenzen, J.K., & Davis, H. (1990, June). Purchasing behavior in embedded markets. *Journal of Consumer Research, 17,* 1-12.
Frenzen, J.K., & Nakomoto, K. (1993, December). Structure, cooperation, and the flow of market information. *Journal of Consumer Research, 20,* 360-375.
Galaskiewicz, J. (1985). Interorganizational relations. *Annual Review of Sociology, 11,* 281-304.
Galaskiewicz, J., & Burt, R.S. (1991). Interorganization contagion in corporate philanthropy. *Administrative Science Quarterly, 36,* 88-105.
Galaskiewicz, J., & Wasserman, S. (1989). Mimetic processes within an interorganizational field: An empirical test. *Administrative Science Quarterly, 34,* 454-479.
Geertz, C. (1992). The bazaar economy: Information and search in peasant marketing. In M. Granovetter & R. Swedberg (Eds.), *The sociology of economic life* (pp. 225-232). Westview Press.
Goodman, P.S. (1974). An examination of referents used in the evaluation of pay. *Organizational Behavior and Human Decision Processes, 12,* 170-195.
Goodman, P.S. (1977). Social comparison processes in organizations. In G.R. Salancik & B.M. Staw (Eds.), *New directions in organizational behavior.* Chicago: St. Clair Press.
Goodman, P.S., Fichman, M., Lerch, F.J., & Snyder, P.R. (1995). Customer-firm relationships, involvement, and customer satisfaction. *Academy of Management Journal,* in press.
Goodman, P.S., & Garber, S. (1994). *The impact of objective and contextual factors on perceptions of organizational responsiveness.* Working paper, Graduate School of Industrial Administration, Carnegie Mellon University.
Granovetter, M.S: (1973). The strength of weak ties. *American Journal of Sociology, 78*(6), 1360-1380.
Granovetter, M. (1985). Economic action and social structure: The problem of embeddedness. *American Journal of Sociology, 91*(3), 481-510.
Heide, J.B. (1994). Interorganizational governance in marketing channels. *Journal of Marketing, 58,* 71-85.
Heide, J.B., & Miner, A.S. (1992). The shadow of the future: Effects of anticipated interaction and frequency of contact on buyer-seller cooperation. *Academy of Management Journal, 35*(2), 265-291.
Heinz, J., & Laumann, E. (1982). *Chicago lawyers: The social structure of the bar.* New York: Russell Sage Foundation; American Bar Foundation.
House, R., Rousseau, D.M., & Thomas-Hunt, M. (1995). A meso paradigm: A framework for the integration of micro and macro organizational behavior. In L. Cummings & B. Staw (Eds.), *Research in organizational behavior* (Vol. 17, pp. 71-114). Greenwich, CT: JAI Press.
Iacobucci, D., Grayson, K., & Ostrom, A. (1994). The calculus of service quality and customer satisfaction: Theoretical and empirical differentiation and integration. In T. Swartz, D. Bowen, & S. Brown (Eds.), *Advances in service, marketing and management: Research and practice* (Vol. 3, pp. 1-67). Greenwich, CT: JAI Press.

Iacobucci, D., & Hopkins, N. (1992, February). Modeling dyadic interactions and networks in marketing. *Journal of Marketing Research, 29*, 5-17.

Johnston, W.J., & Bonoma, T. (1981, Summer). The buying center: Structure and interaction patterns. *Journal of Marketing, 45*, 143-156.

Johnston, W.J., & Spekman, R.E. (1987). Industrial buying behavior: Where we are and where we are going. In J.N. Sheth & E. Hirschman (Eds.), *Research in consumer behavior* (Vol. 2). Greenwich, CT: JAI Press.

Kanter, R.M. (1989). *When giants learn to dance: Mastering the challenge of strategy, management, and careers in the 1990s*. New York: Simon & Schuster.

Kiesler, S., & Sproull, L. (1982). Managerial response to changing environments: Perspectives on problem sensing from social cognition. *Administrative Science Quarterly, 27*, 548-570.

Kohli, A. (1989). Determinants of influence in organizational buying: A contingency approach. *Journal of Marketing, 53*, 50-65.

Larson, A. (1992). Network dyads in entrepreneurial settings: A study of the governance of exchange relationships. *Administrative Science Quarterly, 37*(1), 76-104.

Levinthal, D.A., & Fichman, M. (1988). Dynamics of interorganizational attachments: Auditor client relations. *Administrative Science Quarterly, 33*, 345-369.

Macaulay, S. (1963). Non-contractual relations in business. *American Sociological Review, 28*, 55-70.

McGill, A., & Iacobucci, D. (1992). The role of post-experience comparison standards in the evaluation of unfamiliar services. In J. Sherry & B. Sternthal (Eds.), *Advances in consumer research: Diversity in consumer behavior* (Vo. 19, pp. 57-578). Provo, UT: Association for Consumer Research.

Powell, W. (1990). Neither market nor hierarchy: Network forms of organization. In B. Staw & L. Cummings (Eds.), *Research in organizational behavior* (Vol. 12, pp. 295-336). Greenwich, CT: JAI Press.

Robinson, S.L., Kraatz, M.S., & Rousseau, D.M. (1994). Changing obligations and the psychological contract: A longitudinal study. *Academy of Management Journal, 37*, 137-152.

Ronchetto, J.R., Hutt, M.D., & Reingen, P.H. (1989, October). Embedded influence patterns in organizational buying systems. *Journal of Marketing, 53*, 51-62.

Rousseau, D., & Parks, J.M. (1993). The contracts of individuals and organizations. In L. Cummings & B.M. Staw (Eds.), *Research in organizational behavior* (Vol. 15). Greenwich, CT: JAI Press.

Salancik, G.R., & Pfeffer, J. (1978). A social iniormation processing approach to job attitudes and task design. *Administrative Science Quarterly, 23*, 224-253.

Schneider, B., & Bowen, D.E. (1985). Employee and customer perceptions of service in banks: Replication and extension. *Journal of Applied Psychology, 70*(3), 423-433.

Schneider, B., & Bowen, D.E. (1995). *Winning the service game*. Boston: Harvard Business School Press.

Seabright, M.A., Levinthal, D.A., & Fichman, M. (1992, June). The role of individual attachments in interorganizational attachments. *Academy of Management Journal, 35*, 122-160.

Silk, A.J., & Kalwani, M.U. (1982, May). Measuring influence in organizational purchase decisions. *Journal of Marketing Research*, pp. 165-181.

Simon, H.A. (1957). *Models of man*. New York: Wiley.

Spekman, R.E., & Johnston, W. (1986). Relationship management: Managing the selling and the buying interface. *Journal of Business Research, 14*, 519-531.

Srinivasan, K., Kekre, S., & Mukhopadhyay, T. (1994). Impact of electronic data interchange technology on JIT shipments. *Management Science, 40*(10), 1291-1304.

Stinchcombe, A.L. (1965). Organizations and social structure. In J.G. March (Ed.), *Handbook of organizations*. Chicago: Rand-McNally.

Thibaut, J.W., & Kelley, H.H. (1959). *The social psychology of groups.* New York: John Wiley.
Tse, D.K., & Wilton, P. (1988). Models of consumer satisfaction formation: An extension. *Journal of Marketing Research, 25,* 204-212.
Webster, F.E. (1992). The changing role of marketing in the corporation. *Journal of Marketing, 56,* 1-17.
Weick, K.E. (1979). *The social psychology of organizing.* Reading, MA: Addison-Wesley.
White, H.C. (1980). Where do markets come from? *American Journal of Sociology, 81,* 730-780.
Williamson, O.E. (1975). *Markets and hierarchies: Analysis and antitrust implications.* New York: Free Press.
Williamson, O.E. (1985). *The economic institutions of capitalism: Firms, markets, relational contracting.* New York: Free Press.
Wilson, T.D., Dunn, D.S., Kraft, D., & Lisle, D.J. (1991). Introspection, attitude change and attitude-behavior consistency: The disruptive effects of explaining why we feel the way we do. In L. Berkowitz (Ed.), *Advances in experimental social psychology* (Vol. 22, pp. 287-343).
Woodruff, R.B., Cadotte, E.R., & Jenkins, R.L. (1983). Modeling consumer satisfaction processes using experience-based norms. *Journal of Marketing Research, 20,* 296-304.
Zeithaml, A.V., Parasuraman A., & Berry, L.L. (1985, Spring). Problems and strategies in services marketing. *Journal of Marketing, 49,* 33-46.
Zeithaml, V.A., Parasuraman, A., & Berry, L.L. (1990). *Delivering quality service: Balancing customer perceptions and expectations.* New York: Free Press.

INTERFIRM RELATIONSHIPS:
A GRAMMAR OF PAIRS

Blair H. Sheppard and Marla Tuchinsky

ABSTRACT

Historically, in U.S. management theory and practice, market and hierarchy have been the dominant organizing principles for economic activity. These concepts served as grammars or building blocks for a wide range of theories on motivation, control, governance, dispute resolution, and organizational design. However, as new organizational forms become more prevalent, market and hierarchy are insufficient grammars. They cannot fully explain how people and systems behave, and often serve to limit our thinking about organizational behavior and interfirm relationships. We need alternate relational grammars to provide complementary assumptions about behavior within and between firms. Fiske (1991) outlined four fundamental relational grammars, robust across cultures and academic disciplines: *market pricing, authority ranking, equality matching,* and *communal sharing.* Traditional organizational behavior (OB) primarily has relied on the first two. In this paper, it is argued that the last two also underpin present-day economic activity. We describe four types of buyer-supplier relationships as an example of how Fiske's grammars map onto interfirm relationships. In developing illustrative models of alternative relational grammars, several key issues are addressed: (a) how to sustain trust in long-term, nonhierarchical relationships, (b) why interdependence without complete integration is strategically useful, and (c) how adopting alternative grammars affects OB research.

Phil Laskaway, the Chair of Ernst & Young, is confronting a dilemma that all of his Big 6 accounting firm colleagues are facing. The total revenue and margins in auditing, his core business, are declining. A central solution for Ernst & Young's search for further sources of revenue is to use relationships developed over the course of repeated audit business to develop and sell additional financial, tax, and consulting services to its audit clients. A key to this strategy is to understand well enough the nature of the relationships Ernst & Young has with its clients to know what service capacity it can and should develop.

Gus Watanabe, Executive Vice President of Eli Lilly and President of Lilly Research Laboratories, also has a problem. Eli Lilly, the world's eleventh largest pharmaceutical company, has historically conducted most of its discovery drug research at its headquarters in Indianapolis, with some done in Basingstoke, England. However, today, with the advent of major changes in the science of drug discovery, such as the emergence of biotechnology and distributed information processing capacity, research intelligence is distributed far more broadly than within the walls of the major pharmaceutical firms. Drugs discovered by the over 1,000 smaller biotechnology companies in the United States are reaching the market at a rate comparable to those discovered at larger firms such as Merck, Glaxo, or Lilly (Weisbach & Moos, 1995). A strategy for tapping into this broader market of pharmaceutical research ideas is to develop alliances with some of the more successful biotech firms. At Lilly, they dub this strategy "science without walls."

Neil Ressler, Vice President of Advanced Vehicle Technology at Ford, has an equivalent problem. Historically, Ford engineers did most of the engineering for Ford's new car parts (estimates in the mid-1980s ran as high as 80% of parts engineering done by U.S. manufacturers; see Womack, Jones, & Roos, 1990). Many potential supplier companies would bid on manufacturing the part, with the contract regularly going to the lowest priced bidders. Recent years have seen a shift from that strategy. Now, a few suppliers are designing and manufacturing whole dashboards, steering systems, fluid control systems, braking systems, and engine management systems. Thus, much of the innovation, cost, and quality that will arise in future Ford cars and trucks will not be designed by Ford, but Ford's key suppliers. Neil Ressler's problem is how best to develop relationships with these suppliers so that inexpensive, innovative, and customer friendly components make up Ford cars and trucks. Ford's future rests not just in how well it manages its own assets, but also in how well it can develop and manage relationships with key suppliers (for a broader discussion of the role of suppliers in the product development process, see Ancona & Caldwell, 1990; Brown & Eisenhardt, 1995; Wheelwright & Clark, 1992).

Each of these scenarios, while quite different, represents a similar challenge for the protagonist. The future of his company rests in large part on how well that firm can manage its relationships with other firms, a task at which most members of the firm are not well practiced. Ford's future product development rests on how well it can pair with a few critical suppliers, a task with which most employees at Ford are not experienced. Eli Lilly's future research success depends on how well it can manage to pair with a diverse set of biotechnology companies, a relatively recent strategy at Lilly. Ernst & Young's growth potential depends on how well it can build and leverage existing pairings with clients, clients who historically were jealously guarded from interference from other parts of the firm for fear of losing the audit engagement.

Unfortunately, there is not much we can tell these companies about how to behave in these evolving interfirm circumstances. Historically, in U.S. business theory and practice, market and hierarchy have dominated as mechanisms for organizing and thinking about economic activity (Arrow, 1974; Barnard, 1938; Ouchi, 1980). Hierarchy and market have served as the assumed relationships in which business behavior occurs. Thus, for example, in perusing any introductory organizational behavior textbook one will see extensive discussion of topics such as motivation, goal setting, performance appraisal, and leadership. The assumed perspective of the reader is that of a manager responsible for directing and controlling the behavior of subordinates so that those subordinates achieve the stated ends of the organization. The works of Hackman and Oldham (1976), Vroom (1964), Maslow (1943), and Staw (1977) are all cast in the frame of exercising control in the form of authority. One thing that is clear about network organizations, colocated teams, strategic alliances, and long-term supplier relations: control is not exercised in the form of hierarchical authority. You are not your peer's boss, your allies report through a different authority structure, and suppliers are not your employees.

In economics, network research and organizational behavior, market and hierarchy have served as the basic grammars on which models of interfirm relations have been built. As grammars, they have provided basic rules and essential assumptions about human motivation, the purpose of relationships, and expected social behavior. They have provided the building blocks, the foundation upon which our theories of interfirm relations exist. For example, first steps at developing notions of interfirm behavior in economics have considered interfirm relations as progressive steps away from either market or hierarchy (see, for example, Williamson, 1985). Relationships are understood as the absence of market or hierarchy, not as the presence of some alternative. It is our contention that little progress will be made in the development of effective theories of interfirm relationships until alternative relational grammars to market and hierarchy are identified. It is further our contention that researchers can develop such grammars by elaborating upon work already done in social psychology and social anthropology. We draw upon Alan Fiske's (1991) summary of years of research in these fields in identifying two alternative grammars that pervade human social discourse and serve as important paradigmatic contexts for understanding interfirm relationships. The goal of this paper is very ambitious—to identify and compellingly illustrate two alternatives to market and hierarchy as building blocks for our theories of interfirm behavior. Before outlining these two grammars, it is necessary to provide some historical perspective on how interfirm relationships have been studied in economics, social network research, and negotiation research, both to motivate the need for alternative grammars and to outline some of the issues they need to address. We also address how we see relationships as differing from transactional exchanges.

Definition

Throughout this paper, we will be discussing levels of relationships, ranging from a contractual level to deep, forwarding-looking interdependence. Relationships have been defined in many ways (Berschied, 1985), often indicating that those involved in a relationship have a causal influence on one another's behavior; people behave differently depending on the nature of their relational ties (Kelley et al., 1983). We subscribe to this general assumption about relationships and define a relationship as *a pairing of entities that has meaning to the parties, in which the understood form of present and future interactions influences their behavior today*. For the purposes of this paper, there are two key ideas in the conceptualization of a relationship: (1) parties have a history and an expected future shaping their present interactions, and (2) in a relationship, the link itself has meaning. Grammars provide such meaning; so, as students of organizations, it behooves us to be complete in our understanding of relational grammars.

Economic Models of Interfirm Relationships

In recent years, economists have developed significant interest in the study of long-term interfirm relationships (see especially Jensen & Meckling, 1976; Williamson, 1985). This is quite a shift, as for many classically trained economists, a relatively pure market, in which parties engage in transactions with minimal interdependence and little expectation of future interaction, is optimal. As Williamson (1991a) wrote, "The ideal transaction ... obtains when asset specificity is zero" (p. 282). But, parties do engage in long-term relationships in which each makes investments of greater value to one another than to other parties. Two schools of thought in particular have emerged in economics to account for and describe how best to deal with long-term relationships between firms: agency theory and transaction cost economics.

Agency Theory

Agency theory concerns the implicit or explicit contracts governing principal-agent relationships (Eisenhardt, 1989; Hill & Jones, 1992; Jensen & Meckling, 1976). The central objective of agency theory is to define an "optimal" contract—specifying its contingencies under different levels of information, uncertainty, risk aversion, and incentive structures (Eisenhardt, 1989). Principals should design agent contracts to combat two main problems in agency relationships: goal conflict and differences in risk propensities (Eisenhardt, 1989). Thus, the fundamental assumption of agency theory is that principals cannot trust their agents, that agents will shirk their duties and behave opportunistically if given the chance (Eisenhardt, 1989; Gomez-Mejia & Balkin, 1992; Harrison & Harrell, 1993; Leatherwood & Spencer, 1991). It is likely that much of this preoccupation with distrust emerges from a focus on the market as the assumed relational grammar in agency theory. Independent egoists who view relationships as dependencies and not interdependencies (the assumed orientation of market participants) will act in an untrustworthy and self-interested manner. It is the premise of this paper that trust in long-term interfirm relationships does exist in some relationships, because those relationships are built upon other assumptions. Not all pairs consist of independent egoists. But, it remains that unless another compelling, real grammar can be identified, assumptions of self-interested behavior with guile are quite reasonable.

Transaction Cost Economics

Like agency theory, transaction cost economics is concerned with opportunistic behavior. However, transactions cost economics is concerned with two other factors that critically determine the structure of the contract between parties and firms: bounded rationality and asset specificity (Williamson, 1985, 1991b, 1993). Bounded rationality is the acknowledgment that in highly complex, uncertain environments parties cannot plan for all contingencies; in other words, one cannot write a perfect contract. Asset specificity concerns the degree to which parties have developed assets that are of greater value to their partner than to others in the market, such as when a supplier locates a plant near one of its key customers that is quite distant from other customers. This concern with asset specificity places transactions cost economics squarely in the middle of studying interfirm relationships, as one makes an investment in some asset anticipating the other's existence as a partner in the future. Unfortunately, it is especially under circumstances of bounded rationality and a high degree of asset specificity that opportunism is likely to occur; in such circumstances there is likely to exist an asymmetry in knowledge from which a party engaged in self-interested behavior can take advantage (Williamson, 1985; for an alternative view, see Bromiley & Cummings, 1995). Thus, because contracts cannot be written to protect against all contingencies in times of change and uncertainty (people are boundedly rational) and because opportunism is also most likely in such circumstances, firms invoke governance mechanisms as a replacement for explicit contracts.

During the course of long-term relationships, parties build in dispute settlement methods, contract safeguards, information disclosure conditions and administrative apparatus, all aimed at reducing opportunistic behavior (Williamson, 1991a). With sufficiently deep asset specificity and with sufficient uncertainty, integration within the firm is the best option, as governance mechanisms are most easily applied in the context of one organization. However, several examples provided at the paper's beginning illustrate deeply interdependent relationships between independent firms (i.e., one firm did not acquire the other). In attempting to deal with these different types of relationships, transaction cost economists have represented them as intermediates lying on a continuum between market and hierarchy. They are thought of as synthetic combinations of the two. Thus, for economists market and hierarchy are the building blocks from which a theory of interfirm relations is built. A central premise of this paper is that many interesting forms of relationship can be identified when using grammars other than market and hierarchy, relationships in which the issue of sustainable trust can be successfully resolved.

Network Theory

A field of sociology, network theory has some answers to how trust is sustained in interfirm relationships. Network theory has as its primary concern the structural features of networks and their impact on what members expend and gain through participating. Firms are considered nodes in a series of interlocked connections, the pattern of which has great implications for the firms. Granovetter (1985) argued that firms are embedded; ongoing social ties so constrain institutions and their behavior that they are no longer independent actors. It is not relationships per se that are the primary focus of network researchers, but the structural pattern of those relationships. For example, network research concerns the impact of such structural features as network density (Burt, 1983), or qualitative features such as the basis of the network (e.g., differentiating networks built around geography, or a financial source, or professional affiliations; see Powell, 1990; Saxenian, 1994). This perspective has yielded significant insight about the context in which firm relationships are embedded. For example, entrepreneurial firms are found in structural holes in the networks of more traditional firms, where they can derive significant benefit from linking previously unlinked but conceptually connected networks (Burt, 1992). It is also clear that the rules of relating are different for networks having different fundamental bases (modes of interfirm engagement are different for kieretsu than for firms sharing scientific focus and different again from regional networks; see Powell, 1990).

One of the primary assumptions underlying this literature is that networks rely on coordinated market mechanisms to control member behavior rather than on formal command or authority structures (Miles & Snow, 1992; Powell, 1992). Economic pragmatism explains why some people or companies cooperate with and trust others in their networks. Members fear sanctions and risk having their reputations damaged should they not act honorably (Provan, 1993). Members' performance and success is contingent on that of the others; this interdependence creates incentives for cooperation and long-term commitment (Provan, 1993). Additionally, given the benefits of membership, such as reduced costs, gaining external expertise, faster reaction times and improved performance, network participants are loathe to risk alienation (Powell, 1992). While members recognize their increased adaptability and availability of resources, they also acknowledge the added risks, reduced control, and monitoring costs; they share information, technology and distribution reach primarily so they can maintain their network position and favored access to others (Michael & Yukl, 1993; Powell, 1990; Snow, Miles, & Coleman, 1992).

In summary, network theories contribute greatly to our understanding of interfirm relationships. From these models it is clear that a given relationship is embedded in a broader context of relationships. This is important, both because the value of a given relationship is at least partly dependent upon the other relationships a given firm has, and because other members in a network have an impact upon any pair in the network. But, with the exception of very early work (for a review, see Tichy, 1981), most research on networks has focused upon individual firms in a network or characteristics of a network itself. The nature of a given relationship in a network has not been the target of research and thus is not well understood. Moreover, network models seem to cede too much importance to the network in which firms are embedded rather than to the relative power or importance of each of the relationships within the network. A set of data the first author has been gathering over the last six years provides one example of the importance of understanding specific relationships within a network. Managers in our executive programs have been asked to indicate who, other than themselves, they trust most in the world. With a sample of 4,800 managers, there is a visible ordering:

$$\text{mother} \approx \text{spouse} > \text{child} \approx \text{best friend} > \text{father} \approx \text{dog}.$$

The critical comparison in this set is mother versus father. They are in the same network, but their children feel very different levels of trust in these relationships. Something about the relationship between mother and child, and father and child, seems to matter beyond the structure of the network in which the relationship is embedded. While self-evident to any child, this discrepancy suggests that we should not cede too much credence to the power or importance of networks alone. It is necessary to understand the particular relationships within a network if a full explanation of interpersonal or interfirm relationships is to exist.

Behavioral Negotiation Theory

The one area that has considered the pair specifically in interfirm relations is the field of negotiation. Many have argued that the changing nature of organizations and organizational relationships called for the increased study of negotiation (among them Greenhalgh, 1987; Lewicki, Sheppard, & Bazerman, 1986; Sheppard, 1995). It simply follows that within relationships among relative equals, where traditional authority mechanisms do not exist for resolving strategic, operational, and coordination issues among a pair, negotiation becomes a paramount mechanism for decision making. Bargaining is the sine qua non of interfirm decision making.

Researchers have focused on the outcome a dyad or multiple parties achieve: analyzing interaction or communication patterns during the negotiation (for a review, see Chatman, Putnam, & Sondak, 1991), uncovering and classifying persuasion tactics (see Lewicki, Litterer, Minton, & Saunders, 1994) and judgment errors (see Neale & Bazerman, 1992). A great deal has been learned from this research, especially about the determinants of integrative outcomes (see Pruitt, 1983) and the cognitive limitations of negotiators (see Neale & Bazerman, 1992), but a curious trend occurred over time in negotiation research. Research on negotiation has become increasingly arelational. This research has increasingly taken as its model either game theory (e.g., Murnighan, 1991) or decision theoretic models of negotiation (e.g., Bazerman & Neale, 1992). Each of these points of view is primarily transactional. They have as their model maximizing return to self in each negotiation. They do not address, as their primary focus, negotiation as a means of establishing and growing long-term relationships nor how the context of a given relationship changes the nature of a negotiation.

This problem also pervades the methodologies of negotiation research. For example, a fairly typical study involves two relative strangers engaging in a simulated negotiation over a few dimensions where each has been given a set of information outlining the returns to him/her for a set of settlement points on each dimension. The most frequently used simulation is a variant on the two-person, three-issue negotiation developed by Pruitt and Lewis (1975) for the study of integrative bargaining. These are poor proxies for the study of negotiations in relationships for at least three reasons: (1) the negotiation is not in the context of a relationship, (2) the simulation entails a predefined, highly stylized problem, and (3) there is no past and no future interaction for the subjects. Negotiations among strategic allies and parties to a long-term customer-supplier relationship have a past and a future, occur in the context of a very elaborate relationship and even messy problems. Therefore, the field has attempted to address a very important question—how negotiations occur within the context of an ongoing relationship among relative equals—but given its limiting set of perspectives and methodologies, it really has not. Research has concentrated on transactional exchanges, not relationships.

The absence of relationships in the study of negotiation has not gone unnoticed. Recent research has attempted to insert relational considerations into established negotiation models (for reviews see Greenhalgh & Chapman, 1994; Valley, Neale, & Mannix, 1995). But, to this point, relationship has been studied as a variable within the context of existing theories and methodologies, theories developed with the market in mind. Thus, for example, relationships are discussed as a reason why people act irrationally and give more to a partner they know in a negotiation than to a stranger (for an exception and an illustration of the potency of adopting a simple relational grammar, see Sondak, Pinkley, & Neale, 1994). As Greenhalgh (1995) stated,

> some will argue that such an investigation has been progressing for many years and will cite as evidence the research on economic exchange, power "relationships," and multi-trial games. What this argument misses is that existing paradigms posit the essential character of relationships and thereby preclude investigation of variability across relationships. As a result, instead of making progress in this area, research been narrowly constrained by paradigm. (pp. 4-5)

While it is useful to illustrate liabilities of market and hierarchy as limiting views of emerging business relationships, equally compelling alternatives need to be posited if we are to advance the state of the field.

Summary

In summary, while neither economics, network theory, nor behavioral negotiation theory provides a compelling grammar of alternatives to market and hierarchy, they together outline some features that such a grammar must contain and questions it must address. From this brief review it is clear that an acceptable theory of interfirm pairs must minimally:

- Elaborate a comprehensive set of building blocks from which interfirm pairings can be built. This requires delineating grammars of relationships that are as pervasive and compelling as market and hierarchy, that can serve as the basis of interfirm linkages.

- Illustrate how trust or control can exist in long-term pairings among relative equals outside of the trust created by the pair being embedded in a network of interfirm relations. In essence, a theory of interfirm pairs needs to address the forms of trust that exist at a dyadic level.
- Explain why firms would choose to become increasingly interdependent without complete horizontal or vertical integration. In many economic models in particular, this status of independent but highly connected is considered quite unstable and even undesirable.
- Provide a useful background against which to develop more advanced micro research on topics such as negotiation and communication in ongoing interfirm relationships.
- Be managerially relevant; that is, to outline the set of choices a firm must make regarding the what and how of interfirm relationships and provide some insight about how to make them.

A THEORY OF PAIRS

There has been a great deal of research in social psychology and allied fields attempting to understand the fundamental grammars of social relationships. There does appear to be emerging consensus about the set of grammars upon which social relations are built, a set argued in the next section of this paper as quite relevant to the understanding and study of interfirm relations. From an exhaustive review of the major thinking on relationships in sociology (such as Blau, 1964; Buber, 1987[1923]; Durkheim, 1966[1897]; Tönnies, 1988[1887]; Weber, 1975[1916]), social anthropology (such as Malinowski, 1961[1922]; Polanyi, 1957[1944]; Sahlins, 1965; Udy, 1959), social psychology (such as Clark & Mills, 1979; Krech & Crutchfield, 1965; Leary, 1957; Piaget, 1973[1932]), and theology (Ricoeur, 1967), Fiske argues for the existence of four elemental forms of human relationships: communal sharing, authority ranking, equality matching, and market pricing. His own definitions of these four forms is quite elegant.

> Communal Sharing is a relation of unity, community, undifferentiated collective identity, and kindness, typically enacted among close kin. Authority Ranking is a relationship of asymmetric differences, commonly exhibited in a hierarchical ordering of statuses and precedence, often accompanied by the exercise of command and complementary displays of deference and respect. Equality matching is a one-to-one correspondence relationship in which people are distinct but equal, as manifested in balanced reciprocity (or tit-for-tat revenge), equal share distributions or identical contributions, in-kind replacement compensation, and turn taking. Market Pricing is based on an (intermodal) metric of value by which people compare different commodities and calculate exchange and cost/benefit ratios. (1991, p. ix)

These four forms surface repeatedly in writing on human relationships and can be found in anthropological research on a diverse set of peoples. Fiske's assertion about the pervasiveness and importance of these four forms of human relationships is not a modest one, but it speaks to the notion of being foundational which is essential to the argument in this paper:

> My hypothesis is that these models are *fundamental*, in the sense that they are the lowest or most basic-level "grammars" for social relations. Further, the models are *general*, giving order to most forms of social interaction, thought, and affect. They are *elementary*, in the sense that they are the basic constituents for all higher order social forms. It is also my hypothesis that they are *universal*, being the basis for social relations among all people in all cultures and the essential foundation for cross-cultural understanding and intercultural engagement. (1991, p. 25)

That they are foundational implies that market (market pricing) and hierarchy (authority ranking) are only two of four well understood and well practiced relational grammars. All four forms of relationships are fundamental to human discourse from the Moos in Africa to the streets of Durham, North Carolina. According to Fiske, we have all experienced these four grammars with regularity; it is only organizational and economic theory that have ignored them. In fact, developing a working knowledge of these four fundamental forms of social relations is at the heart of childhood socialization.

Of course, there are several issues that need to be addressed before applying Fiske's notions to interfirm relations. For one thing, alternative representations of relationships exist in social psychology. For example, some adopt a personality perspective. The most well known scheme entails an empirically derived interpersonal circumplex, that divides interpersonal behavior into octants based upon the two dimensions of affiliation and power (Kiesler, 1983; Wiggins, 1980). Others look at the nature of resources exchanged in relationships. Foa (1961; Foa & Foa, 1980) differentiates the content of exchanges in relationships in terms of love, status, information, money, goods, and services. Still others consider social motives (Kelley & Thibaut, 1978; MacCrimmon & Messick, 1976) and differentiate relationships in terms of the motives people have concerning the distribution of resources including altruism, cooperation, individualism, competition, and aggression. Finally, Clark and Mills (1979) differentiate communal from exchange relationships, two notions with origins at least as early as when Tönnies (1988[1887]) distinguished gemeinschaft from gesellschaft.

A serious issue concerns why Fiske's model is preferable to these other models as a basic grammar of relationships. First, with the exception of Clark and Mills, these models all relate to components of relationships or motives of people in relationships. Thus, they are not as general as Fiske's grammars. Second, recent evidence suggests that Fiske's notions are quite consistent with people's cognitive structures of social relationships (Haslam, 1995; Haslam &

Fiske, 1992). Further, most of the key ideas captured by other models can be encompassed within Fiske's grammars. For example, altruism is a natural consequence of communal sharing relationships, while individualism and competition are the hallmarks of market pricing. Affiliation and power are two key dimensions differentiating Fiske's grammars (Haslam, 1995). Clark and Mills (1979) essentially outline two of Fiske's four, as exchange relationships have much in common with market pricing, and communal relationships have much in common with communal sharing. As such, Clark and Mills miss one form of relationship that would appear particularly important for understanding interfirm relationships, that is, equality matching. It is our real sense, and there is emerging consensus, that Fiske's grammars are superordinate to these other models.

There are two other more direct concerns about Fiske's grammars and their relevance to interfirm relations that need to be addressed before considering his four relational grammars in an interorganizational context. First, Fiske has not developed a typology specific to interfirm relations. His interest has been to develop a set of relatively universal grammars that apply well in family, community, and business contexts across cultures. To make a compelling case, specific forms of interfirm relations need be illustrated that map well onto Fiske's grammars. Second, he does not address the concern of sustainable trust. It is not clear from Fiske's work how trust evolves or is sustained in these four fundamental forms. Without addressing how trust can be sustained, the essential critique of transactions cost economists is not addressed. Concerning both of these points, Fiske's ideas have a remarkable parallel to a simple typology of trust and interfirm relations we have been developing over the last few years based on field research with firms attempting to develop new forms of interfirm relationships (Lewicki & Bunker, 1995; Shapiro, Sheppard, & Cheraskin, 1992; Sheppard & Tuchinsky, 1995). We will now turn to describing these notions and illustrating the parallel to Fiske's model. We will then turn to the implications of these four forms for the evolution of interfirm relationships, and the implications for micro-OB.

Application of Fiske's Grammars to Customer-Supplier Relationships

At the heart of a customer-supplier relationship is the nature of the product or service a supplier provides for a customer. It is our sense that a remarkable parallel emerges when one differentiates relationships in terms of how much tailoring a supplier does to a product or service for a customer and the notions of Fiske. Consider four quite distinct levels of accommodation suppliers perform to meet a customer's unique needs. A summary of the key characteristics of each of these four forms of accommodation is provided in Table 1.

Table 1. Typology of Relational Forms

	Transact	Tinker	Tailor	Align
WHAT DOES THE RELATIONSHIP LOOK LIKE?				
Equivalent Fiske Form Form of relationship identified by Fiske's typology	Market Pricing	Market Pricing	Equality Matching	Communal Sharing
Degree of Customization To what degree is the product/service tailored?	*Off the Shelf* Predesigned product sold on market; customer selects from existing models	*Modified* Supplier modifies core to meet customer specifications	*Joint Design* Product or service tailor designed for customer	*Aligned* Supplier adjusts core processes, competencies, systems, strategy to better meet specific customer's long-term needs
Supplier Selection Criteria How do suppliers choose a partner?	*Ease of Transaction* Ability to pay and not excessively demanding	*Beverly Hills* Customer is willing to pay for value added features	*Growth and Knowledge* Customer represents learning opportunity, has intellectual capital, access to technology/industry info that supplier wants	*Organization Quality* Quality of customer management, knowledge/insight re: where market/industry is heading, technology, processes
Customer Selection Criteria How do customers choose a partner?	*Cost* Price for product features or service performance level	*Cost and Features* Total price and ability to incorporate desired features/performance levels	*Speed and Quality* Responsiveness, expertise, quality, willingness to dedicate best resources	*Organization Quality* Quality of supplier's organization: management, personnel intellectual capital, processes, cost structure, other relationships, long-term viability
Form of Agreement What type of formal agreement do parties have?	*Standard Contract* Exchange money for product/service at time of transaction	*Modified Standard Contract* Specifies product features, delivery specs, form of modifications, costs; may include dispute resolution mechanisms	*Structured Letter of Understanding* Specifies basic product/service qualities and processes for codeveloping product	*Open Letter of Understanding* Incorporates intent of relationship, governance form, criteria for assessing relationship success

(*continued*)

Table 1. (Continued)

	Transact	Tinker	Tailor	Align
HOW DO THE PARTICIPANTS BEHAVE?				
Buyer Control Mechanisms	*Exit* Buyer stops doing business with a supplier	*Voice* Buyer has input, before delivery, into product/service modifications and quality	*Decision Authority* Buyer jointly makes decisions through codesign, integrated systems, shared intelligence, and shared approval	*Strategic Alignment* Seller integrates with buyer strategy; shared decision process, structure, design; often entails some form of equity
Basis of Trust	*Contractual* Trust based on formal contract, legal system, social norms	*Calculative* Network and reputation concerns; personal links between firms	*Understanding* Shared understanding of each party/mutual goals, needs and capacities	*Identity* Congruent values, culture, and preferences
Operating Mechanism	*Seller Driven* Seller determines product, price, condition of sale	*Joint Definition of Need* Jointly determine modifications seller will make	*Codevelopment* Joint development within a defined scope	*Linked* Joined or tightly linked processes, communication, personnel
Typical Basis of Conflict Over what do parties disagree?	*Performance* Product returned for nonperformance	*Value* Haggle over price, unmet expectations	*Process* How to allocate work, design features, skill deficits, nonconformance, quality, and innovation	*Strategic Direction* Future trends, strategic differences, management quality
WHY PAIR?: THE SUPPLIER'S PERSPECTIVE				
Advantages Why would a supplier choose this relationship?	*Volume* High volume, easy transactions	*Customer Intelligence* (Limited) intelligence re: customer needs, preferences	*Customer Loyalty* Reduced risk, access to technology, capacity to cross sell, increased loyalty and significant customer intelligence	*Product/Service Evolution* Access to customer capital, ideas, technology; risk sharing; opportunity to develop new/refine existing competencies
Cost for Supplier What is the nature of supplier costs?	*Weak Intelligence* Limited intelligence re: customer preferences	*Costs* Redesign costs, customer intelligence gathering costs	*Investment* Detailed research, codevelopment, coordination, relationship mgmt costs; may restrict	*Restructure* Opportunity costs; deep relationships only possible with a few customers

Risks for Supplier Where is the seller vulnerable?	*No Loyalty* Low switching costs reduces customer loyalty	*Low Profitability* Production/delivery inefficiencies, inability to recoup modification costs	*Low Investment Payoff* Agreement ends before recover costs, customer steals core ideas, customer cannot sell own product	*Overdependence* Align with loser, loss of innovation, identity, core competencies; organization features misspecified for future

WHY PAIR? THE CUSTOMER'S PERSPECTIVE

Advantage for Customer Why would a customer choose this relationship?	*Ease* Easy to conduct transactions, shift with market changes	*Fit and Focus* Better product/service fit, focus on customer needs; less need for customer changes	*Access* Access to supplier design and development, insight into processes, can close out competitors to best supplier	*Strategic* Ability to integrate seller competencies over a long-term, focus on own best skill, shape the future
Cost for Customer What is the nature of customer costs?	*Unmet Needs* Product may not meet needs, cost to adjust internal processes to fit product/service	*Price and Time* More expensive product; time required to share needs with supplier	*Time and Resources* Time, resources tied up in codevelopment process; may lose access to other suppliers	*Reduced Options* Lost access to other suppliers, drastically reduced choice, less bargaining power
Risk for Customer Where is the customer vulnerable?	*Competitor Gains* Competitors accrue advantages of tailored product, better aligned supplier	*Cost > Value* Lower quality due to special production, insufficient value in features for price, supplier not deliver to specs, supplier steals customer intelligence	*Time and Intelligence* Expensive process, lose intelligence to supplier, key skill may atrophy, competitor picked better supplier	*Loser* Aligned with wrong long-term partner, smothered supplier innovation, permanent loss of valued skill, limited ability to switch markets or technology

Transacting

In the purest form of *market pricing*, in this paper termed *transacting*, a supplier sells a predesigned product to a customer, who chooses a model "off the shelf" with no product or service specialization. The supplier has a stock product; the customer either buys it or does not buy it. This form resembles a spot market (Ouchi, 1980): all obligations are fulfilled immediately, and parties exchange products or service for money. Standard purchase and delivery terms prevail. The contract lies in the exchange of money for a product or service at the transaction point. There is little consideration of past or future; the supplier is self-contained and the customer is free to shop elsewhere. Transacting is market pricing in its simplest form. Suppliers compete on the basis of design, production, and delivery of a product or service with some ratio of [(quality + features + service)/price] determining who will win customers. Customers are choosing among products with their primary or sole focus being the product itself.

Tinkering

But many customers, in fact, most industrial customers, are not happy with buying parts or services off the shelf. They expect some tailoring of the product to their particular needs. The need for such product modification most frequently arises when the service is somewhat complex, especially in terms of how it interacts with other parts of the customer's products or activities. The capacity to appear to tailor a product to customer needs is also an increasingly important source of differentiation today. It is possible to stay true to the fundamental principles of market pricing and still permit some modification to meet customer needs, labeled *tinkering* in this paper. In tinkering a supplier modifies a core product to meet a customer's specifications. Tinkering may involve changes in either the product or how it is delivered. For example, if a customer wants an unusual color or feature, to buy larger or smaller than customary lots, to delay billing, or additional warranties, these would require a relationship extending beyond standard transactions. Customer and supplier must reach agreement that each is willing to assume the risk such modification requires. Suppliers alter processes, make limited production runs, and/or tie up designers or service personnel, all of which have real and opportunity costs. Customers rely on the supplier to perform, and may also forgo other opportunities. Parties' transaction costs rise, and opportunities are constrained. They typically draft a contract specifying product or service features, modifications, compensation terms, and guarantees on both sides. Relative to the first level, parties each assume greater cost and risk, but with the potential for greater benefit than a spot market transaction offers. Parties are connected for the length of a product run or length of a service contract.

The critical characteristic of tinkering is that a supplier still primarily designs, produces, and delivers a product derived from a base product developed before the customer became involved. The platform existed before the customer placed demands, and thus customer options are constrained by what is possible in the context of a predesigned core product. In addition, the customer is still shopping products or services comparatively. Compensation is based on market forces and follows the rules of market pricing. Contracts serve as the vehicle of control and discussions look very much like negotiations over price versus terms, typical of negotiation research conducted today.

Insufficiency of Market Pricing at Further Levels of Integration

To this point this paper has described two distinct forms of market pricing: transacting and tinkering. Before turning to outline the application of alternative grammars to customer-supplier relationships, we will first formally consider the circumstances under which market pricing is insufficient. Often, tinkering is insufficient, as customers need a truly tailor designed product. This need arises when a part or service is highly linked to other components of an integrated product assembled by the customer. Automotive assembly is a clear example of the need for and value of a tailor designed product, as is any other complex assembling task requiring the integration of relatively novel technology. In many industries, this process has historically been conducted in the form of an auction. Auctions are the natural extension of market pricing assumptions and forms of control to the need for a highly tailored product or service. Auctions involve the customer developing detailed drawings over which competing suppliers would bid for the opportunity to manufacture the part. But, auctions do not work well under just the circumstances that call for a tailored product and that are arising with increasing regularity today.

When a part or service is complex, based on rapidly changing technology, the knowledge of which is widely dispersed, and there exists considerable interdependence between that part and other parts, it is next to impossible to effectively provide complete and accurate part design and specifications in advance. Auctions based on improper specifications lead to troublesome post-purchase negotiations and potentially large losses from incorporating new part features midstream. Why is specification so hard? First, it is quite unlikely that all relevant knowledge exists among a customer's design team. Highly complex parts or systems require both broad and deep knowledge, which with complex, rapidly changing technology is often widely dispersed around the world. It is possible to seek information from others, but competitors are unlikely to share it and others in the supply chain are unlikely to provide that advice unless they have a relationship with the customer. Second, if change in relevant technology occurs rapidly, then an optimal design at any one point in time is likely to be less optimal as time progresses. Thus, the capacity to flexibly and in a coordinated manner adapt technology is essential with complex, changing, integrated parts. An effective auction, then, requires a relatively complete and immutable design, at least over the period of the contract, and is likely to lead to outdated technology and a competitive disadvantage. Interconnectedness makes shopping the world difficult as well unless a firm is in a position to impose standards upon the industry, or someone else is doing it for them (see Pitta, 1995 regarding Intel and Microsoft consortium).

If an auction is impossible to effectively conduct, one argument is that a firm can stay current by developing fast, effective means of integrating the best generally available parts into a product. Thus, complete expertise is not essential, as suppliers are providing much of the design expertise. A firm could also switch suppliers rapidly as one gains a technological edge over others. Sun Microsystems had as its original strategy to regularly make its own product line obsolete by integrating the best available parts to a computer on the market at all times. Complexity, distributed knowledge, interdependence, rate of change in underlying technology, and need for speed mitigate against this transactional option as well. Given the interdependence between parts and need for speed, it is important that the designers of one part be heavily linked to designers of other parts during design; the greater the interdependence, the longer it takes to redesign all steps in a product chain (Wheelwright & Clark, 1992). If speed is important, this time is too long. Someone needs to coordinate design among component parts to keep all as current as necessary to satisfy the market.

If conducting an auction, or buying on the open market is not possible, then classical theorists would argue that a firm should acquire the capacity to make that product internally (Williamson, 1985). When markets fail, invoke hierarchy. Again, complexity, distributed knowledge, rapid change in underlying technology base, parts interdependence, and need for speed mitigate against owning that capacity. Increasingly complex products demand broader domains of deep expertise. Expertise is expensive to acquire and difficult to manage and keep current if the underlying technology is changing quickly. Unless one is willing to manage that expertise extremely closely, acquiring internal capacity is problematic when obsolescence is highly likely. Finally, the incentives are somewhat misplaced if one step in a chain acquires most of the suppliers in the preceding step. A supplier has an incentive to stay current, lean, and competitive in its specific core business. If someone only manufacturers chips, then staying current and maximizing the value of custom designed chips is likely to be that firm's primary focus. If, however, the firm were both to integrate the chip into other parts it manufactures internally and parts acquired externally, that firm now has many foci. Generally, an integrating step will take priority and, over time, parts expertise, price, and value will suffer.

Taken together, this discussion suggests a quandary. When complexity, distributed knowledge, change in underlying technology, parts interdependence and need for speed are high, then it is best to remain separate but integrated. *To separate too far leads to obsolescence, slowness, and incompleteness. To link too closely leads to obsolescence, slowness, and incompleteness.* It is necessary to maintain the tension between being separate, but allied. In essence, this argument has much in common with the classic notions of differentiation and integration (Lawrence & Lorsch, 1967), but applied to interfirm rather than intrafirm relations.

Many people are adopting separate yet tied practices. Retail chains such as Wal-Mart have integrated their information systems with key suppliers to the extent that point of sale information is immediately available to the manufacturer. Medical products companies such as Johnson & Johnson have been involved in intensive supplier qualification efforts to ensure devices and other materials meet the necessary stringent standards for use in living patients. Ford, Chrysler, and Saturn have strong supplier relations programs underway. But, do these practices really work? Table 2 shows performance of Japanese and U.S. automotive suppliers in the early 1980s. At that time, U.S. manufacturers used hostile bidding practices and arm's length interactions with their suppliers while the Japanese kept tight partnerships with a small set of suppliers, sharing information, technology and profits gained through process

Table 2. Cross-Regional Comparison of Automobile Suppliers

Averages for Each Region	Japan	United States
Supplier Performance		
Die change times (minutes)	7.9	114.3
Lead time for new dies (weeks)	11.1	34.5
Job classifications	2.9	9.5
Machines per worker	7.4	2.5
Inventory levels (days)	1.5	8.1
Number of JIT deliveries	7.9	1.6
Parts defects (per car)	.24	.33
Supplier Design Involvement		
Supplier percentage of total engineering	51	14
Supplier proprietary parts (%)	8	3
Black box parts (%)	62	16
Assembler designed parts (%)	30	81
Supplier/Assembler Relations		
Suppliers per assembly plant	170	509
Inventory level (days, 8 parts)	0.2	2.9
Percentage of parts JIT	45.0	14.8
Percentage of parts single sourced	12.1	69.3

Source: Womack, Jones, and Roos (1990).

improvement (Womack et al., 1990). On all counts, the Japanese suppliers outperformed those of the United States. Even more compelling, perhaps, is the recent reemergence of Chrysler and Ford, who among other things have dramatically shifted the level of supplier involvement in parts design, while simultaneously attempting to focus internal parts divisions on supplying external customers.

This story with cars illustrates the value of treating some suppliers in terms other than typical market pricing or hierarchy and leads to two propositions.

Proposition 1. Interfirm relationships other than market pricing are especially likely to arise when four conditions hold: (a) when the part or service is complex and (b) based on rapidly changing technology, (c) there exists considerable interdependence between the given part or service and other features of the customer's product or activities, and (d) there exists a need for quick integration of design and production between supplier and customer.

Proposition 2. Interfirm relationships other than vertical integration are especially likely to arise when three conditions hold: (a) the customer's core product is complex, (b) the part or service a customer supplies is based upon rapidly changing technology, and (c) the knowledge upon which it is based is widely dispersed.

It is clear that the conditions suggesting the need for separate but highly integrated customer and supplier are increasingly prevalent today. Complexity, interdependence, dispersion of knowledge and need for speed are the cornerstones of what, for example, D'Aveni (1994) has called hypercompetition. Thus, it is not surprising that we see increasing use of interfirm relations other than market pricing. Consistent with Fiske's notions of *equality matching* and *communal sharing* there are really two quite distinct options for solving this need to integrate, but keep separate: tailoring and aligning.

Tailoring

The first, call it *tailoring*, involves customer and supplier teaming up to design a unique product or service. Instead of ordering a McDonald's hamburger (transacting), or a Burger King "have it your way" Whopper (tinkering), this is akin to a pair going shopping for ingredients, heading into one's kitchen to plan mutually how the burger is likely to be cooked, and then letting the kitchen owner prepare the burger. Parties generally have a history of interaction before undertaking such a connection. Such prior ties allow "cautious contracting [to give} way to looser practices as partner firms build confidence in each other" (Gulati, 1995, p. 105). Such a relationship tends to

Interfirm relationships 351

use a letter of understanding instead of exhaustive contracts. The letter establishes parties' basic expectations and responsibilities: product qualities, who assumes which costs, what information parties may share with one another and with outside parties, basic coordination mechanisms, and possible dispute resolution methods. Supplier and customer discuss process and jointly make design decisions. Typically, such a relationship has a longer time frame than the forms discussed above. The supplier needs a longer time horizon in which to develop efficiencies, and both need time to amortize investments. Company structures may shift to accommodate joint activities—personnel may change location and they may open communication channels, for instance—but each firm remains separate. Each maintains its own core competence, strategy, and identity.

There are three critical shifts in the emergence of tailoring relationships from market pricing mechanisms, quite typical of equality matching. First, customer focus shifts from buying a product or service to buying the talents and organizational skills of the supplier. The focus shifts from the product to the producer of the product. Second, there becomes an intimacy and interdependence quite unlike market exchanges. Parties come to see the need to better understand one another. Finally, an air of equality comes to lay over the pair. While it remains clear that each is separate, and that one in particular is the customer, parties come to think of themselves as mutually engaged in delivering the needs of the ultimate consumer. Discussions shift from discussions of price, delivery terms, and so forth to discussions of equality of input, relevant balance of activity, appropriate sharing of information and resources. The central question is how supplier and customer can remain separate but relatively equal contributors to the design, production, and integration of the supplied product.

An especially diagnostic indication of the differences between market pricing based mechanisms of supplier/customer integration and tailoring concerns the nature of disagreements in the three instances. Transactions entail discussions of price, quantity, terms of delivery, and product features. A typical conflict would be over returning a product for nonconformance, or seeking compensation for poor service. In tinkering, parties argue over unmet expectations, or haggle over the proper pricing of service or options added to the core product. Buyers rely on voice to control suppliers. They offer input into features and forms of product or service modifications, both before delivery and on a continuing basis. In tailoring, with the increase in range of activities and interaction, potential sources of conflict also increase. Typical conflicts are over work allocation, skill deficits, and nonconformance, design feature qualities, level of innovation, and coordination problems.

It is also worth considering how dissolution occurs in each of these instances. In both transacting and tinkering the central condition for continuing the relationship is the continued performance of the product relative to the competition. Thus, the relationship will be discontinued as soon as an alternative becomes more attractive. Because of the value of breadth and continuity of relationship in tinkering, this shift will be stickier. Customers will exercise efforts to improve the performance of a product before leaving, but once it is clear that a better alternative exists and will continue to exist, the customer will leave. Forgiveness is not forever. In transacting, exit is nearly instantaneous; in tinkering voice is exercised first. The ability to retain a customer in such circumstances is highly related to the perceived responsiveness a supplier has to exercised voice. In tailoring, things become more complicated. The relationship ends when one party concludes that the other is no longer up to the demands of the design and implementation task. Thus, dissolution is a result of concluding one's partner is not as good as an alternative and will continue to not be as good. So, dissolution is a more traumatic and costly event. It is a statement about inherent qualities of the other and an admission of one's own poor selection or relationship management skills. Dissolution is generally associated with phrases such as "this is not the company I thought it was," or "my how my partner has changed." Of course, tailored relationships are not always intended to last forever. It may just be that time has come to part ways. In the form of relationship we are about to turn to discuss, dissolution is significantly harder. Linkages are deeper and of strategic import. Dissolution only comes after great reflection and at some real personal, organizational, and strategic costs. Such dissolutions are like the loss of an old friend or sibling, someone intimately linked to one's sense of self. In such instances, dissolution is associated with phrases such as "we failed," "we are no longer assets for one another," "isn't it a shamem."

Aligning

At a still deeper level, call it *aligning*, a supplier adjusts core processes, systems and strategic focus to better align with the customer's overall systems and needs, both present and future. Such alignment is necessary for a supplier to engage in black box design, that is, to produce a part or service that is to be integrated into a highly complex assembled part with little design input from the customer. Alignment occurs so that a customer can cede control over a critical aspect of a product to a given supplier. Such a requirement is inevitable when products get complex enough and technology changes rapidly enough. Customers, even the largest and wealthiest, cannot stay on top of everything in those circumstances and thus encumber certain key suppliers with some of their strategic future. In a very real sense, then, while tailoring is about increasing level of codesign or coproduction, alignment is about permitting very risky independent action on the part of suppliers. Customer involvement in design and production is replaced with intense alignment of supplier interests, capital, human resources, and strategy with customers' interests and strategies. A second notable feature about alignment is that with alignment it is in the best interest of the customer to invest in the improvement, development, and future of the supplier. In alignment both parties consider one another when making capital investment decisions, strategic market decisions, hiring, and technology adoption. Each may supply people or other resources to the other to help improve quality, processes or systems. Information systems, planning systems, product development, and logistics are often integrated activities.

As with tailoring, an exhaustive contract would be impossible to specify and would likely prove detrimental to enforce. Parties rely on informal negotiations at many levels with each firm. Alignment tends to emerge from past fair dealings, so informal control mechanisms prove stronger than formal legal contracts (Granovetter, 1985; Ring & Van de Ven, 1994). This relational form resembles what Eccles (1981) described as a quasifirm, Ouchi (1980) called a clan and some others have called a strategic alliance (e.g., Yoshino & Rangan, 1995).

In both form and substance, aligning shares much in common with Fiske's notion of communal sharing. Parties are focused on mutual long-term improvement. One member's needs become the other's. The futures of the two firms become deeply intertwined. Alignment is not an altruistic act, however. Each is aligning with what it hopes to be a winner for the purpose of deriving long-term benefit from a deep relationship with the best customer or supplier. There is also a secondary purpose of improving internal capacities under the guidance of a competent and demanding partner. Communal sharing is not just about communal activities, but also the advantages of a community as an anchor from which to foray into the world.

Relation to Fiske

It is now worth returning to Fiske and considering explicitly how the four forms of supplier accommodation to customer relate to his ideas. Perhaps most illustrative is to consider the principle of justice upon which partners engaged in each form of accommodation would base their discussions or disagreements. In both transacting and tinkering the focus is on features of the product or service. Thus, discussions would center upon the ratio of product features and quality to price. Such comparisons of ratios are at the heart of the principle of equity, in which people compare relative inputs and outputs in determining what is fair. Higher prices demand higher quality and better featured products. Because of the emphasis on codesign in tailoring, and the need for creating a sense of unity between customer and supplier, the emphasis shifts from a focus on relative contribution to one of shared and equal contribution. Thus, equality is raised with far greater frequency in tailored relationships than with tinkering or transacting. Sometimes it galls the customer that a supplier considers it a right to take an equivalent share of the margin as a requirement for assuming the costs and risks of codesigned products. Executives at Boeing, for example, are regularly engaged in discussing the merits of tailoring given the impact on their profitability that comes from sharing profits with key partners (personal communication). Aligned relationships focus more on the individual needs of the parties to the relationship. What sort of margin is necessary for a key supplier to continue to be a world leader in its respective domain? What capital investments are required? What sorts of human resource investments are required? Discussions center on the needs of the respective partners to remain among the best and to improve and innovate. Thus, the relationship turns a corner from a concern over the relative division of spoils to mutual investment in creating larger spoils to divide. The central assumption of aligned relationships is that by investing in the other, each firm becomes stronger and more profitable.

It is important to realize that while the structure and assumptions of these forms of interfirm relationships are different, they are also psychologically quite different. Transacting and tinkering are individualized and competitive modes of engagement; social motivation and interpretive relational schemes are egoistic. Tailoring is a relationship of separate but linked equals. Tailoring is a relationship built upon tit for tat, balance and cooperation. Alignment is a relationship based upon deep connection. Partners are no longer focused on separation, but on being a part of something larger. Each partner derives some real sense of identity through its linkage with the other. The psychological scales are also different—tinkering and transacting are built on a ratio scale, tailoring on an interval scale, and aligning largely on a nominal scale (see Fiske, 1991). These differences serve as the basis of very different underpinnings for the development of a micro-OB of interfirm relations. The psychology of markets is not the same as the psychology of partnerships. Relationship discourse, conflict, metrics and behavior are based on quite distinct grammars in each instance.

As a summary of this description of the forms of customer integration we offer two further propositions.

Proposition 3a. The emergence of codesign and coproduction activities will arise with moderate levels of (a) supplier product complexity, (b) required integration with other components of customer product or activities, (c) rate of change in basic technology underlying core features of the supplier product or services, (d) dispersed intelligence, and (e) need for speed of integration and introduction of product into the market.

Proposition 3b. The basis of discussion of distributing goods and costs in such instances is based on equality matching, represented by tallying of contributions, chit keeping and concern for keeping things relatively balanced.

Proposition 4a. Deep alignment of strategies, investments, information systems and people will arise with high levels of (a) supplier and customer product complexity, (b) required integration with other components of customer product or activities, (c) rate of change in basic technology underlying core features of the supplier product or service, (d) dispersion of intelligence around core technologies in supplier products, and (e) need for speed of integration and introduction into the market.

Proposition 4b. In aligning, the basis of discussion of distributing goods and costs entails issues of need. This is represented by concern for the necessary investment, margin, skills and organizational capacities to remain among the best and to sustain necessary innovation.

An Example

As an illustration of these forms of supplier/customer relationships and as an illustration of their respective advantages, consider Ernst & Young's strategy for developing customer relationships in its consulting business (personal communication with Mike Powers, Vice Chairman). Ernst & Young thinks of customers as fitting into four categories, the first of which is those most important, preferred customers around whom Ernst & Young redefines its core strategies and practices. These are typically very large, multinational clients considered models of future success for a given industry. Ernst & Young goes to school on these clients so that they may retain a deep and lucrative relationship with future successful companies, and also to be better positioned to provide services to those who follow their preferred client's lead. A second type of customer also tends to be a larger account for whom it makes sense to develop tailor designed services and products. Unlike preferred clients, these companies are not the basis of E&Y's long-term organizational strategy and alignment, but E&Y develops unique products and services for them. Such clients need to be large enough that they require and can afford to pay for a deeply tailored service or product. The next level client is frequently smaller and cannot afford to hire the most expensive and talented of Ernst & Young's consulting partners. Instead, they benefit from the design work done for the larger, more affluent clientele. They do expect some modifications of a core product or service, however, to meet their needs. Too packaged a solution leads them to distrust its relevance for their perceived unique problems. Finally, sometime later the product or service will often be packaged or formatted for mass sale, often as a book or CD or service provided by a manager to much smaller clients. With this mix of clients, E&Y gets the benefits of critical review of its strategy, personnel, processes and systems by very sophisticated clients, codevelopment of products with very discerning clients, and volume sales from tinkering and packaging of these unique solutions for broader market application. Thus, the proper strategic mix of clients results in a trickle down of strategic posture and product from the most future oriented and discerning customers to those many who can afford only a derivative solution. Without such volume, deep codevelopment would be too expensive for E&Y to engage in. Thus, each level of relationship supplements the other. Less entangled relations derive intelligence and design from more entangled relationships, and the highest order relationships are made possible by the derived profits with higher volume transactions.

SUSTAINABLE TRUST

We have attempted to illustrate how two increasingly prevalent forms of customer-supplier relationships share much in common with equality matching and communal sharing, the two basic relational grammars Fiske identified as alternatives to market pricing and authority ranking. Thus, to this point we have provided evidence for the existence and relative advantage in certain circumstances of these two forms of relationship. However, the question still arises concerning the sustainability of these relationships given the incentive to cheat (Williamson, 1985) and other risks associated with them. Can sustainable trust be created? To develop the bases of trust that we think create sustainability, consider first more seriously the risks associated with each form of accommodation to client.

With tinkering, suppliers work to build customer loyalty. They gather more information about customer preferences and needs, and adjust to serve unique customer interests. The modifications required of tinkering may help suppliers re-design their products to incorporate new features or technology, either by directly transferring a customer's modifications or through engineers being inspired by the required changes. Thus, tinkering mitigates some of the risks of spot markets, but with its own associated risks. In particular, suppliers risk losing money if they cannot recoup investment costs, especially if the customer does not reorder the special items. With tinkering, a customer gets a better fitting product, from a firm focused on meeting customer demands. The supplier bears design costs. However, obtaining products or services in this type of relationship takes longer; suppliers need to assess customer needs and preferences and then create a tailored product. Such a product can be priced too high for the value of additional tinkering and there is a risk that the supplier cannot perform up to expectations. Customers cannot feel and smell the exact product before a contract is negotiated. Quality may drop as well with the demands that unique features place on product manufacturing or service delivery. Finally, customers run the risk of suppliers stealing design features and intelligence for sale to customer competitors. In essence, customers run the risk that suppliers will not be sufficiently reliable, and that they will not maintain confidentiality when critical information is shared.

With tailoring, suppliers share even larger risks with the customer. Greater intelligence comes with tailoring. Not only do suppliers come to understand customer needs extremely well through codesign, but suppliers also have access to customer technology and design intelligence. Customers are more loyal and open to cross-selling. Suppliers are both more and less attentive—in these relationships, a customer is more demanding but also more forgiving of minor lapses. This level of relationship offers supplier personnel real learning opportunities. But, tailoring comes with several risks. Codesign teams may have difficulty specifying costs each side incurs. A customer may exit before the supplier recovers development costs, or worse, the customer may steal product or design intelligence or carry it to a supplier competitor. A supplier also risks that the customer cannot sell its product. Finally, a supplier risks misjudging a partner and having all the downside costs and no upside potential gained. Through tailoring, a customer gains a specific, integrated part or service, insight and access into supplier design and development processes, network and resources. The customer has active control over the final product or service content and specifications. Customers also get a chance to shut out competitors from a best supplier. Primary costs include time and resources tied up in codevelopment processes, potentially higher prices, and various opportunity costs, such as losing access to other suppliers. Customers risk a weak product (because first runs and prototypes may have kinks or bugs in them) from an inefficient process. Customers who hand off work previously done internally risk having those internal skills atrophy or grow out of date. They may lose intelligence or key employees to a supplier, or risk having chosen the wrong supplier, which gives a competitor an advantage.

With aligning, suppliers share still more risk and rewards with their customers. They have access to their own resources and most of the customer's as well: technology, capital, network ties, personnel. They have stabilized their customer base too. Suppliers gain an intimate knowledge of customer preferences and plans, and can redefine or develop their competencies in light of a customer's strategic direction. (Customer competitors may choose similar directions later, so a supplier will subsequently better match with other customers.) Suppliers learn a great deal from these types of relationships, and can use the opportunity to reinvent themselves, their technology, product, service, and processes. But, these relationships carry high risks. It is only possible to closely tie with a few customers. Such bonds entail opportunity costs vis-à-vis other customers, other strategic directions for the supplier firm, and other deep relationships. Similarly, this relationship type is predicated on both firms surviving into the future; a supplier who aligns its strategy and competencies around another who goes out of business is at risk. Parties must take care not to bet the store. Suppliers carry other risks as well. A supplier may lose its core competencies, making it less attractive to other customers. It may not correctly anticipate future needs and consequently retools for a future that never arrives. The firm may risk merging too much with the customer firm, losing its own identity in the process. Finally, it may lose its innovativeness, relying too heavily on the customer to navigate strategic direction.

In aligning, a customer gains all the advantages of a tailoring relationship plus the capacity to integrate supplier competencies into its long-term plans. This stabilizes the customer's environment, allowing greater control over the future, and speeds up future product development. A customer knows what the supplier can or will be able to do, and has access to its design and production teams. The customer can focus on its own best skills and strategic direction. However, such arrangements drastically reduce customer choice, because it is costly to align closely with another. A customer may lose access to other suppliers as well as access to new markets or technology. If the customer chooses badly, it may align with a loser who cannot make needed investments or develop appropriately. Customers risk losing their identity should the firms become too interdependent, and risk smothering supplier innovation by isolating them from other buyers. Customers also risk permanently losing a valuable skill or asset through relying on a supplier to perform some critical task.

Bases of Trust

Thus, both the rewards and risks of tailored and aligned relationships are quite high. This observation returns us to the question of trust. Without the ability to identify a winner and create sufficient trust, deep interfirm relationships entail too many risks to merit their development. Proper selection of a partner can mitigate some of the concerns for sustainability of trust between firms. Trust is partially related to the degree to which each side of the pair believes in its ability to use the proper criteria for partner selection and evaluate potential partners against those criteria. Trust in this instance is a product of one's capacity to assess the trustworthiness of one's potential partner (what Zucker, 1986, would call individual trust). However, selection is not enough. Trust also emerges from qualities of the relationship itself. Different forms of relationships demand different primary bases of trust. This notion of relational trust is quite distinct from the conceptualization of relational trust typically used in sociology (e.g., Zucker, 1986). Zucker describes relational trust as trust that evolves from the cultural similarity of the parties that arises from their shared participation in a broader common society. Thus, relational trust is something that parties carry with them to the relationship. Our notion is quite different, and concerns the features of a relationship that create trust in the pair. It is our sense that different forms of trust are required for different levels of relationships.

For example, in transactions it is only necessary for parties to believe that others will act in accordance with fair and reasonable business practice, things typically assured by factors outside of the pair, such as the presence of the courts, lending institutions, credit bureaus, and so forth (e.g., Galaskiewicz, 1985; Ring & Van de Ven, 1994; Zucker, 1986). In tinkering, institutional factors may not be enough. Given large amounts of tinkering it is often not possible to develop an explicit enough contract to cover all contingencies. For example, a customer may need to share some critical strategic information for effective product redesign to occur. In such instances, it is useful for there to exist some agreement that a supplier will not share strategic information with one of the customer's competitors. Court enforcement is not always a solution in such a situation. Further, complete specification of features and cost may not be possible; hence, some trust in the reliability of the other is needed. As argued above, it is possible to select partners for their history or reliable and discreet behavior. But, it is also useful to have incentives in the relationship favoring keeping mum and being reliable. The necessary form of trust in such circumstances we have previously called calculative or deterrence-based trust (Lewicki & Bunker, 1995; Shapiro, Sheppard, & Cheraskin, 1992; Sheppard & Tuchinsky, 1995). Deterrence in a relationship arises when the potential costs of discontinuing the relationship in whole or in part outweigh the short-term advantage of acting in a distrustful way. This is achieved in a relationship when either many different forms of valuable exchange are being conducted between parties, such that the benefits of cheating in any one exchange pales in comparison to the advantages created through the many other exchanges, or through building future dependency, such that existing investments lose a great deal of value in the future if the other party is not present. This argument is similar, but not identical to that of political scientists such as Axelrod (1984) who argues that the long shadow of the future serves to induce cooperative behavior, and to sociologists such as Granovetter (1985) who claims that personal trust arises from continuity and interdependence in relationships (see also Shapiro, 1987).

Trust in a tailoring relationship also requires that one's partner be reliable and mum, but it goes further. In tailoring, speed and quality of adaptation are also essential features of a sufficiently trustful relationship. A customer needs to trust that codevelopment will occur well and be truly consistent with its needs. As argued earlier, tailoring relationships are most likely to evolve in complex, rapidly changing environments. In such instances, tailoring is only an advantage the degree to which it allows faster, better coordinated product development and integration. In such instances, knowledge-based forms of trust are essential. A second basis of trust is the capacity to predict one's partner.

The capacity to predict a partner's behavior means that it is possible to make plans, investments, or other decisions contingent upon that partner's behavior. This capacity improves both the speed of decision making, as it is possible to decide knowing the other's response, and quality of performance, as the other's likely response can be incorporated into one's actions.

Two approaches described above contribute to one's ability to predict a partner's behavior: repeated and multifaceted relationships. The more points of contact parties have, the better the chances are that they will come to understand and predict each other's behavior. Also useful are regular communication and actively researching one's partner. Firms, functions, and individuals that have the opportunity for ongoing communication improve trust. For example, Bose Corporation has begun stationing a full-time employee in its suppliers' plants. By having someone on site, these suppliers get a feel for Bose's needs and can better meet them, while Bose learns what its suppliers' capacities are. As one supplier commented, "any time you get two companies literally sitting with one another and knowing each other's problems and expectations, there are bigger wins than there are almost anywhere else" (Stein, 1993, p. 545).

Finally, with the level of relationship we call alignment two additional requirements are essential. A primary advantage of trust relationships is that they permit both parties to focus on the work they are performing, realizing that integration of the final product will be relatively seamless. Deep trust permits agency, the ability to allow another firm to make decisions over factors of strategic importance to one's own firm. As argued earlier, this condition of highly linked independence is especially critical when a part or service is complex, based on rapidly changing technology, the knowledge of which is widely dispersed, and there exists considerable interdependence between a given part or service and other parts. In such situations, both a supplier and customer need to focus on staying state of the art in their respective domains, but doing so in a manner that permits fast and effective integration of components. Thus, the shift from tailoring to trusting relationships is captured by a shift from codevelopment of a product to black box development in which a supplier produces a part matching a firm's needs with very little direction or specifications (see Table 2 for evidence of the advantages in terms of speed and quality of black box design). In black box design, the relationship must be such that a supplier knows extremely well what the customer's needs are and that those needs will be treated as sacrosanct. It is also essential that one's partner firm be sufficiently trustworthy such that developing long-term strategic and systemic integration does not leave either firm exposed to opportunistic behavior. In circumstances of deep systemic and temporal linkage, in which each side acts quite independently, there will exist many chances for opportunism. From this perspective, a paradox exists such that deeper, longer commitment relationships are most at risk for dissolution resulting from opportunism.

This highest order of trust, called identification-based trust, assumes that one party has fully internalized the other's preferences. In social psychology, it has been well demonstrated that people in the same group tend to behave in a more trustworthy manner toward each other than toward others not in the group (see Kramer & Brewer, 1984 for a review of this literature). Membership in a firm has a similar effect. Knowing that someone is from the same company somehow makes him or her more trustworthy. Identity-based trust is likely one of the advantages of vertical integration; after all, the supplier and the customer now work for the same company and are psychologically identified. Identification-based trust can be achieved, however, without integrating the two firms. The factors inducing a sense of identity are many; among the most important are the existence of joint products, goals and strategy, having a shared name or legal status, proximity, the presence of a long and entangled history, and common values (Sheppard & Tuchinsky, 1995).

The investment required to engender identification-based trust is greater than that required to establish deterrence-based trust, or trust based on knowledge. The rewards, however, are commensurably greater. The benefits go beyond quantity, efficiency and flexibility that accrue from deterrence and knowledge. When an identity relationship exists, it is possible for one's partner to act in one's stead. Thus, just as knowledge and deterrence-based trust allow a customer to become more dependent on a supplier, identity-based trust makes it possible for a firm to permit a partner to act independently—knowing its interests will get met. The agency problem is mitigated.

Taking these four levels of trust together, it should be quite apparent that relational trust evolves from significant investment in a relationship. Ernst & Young does not create effective knowledge-based trust by learning what a corporate comptroller's vicissitudes and interests are, but by understanding well many critical components of the firm. Without such knowledge, it is not possible to know what additions to their typical procedures and services are truly valuable to the client. If Maslan Carpet is to truly align with Ford and shift from being one of many carpet suppliers to becoming an integral part of Ford's long-term sound management systems strategy, then it will require significant investment in capital, technology, systems, and people to become truly integrated with Ford's long-term plans. This will include building carpet plants near Ford locations, even if they are far from other Maslan clients, developing real expertise in sound management, and aligning product design activities with Ford and Ford's other key suppliers. All of this comes at significant cost; the decision to evolve a relationship to a given level should not be taken lightly. The decision to create an identity relationship with a partner through serious investment in time, people, systems, and capital should only be made if that partner is truly likely to be a trend setting winner in the future and if they also wish a significant relationship.

Residual Issues

We have attempted to illustrate how concepts quite similar to equality matching and communal sharing map well onto recent trends in the evolution of long-term interfirm relationships. Further, we illustrated how trust can be sustained in these long-term relationships. These are essential ingredients to the construction of a compelling argument that alternative and useful grammars exist to market and hierarchy. However, three residual questions need to be addressed before this task is complete:

1. Do these grammars apply to interfirm relations other than customer-supplier relations?
2. Are Fiske's four grammars really as distinct as implied by the preceding discussions? Are relationships so simple? Do they not often connect?
3. Do they really matter for the study of OB?

Consider each in turn.

Other Contexts for Interfirm Relations: The Case of Competitor Alliances

Four forms of relationships were delineated using supplier-customer relationships as the backdrop. The central ideas apply as well to relationships between competitors with some tweaking and a very important qualification. In pairings among competitors the problem is significantly a more mixed motive (for the best representation of this problem see Hamel, Doz, & Prahalad, 1989). The dilemma for cooperating competitors is to find ways of establishing an effective form of collaboration in one venue, while continuing to be deep competitors, even mortal enemies in other venues. This next section of the paper will provide a brief analysis of the comparability of customer-supplier pairings with competitor pairings and then turn to the task of illustrating how to resolve the mixed motive problem.

Among pairs of competitors, there is a less clear delineation of who is a customer and who is a supplier. However, both the four forms of relationship and the bases of trust are quite useful for delineating the possible types of connection between competitors. In the first instance, transacting, one company may need a part, service or product already designed by a competitor. In such cases, there will be negotiations over price, delivery terms, relative priority of production for internal and competitor consumption—the exchange looks very much like a transaction. General Motors' efforts to flesh out its small car product line with Isuzu cars was an example of such a transaction. Isuzu derived the benefits of increased volume and market access, General Motors was able to provide a more complete line of entry-level vehicles and achieve some margin in the sale of another manufacturer's product under the

GEO label. Another example is when IBM bundles Microsoft software into its PC. Microsoft accrues the benefits of volume and another channel for distribution of its operating system, as well as accruing some gain through excluding OS/2 from IBM machines. IBM adds a desirable feature to its product line, which it must do if it is to compete with the likes of Compaq, Dell, and Gateway, all of whom bundle Microsoft products with their machines. Notice the mixed motive nature of this relationship: IBM personal computer sales are benefited at a cost to sales of its own operating system. One arm of IBM wishes to link with a competitor of another arm of IBM. Trust in this instance is achieved in the same manner as all transactions: through the institutional factors inducing fair and reasonable business practice.

The next level of integration occurs when a competitor specifically chooses to modify its platform product to enhance the value of a competitor's product. For example, Ford Automotive Components Group may redesign a component for Volkswagon; a Synovus bank card servicing center may add a feature to a card that another bank offers. Again, the form of this relationship looks very much like tinkering. However, the specter of a mixed motive problem becomes significantly more problematic. In tinkering, the tinkerer is directly advantaging a competitor, but is also learning something critical about the basis of competition of that competitor. Providing temporary advantage may yield important strategic intelligence.

Tailoring, too, looks much the same. Competitors join together in the design of a product or service. IBM and Apple's collaboration with Motorola illustrate this form of cooperation. Both hardware manufacturers felt a need to find a viable alternative to the Intel x86 microprocessor series. Thus, their common fear of another caused them to join forces in codesigning and developing the PowerPC microprocessor. This too is a very mixed motive game. While both serve to benefit by having an alternative to Intel microprocessors, both also learn a great deal about and from a key competitor in the process. Without a reasonable solution to this mixed motive problem trust is extremely hard to sustain. Knowledge-based trust needs a supplement.

Finally, long-term multiproduct collaboration is increasingly occurring between competitors. Figure 1 illustrates one example of the growth in these forms of competitive alliances. The figure shows a dramatic growth in alliances between competing firms located in the United States, Japan, and the EEC from 1979 to 1985. Ford is bidding on the possibility of entering a joint venture with Shanghai Automotive Works in developing a midsize car for the Chinese market. This would be the first of many products these partners will develop. Many reasons exist for engaging in such a venture. Shanghai VW now accounts for more than one-half of all car sales in China. Ford would like to take some of that share. Ford could not enter the market alone, primarily for political reasons. A joint venture in assembly also provides an opportunity for the market share winner to dramatically increase component part sales to other

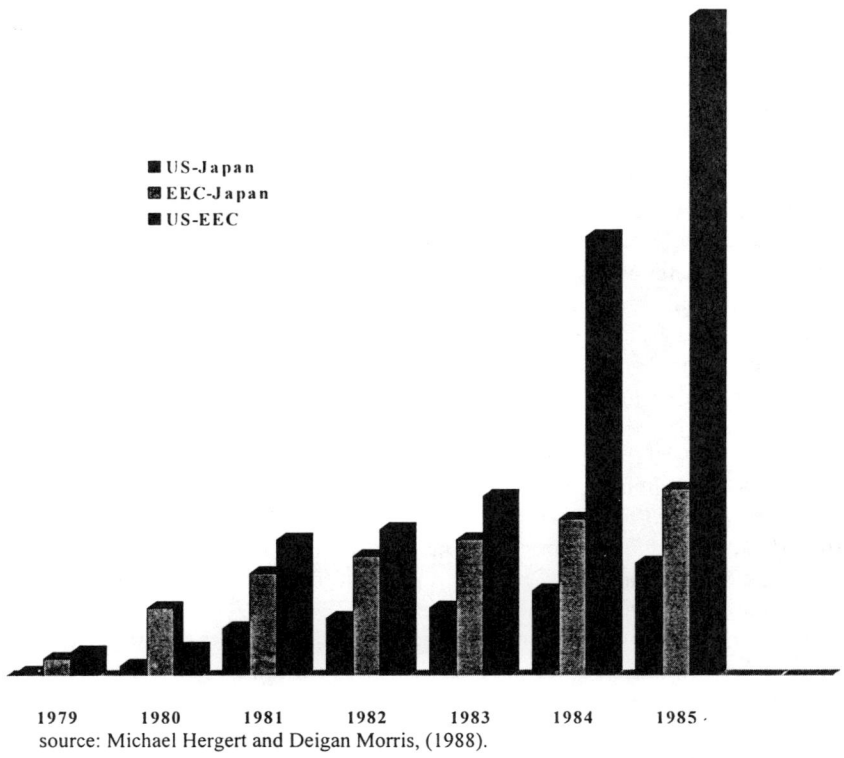

Source: Hergert and Morris (1988, p. 101).

Figure 1.

cars developed in China. Finally, the winner gets an opportunity to establish a manufacturing base in a low labor cost country with large numbers of increasingly highly educated employees. The gains are potentially huge, but so too are the risks. A primary goal of Shanghai Automotive is to acquire design, engineering, manufacturing, marketing and management expertise from its partner. In essence, Ford would be arming its future competitor. With that wrinkle, however, the necessary pairing looks very much like a deep trust relationship with all of its requisite investment.

Solutions to the Mixed Motive Problem

A critical additional dilemma arises when pairing with another who makes the same (or very similar product)—creating effective collaboration in the context of an otherwise competitive relationship. As evidenced above, this problem becomes more significant as relationship depth increases, as both the level of collaboration increases and the threat of releasing critical strategic information grows. Three answers have been articulated for solving this problem, each with allied benefits and risks. The simplest answer is to isolate the collaborative activity from the more competitive aspects of the pair's relationship, most frequently through creating a joint venture with a separate management structure (see Harrigan, 1986, for a thorough treatment of this problem). Creating a separate legal entity is not always necessary for acceptable isolation, however. Large project activities such as collaborative oil exploration may not entail a true joint venture, but only a temporary collaborative management structure that exists at quite a distance from the parent firms. Also, colocating the respective individuals at a site quite distinct from the parent firms may achieve much of what a formal joint venture does. The key is to provide those people and systems involved in the collaboration sufficient isolation that they are focused on how to make the pairing work. Thus, for example, joint ventures in which the members are on very short assignments with instructions to protect their parent's interest may be less effectively isolated than a colocated joint product design group whose members have been assigned for the project's duration and who have been told their future career success and present compensation are dependent on the project's success.

The second option was just alluded to: create the right incentives and protections, a direct application of the principles of agency theory (Eisenhardt, 1989). This option is generally less viable, as the competitive background of the pair is omnipresent and thus difficult to drown out with local security protections and incentives. Finally, a viable solution is to have both sides acknowledge and accept that intelligence gathered from this project is part of what each is seeking (Hamel, Doz, & Prahalad, 1989). In the NUMMI joint venture between Toyota and General Motors, for example, it was clear to both sides that General Motors wished to directly study Japanese management and manufacturing practices and Toyota wished to gather GM's market intelligence. It was up to each to construct a contract that permitted the forms of access necessary to gather the desired intelligence and to learn to transfer that intelligence effectively.

Relationships among Grammars: A Process View

This paper has concerned four distinct grammars of relationships. It could be inferred, therefore, that all relationships fit within one and only one of these grammars. Exactly the opposite is true, however. Most interesting relationships are really combinations of these grammars. The grammars are just that, building blocks from which very rich and complex relationships are formed. For example, sibling relationships entail components of market pricing, such as when they are squabbling over the value of a precious item one lost; equality matching, illustrated by turn taking in household chores or trading toys; communal sharing, as when they graciously allow the last scoop of ice cream to the hungriest or yield the couch to the one most tired; and authority ranking, occurring when the eldest asserts knowledge or privileges the youngest does not have. At times sibling concerns are about equity, at times about equality, at times about need and at times about relative power. Similarly, deep interfirm relationships entail combinations of these fundamental grammars. Most clear is that market pricing is present in some form in almost all interfirm relationships, at least, in the United States. Given that business is the backdrop against which all interfirm relationships exist, concerns for appropriate distribution of margin is never too far away. Thus, tailoring and aligning are in practice usually hybrids of market pricing and equality matching and communal sharing. As such, they are very complex multimotivational relationships that entail a delicate balance among competing relational perspectives. Thus, the four grammars are really the building blocks of relationships.

Tinkering, tailoring, and aligning also typically occur in some combination. Consider, for example, how aligned relationships evolve. Like successful marriages, aligned interfirm relationships do not occur overnight. Generally, they progress through steps of dating, going steady and engaging before the marriage occurs. Similarly, market transactions, tinkering and tailoring inevitably precede healthy aligned relationships. In fact, this sequence is somewhat essential. The level of communication necessary to develop the trust that serves as the basis of tailored relationships is not possible if some of the protections that accrue from calculative trust are not present. A partner will not wisely share information with another firm that has no real incentive to act carefully on that information and remain appropriately confidential. Similarly, deep alignment is only possible with the level of understanding that accrues from tailoring relationships. The basis of trust in alignment grows from the trust developed in tailoring and tinkering (see Lewicki & Bunker, 1995, for elaboration of this point).

This suggests that there are two needs for further conceptual and empirical development. First, it is necessary to better understand the managerial implications of equality matching and communal sharing relationships as relatively pure forms. Second, it is critical to understand how they work in combination with each other and with market pricing and hierarchy.

Research Agenda

Thus, there is much that needs to be done. The ideas in this paper suggest that a very large research agenda is required to better understand the theoretical and managerial implications of placing equality matching and communal

Interfirm relationships 367

sharing alongside market pricing and authority ranking as assumed relational grammars. To illustrate all of the substantive research questions suggested by these new grammars is not possible in one paper and would be somewhat redundant with other recent papers (Sheppard, 1995; Sheppard & Tuchinsky, 1995). As an example, Table 3 provides a summary of some of the questions for the study of negotiation arising from considering alternative relational grammars. It is more possible and perhaps more useful to conclude by addressing a related, but more fundamental question and consider how our thinking and research in OB may need to shift as we introduce these ideas into our research.

Most obviously, it will be critical in the future to consider the basic relational form one is assuming in doing most research. Negotiation, for example, is quite different in transactional versus alignment relationships. In one case, discussing an issue is discussing the terms of a one-time contract; in the other, the same

Table 3. Research Questions Concerning Negotiations in Relationships

What is the impact of anticipated deep future interaction on:
    the nature of discourse between negotiators?
    the substance of negotiation?
    choice of negotiation partner?
How do open ended, ongoing negotiations differ from discreet, closed negotiations?
What is the impact of the existence of a past and related history on:
    the emergence of patterns in negotiation?
    evolution of negotiations?
    frames adapted in negotiation?
How do parties conduct parallel, but related negotiations?
What sorts of artificial walls effectively permit appropriate bleeding of discussion across related negotiations?
What do people consider appropriate transgressions to become involved in? What is my business and what is private between parties in my network?
How do people restart negotiations?
How do negotiations change as external relationships change?
What is the impact of the addition of a new member to an ongoing relationship?
What types of social networks exist, and how do they influence negotiation behavior?
How does the integration of information systems between firms or functions within a firm influence negotiation?
How are negotiations different when the subject is essential qualities of the other person or firm?
How do people negotiate the giving up of a critical skill?
How do we negotiate so as to ensure growth in another and not smothering?
How do distinct cultures merge or accommodate over time?
How do different forms of trust color a negotiation?
How do people fight productively?
What strategies are used to discuss a highly sensitive issue without offending a partner: tacit negotiation, proxies?
Is negotiation the right metaphor for considering discussions among partners?

apparent issue may be serving as a proxy for a critical precedent setting discussion, about the fundamental strengths and weaknesses of one of the partners that has implications for important capital investment decisions, long-term strategy and sources of advantage for both firms. The former can, even should, be an economically rational, egoistic discussion of objective issues in which the person is separated from the problem. The latter is an embedded, potentially highly emotional, complex and firm-determining experience. As one shifts from transactions to aligned relationships, the ground on which a theory and science of negotiation is built also shifts. So too do our theories of control, motivation, self, satisfaction, justice and even group behavior, which need to be more self-conscious about the assumed relational bases upon which they are built.

It will also be crucial to incorporate relational history and future into our theories and research than has traditionally been the case. Considerations of the future have been central in many important notions in micro OB, especially expectancy theory (see Mitchell, 1982; Staw, 1977; Vroom, 1964), or behavioral decision theory (see Bazerman, 1994, for a straightforward review). However, this has taken the form of expectations or beliefs about likely future events. Such research, therefore, has been cross-sectional in nature involving assessing how expectations of future events influence decisions made at a given point in time. Research on relationships will need to be more dynamic, evaluating how both expected and unexpected behavior and decisions at one point influence future levels of trust, social behavior and even the nature of the relationship itself. Trust, for example, is probably most interesting when studied as an evolutionary or devolutionary phenomena; thus, questions such as how does trust build, what is a credible commitment and how does it play out, is loss of trust abrupt or slow, and how is trust regained after it is threatened or lost are all questions that are best assessed dynamically.

Third, part of the persuasiveness of Fiske's approach comes from his invocation of rich cross-cultural data. We can learn a great deal about western business practice by understanding economic exchange in other cultures. Thus, fields such as anthropology may be as important for future OB researchers to be conversant with as psychology or sociology, the two fields from which OB has drawn most in the past. The need for comparative research may be especially important in early research involving relational grammars to facilitate self-consciousness about our deep seated relational assumptions. It is quite likely we are not well aware of how market and hierarchical assumptions have permeated our thinking.

Finally, the relationship itself will often need to shift from a piece of contextual background to the primary unit of analysis. Organizational behavior will need to concern not just the behavior of individuals within the firm, but the qualities, features and behavior of pairs of firms within the broad economy. In many ways, all four of these trends are emerging quite strongly in organizational behavior, as people have been recently engaged in research on emotion, relationships, comparative management, and dynamic processes. The value of this paper, therefore, is less as a call to arms as it is as a template for amassing the troops.

ACKNOWLEDGMENT

The authors are indebted to Martha Putallaz for her assistance with an earlier version of this manuscript.

REFERENCES

Ancona, D.G., & Caldwell, D.F. (1992). Bridging the boundary: External activity and performance in organizational teams. *Administrative Science Quarterly, 37,* 634-665.
Arrow, K. (1974). *The limits of organization.* New York: Norton.
Axelrod, R. (1984). *The evolution of cooperation.* New York: Basic Books.
Barnard, C.I. (1938). *The functions of the executive.* Cambridge, MA: Harvard University Press.
Bazerman, M.H. (1994). *Judgement in managerial decision making.* New York: John Wiley & Sons.
Bazerman, M.H., & Neale, M.A. (1992). *Negotiating rationally.* New York: Free Press.
Berscheid, E. (1985). Interpersonal attraction. In G. Lindzey & E. Aronson (Eds.), *The handbook of social psychology* (3rd ed.). New York: Random House.
Blau, P.M. (1964). *Exchange and power in social life.* New York: Wiley.
Bromiley, P., & Cummings, L.L. (1995). Transactions costs in organizations with trust. In R.J. Lewicki, R. Bies, & B.H. Sheppard (Eds.), *Research on negotiation in organizations* (Vol. 6). Greenwich, CT: JAI Press.
Brown, S.L., & Eisenhardt, K.M. (1995). Product development: Past research, present findings, and future directions. *Academy of Management Review, 20*(2), 343-378.
Buber, M. (1987[1923]). *I and thou.* Ronald Gregor Smith, trans. New York: Collier-Macmillan.
Burt, R.S. (1983). *Corporate profits and cooptation.* New York: Academic Press.
Burt, R.S. (1992). *Structural holes: The social structure of competition.* Cambridge, MA: Harvard University Press.
Chatman, J.A., Putnam, L.L., & Sondak, H. (1991). Integrating communication and negotiation research. In M. Bazerman, R.J. Lewicki, & B.H. Sheppard (Eds.), *Research on negotiation in organizations* (Vol. 3, pp. 139-164). Greenwich, CT: JAI Press.
Clark, M.S., & Mills, J. (1979). Interpersonal attraction in exchange and communal relationships. *Journal of Personality and Social Psychology, 37,* 12-24.
D'Aveni, R.A. (1994). *Hypercompetition.* Toronto, Canada: Free Press.
Durkheim, E. (1966[1897]). *Suicide: A study in sociology.* Translated by J.A. Spaulding & G. Simpson. New York: Free Press.
Eccles, R. (1981). The quasifirm in the construction industry. *Journal of Economic Behavior in Organizations, 2,* 335-357.
Eisenhardt, K.M. (1989). Agency theory: An assessment and review. *Academy of Management Review, 14*(1), 57-74.
Fiske, A.P. (1991). *Structures of social life: The four elementary forms of social relationship.* New York: Free Press.

Foa, U.G. (1961). Convergences in the analysis of the structure of interpersonal behavior. *Psychological Review, 68*, 341-353.
Foa, U.G., & Foa, E.B. (1980). Resource theory: Interpersonal behavior as exchange. In K.J. Gergen, M.S. Greenberg, & R.H. Willis (Eds.), *Social exchange: Advances in theory and research* (pp. 77-94). New York: Plenum.
Galaskiewicz, J. (1985). Interorganizational relations. *Annual Review of Sociology, 11*, 281-304.
Gomez-Mejia, L.R., & Balkin, D.B. (1992). Determinants of faculty pay: An agency theory perspective. *Academy of Management Journal, 35*(5), 921-955.
Granovetter, M. (1985). Economic action and social structure: A theory of embeddedness. *American Journal of Sociology, 91*, 481-510.
Greenhalgh, L. (1987). Relationships in negotiations. *Negotiation Journal, 3*(3), 235-243.
Greenhalgh, L. (1995). Competition in a collaborative context: Toward a new paradigm. In R.J. Lewicki, R. Bies, & B.H. Sheppard (Eds), *Research on negotiation in organizations* (Vol. 5, pp. 251-270). Greenwich, CT: JAI Press.
Greenhalgh, L., & Chapman, D.I. (1994). *The influence of negotiator relationships on the process and outcomes of business transactions*. Working paper, Amos Tuck School of Business Administration, Dartmouth College.
Gulati, R. (1995). Does familiarity breed trust? The implications of repeated ties for contractual choice in alliances. *Academy of Management Journal, 38*, 85-112.
Hackman, J.R., & Oldham, G.R. (1976, August). Motivation through the design of work: Test of a theory. *Organizational Behavior and Human Performance*, pp. 250-279.
Hamel, G., Doz, Y.L., & Prahalad, C.K. (1989). Collaborate with your competitor—and win. *Harvard Business Review, 67*, 133-139.
Harrigan, K.R. (1986). *Managing for joint venture success*. Lexington, MA: Lexington Books.
Harrison, P.D., & Harrell, A. (1993). Impact of "adverse selection" on managers' project evaluation decisions. *Academy of Management Journal, 36*(3), 635-643.
Haslam, N. (1995). Factor structure of social relationships: An examination of relational models and resource exchange theories. *Journal of Social and Personal Relationships, 12*(2), 217-227.
Haslam, N., & Fiske, A.P. (1992). Implicit relationship prototypes: Investigating five theories of the cognitive organization of social relationships. *Journal of Experimental Social Psychology, 28*, 441-474.
Hergert, M., & Morris, D. (1988). Trends in international collaborative agreements. In Contractor & Lorange (Eds.), *Cooperative strategies in international business*. Lexington, MA: Lexington Books.
Hill, C.W.L., & Jones, T.M. (1992). Stakeholder-agency theory. *Journal of Management Studies, 29*(2), 131-154.
Jensen, M.C., & Meckling, W.H. (1976). Theory of the firm: Managerial behavior, agency costs and ownership structure. *Journal of Financial Economics, 3*, 305-360.
Kelley, H.H., Berscheid, E., Christensen, A., Harvey, J., Houston, T.L., Levinger, G., McClintock, E., Paplau, A., & Peterson, D.R. (1983). Analyzing close relationships. In H.H. Kelley et al. (Eds.), *Close relationships* (pp. 20-67). San Francisco: Freeman.
Kelley, H.H., & Thibaut, J.W. (1978). *Interpersonal relations: A theory of interdependence*. New York: John Wiley & Sons.
Kiesler, D.J. (1983). The 1982 interpersonal circle: A taxonomy for complementarity in human transactions. *Psychological Review, 90*, 185-214.
Kramer, R.M., & Brewer, M.B. (1984). Effects of group identity on resource use in a simulated commons dilemma. *Journal of Personality and Social Psychology, 46*, 1044-1057.
Krech, D., & Crutchfield, R.S. (1965). *Elements of psychology*. New York: Knopf.
Lawrence, P.R., & Lorsch, J.W. (1967). *Organization and environment*. Boston, MA: Harvard Business School Press.

Leary, T.F. (1957). *Interpersonal diagnosis of personality: A functional theory and methodology for personality evaluation.* New York: Ronald Cress.
Leatherwood, M.L., & Spencer, L.C. (1991). Enforcements, inducements, expected utility and employee misconduct. *Journal of Management, 17*(3), 553-569.
Lewicki, R.J., & Bunker, B.B. (1995). Trust in relationships: A model of development and decline. In B.B. Bunker & J.Z. Rubin (Eds.), *Conflict, cooperation and justice: Essays inspired by the work of Morton Deutsch* (pp. 133-173). San Francisco: Jossey-Bass.
Lewicki, R.J., Litterer, J.A., Minton, J.W., & Saunders, D.M. (1994). *Negotiation* (2nd ed.). Burr Ridge, IL: Richard D. Irwin.
Lewicki, R.J., Sheppard, B.H., & Bazerman, M.H. (1986). Introduction to this series. In R.J. Lewicki, B.H. Sheppard, & M.H. Bazerman (Eds.), *Research on negotiation in organizations* (Vol. 1, pp. xi-xv). Greenwich, CT: JAI Press.
MacCrimmon, K.R., & Messick, D.M. (1976). A framework for social motives. *Behavioral Science, 21,* 86-100.
Malinowski, B. (1961[1922]). *Argonauts of the Western Pacific: An account of native enterprise and adventure in the archipelagoes of Melanesian New Guinea.* New York: Dutton.
Maslow, A.H. (1943, July). A theory of human motivation. *Psychological Review,* pp. 370-396.
Michael, J., & Yukl, G. (1993). Managerial level and subunit function as determinants of networking behavior in organizations. *Group & Organization Management, 18*(3), 328-351.
Miles, R.E., & Snow, C.C. (1992, Summer). Causes of failure in network organizations. *California Management Review,* pp. 53-72.
Mitchell, T.R. (1982). Expectancy-value models in organizational psychology. In N.T. Feather (Ed.), *Expectations and action: Expectancy-value models in psychology.* Hillsdale, NJ: Erlbaum.
Murnighan, J.K. (1991). *The dynamics of bargaining games.* Englewood Cliffs, NJ: Prentice-Hall.
Neale, M.A., & Bazerman, M.H. (1992). Negotiator cognition and rationality: A behavioral decision theory perspective. *Organizational Behavior and Human Decision Processes, 51,* 157-175.
Ouchi, W.G. (1980). Markets, bureaucracies, and clans. *Administrative Science Quarterly, 25,* 129-141.
Piaget, J. (1973[1932]). *Le jugement moral chez l'enfant* [*The moral judgement of the child*]. Bibliothèque de philosophie contemporaine. Paris: Presses Universitaries de France.
Pitta, J. (1995, January 16). New hope for computer illiterates? *Forbes,* pp. 88-89.
Polanyi, K. (1957[1944]). *The great transformation: The political and economic origins of our time.* New York: Rinehart.
Powell, P. (1992). Beyond networking: The rise of the nebulous organisation. *European Management Journal, 10*(3), 352-356.
Powell, W.W. (1990). Neither market nor hierarchy: Network forms of organization. In B.M. Staw & L.L. Cummings (Eds.), *Research in organizational behavior* (Vol. 12, pp. 295-336). Greenwich, CT: JAI Press.
Provan, K.G. (1993). Embeddedness, interdependence and opportunism in organizational supplier-buyer networks. *Journal of Management, 19*(4), 841-856.
Pruitt, D.G. (1983). Integrative agreements: Nature and consequence. In M.H. Bazerman & R.J. Lewicki (Eds.), *Negotiating in organizations.* Beverly Hills: Sage.
Pruitt, D.G., & Lewis, S.A. (1975). Development of integrative solutions in bilateral negotiation. *Journal of Personality and Social Psychology, 31,* 621-633.
Ricouer, P. (1967). *The sybolism of evil.* E. Buchanan trans. Boston, MA: Beacon Press.
Ring, P.S., & Van de Ven, A.H. (1994). Developmental processes of cooperative interorganizational relationships. *Academy of Management Review, 19,* 90-118.

Sahlins, M. (1965). On the sociology of primative exchange. In M. Banton (Ed.)., *The relevance of models for social anthropology.* Association of Social Anthropologists, Monograph 1. London: Tavistock.
Saxenian, A. (1994). *Regional advantage: Culture and competition in Silicon Valley and Route 128.* Cambridge, MA: Harvard University Press.
Shapiro, D.L., Sheppard, B.H., & Cheraskin, L. (1992, October). Business on a handshake. *Negotiation Journal,* pp. 365-377.
Shapiro, S.P. (1987). The social control of impersonal trust. *American Journal of Sociology, 93*(3), 623-658.
Sheppard, B.H. (1995). Negotiating in long-term mutually interdependent relationships among relative equals. In R.J. Lewicki, R. Bies, & B.H. Sheppard (Eds.), *Research on negotiation in organizations* (Vol. 5, pp. 3-44). Greenwich, CT: JAI Press.
Sheppard, B.H., & Tuchinsky, M. (1995). Micro OB and the network organization. In R. Kramer & T. Tyler (Eds.), *Trust in organizations* (pp. 140-165). Thousand Oaks, CA: Sage Publications.
Snow, C.C., Miles, R.E., & Coleman, H.J. Jr. (1992). Managing 21st century network organizations. *Organizational Dynamics, 20*(3), 5-20.
Sondak, H., Pinkley, R.L., & Neale, M.A. (1994). *Relationship, input, and resource constraints: Determinants of distributive justice in individual preferences and negotiated agreements.* Working paper, Duke University, Durham, NC.
Staw, B.M. (1977). Motivation in organizations: Toward a synthesis and redirection. In B.M. Staw & G.R. Salancik (Eds.), *New directions in organizational behavior.* Chicago, IL: St. Clair Press.
Stein, M.M. (1993). The ultimate customer-supplier relationship at Bose, Honeywell and AT&T. *National Productivity Review, 12*(4), 543-548.
Tichy, N.M. (1981). Networks in organizations. In P.C. Nystrom & W.H. Starbuck (Eds.), *Handbook of organizational design* (pp. 225-249). New York: Oxford University Press.
Tönnies, F. (1988[1887]). *Comunity and society (Geminschaft und Gesellschaft).* C.P. Loomis, trans. New Brunswick, NJ: Transaction Books.
Udy, S.H. (1959). *Organizaiton of work: A comparative analysis of production among nonindustrial peoples.* New Haven, CT: Human Relations Area File Press.
Valley, K.L., Neale, M.A., & Mannix, E.A. (1995). Friends, lovers, collegues, strangers: The effects of relationships on the process and outcome of dyadic negotiations. In R.J. Lewicki, R. Bies, & B.H. Sheppard (Eds.), *Research on negotiation in organizations* (Vol.5, pp. 65-94). Greenwich, CT: JAI Press.
Vroom, V.H. (1964). *Work and motivation.* New York: Wiley.
Weber, M. (1975[1916]). The social psychology of the world religions. In H.H. Gerth & C.W. Mills (Eds., Trans.), *From Max Weber: Essays in sociology.* New York: Oxford University Press.
Weisbach, J.A., & Moos, W.H. (1995). Diagnosing the decline of major pharmaceutical research laboratories: A prescription for drug companies. *Drug Development Research, 34,* 243-259.
Wheelwright, S.C., & Clark, K.B. (1992). *Revolutionizing product development: Quantum leaps in speed, efficiency and quality.* New York: Free Press.
Wiggins, J.S. (1980). Circumplex models of interpersonal Behavior. In L. Wheeler (Ed.), *Review of personality and social psychology* (Vol. 1). Beverly Hills, CA: Sage.
Williamson, O.E. (1985). *The economic institutions of capitalism.* New York: Free Press.
Williamson, O.E. (1991a). Comparative economic organization: The analysis of discrete structural alternatives. *Administrative Science Quarterly, 36,* 269-296.
Williamson, O.E. (1991b). Strategizing, economizing, and economic organization. *Strategic Management Journal, 12,* 75-94.

Williamson, O.E. (1993). Calculativeness, trust and economic organization. *Journal of Law and Economics, XXXVI,* 453-486.
Womack, J.P., Jones, D.T., & Roos, D. (1990). *The machine that changed the world.* New York: Rawson Associates.
Yoshino, M.Y., & Rangan, U.S. (1995). *Strategic alliances: An entrepreneurial approach to globalization.* Boston, MA: Harvard Business School Press.
Zucker, L.G. (1986). Production of trust: Institutional sources of economic structure, 1840-1920. In B.M. Staw & L.L. Cummings (Eds.), *Research on organizational behavior* (Vol. 8, pp. 53-111). Greenwich, CT: JAI Press.

JAI PRESS

Research in Organizational Behavior
An Annual Series of Analytical Essays and Critical Reviews

Edited by **Barry M. Staw**, *School of Business Administration, University of California, Berkeley* and **L.L. Cummings**, *Carlson School of Management, University of Minnesota*

Volume 17, 1995, 461 pp. $73.25
ISBN 1-55938-743-2

CONTENTS: Towards a Theory of Timing: An Archival Study of Timing Decisions in the Persian Gulf War, *Stuart Albert.* The Meso Paradigm: A Framework for the Integration of Micro and Macro Organizational Behavior, *Denise Rousseau, Melissa Thomas, and Robert House.* Population Level Learning, *Anne S. Miner and Pamela R. Haunschild.* A Paradigm for Confirmatory Cross-Cultural Research in Organizational Behavior, *Anne L. Lytle, and Maddy Janssens.* Extra-Role Behaviors: In Pursuit of a Construct and Definitional Clarity (A Bridge over Muddied Waters), *Linn Van Dyne, L.L. Cummings, and Judi McLean Parks.* The Enactment of Economic Adversity: A Reconciliation of Theories of Failure-Induced Change and Threat-Rigidity, *William Ocasio.* Organizational Forms and Managerial Philosophies: A Descriptive and Analytical Review, *Raymond E. Miles and W. E. Douglas Creed.* Membership Dynamics in Groups at Work: A Theoretical Framework, *Holly Arrow and Joseph McGrath.* Labeling Processes in the Organization: Constructing the Individual, *Blake E. Ashforth and Ronad H. Humphrey.*

FACULTY/PROFESSIONAL discounts are available in the U.S. and Canada at a rate of 40% off the list price when prepaid by personal check or credit card and ordered directly from the publisher.

JAI PRESS INC.
55 Old Post Road # 2 - P.O. Box 1678
Greenwich, Connecticut 06836-1678
Tel: (203) 661- 7602   Fax: (203) 661-0792